D1534818

A BRIEF HISTORY
OF ISRAEL

THIRD EDITION

A BRIEF HISTORY OF ISRAEL

THIRD EDITION

BERNARD REICH

George Washington University
Washington D.C.

Facts On File
An imprint of Infobase Publishing

A Brief History of Israel, Third Edition

Copyright © 2012, 2008, 2005 by Bernard Reich

Facts On File, Inc.
An imprint of Infobase Learning
132 West 31st Street
New York NY 10001

Library of Congress Cataloging-in-Publication Data
Reich, Bernard.
    A brief history of Israel / Bernard Reich. — 3rd ed.
        p. cm.
    Includes bibliographical references and index.
    ISBN 978-0-8160-8341-1
    1. Israel—History. 2. Arab-Israeli conflict. I. Title.
    DS126.5.R37 2012
    956.9405—dc23   2011026397

Text design by Joan M. McEvoy
Composition by Hermitage Publishing Services
Cover printed by Yurchak Printing, Landisville, Pa.
Book printed and bound by Yurchak Printing, Landisville, Pa.
Date printed: March 2012
Printed in the United States of America

10 9 8 7 6 5 4 3 2 1

This book is printed on acid-free paper.

For my grandchildren
Andrew Ryan Reich, Benjamin Hiro Reich
John Alexander Walter, Sidney Elizabeth Walter,
Evan Isaac Reich, and Katherine Isabelle Reich

CONTENTS

Appendixes

LIST OF ILLUSTRATIONS

LIST OF MAPS

LIST OF ABBREVIATIONS AND ACRONYMS

ADP	Arab Democratic Party
CRM	Citizens' Rights Movement (Hatnua Lezhuiot Haezrach)
DA	Democracy and Aliya
DFPE	Democratic Front for Peace and Equality
DMC	Democratic Movement for Change (Hatnuah Hademoratit Leshinui)
DOP	Declaration of Principles
Etzel	Irgun Tzvai Leumi (National Military Organization)
EU	European Union
Gahal	Gush Herut Liberalim (Herut Liberal bloc)
IDF (Zahal)	Israel Defense Forces (Zvah Hagana Leyisrael)
JNF	Jewish National Fund
Lehi (LHY)	Lohamei Herut Israel (Fighters for the Freedom of Israel or Stern Gang)
Mafdal	See NRP
Maki	Miflaga Kommunistit Israelit (Israel Communist Party)
Mapai	Mifleget Poalei Eretz Yisrael (Workers Party of the Land of Israel)
Mapam	Mifleget Poalim Hameuhedet (United Workers Party)
Meimad	Dimension–Movement of the Religious Center
MOU	Memorandum of Understanding
Nahal	Noar Halutzi Lohaim (Fighting Pioneering Youth)
NRP (Mafdal)	National Religious Party (Miflaga Datit Leumit)
NUG	national unity government
NZO	New Zionist Organization
OECD	Organisation for Economic Cooperation and Development
PA	Palestinian Authority
Palmach	Plugot Mahatz (Shock Forces)
PFLP	Popular Front for the Liberation of Palestine
PIJ	Palestine Islamic Jihad
PLO	Palestine Liberation Organization

PLP	Progressive List for Peace
PNC	Palestine National Council
Rafi	Reshimat Poalei Israel (Israel Labor List)
Rakah	Reshima Komunistit Hadasha (New Communist List)
Ratz	Hatnua Lezhuiot Haezrah UleShalom (Citizens' Rights [and Peace] Movement)
Shabak	Sherut Bitahon Klalit (Shin Bet) (General Security Service)
Shas	Sephardi Torah Guardians
Shelli	Shalom Lemaan Israel (Peace for Israel)
SLA	South Lebanese Army
Tami	T'nuah Lamasoret b'Israel (Traditional Movement of Israel)
Tzomet	Movement for National Revival
UAL	United Arab List
UAR	United Arab Republic
UN	United Nations
UNDOF	United Nations Disengagement Observer Force
UNEF	United Nations Emergency Force
UNESCO	United Nations Educational, Scientific and Cultural Organization
UNHRC	United Nations Human Rights Council
UNIFIL	United Nations Interim Force in Lebanon
UNSC	United Nations Security Council
UNSCOP	United Nations Special Committee on Palestine
UNTSO	United Nations Truce Supervision Organization
UTJ	United Torah Judaism
WIZO	Women's International Zionist Organization
WZO	World Zionist Organization
Zahal	*See* IDF

PREFACE

This brief history traces the evolution of Israel from an idea grounded in ancient history and tradition to a modern, democratic, economically prosperous, highly developed state. This is the story of the nation of Israel and its people—its trials and tribulations, its achievements and accomplishments, and its challenges.

The work seeks to encompass, in a short space, a very complex and continuing history. In doing so, it focuses on the main themes of establishing the state and ensuring its continued existence—that is, the history of how it got to where it is today and what challenges remain. Israel's story is about determined and talented individuals working to overcome obstacles and opposition to make Israel a reality that could contribute to the history of the Jewish people and be a positive force in the international system. Given the complex history of the Jewish state, numerous themes are related, but not all can be developed to their full extent in this brief history. Since the publication of the earlier editions of *A Brief History of Israel,* significant changes have occurred in Israel's domestic political arena and its foreign and security policies. A seventh Arab-Israel war, this time with Israel facing a non-state entity based in Lebanon (Hizballah), followed by Operation Cast Lead against Hamas in the Gaza Strip, ushered in a new type of conflict, instability, and political uncertainty. At the same time, Ariel Sharon's incapacitating stroke and Shimon Peres's ouster as Labor Party leader removed the remaining two historic leaders of Israel and ushered in a new generation of leadership and a new political constellation. The continuing efforts to achieve peace took on new dimensions in the Obama administration that, in turn, were affected as the Arab Spring brought dramatic changes to Israel's neighborhood. Then, in July and August 2011, Israel was faced with large-scale protests raising questions about the nature of the Israeli social contract.

The reader will note that this edition does not simply bring the story of Israel up to date but includes numerous additions and changes throughout the volume. All elements of the book have been reviewed and revised. These alterations and modifications reflect changes in the history, the appearance of new literature on the themes considered here, and new sources of information that the reader will find useful and enlightening.

ACKNOWLEDGMENTS

Claudia Schaab of Facts On File recruited me to write this book, and in a moment of weakness, I agreed and took on the task of writing a "brief" history of a country with a long and complex story. Of course, the story continues, and at a rapid pace, hence a second and, now, third edition to carry the history forward. Throughout, Claudia has been an able guide. A host of students and their questions and comments during decades of teaching and lecturing about Israel, its history, society, politics, and international relations have helped shape the content of this volume. Several former students at George Washington University were particularly helpful in the preparation of this work. Ilana Cutler, Aaron Cutler, and Peter Feldman reviewed the manuscript and performed research for its preparation. Daniel Aires shared his impressions of Israel and provided photographs incorporated in the work. Modifications of the book have resulted from the questions and observations of Paul Sullivan and Daniel Weiss, among others.

I have benefited from living through the modern history of Israel and closely studying it from the vantage point of Washington, D.C., and from numerous trips to and sojourns in Israel, as well as in most of the Arab world. Over the years, I have learned a good deal from discussions with Israelis, Arabs, and others about the subject matter of this book. In the preparation of this manuscript, I have greatly profited from the advice and assistance of a number of friends and colleagues in Israel and Canada, as well as the United States. Many of these colleagues, who prefer anonymity, offered criticism and suggestions, information and explanations that helped to shape the final work. At the same time I gladly acknowledge the following individuals (longtime friends and colleagues) whose careful and critical review of my work has greatly improved it: David Ettinger, David H. Goldberg, Ronald L. Turner, Arie Hashavia, Sanford R. Silverburg, Shawn A. Kalis, and Gershon R. Kieval. Individually and collectively they are among the distinguished experts on Israel and the Middle East as well as on the study and teaching of history and on the skills of historical research. But, the errors or analysis and interpretation remain mine alone.

This edition has been further enriched by the comments and observations of numerous readers, including students in my various courses and friends and experts on the subject matter discussed here.

Israel Today

LEBANON

SYRIA

Mediterranean Sea

UNIFIL Zone

UNDOF Zone

Nahariyya

'Akko

Qiryat Shemona

GOLAN HEIGHTS

Haifa

Sea of Galilee (Lake Tiberias)

Yarmuk R.

Nazareth

'Afula

Jordan R.

GILEAD

Hadera

Jenin

Jebel Um ed Daraj

Netanya

Tulkarm

Herzliyya

Nablus

Zarqa R.

Tel Aviv–Jaffa

West Bank*

Rishon le Zion

Ramallah

Rehovot

Amman

Ashdod

Jericho

Jerusalem

Ashqelon

Qiryat Gat

Gaza Strip*

Bethlehem

Khan Yunis

Sderot

Hebron

Dead Sea

JORDAN

Gaza

1950 Armistice Line

1949 Armistice Line

Mujib R.

Beersheba

'Arad

Dimona

Yeroham

Hasa R.

JEBEL ITHRIYAT

Nitzana

N

NEGEV

Wadi al-'Arabah (Wadi el Jeib)

Israeli-occupied

The United Nations and most governments do not recognize Jerusalem as the capital of Israel

UNDOF Zone — United Nations Disengagement Observer Force Zone

UNIFIL Zone — United Nations Interim Force in Lebanon

* — Final status to be determined through negotiations

EGYPT

Eilat

Jebel Ram

0   50 miles

0   50 km

Gulf of Aqaba

SAUDI ARABIA

© Infobase Learning

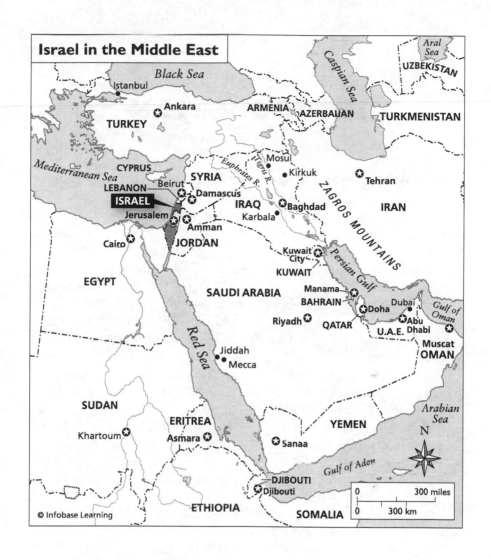

Israel in the Middle East

Black Sea

Istanbul

Ankara

TURKEY

ARMENIA

AZERBAIJAN

Caspian Sea

Aral Sea

UZBEKISTAN

TURKMENISTAN

Mediterranean Sea

CYPRUS

LEBANON

ISRAEL

Jerusalem

Cairo

EGYPT

SYRIA

Beirut

Damascus

Amman

JORDAN

Euphrates R.

Tigris R.

Mosul

Kirkuk

IRAQ

Baghdad

Karbala

Tehran

ZAGROS MOUNTAINS

IRAN

Kuwait City

KUWAIT

Persian Gulf

Red Sea

SAUDI ARABIA

Riyadh

Manama

BAHRAIN

QATAR

Doha

Dubai

Abu Dhabi

U.A.E.

Gulf of Oman

Muscat

OMAN

Jiddah

Mecca

SUDAN

Khartoum

ERITREA

Asmara

YEMEN

Sanaa

Arabian Sea

N

Gulf of Aden

DJIBOUTI

Djibouti

ETHIOPIA

SOMALIA

© Infobase Learning

0   300 miles

0   300 km

INTRODUCTION

Israel's beginnings were inauspicious. Its Declaration of Independence, lofty in ideals and objectives, was promulgated in a land of limited potential and greeted with a declaration of war by its neighbors. More than six decades later, Israel continues to face some, albeit fewer, hostile neighbors and its economic prospects are bright. While its democratic system has been buffeted by challenges never imagined, such as the assassination of a prime minister by a Jewish extremist, it has weathered them to sustain its parliamentary structure and Western-style liberal democracy. Israel's prospects are substantial, although both adversity and challenges seem to grow with each new accomplishment.

The modern State of Israel is the world's only Jewish state and a product of Zionism, an ideology that draws from history and religion, from the ancient connection of the Jewish people to the Jewish state. Israel is small in both size and population. It is located in southwestern Asia on the eastern shore of the Mediterranean Sea and borders Egypt, Jordan, Syria, and Lebanon. It declared its independence on May 14, 1948, within the territory of the Palestine mandate, in accordance with the United Nations partition plan of 1947. Jerusalem is Israel's capital and the seat of its government. Most countries, including the United States, continue to maintain their embassies in Tel Aviv.

The Jewish connection to the "Land of Israel" (in Hebrew, Eretz Yisrael) is a recurrent theme in Jewish tradition and writing and can be traced to the period of the patriarchs of Judaism (Abraham, Isaac, and Jacob) around the 17th century B.C.E. The Exodus of the Jews from Egypt and the conquest of Canaan were followed by the establishment and consolidation of the Kingdom of Israel under Kings Saul, David, and Solomon. Subsequent defeats of the Kingdoms of Israel and Judea, the destruction of the Temple, and the dispersion of the Jews in the Diaspora (Jewish communities outside Israel) provide the base for the linkage of the Jews to the Land of Israel. The desire of the Jews to return to the historical homeland as recorded in the Bible was expressed in the period of the Babylonian exile and became a universal Jewish theme after the destruction of Jerusalem in 70 C.E.

ETERNALLY OPTIMISTIC

Israel's eternal optimism that it will persevere and overcome adversity has emerged in numerous ways, including this widely told story.

Things are going badly for Israel. The economy is in a tailspin, inflation is rising, and immigrants are flooding into the country from all over the globe. Problems, problems, problems, but what to do? The Knesset (parliament) holds a special session to devise a solution. After several hours of debate without progress, one member stands up and says, "Quiet everyone, I've got the solution to all our problems. We'll declare war on the United States. Of course, we'll lose. The United States does what it always does when it defeats a country: It rebuilds everything—our highways, airports, shipping ports, schools, hospitals, factories—and loans us money and sends us food aid. Our problems would be over."

Another member quickly responds, "Sure, that's if we lose. But what if we win?"

For nearly 3,000 years, the Jews yearned to return to the Land of Israel where their early kingdoms existed. Since biblical days, Jews of the Diaspora have hoped that they would return to Zion, the "Promised Land," where the ancient Jewish state had been, as described in the Bible. Over the centuries, Zionism focused on spiritual, religious, cultural, social, and historical links between Jews and the Holy Land. Political Zionism (Jewish nationalism), with the establishment of a Jewish state as its goal, developed in 19th-century Europe, mostly as a response to anti-Semitism then prevalent in those societies.

The Jewish yearning and the Zionist efforts reached culmination in the declaration of an independent Jewish state of Israel in May 1948. But that declaration, lofty in ideals and objectives, was greeted by a declaration of war by its neighbors and their like-minded allies. From that point to this day, Israel has continued to face hostile neighbors not yet reconciled to the existence of a Jewish state in the Land of Israel. The modern history of Israel is thus recounted in the wars it has fought with its Arab neighbors who have challenged its right to exist and with the efforts by terrorists to prevent Israel from sustaining its democratic political system. The democratic and liberal political system marked by dramatic achievements and accomplishments in its economy, science, technology, education, society, and the arts, has nevertheless endured. Israel's exercise of its democratic concepts through elections for parliament and for prime minister, as well as in numerous other ways, have also become significant watersheds in the history of the state.

The special relationship between Israel and the United States is perhaps the most interesting, if complex, element of Israel's diplomacy and foreign policy. Although the United States was a dispassionate, almost uninterested midwife at Israel's birth, it and Israel are joined in an unparalleled relationship aimed at assuring Israel's survival, security, and well-being. This, too, has been a major factor in Israel's modern history.

Israel is a country seemingly always on the move, rushing from issue to issue and problem to problem. Against all odds and despite overwhelming Arab (and other) opposition, in six decades Israel became a modern, democratic state with substantial economic accomplishments and scientific achievements. However, the quest for peace continues and—despite peace treaties with Egypt and Jordan—Israel remains at war with other Arab neighbors and faces threats from Iran. These factors are all connected in the story that is told here.

1

FROM BIBLICAL TIMES
TO THE OTTOMAN PERIOD

Biblical Period

According to the Bible, Jewish history began with the patriarch Abraham, his son Isaac, and his grandson Jacob. The Book of Genesis relates how Abraham (Abram) was summoned to be the founder of a new people in a new land (Genesis 12:1) with a new belief in one God. God made a covenant with Abraham promising to protect, aid, and support him and his descendants. The area referred to in the Bible is generally believed to be the land of Canaan, approximately modern-day Israel and the West Bank. It could be defined then as an area with the Mediterranean Sea to the west, the desert of Arabia to the east, Egypt to the south, and Mesopotamia to the north. It existed between the Nile and Euphrates river valleys, between the great civilizations and cultures of Egypt and Mesopotamia. Abraham left Ur of the Chaldees, traveled through Haran, in Mesopotamia, and eventually settled in Canaan sometime between the 20th and 19th centuries B.C.E. Once in Canaan, he was told "to thy seed will I give this land" (Genesis 12:7).

Among the peoples who moved from Mesopotamia to the Mediterranean were those who spoke various western Semitic languages, including Hebrew. The term *Hebrew* apparently derives from the word used for semi-nomads who lived separate from existing sedentary settlements. Abraham was the leader of one of these groups. The Bible describes him in terms that suggest he was a wealthy semi-nomad with a group of followers who had large flocks of cattle, sheep, goats, and other animals.

Abraham chose to remain in Canaan and eventually settled there with a large and growing family. He chose a burial place in Hebron for his wife, Sarah, and later, he was buried there in the Cave of Machpela as well, along with his son Isaac and grandson Jacob and their wives, except for Jacob's wife Rachel, whose tomb is located near Bethlehem.

Abraham's grandson Jacob was renamed "Israel," Hebrew for one who "hast striven with God and with men, and has prevailed" (Genesis 32:28–29). Jacob established the close and permanent links of the Jews to the area then referred to as Canaan. The 12 sons of Jacob, the children of Israel, became the progenitors of the 12 tribes of Israel and provided the foundations of the Jewish people. The term *Jew* derives from the name of the large and powerful tribe of Judah, from which King David emerged. The Bible relates that when a drought and famine spread in the area of Canaan in the 16th or 15th century B.C.E., Jacob, his 12 sons, and their families established themselves in Goshen, east of the Nile delta in Egypt. At first they enjoyed a favorable existence, but as rulers changed, so did conditions, and their situation began to deteriorate. Eventually their descendants were reduced to slavery and pressed into forced labor. It is during this sojourn in Egypt that a nation emerged called the children of Israel, or Israelites.

After some 400 years of bondage and Egyptian oppression, the Israelites revolted, escaped, and were led to freedom by Moses, who according to the Book of Exodus, was chosen by God to take his people out of Egypt, back to the Land of Israel (Eretz Yisrael). To them, Eretz Yisrael was the Promised Land, that land promised to their forefathers. The Exodus from Egypt is celebrated in the Jewish festival of Passover. The event probably occurred during the rule of Ramses II or his successor and is often dated about 1266 B.C.E. According to the Bible, during 40 years of wandering in the Sinai Desert, the children of Israel received the Law of Moses, including the Ten Commandments and the Torah. The Book of Exodus describes this period in great detail. The Exodus from Egypt and the events during the wanderings in Sinai left a substantial imprint on the national history of the Jewish people and subsequently became a symbol of liberty and freedom. The Jewish festivals of Shavuot (Festival of the Giving of the Law) and Succot (Feast of Tabernacles) commemorate these events and the Jewish identity that has its roots in these events. Moses and much of the generation of the Exodus perished in the wilderness en route from Egypt to the Promised Land.

One of Moses' followers, Joshua, became a military hero who led the conquest of Canaan. The biblical description tells of a confederation of tribes conquering territory from a sedentary population, mostly Canaanites, living in walled cities. The Jewish tribes gained control of much of the land but failed to take the mountainous area and the coastal towns. They were often separated from one another by territory

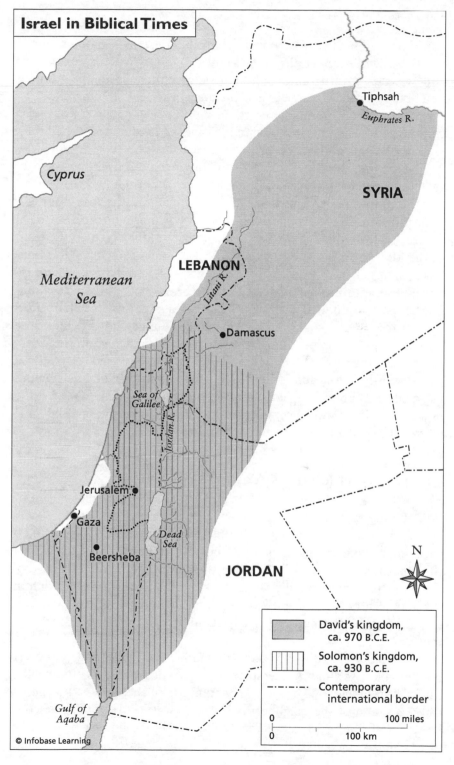

Israel in Biblical Times

Tiphsah

Euphrates R.

SYRIA

Cyprus

LEBANON

Mediterranean Sea

Litani R.

Damascus

Sea of Galilee

Jordan R.

Jerusalem

Gaza

Dead Sea

Beersheba

JORDAN

N

Gulf of Aqaba

© Infobase Learning

David's kingdom, ca. 970 B.C.E.

Solomon's kingdom, ca. 930 B.C.E.

Contemporary international border

0   100 miles

0   100 km

3

controlled by hostile inhabitants. The Bible describes conflict among the tribes while under the judges, the leaders who followed Joshua and were to govern the people and deliver them from their hostile neighbors. Periods of relative calm and peace were punctuated by times of war with unfriendly neighboring peoples. During the next two centuries, the Israelites conquered most of the land, relinquished their nomadic ways, and became farmers and artisans.

The inherent weakness of this tribal organization eventually accentuated the need for a ruler who would unite the tribes and convert his position into a permanent institution, especially in the face of threatened invasion. The Philistines, a non-Semitic people who are believed to have come from the Aegean Sea (probably Crete), emerged on the coast of the Mediterranean and settled in the area in what is today the Gaza Strip. They generally are described as a warlike people with iron weapons and superior military discipline. Having eliminated the Canaanites on the coast, around 1050 B.C.E., they began a large-scale military effort against the interior areas, where they encountered the Israelites. The Philistines proved to be militarily dominant and gained control of these areas. The prophet Samuel, the last of the judges, anointed the guerrilla captain Saul of the tribe of Benjamin as the first king of the Israelites in an effort to unite the people and expel the Philistines. However, the newly united army was not successful in its efforts to end the Philistine threat, and Saul and his son Jonathan were killed.

The Israelite Monarchy (ca. 1020–930 B.C.E.)

The first king, Saul, bridged the period between loose tribal organization and the establishment of a monarchy under his successor, David. David, the son of Jesse, was a shepherd who became a warrior and a successful unifier of the disparate tribes. He is perhaps best known for the biblical story in which he killed the giant Goliath, a champion of the Philistine army. Initially David took control of the area of Judah in the southern portion of the kingdom and eventually united the north and the south under his rule. His reign as king of all of Israel was momentous.

King David (ca. 1004–965 B.C.E.) established Israel as a major power in the region through successful military expeditions—including the final defeat of the Philistines, the conquering of the mountainous central areas, and of the neighboring states—as well as through the construction of a network of alliances with nearby kingdoms. The whole of the land west of the Jordan River was now under his control and

4

rule. He conquered the city of Jerusalem, a city that controlled the main north-south route in the interior of his kingdom, from the Jebusites. Consequently, his authority was recognized from the borders of Egypt and the Red Sea to the banks of the Euphrates River. He created a powerful and professional army that ended tribal unrest and provided a strong foundation for his rule. At home, he set up a new administration, made Jerusalem his capital, united the 12 tribes of Israel into one kingdom, and placed Jerusalem and the monarchy at the center of the country's national life. He established control over the regional trade routes and economic contacts with the Phoenician cities along the Mediterranean coast. According to the Bible, David brought the Ark of the Covenant, a wooden chest containing the tablets of the covenant and a symbol of Jewish faith and unity, to Jerusalem, helping to establish that city as the center of his united kingdom. Jerusalem became the religious and political heart of Israel. David's impressive kingdom was passed on to his son and successor, Solomon.

King Solomon (ca. 965–930 B.C.E.), directed most of his activities toward strengthening the kingdom. Treaties with neighboring kings, reinforced by politically motivated marriages, helped to ensure tranquility within Israel and made it equal among the great powers of the period. Solomon expanded foreign trade and promoted economic progress by developing major enterprises such as copper mining and metal smelting. He fortified towns of strategic and economic importance and established new ones. Crowning Solomon's construction activities were the royal palace and the Temple in Jerusalem. Jerusalem developed as the center of the people's national and religious life, and the Temple's priests became the central religious authority.

Divided Monarchy (930–586 B.C.E.)

Solomon's rule was marred toward the end by discontent on the part of the populace. With Solomon's death, the northerners refused to recognize his son and successor, Rehoboam. Open insurrection led to the breaking away of the northern tribes and the division of the country into a northern kingdom, Israel, and a southern kingdom, Judah.

The Kingdom of Israel, encompassing the territory of 10 of the Israelite tribes, with its capital in Samaria, lasted more than 200 years under 19 kings, while the Kingdom of Judah, made up of the territory of the tribes of Judah, Simeon, and part of Benjamin in the south, was ruled from Jerusalem for 400 years by kings of the lineage of David. The northern kingdom flourished and prospered more than its southern neighbor because it was more populous, had more fertile land, and was closer to the trading centers. The expansion of the Assyrian and Babylonian Empires brought first Israel and later Judah under their control. The Kingdom of Israel was destroyed by the Assyrians between 740 and 722, and its people (who came to be known as the 10 lost tribes) were carried off into permanent exile and oblivion.

With the end of the northern kingdom, perpetuation of Jewish history and tradition depended on the southern kingdom and its component tribes; in fact, the term *Jew* derives from the Hebrew word *Yehudi,* meaning "a man of Judah." But at the end of the sixth century B.C.E., the Assyrian Empire collapsed. The Babylonians under Nebuchadnezzar besieged Jerusalem, captured the king, and ended the Kingdom of Judah. Babylonia razed the Temple in 586 and exiled most of Judah's inhabitants. From that point to the present day, most Jews have lived outside the Holy Land, in the Diaspora.

The First Exile (586–538 B.C.E.)

The Babylonian conquest, with the destruction of the Temple, brought an end to the first Jewish commonwealth and marked the beginning of the Jewish Diaspora, in which Judaism as a unique system of ideas and a way of life outside the Land of Israel started to grow. In exile there developed a cohesiveness in Jewish identity that seemed not to have existed while in Eretz Yisrael, and Jerusalem's significance gained new centrality in Jewish thought. The biblical Psalm 137 suggests this while foreshadowing the emergence of Zionism: "If I forget thee, O Jerusalem, let my right hand forget her cunning. If I do not remember thee, let my tongue cleave to the roof of my mouth; if I prefer not Jerusalem above my chief joy."

Persian and Hellenistic Periods (538–142 B.C.E.)

In the sixth century B.C.E., the Persian king Cyrus the Great defeated the Babylonians and allowed the Jews to return to their homeland and rebuild their temple, and while some did, most remained in the Diaspora. In 538, an estimated 40,000–50,000 repatriates embarked on the First Return, led by Zerubabel, a descendant of the house of David, to create the second Jewish commonwealth. The Temple was rebuilt between 520 and 515. Less than a century later, in about 450, the Second Return was led by Ezra the Scribe. Over the next four centuries, the Jews knew varying degrees of self-rule under Persian (538–333) and later Hellenistic (Ptolemaic and Seleucid) control (332–142).

The repatriation of the Jews, Ezra's inspired leadership, the rebuilding of the Temple, the refortification of Jerusalem's walls, and the establishment of the Knesset Hagedolah (Great Assembly) as the supreme religious and judicial body of the Jewish people marked the beginning of the second commonwealth (Second Temple period). Within the confines of the Persian Empire, Judah was a nation centered in Jerusalem, whose leadership was entrusted to the high priest and the Council of Elders.

In 332, Alexander the Great destroyed the Persian Empire and ended its rule over Judah. After he died, his generals divided the empire. In 301, Ptolemy I took direct control of the Jewish homeland. Ptolemy's successors were replaced by the Seleucids. Antiochus IV (Antiochus Epiphanes) seized power in 175 and launched a campaign against Judaism.

In the course of the Hellenistic period, the Syrian-based Seleucid rulers prohibited the practice of Judaism and desecrated the Second Temple in 167 in an effort to impose Greek-oriented culture and customs on the entire population. In response, the Jews rose in rebellion (166), led at first by Mattathias of the priestly Hasmonean dynasty and upon his death by his son, Judah, known as the Maccabee. The latter won a number of victories against the Seleucid army, the Temple was purified, and freedom of worship was restored (164). These events are celebrated each year during the Festival of Hanukkah (the Feast of Lights).

Hasmonean Dynasty (142–63 B.C.E.)

Following further Hasmonean victories, the Seleucids restored political and religious autonomy to Judea (as the area was now called) in 142, and with the collapse of the Seleucid kingdom in 129, complete independence was achieved. Judah was succeeded by his brother Simon, and the Hasmonean rulers, who became hereditary kings, regained boundaries similar to those of Solomon's kingdom. During the period of the Hasmonean dynasty, which lasted about 80 years, political consolidation under Jewish rule was attained, and Jewish life flourished again.

Roman Rule (63 B.C.E.–313 C.E.)

The expanding Roman Empire became interested in Judea, and in 63 B.C.E., under Pompey, the Roman legions seized Jerusalem. When the Romans replaced the Seleucids, they granted the Hasmonean king,

Hyrcanus II, limited authority under the Roman governor of Damascus. The Jews did not willingly accept the new regime, and the following years witnessed frequent insurrections. The last attempt to restore the former glory of the Hasmonean dynasty was made by Mattathias

MASADA

A large natural rock fortress in the Judean desert on the shore of the Dead Sea south of Ein Gedi, Masada is where a group of Jewish Zealots sought refuge and held out against a Roman siege for seven months in 73 C.E. When the Romans finally entered the fortress, they found that the defenders had committed suicide rather than be taken alive and submit to slavery. This heroic stand and the Zealots' valiant defiance of the Romans is remembered in the oath made by Israeli army recruits that "Masada shall not fall again." Excavations of the site by archaeologist Yigael Yadin in the mid-20th century documented much of the writings of the Jewish historian Flavius Josephus (ca. 37–100 C.E.) concerning Masada.

Masada, the rock fortress in the Judean desert (Courtesy Embassy of Israel, Washington, D.C.)

Antigonus (40 B.C.E.). His defeat and death three years later at the hands of the Romans brought Hasmonean rule to an end, and the land became a vassal state of the Roman Empire.

In 37 B.C.E., Herod, a Jewish convert from a politically influential family, was made king of Judea by the Roman senate, and although nominally independent, he had no authority in foreign policy. Herod was however granted almost unlimited autonomy in the country's internal affairs and became one of the most powerful monarchs in the eastern part of the Roman empire. An admirer of Greco-Roman culture, Herod launched a massive building program that included the cities of Caesarea and Sebaste and the fortresses Herodium and Masada. He also remodeled the Temple.

After Herod's death in 4 B.C.E., the authority of his heirs was progressively diminished, mainly due to popular opposition, until Judea was brought under direct Roman administration in 6 C.E.. Rome granted the Jews a degree of religious autonomy and some judicial and legislative rights through the Sanhedrin, the highest Jewish legal and religious body under Rome. Its exact composition and role remains in some doubt and controversy. When increasingly harsh and insensitive Roman rule became intolerable, a group of Jews, later referred to as the Zealots, launched a revolt in 66 C.E. in the last days of the Roman emperor Nero. It was during this rebellion that followers of Jesus Christ established Christianity. This First Roman War ended with the total destruction of Jerusalem and the Second Temple (in 70 C.E.) and the defeat of the last fortress of the Jews at Masada (in 73 C.E.). The ruthless destruction of Jerusalem and the Temple by Titus, head of the Roman forces, gravely affected the Jewish people. Hundreds of thousands of Jews were killed or taken captive.

A last brief period of Jewish sovereignty followed the revolt of Shimon Bar Kochba in 132 during which Judea and Jerusalem were regained, but only for three years. In conformity with Roman custom, Jerusalem was then "ploughed up with a yoke of oxen," and to blot out all Jewish ties with the land, Judea was renamed Syria Palaestina and Jerusalem, Aelia Capitolina. The Temple was destroyed, and Jerusalem, burned to the ground. A small and impoverished Jewish community remained primarily in Safed and in Galilee.

Under Byzantine Rule (313–636)

By the end of the fourth century, following Emperor Constantine's conversion to Christianity (313) and the founding of the Byzantine Empire,

Men pray at the Western Wall (Kotel Hama'aravi), sometimes referred to as the Wailing Wall (derived from the sounds of Jews praying and weeping over the destruction of the Second Temple and Jerusalem by the Romans), the holiest shrine of Judaism. It is all that remains of the wall that encircled the Temple compound. (Courtesy Embassy of Israel, Washington, D.C.)

the area had become predominantly Christian. The Persian invasion of 610–614 was welcomed and aided by the Jews, who were still inspired by messianic hopes of deliverance. In gratitude for their help, the Jews were granted the administration of Jerusalem; this interlude, however, lasted only about three years. Subsequently, the Byzantine army reentered the city (629) and again expelled its Jewish population.

Under Arab Rule

In 638, Muslim Arabs captured Jerusalem. Their reign lasted more than four centuries, with caliphs ruling first from Damascus, then from Baghdad, and later Egypt.

The Muslim caliph Umar designated Jerusalem as the third holiest place in Islam after Mecca and Medina. The Dome of the Rock was built in 691 on the site of the Temple of Solomon to mark where the prophet Muhammad was believed to have ascended to heaven. Nearby the al-Aqsa Mosque was constructed. At the outset of Islamic rule, Jewish settlement in Jerusalem was resumed, and the Jewish community was granted permission to live under "protection," the customary status of non-Muslims under Islamic rule, which safeguarded their lives, property, and freedom of worship in return for payment of special poll and land taxes. However, the introduction of restrictions against non-Muslims in 717 affected the Jews' public conduct, religious observances, and legal status, while the imposition of heavy taxes on agricultural land compelled many of them to leave their rural communities and move to towns, where their circumstances hardly improved. Increasing social and economic discrimination forced many Jews to leave the country. Other non-Muslims were similarly affected, and there was substantial conversion to Islam in the Holy Land. Abbasid dynasty caliphs furthered the process of Islamization of the people of the area. The Abbasids were replaced by the Fatamids who were engaged in seemingly constant conflict, and the area was one of virtual continuous warfare. In 1071, the Seljuk Turks captured Jerusalem. The Fatamids recaptured it in 1098 only to lose it to the crusaders.

The Crusader Period (1099–1291)

In July 1099, the knights of the First Crusade captured Jerusalem, and in 1100 established the Latin Kingdom of Jerusalem. Most of the city's non-Christian inhabitants were massacred; barricaded in their synagogues, the Jews defended their quarter, only to be burned to death or sold into slavery. During the next few decades, the crusaders extended their power over the rest of the country.

When the crusaders were defeated by the Ayyubid sultan of Egypt, Saladin (Salah ad-Din), at the Battle of Hittin (1187), the Jews were again accorded a certain measure of freedom, including the right to resettle in Jerusalem. Although the crusaders eventually regained control of much of the area after Saladin's death (1193), their presence was limited to a network of fortified castles. A final defeat in 1291 at Acre by the Mamluks, a Muslim military class originally from Turkey that had come to power in Egypt and Syria, put an end to crusader domination of the land.

Under Mamluk Rule (1291–1516)

The land under the Mamluks became a backwater province ruled from Damascus. By the end of the Middle Ages, its urban centers were virtually in ruins, most of Jerusalem was abandoned, and the small Jewish community was poverty stricken.

In 1516, the Ottoman Turks, under Sultan Selim I, routed the Mamluks and inaugurated four centuries of Ottoman rule over the area. Ottoman rule varied over the centuries with links to other portions of the empire, most notably to Damascus until about 1830, and during these centuries, the region was significantly insulated from outside influences and international issues.

Under Ottoman Rule (1517–1917)

For the next four centuries, the area was ruled from Constantinople by the Ottoman Turks. The region of Palestine was divided into districts and attached administratively to the province of Damascus. At the outset of the Ottoman era, an estimated 2,000 Jewish families lived in the region, residing mainly in Jerusalem, Nablus (Nabulus), Hebron, Gaza, Safed, and the villages of Galilee. The community consisted of descendants of Jews who had never left the area, as well as immigrants, primarily from North Africa and Europe.

Orderly government, until the death of the Ottoman sultan Suleiman (Sulayman) the Magnificent (1566), brought improvements and stimulated Jewish immigration. Some newcomers settled in Jerusalem, but the majority went to Safed, where by the mid-16th century, the Jewish population had grown to about 10,000, and the town had become a thriving textile center as well as the focus of intense intellectual activity.

With a gradual decline in the quality of Turkish rule, the area was brought to a state of widespread neglect. By the end of the 18th century, much of the land was owned by absentee landlords and leased to impoverished tenant farmers. Taxation was crippling and capricious. The great forests of Galilee and the Carmel mountain range were denuded of trees; swamp and desert encroached on agricultural land.

Napoléon Bonaparte's Middle Eastern foray at the end of the 18th century led to increased involvement by European powers in the region, including Palestine. In the 19th century medieval backwardness gradually gave way to the beginnings of Western progress. The European powers jockeyed for position in the empire, often through missionary activities. The condition of Palestine's Jews slowly improved, and their numbers substantially increased.

Despite this, Palestine in the 19th century was essentially a backwater of the Ottoman Empire—a mainly poor and rural society generally isolated from the international community except for the growth of Christian missionary influence in the area and the establishment of Christian missions, schools, and medical facilities in the region.

The population of Palestine was overwhelmingly Muslim Arab with a Christian Arab merchant and professional class that was primarily urban. The Jewish population was small but nonetheless a mixed one— the descendants of Jews who had remained in the area since earliest times and recent immigrants, many of whom were religiously observant Orthodox Jews who sought to live a religious life, study the holy works, and die in the Holy Land.

2

THE PREHISTORY OF THE STATE OF ISRAEL (CA. 1880–1948)

The Roots of Zionism

Israel's modern history begins before statehood, with the migration of Jews to Palestine (as the area was then called) in the 19th century from eastern Europe, primarily Russia and Poland, and with the establishment of the modern political Zionist movement.

In 1880, the total number of Jews in Palestine was estimated at under 25,000. Some two-thirds lived in Jerusalem with most of the remainder in other cities considered holy by the Jews, such as Safed, Tiberias, and Hebron. There were also small Jewish communities in Jaffa and Haifa. Most of the Jews were Orthodox and generally subsisted on charitable donations from Jews abroad.

In the early 1880s, a wave of *aliyah* (immigration to Palestine or Israel), known as the First Aliyah, brought Jews from Russia and eastern Europe who wanted to settle the land. The Second Aliyah, which began in 1904 and lasted until Word War I, brought additional immigrant settlers from eastern Europe. This increased the Jewish population in Palestine to approximately 85,000 (about 12 percent of the total population) by 1914, with about half of the Jews residing in Jerusalem.

During these waves of migration, Jews came to Palestine for a variety of reasons. Some came primarily for religious reasons and joined existing Jewish communities, primarily in Jerusalem, but also in other holy cities, where they could study and practice their religion. Others sought to escape the pogroms (organized massacres) prevalent in Russia or the generally poor economic and social conditions in eastern Europe and often were motivated by socialist ideas and concepts. Some were drawn by the Zionist ideology that sought the creation of a Jewish state as a response to anti-Semitism (discrimination against or hostility toward Jews) in their native lands.

Nineteenth-century western Europe provided some opportunities for Jews to move from the ghettos and be assimilated, or incorporated, into general society. Some Jews prospered and were seen as an economic threat to the local populace, fueling anti-Semitism. Political Zionism was the nationalist response of the Jewry of western and central Europe to the pervasiveness of anti-Semitism. Its objective was the establishment of a Jewish homeland in any available territory—not necessarily in Palestine—through cooperation with Western powers (the Great Powers). These Zionists believed that the new state, which they envisioned as a secular nation modeled after the postemancipation European states, would attract large numbers of Jews and resolve the problem of anti-Semitism.

In the Russian Empire, the situation of the Jews was different. Under Czar Alexander II (1855–81), Jews gained access to educational institutions and professions previously closed to them, and a class of Jewish intellectuals began to emerge in some cities, as they had in western Europe. However, all hopes for emancipation were dashed when Alexander II was assassinated in 1881. His reign was followed by renewed anti-Semitism and pogroms throughout the Russian Empire as Alexander III instituted oppressive policies. This led to substantial emigration of Jews from the empire. Between 1881 and 1914, some 2.5 million Jews left Russia. Most went to the United States, but some chose Palestine, where they sought refuge in the idea of reconstituting a Jewish state—but a secular and socialist one.

Zionism as a Political Movement

Modern Zionist writings emerged in Europe in the mid-1880s. A number of Jewish writers were impressed by the nationalist fervor developing in Europe that led to the creation of new nation-states and also by the resurgence of messianic expectations among Jews that, some believed, might include the return of the Jews to the Holy Land. In *Rome and Jerusalem* (1862), Moses Hess, a German Jew, called for the establishment of a Jewish social commonwealth in Palestine as a solution to the Jewish problem. Leo Pinsker, a Russian physician living in Odessa, wrote in *Auto-Emancipation* (1881) that anti-Semitism was a modern phenomenon and that Jews must organize themselves to find their own national home wherever possible. Pinsker's work attracted the attention of Hibbat Zion (Lovers of Zion), an organization devoted to Hebrew education and national revival. It took up his call for a territorial solution to the Jewish problem and helped establish Jewish agricultural settlements in Palestine at Rishon le Zion, south of Tel Aviv, and Zikhron Yaaqov, south of Haifa. Although the numbers were small—only 10,000 settlers by 1891—the First Aliyah (1882–1903) was important because it established a Jewish position in Palestine espousing political objectives.

Theodor Herzl is widely recognized in Israel and elsewhere as the founder of political Zionism and the prime mover in the effort to found a Jewish state. Modern political Zionism as conceived by Herzl sought the creation of a Jewish state in Palestine as a solution to the "Jewish Question" (essentially anti-Semitism). In *Der Judenstaat (The Jewish State)*, published in Vienna, Austria, on February 14, 1896, Herzl assessed the situation of the Jews and proposed a practical plan for a resolution by creating a state in which Jews would reconstitute their national life from biblical days in a territory of their own. His assessment of the problem saw anti-Semitism as a broad-scale and widespread phenomenon that appeared wherever Jews were located. He wrote: "Let sovereignty be granted us over a portion of the globe large enough to satisfy the rightful requirements of a nation" (Reich, ed., 1995, p. 18). He suggested that the preferred location was Palestine: "Palestine is our ever-memorable historic home. The very name of Palestine would attract our people with a force of marvelous potency" (ibid.). But initially, Palestine was not the only location considered by the Zionist movement.

On August 23, 1897, in Basel, Switzerland, Herzl convened the first World Zionist Congress, representing Jewish communities and organizations throughout the world. The congress established the World Zionist Organization (WZO), whose primary goal was enunciated in the Basel Program: "to create for the Jewish people a home in Palestine." Herzl believed the meeting to have been a success and wrote in his diary on September 3, 1897:

> Were I to sum up the Basel Congress in a word . . . it would be this: At Basel I founded the Jewish State. If I said this out loud today, I would be answered by universal laughter. Perhaps in five years and certainly in 50, everyone will know it.

Thus, by the beginning of the 20th century, there was a movement whose goal was a Jewish state in Palestine, and there was Jewish immigration to Palestine, primarily from eastern Europe and Russia. Herzl

THEODOR HERZL
(MAY 2, 1860–JULY 3, 1904)

Theodor Herzl, the founder of political Zionism, was an unlikely choice to create the ideology and movement that led to the creation of the modern Jewish state. An assimilated Jew, he was born in Pest, Hungary, in 1860. He later moved to Vienna and studied law but soon wrote short stories and plays. He worked as the Paris correspondent of the Viennese daily newspaper *Neue Freie Presse* from 1891 to 1895. Growing anti-Semitism in France contributed to Herzl's interest in the "Jewish Question." As a journalist, he observed the trial of Captain Alfred Dreyfus and was affected by the false accusations of "traitor" lev-

Theodor Herzl in Basel, Switzerland
(Courtesy Embassy of Israel, Washington, D.C.)

eled against the French Jewish army officer and by the episodes of anti-Semitism that accompanied the trial and the disgrace of Dreyfus. Herzl wrote *Der Judenstaat* (*The Jewish State*), in which he proposed the establishment of a Jewish state. Subsequently, Herzl traveled widely to publicize and gain support for his ideas. He found backing among the masses of eastern European Jewry and opposition among the leadership and wealthier segments of the western Jewish communities.

In 1897 Herzl convened the first World Zionist Congress, in Basel, Switzerland. The congress established the World Zionist Organization (WZO) and founded a Jewish national movement with the goal of establishing a home in Palestine for the Jewish people. Zionism rejected other solutions to the Jewish Question and was the response to centuries of discrimination, persecution, and oppression. It sought redemption through self-determination. Herzl died in Austria in 1904 and was buried in Vienna. In August 1949, his remains were reinterred on Mount Herzl in Jerusalem.

BASEL PROGRAM
(AUGUST 23, 1897)

The aim of Zionism is to create for the Jewish people a home in Palestine secured by public law. The [World Zionist] Congress contemplates the following means to the attainment of this end:

1. The promotion, on suitable lines, of the colonization of Palestine by Jewish agricultural and industrial workers.
2. The organization and binding together of the whole of Jewry by means of appropriate institutions, local and international, in accordance with the laws of each country.
3. The strengthening and fostering of Jewish national sentiment and consciousness.
4. Preparatory steps towards obtaining Government consent, where necessary, to the attainment of the aim of Zionism.

negotiated for land with a number of world leaders, including the pope, Germany's kaiser Wilhelm, the Ottoman sultan Abdul Hamid II, various princes, and other European political figures.

Herzl's political Zionism and the WZO that he established to secure a Jewish state in Palestine were not universally welcomed in the world's Jewish communities. Only a small number of individuals joined his cause at the outset, and the growth of the movement was slow, especially outside western Europe. The primary opposition to political Zionism came from Orthodox Jews who saw it as a rewriting of Jewish tradition. They rejected the idea that the Jews would return to the Holy Land before the coming of the Messiah. Zionism was seen as a secular (and socialist) movement that contradicted Jewish belief and tradition. Many Jews were also of the view that Zionism had altered Judaism by its focus on a political objective, a Jewish state, rather than sustaining a central sense of devotion and Jewish ritual observance.

World War I

The migration of Jews to Palestine from Europe and Russia continued in the earliest years of the 20th century, and the Jewish population of the Holy Land continued to grow both in the cities and in rural areas.

Similarly, the Zionist movement continued its growth and development despite the death of Herzl in 1904. Growth of population was not matched by progress toward the goal of a Jewish state, and Ottoman control of the area remained the primary obstacle to Jewish self-government.

By World War I (1914) there were some 85,000 Jews in Palestine, both longtime residents and recent immigrants. At that time, there were some 600,000 Arabs in Palestine. The war provided an opportunity for substantial political maneuvering by the great powers seeking enhanced positions in the region as well as by indigenous peoples and leaders. During the war, Palestine was an area of particular focus. Both the Zionist movement and its supporters on the one hand and the Arab populations of the region under the leadership of Sherif Hussein ibn Ali, the emir of Mecca, on the other hand sought eventual control over Palestine. As part of wartime maneuvering, the British and French, initially with their Russian ally and later without it, developed schemes for the division of the territories of the defeated Ottoman Empire after the war's end. In the Sykes-Picot Agreement, Britain sought a sphere of influence in those parts of the empire that became Palestine and Iraq, while the French focused on the more northern territories that became Syria and Lebanon.

In their victory over the Ottomans, the British sought assistance from various groups in the region and beyond. A basic strategy was to encourage an Arab revolt against the Ottomans thereby forcing the empire to divert attention and forces from the war in Europe to the conflict in the Middle East. The British concluded that this would facilitate the Allied war effort against its adversaries.

In exchange for Arab assistance, the British pledged support for Sherif Hussein ibn Ali and his plans for an Arab kingdom under his leadership. In an exchange of correspondence between Hussein and the British high commissioner in Egypt, Sir Henry McMahon, between July 14, 1915, and March 1916, Hussein claimed Palestine as part of that territory. Although the British excluded that area from Hussein's proposed domain, McMahon's remarks left this pledge somewhat ambiguous during the hostilities so as to ensure Arab support against the Ottomans. Indeed, the ambiguities continued in the various negotiations for the postwar settlement. It was not until 1922, in the so-called Churchill Memorandum (also known as the Churchill White Paper), that the British government clarified that the pledge by McMahon to Hussein excluded the area west of the Jordan River (in other words, the area that later became Israel, the Gaza Strip, and the West Bank).

CHAIM WEIZMANN
(NOVEMBER 27, 1874–NOVEMBER 9, 1952)

Chaim Weizmann was born in Motol, near Pinsk, Russia, in 1874 to an ardent Zionist family. He was educated at the University of Freiburg in Germany where he received a doctor of science degree in 1900. Weizmann moved to England in 1904 and began his career as a faculty member in biochemistry at the University of Manchester. As director of the Admiralty Laboratories during 1919, he discovered a process for producing acetone, a vital ingredient of gunpowder.

Chaim Weizmann, president of Israel, 1949–52 (Courtesy Embassy of Israel, Washington, D.C.)

Weizmann became the leader of the English Zionist movement and was instrumental in securing the Balfour Declaration. In 1919, Weizmann headed the Zionist delegation to the Paris Peace Conference. Following World War I, Weizmann emerged as the leader of the World Zionist Organization and served as its president from 1920 to 1946, except for the years 1931–35. He helped found the Jewish Agency, the Hebrew University of Jerusalem, and the Sieff Research Institute (now the Weizmann Institute of Science) at Rehovot. In the fall of 1947, he addressed the United Nations General Assembly to plead for the establishment of a Jewish state. Weizmann also met with U.S. president Harry Truman and appealed for assistance in the effort to secure a Jewish state. Weizmann became president of Israel's provisional government in May 1948, and in February 1949, the first elected Knesset selected Weizmann as the first president of Israel. He was reelected in November 1951 but died a year later.

World War I also provided opportunities for the Zionist movement to make progress toward its objectives. Material aid to the Allied cause was provided by Jewish fighters, with the notable contribution of Dr. Chaim Weizmann in aiding the British war effort. A Russian Jewish immigrant to Great Britain and a leader of the World Zionist Organization who gained access to the highest levels of the British government, Weizmann helped secure the issuance of the Balfour Declaration by the British government in November 1917. The declaration's core point was that "His Majesty's Government view with favour the establishment in Palestine of a national home for the Jewish people . . ." This declaration was seen as expressing support for the Zionist position and laying the basis for a Jewish state in Palestine. But it was a short and somewhat ambiguous document: The declaration suggested that the British government would view such an event "with favour"; furthermore, it spoke not of a state but of "a national home." There was no timetable, no clear articulation of the end result, and no description of the area in question beyond noting "in Palestine." The ambiguity allowed for numerous and various interpretations.

BALFOUR DECLARATION
(NOVEMBER 2, 1917)

Dear Lord Rothschild,

I have much pleasure in conveying to you, on behalf of His Majesty's Government, the following declaration of sympathy with Jewish Zionist aspirations which has been submitted to, and approved by, the Cabinet:

'His Majesty's Government view with favour the establishment in Palestine of a national home for the Jewish people, and will use their best endeavours to facilitate the achievement of this object, it being clearly understood that nothing shall be done which may prejudice the civil and religious rights of existing non-Jewish communities in Palestine, or the rights and political status enjoyed by Jews in any other country.'

I should be grateful if you would bring this declaration to the knowledge of the Zionist Federation.

Yours Sincerely,
Arthur James Balfour

The British found advantages to a Jewish presence in Palestine. Some believed it was economically, politically, and strategically desirable; others saw the Jews in the Holy Land as having religious significance, with the Jews rightfully in Zion. The combination of British political and strategic calculations and Zionist efforts led to the British government's decision.

The Balfour Declaration dramatically altered the Zionist movement's efforts to create a Jewish state in Palestine. It pledged British support for the primary Zionist objective and thereby generated widespread international recognition of the objective and additional support for the goal. U.S. president Woodrow Wilson personally endorsed the declaration and the U.S. Congress, in 1922, unanimously approved a joint resolution supporting the Balfour Declaration.

The Mandate for Palestine and the Prestate Period

On December 9, 1917, British troops under General Edmund Allenby took Jerusalem from the Turks, ending four centuries of Ottoman rule. Included in the British army were three battalions of the Jewish Legion, consisting of thousands of Jewish volunteers. An armistice was concluded with Turkey on October 31, 1918, and all of Palestine came under British military control.

The Ottoman Empire, defeated by the Western alliance of Great Britain, France, the United States, and others, was forced to relinquish much of its empire. Competing arguments, supporting either the Jewish (Zionist) claim or the Arab claim, were advanced at the various peace conferences and other venues where the postwar settlement and the future of Palestine was considered. Eventually, the British decided not to grant control of the area to either the Arabs or the Zionists and thereby incurred the displeasure of both parties. Instead of making the decision soon after the cessation of hostilities, the British effectively postponed it and instead took upon themselves to retain control of Palestine. At the San Remo Conference of April 1920, the details of the mandate system were structured. The British mandate for Palestine was approved by the Council of the League of Nations on July 24, 1922, and became official on September 29, 1923.

The mandate for Palestine provided the legal foundation and the administrative and political framework for the ensuing quarter of a century. The history of the modern Jewish state, from an administrative and bureaucratic perspective, begins with the creation of the mandate.

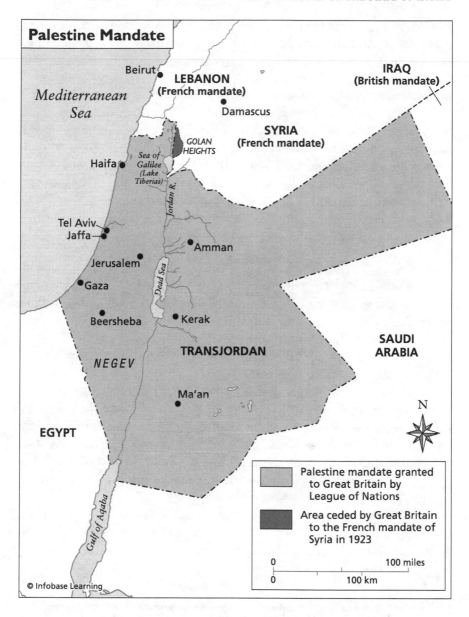

The mandate recognized the "historical connection of the Jewish people with Palestine," called upon the mandatory power to "secure establishment of the Jewish national home," and recognized "an appropriate Jewish agency" for advice and cooperation to that end. The WZO, which was specifically recognized as the appropriate vehicle, formally established the Jewish Agency in 1929. Jewish immigration was to be facilitated, while ensuring that the "rights and position of other sections of the population are not prejudiced." English, Arabic, and Hebrew were all to be official languages.

The objective of the British mandate administration was the peaceful accommodation of Arabs and Jews in the mandate and the development of Palestine by Arabs and Jews under British control. Sir Herbert Samuel, the first high commissioner of Palestine, was responsible for keeping order between the two antagonistic communities. He called for Jewish immigration and land acquisition, which enabled thousands of highly committed and well-trained socialist Zionists to enter Palestine between 1919 and 1923. The Third Aliyah, as it came to be called, made important contributions to the development of Jewish agriculture, especially collective farming.

The Jewish Community under the Mandate

The British mandate authorities granted the Jewish and Arab communities the right to run their own internal affairs. During the mandate period, the Jewish community in Palestine (known as the Yishuv) established institutions for self-government and procedures for implementing decisions. The organized Jewish community chose by secret ballot the Assembly of the Elected (Asefat Hanivcharim) as its representative body. It met at least once a year, and between sessions its powers were exercised by the National Council (Vaad Leumi), which was elected by the assembly. The mandatory government entrusted the National Council with responsibility for Jewish communal affairs and granted it considerable autonomy. Financed by local resources and funds provided by world Jewry, these bodies maintained a network of educational, religious, health, and social services for the Jewish population. The council and its component units were responsible for administration within the Jewish community and created institutions to perform the requisite functions.

In addition to the standard departments and agencies of the government, a clandestine force, the Haganah, was created in 1920 as a wide-ranging organization for the defense of Jewish life and property in Palestine following a series of serious Arab actions in Jerusalem and elsewhere in Palestine. After independence, the Haganah formed the core of the Israel Defense Forces (IDF), Israel's military. Arms were smuggled to the Haganah, and training was provided. The Haganah guarded settlements, manufactured arms, and built stockades and roads for defense.

Other political and social institutions were created within the framework of the Yishuv, and many of these continued to function long after the creation of the State of Israel. These included the Histadrut, the General Federation of Labor, which coordinated labor-related matters and engaged in various social welfare and economic endeavors. The Histadrut, established in 1920, was more than a traditional labor union. It established training centers, helped to absorb new immigrants, and funded and managed large-scale agricultural and industrial enterprises. It set up agricultural marketing cooperatives, banks, and the construction firm Solel Boneh.

Political parties, many of which continue to exist today, albeit after various reinventions of themselves, were also created within the Yishuv structure. Among these institutions was also the Jewish Agency, created by the terms of the Palestine mandate, which eventually became the basis for the foreign ministry and other agencies with diplomatic missions outside Israel and for the functions relating to immigrants and liaison with the Jewish Diaspora.

The central figure and the architect of the Yishuv administration throughout the period of the mandate and into the first decades of the new State of Israel was David Ben-Gurion. In 1919, he founded a Zionist labor party, Ahdut Ha'avodah (Unity of Labor). Ben-Gurion and Ahdut Ha'avodah dominated the Histadrut and, through it, the Yishuv. As secretary-general of the Histadrut, Ben-Gurion oversaw the Jewish economy in the mandate.

Division in Zionism

The Jewish community in the mandate was not wholly cohesive. Internal divisions over domestic and foreign policies periodically developed. Revisionist Zionism, led by Vladimir Ze'ev Jabotinsky, challenged the views and policies of Ben-Gurion and the Zionist leadership of the Yishuv on a number of levels. Jabotinsky espoused a less socialist economic structure and a more activist defense policy against Arab riots and demonstrations. He also disagreed over the British decision to divide the Palestine mandate and create a new Arab state in the territory of the mandate east of the Jordan River, then known as Transjordan.

In the Revisionist conception, the Zionist aim was to provide an integral solution to the worldwide Jewish problem in all its aspects—political, economic, and spiritual. To attain this objective, the Revisionists demanded that the entire mandated territory of Palestine, on both sides of the Jordan River, be turned into a Jewish state with a Jewish majority.

DAVID BEN-GURION
(OCTOBER 16, 1886–DECEMBER 1, 1973)

David Gruen (or Green) was born in Pło′nsk, Russia (present-day Poland), in 1886. Under the influence of his father and grandfather, he became a committed Zionist in childhood. He studied in Warsaw and arrived in Jaffa in September 1906. There, he was elected to the central committee of the Poalei Zion (Workers of Zion), a socialist party, and began organizing workers into unions. In 1910, he joined the editorial staff of a new Poalei Zion paper, *Ahdut* (Unity), in Jerusalem and began publishing articles under the name Ben-Gurion (Hebrew for "son of the young lion"). In 1912, he went to study at the University of Constantinople, where he earned a law degree with highest honors. In 1914, he returned to Palestine and resumed his work as a union organizer but in 1915 was exiled by Ottoman authorities. In May 1918, he enlisted in a Jewish battalion of the British Royal Fusiliers and sailed to Egypt to join the expeditionary force. After the war, from 1921 to 1935, Ben-Gurion was the secretary-general of the Histadrut (General Federation of Labor) and was instrumental in the founding of the Unity of Labor party (Ahdut Ha'avodah), in 1919, which eventually would merge with other labor factions in 1930 to become Mapai (Israel Workers Party).

In the 1920s and 1930s, Chaim Weizmann, the head of the World Zionist Organization and chief diplomat of the Zionist movement, ran overall Zionist affairs, while Ben-Gurion headed Zionist activities in Palestine, where his major rival was Vladimir Ze'ev Jabotinsky, leader of the Revisionist Zionists. Ben-Gurion was convinced that the Revisionists and their more militant stance were endangering the drive toward eventual statehood and sought to undermine and discredit Revisionism. When Menachem Begin replaced Jabotinsky as the leader of Revisionism in the 1940s and increased militant actions against the British, Ben-Gurion intensified these efforts. In 1935, Ben-Gurion defeated the supporters of Chaim Weizmann and was elected chairman of the Jewish Agency's executive committee, a post he held from 1935 to 1948.

After World War II, Ben-Gurion supported an activist policy against the British in Palestine and, later, the United Nations partition plan of 1947. He declared the independence of Israel in May 1948 and became prime minister. He led Israel during the War of

David Ben-Gurion, leader of the Jewish community in mandatory Palestine and first prime minister of Israel (Courtesy Embassy of Israel, Washington, D.C.)

Independence and encouraged immigration. He served as prime minister from 1948 to 1963, except for a period of two years from December 1953 to 1955, when he voluntarily retired to Sde Boker in the Negev to seek respite from the rigors of his long political career and to dramatize the significance of pioneering and reclaiming the desert. In 1955, Ben-Gurion left Sde Boker to become minister of defense in the government headed by Moshe Sharett.

After the election of 1955, Ben-Gurion undertook to form a new government. The eruption of the Lavon Affair in 1960 brought disarray to Mapai, and Ben-Gurion's political strength eroded. He resigned as prime minister in June 1963, ostensibly to study and write, but remained in the Knesset. In 1965, he founded a new political party, Rafi (Israel Labor List), which won 10 seats in parliament. Rafi rejoined the government in 1967 and soon thereafter became part of the Israel Labor Party, but Ben-Gurion did not participate. In the October 1969 Knesset elections, he and some followers contested the election as the State List party and won four mandates. He remained in the Knesset until he resigned in 1970. He died in 1973.

They stressed the necessity of bringing to Palestine the largest number of Jews within the shortest possible time. Revisionism met with increasingly strong resistance, particularly from labor groups. The World Union of Zionists-Revisionists was founded in 1925 as an integral part of the WZO with Jabotinsky as president. In 1935, a referendum held among Revisionists resulted in their secession from the WZO and the establishment of an independent New Zionist Organization (NZO). Eleven years later, when ideological and tactical differences between the NZO and the WZO had diminished, the NZO decided to give up its separate existence and participated in the elections to the 22nd World Zionist Congress in Basel in 1946.

During the Mandate

Successive waves of Jewish immigrants arrived in Palestine between 1919 and 1939, each contributing to different aspects of the developing Jewish community. Some 35,000 who came between 1919 and 1923, mainly from Russia, strongly influenced the community's character and structure. These pioneers laid the foundations of a comprehensive social and economic infrastructure, developed agriculture, established kibbutzim (communal settlements) and moshavim (cooperative settlements), and provided the labor for the construction of housing and roads.

The following influx, between 1924 and 1932, of some 60,000 immigrants, primarily from Poland, was instrumental in developing and enriching urban life. They settled mainly in Tel Aviv, Haifa and Jerusalem, where they established small businesses, construction firms, and light industry. The last major wave of immigration before World War II took place in the 1930s, following Adolf Hitler's rise to power, and consisted of some 165,000 people, mostly from Germany. The newcomers, many of whom were professionals and academics, constituted the first large-scale influx from western and central Europe. Their education, skills, and experience raised business standards, improved urban and rural lifestyles, and broadened the community's cultural life.

During the British mandate, agriculture expanded, factories were established, the waters of the Jordan River were harnessed for the production of electric power, new roads were built throughout the country, and the Dead Sea's mineral potential was tapped. Furthermore, a cultural life was emerging. Activities in art, music, and dance developed gradually with the establishment of professional schools and studios. Galleries and halls were set up to provide venues for exhibitions and performances. The Hebrew language was recognized as one of the

VLADIMIR ZE'EV JABOTINSKY
(OCTOBER 18, 1880–AUGUST 4, 1940)

Vladimir Ze'ev Jabotinsky was born in Odessa, Russia, in 1880. He studied law in Bern, Switzerland, and Rome, Italy, and became interested in the Zionist cause with the pogroms in Russia. After the beginning of World War I, Jabotinsky promoted the idea of a Jewish Legion as a component of the British army, and he later joined it. In March 1921, he was elected to the Zionist Executive, which carried out policies established by the World Zionist Congress, but resigned in January 1923 to protest the perceived lack of resistance on the part of the Zionist leadership to British

Vladimir Ze'ev Jabotinsky, leader of Revisionist Zionism (Courtesy Embassy of Israel, Washington, D.C.)

Middle East policy, specifically the unilateral secession of Transjordan from the Palestine mandate in 1922. In 1923, Jabotinsky founded the youth movement Betar, and in 1925 the World Union of Zionists-Revisionists was formed in Paris, with Jabotinsky as president. He later seceded from the World Zionist Organization and founded in Vienna in 1935 the New Zionist Organization (NZO), which advocated the establishment of a Jewish state, increased Jewish immigration to Palestine, and militant opposition to the British mandatory authorities. Jabotinsky became president of the NZO. His philosophy provided the ideological basis for the Herut Party. He campaigned against the British plans for the partition of Palestine. He died in New York in 1940; his remains were transferred to Israel and reburied on Mount Herzl in Jerusalem in July 1964. Jabotinsky's influence on Israel's history and politics is substantial as indicated by his role as the ideological forebear of the Herut and Likud political parties and especially the influence of his ideas on the thinking and policies of Menachem Begin, Yitzhak Shamir, Benjamin Netanyahu, and Ariel Sharon.

THE KIBBUTZ

Jewish immigrants to Palestine in the 19th and early 20th centuries sought to create conditions for a Jewish state to prosper in an area of limited economic potential. To facilitate their efforts, these early pioneers *(halutzim)* developed a new type of communal settlement called the kibbutz. The first kibbutz had its origins in the founding, in December 1909, of an experimental collective settlement in the Jordan River Valley near the Sea of Galilee. Although the experiment proved successful, its original members dispersed, and it was taken over by a group of pioneers from Russia, who named it Degania. The kibbutz soon came to symbolize the pioneering spirit of Israel and even became synonymous with Israeli society although it never represented more than a small proportion of Israel's population.

The word *kibbutz* comes from the Hebrew for "group." The kibbutz is a socialist experiment: a voluntary grouping of individuals who hold property in common and have their needs satisfied by the commune. Every kibbutz member participates in the work. All the needs of the members, including education, recreation, medical care, and vacations, are provided by the kibbutz. The earliest kibbutzim were founded by immigrant *halutzim* from eastern Europe who sought to join socialism and Zionism to build a new kind of society and have been maintained by successive generations as well as new members. Initially, the kibbutzim focused on working the land and became known for their crops, poultry, orchards, and dairy farming. As modern, especially automated, techniques were introduced and as land and water became less available, many of the kibbutzim shifted

three official languages of the territory, along with English and Arabic, and was used on documents, coins, and stamps, and on the radio. Publishing proliferated, and Palestine emerged as the dominant center of Hebrew literary activity. Theaters opened and there were attempts to write original Hebrew plays. The Palestine Philharmonic Orchestra was also founded during this time.

Arab-Jewish Conflict under the Mandate

The history of the mandate period is one of tension and conflict between the Jewish and Arab communities in Palestine and between them and the British. Each community believed that it had the right

their activities or branched out into new areas, such as industry and tourism, to supplement their agricultural pursuits. Kibbutz factories now manufacture electronic products, furniture, plastics, household appliances, farm machinery, and irrigation-system components. Some operate large shopping centers.

A type of cooperative agricultural settlement often confused with the kibbutz is the moshav, which allows its members to live individually and to farm their own land but cooperatively owns the heavy machinery and handles the purchasing of supplies and market-ing products. The first moshav, Nahalal, was founded in 1921 in the Jezreel Valley.

The kibbutz, a social and economic framework that grew out of the pioneering society of the early 20th century, became a perma-nent rural way of life based on egalitarian and communal principles. It set up a prosperous economy and distinguished itself through the contribution of its members in the establishment, and building, of the state. Given the small percentage of the population who participated in kibbutzim, however, the kibbutz was over-represented in social importance and political strength.

Prior to Israel's independence and its initial years of statehood, the kibbutz assumed a number of important functions and activities dealing with settlement, immigration, agriculture and defense. This was important in creating both a new state and a new society. Later these became state functions and the role of the kibbutzim in society, especially since the 1970s, has declined, as has its political strength. Nevertheless, its role in the economic sphere has remained signifi-cantly greater than the percentage of the participating population.

to the entire territory and had been so promised by the British govern-ment and its World War I Allies, yet neither got it as the British retained control. The efforts of the Jewish community to build a country for themselves primarily through Jewish immigration and land purchases were opposed by the Arabs and led to unrest, in 1920 and 1921, that continued to escalate.

Violence erupted again in the late 1920s. In 1928 and 1929, there were disturbances and riots associated with the Western, or Wailing, Wall, and Jews were killed in Jerusalem, Hebron, and Safed, with more injured there and elsewhere. A tenth of the Jewish community in Hebron was massacred, and the remainder left the city. The British

HEBREW

Hebrew is one of the oldest living languages. Its history spans a period of some 3,300 years, during which it has served as the language of the Bible and many other works of thought and ethics. In addition, Hebrew represents the only instance of a language successfully revived as a spoken language after it had ceased to be spoken.

Between the years 200 C.E. and 1880, Hebrew was not spoken in everyday life, although it was used as a means of communication between Jews of different countries who could not understand each other's native languages and among some pious Jews who spoke Hebrew on the Sabbath. The use of Hebrew in writing was however widespread throughout that period. In some parts of Jewry, Hebrew was used side by side with another written language. In eastern Europe, Hebrew was the language of the educated classes. When, in the late 18th century, modern European civilization began to penetrate among the Jewish masses, it did so largely through the Hebrew writings of the Haskalah (Enlightenment) movement, which encouraged secularization and assimilation as a route of Jewish emancipation. In 1856, there appeared the first Hebrew newspaper, the weekly *Ha-Maggid.*

When it became clear that the solution to anti-Semitism would include the rebuilding of a Jewish state, the importance of a national language in this reconstruction was recognized. Hebrew became the language of Hibbat Zion, the forerunner of Zionism. The immediate result was a spectacular development of Hebrew literature after 1880. This period, which included such writers as Ahad Ha'am (Asher Ginzberg), Chaim Nachman Bialik, and Saul Tchernichowsky, is generally considered the classical age of Hebrew literature. It also saw the rise of a Hebrew daily press.

The connection between the language and national revival was drawn by Eliezer Ben-Yehuda, considered the father of the modern Hebrew language. In spring 1879, he published an article in which he proposed the foundation of a Jewish state in Palestine as a national center where the literary language would be Hebrew.

The Palestine mandate recognized Hebrew as one of the official languages of the country. Thereafter, it was used in the administration of the mandate and especially by the autonomous Jewish institutions. Numerous daily and weekly papers emerged, a network of schools was created, the Hebrew University was founded in 1925, and a vigorous literature developed.

In May 1948, when the State of Israel was established, Hebrew regained a position it had lost nearly 2,000 years earlier, when the Hasmonean dynasty fell. It became the official language of the state.

government established a commission in September 1929 to investigate the cause of the anti-Jewish riots and to suggest policies that might prevent such occurrences in the future.

The Shaw Commission report suggested that the disturbances resulted from Arab fears of Jewish domination of Palestine through Jewish immigration and land purchases. It recommended that the British government issue a clear statement of policy on the meanings of the mandate provisions and on such issues as land ownership and immigration. The British continued to debate the issue of immigration and land purchases in the early 1930s but reached no definitive policy. Nevertheless, for several years Palestine remained relatively calm.

In November 1935, the Arabs in Palestine petitioned the British authorities to halt land transfers to the Jews, to establish a form of democratic leadership, and to terminate further Jewish immigration until there was an evaluation of the absorptive capacity of the country. Their demands were rejected, and in April 1936, the Arab Higher Committee, which consisted of representatives from the major Arab factions or groups in Palestine, called for a general strike. The Arab revolt soon escalated into violence as marauding bands of Arabs attacked Jewish settlements and Jewish paramilitary groups responded. After appeals from Arab leaders in the surrounding states, the committee called off the strike in October 1936.

The British government appointed a commission under Lord Robert Peel to assess the situation. The Peel report, published in July 1937, noted that because the British had made promises to both the Arabs and Jews during World War I and in return had gained the support of both, each party had drawn its own expectations from those promises. Although the British had believed that both Arabs and Jews could find a degree of compatibility under the mandate, this belief had not been justified nor would it be in the future. However, Britain would not renounce its obligations; it was responsible for the welfare of the mandate and would strive to make peace:

> In the light of experience and of the arguments adduced by the Commission . . . [the British government is] driven to the conclusions that there is an irreconcilable conflict between the aspirations of Arabs and Jews in Palestine, that these aspirations cannot be satisfied under the terms of the present Mandate, and that a scheme of partition on the general lines recommended by the Commission represents the best and most hopeful solution to the deadlock.

Cantonization (the division of Palestine into cantons, or territories) was examined as a possible solution and found not to be viable because it would not settle the question of self-government. The commission suggested the partition of Palestine into three zones: a Jewish zone, an Arab section, and a corridor that went from Tel Aviv–Jaffa to Jerusalem and Bethlehem, which was to be under a continued British mandate. The drawbacks of partition, it was believed, would be outweighed by the advantages of peace and security. The mandate would thus be dissolved and replaced by a treaty system identical to that of Iraq and Syria. Access to and the protection of the Holy Places in Jerusalem and Bethlehem would be guaranteed to all by the League of Nations. The principle guiding the partition of Palestine was the separation of Jewish areas of settlement from those completely or mostly occupied by the Arabs.

The partition plan proposed by Peel, the first recommendation for the partition of Palestine, was a reversal of British policy on the mandate and the Balfour Declaration. Anger and protest from both the Arabs and the Zionists ensued. The Arabs did not want to have to give up any land to the Jews, and the Zionists felt betrayed in their pursuit of all of Palestine as a national home.

Britain endorsed the Peel plan. After reviewing the Peel Commission report in July/August 1937, the League of Nations Permanent Mandates Commission in Geneva objected to the partition. The Jewish Agency accepted the plan even though it was not happy with the exclusion of Jerusalem and with the amount of territory allotted to the Jewish state. The Arab Higher Committee rejected the plan and the division of Palestine, and a new and more violent phase of the Arab revolt began.

Yet another commission was established. The Woodhead Commission published its findings in October 1938, which held that the Peel Commission's proposals were not feasible, primarily because it would leave a large Arab minority within the boundaries of a Jewish state, which also would be surrounded by other Arab states. The Woodhead Commission concluded that there were no feasible boundaries for self-supporting Arab and Jewish states in Palestine but suggested a number of partition plans. The British government responded on November 9, 1938, noting that partition was not feasible: "His Majesty's Government . . . have reached the conclusion that . . . the political, administrative and financial difficulties involved in the proposal to create independent Arab and Jewish States inside Palestine are so great that this solution of the problem is impracticable."

On February 7, 1939, the British government convened the St. James Conference in London to see if a solution could be developed through negotiations with the Arabs and the Jews. The failure of the conference led to a White Paper of May 17, 1939, that called for severe restrictions on Jewish immigration: "His Majesty's Government believe that the framers of the Mandate in which the Balfour Declaration was embodied could not have intended that Palestine should be converted into a Jewish State against the will of the Arab population of the country." It called, therefore, for the establishment of a Jewish National Home in an independent Palestinian state. Jewish immigration would be restricted, as would be land transfers. The White Paper foresaw an independent Palestinian state within 10 years.

The House of Commons debated the White Paper on May 22, 1939, and it was approved. The House of Lords also approved it. The response was outrage in both Arab and Jewish communities. The Arabs wanted an immediate end to all Jewish immigration and the review of all immigrants who had entered Palestine since 1918. The Zionists felt that the British had backed away from previous commitments to work toward a Jewish homeland and that this policy was a breach of faith. Peace in Palestine seemed improbable, as both the Arabs and the Jews rejected the White Paper.

On the eve of World War II, the British realized they could not end the conflict in Palestine and that their role in the country was over. The animosity and the violence between Jews and Arabs had become unmanageable.

World War II and the Holocaust

During World War II, the National Socialist (Nazi) regime under Adolf Hitler in Germany systematically carried out a plan to liquidate the European Jewish community. As the Nazi armies swept through Europe, Jews were persecuted, subjected to pain and humiliation, and herded into ghettos. From the ghettos, they were transported to concentration camps and murdered in mass shootings or in gas chambers. In 1939, some 10 million of the estimated 16 million Jews in the world lived in Europe. By 1945, almost 6 million had been killed, most in the major concentration camps. In Czechoslovakia, about 4,000 Jews survived out of 281,000; in Greece, about 200 survived out of 65,000–70,000. In Austria, 5,000 of 70,000 escaped death. Some 4.6 million were killed in Poland and German-occupied areas of the Soviet Union.

During World War II, the Yishuv generally pursued a policy of cooperation with the British in the war effort against Germany and other Axis powers. Some 32,000 Jews in Palestine volunteered to serve

The Hall of Remembrance at the Yad Vashem Holocaust memorial (Courtesy Bernard Reich)

in the British forces. In 1944, the Jewish Brigade (composed of some 5,000 volunteers) was formed and later fought. As a consequence, the Yishuv leadership formed a mobile defense force to replace the Haganah members who had gone to fight with the British. The Plugot Mahatz (Shock Forces), or Palmach, were a mobile force designed to defend the Yishuv, and the British helped train them. The Jewish Brigade and Palmach veterans would later constitute the core of the IDF officer corps.

After World War II

World War II and its associated horrors created a greater need for a resolution to the Palestine issue, and the struggle for Palestine intensified. At the end of World War II, hundreds of thousands of desperate Jews who had populated Europe's concentration camps wanted relocation to Palestine, but the British were still unwilling to allow it. A change of government in Britain brought Ernest Bevin, widely regarded as anti-Semitic, into the position of foreign secretary, and he opposed any new Jewish immigration to Palestine. British policy united the various elements of the Yishuv leadership, who saw no alternative but to launch a full-fledged campaign against the British, which took several forms. One was diplomatic. Another was an appeal to the compassion of the world by launching an illegal immigration effort, bringing tens of thousands of refugees from Europe in refugee boats. The campaign against the British also used violence, with the first shots fired on British military and government facilities by armed underground groups.

On July 22, 1946, the southwest corner of Jerusalem's King David Hotel, headquarters of the British military and civilian command in Palestine, was destroyed by a bombing committed by the Irgun Zvai Leumi. A total of 91 people were killed in the attack: 41 Arabs, 28 British, 17 Jews, and five others. According to the Irgun's leader, Menachem Begin, the bombing was a political act, a demonstration that the Irgun could strike at the very heart of the British mandate in Palestine. The attack was condemned by the Jewish Agency leadership. Nevertheless, it prompted a crackdown by British security authorities on Zionist activities in Palestine.

During World War II, the focus of the Zionist movement's activities and leadership shifted from Europe to the United States, creating a new set of opportunities to achieve the Zionist objective as well as a fortuitous linking of Zionism to the United States, which would emerge a superpower from World War II and help guide the creation of a new world environment. The Biltmore Conference of 1942 marked the public manifestation of the move in Zionist focus to the United States. Subsequently, Chaim Weizmann secured U.S. support for the creation of a Jewish state in Palestine, paralleling his role with the British during World War I.

The Zionist movement had been primarily a European one until World War II when its membership and leadership was destroyed and dislocated by the Holocaust and by the war. In the United States, the Jewish community, whose focus generally had not been on Zionism as a solution to anti-Semitism but rather on the civil rights concerns of American Jews, emerged as interested in and concerned about the fate of their coreligionists in Europe and Palestine.

The Holocaust and World War II emerged as public policy issues in the United States at the end of the war. The practical and humanitarian problems were faced by U.S. military forces confronting large numbers of displaced European Jews and the problems associated with their survival and future. It was at this point that U.S. president Harry Truman determined that allowing some of these Jewish refugees to find refuge in Palestine would make good sense and good policy. Truman suggested the need to open the gates to Palestine for displaced Jews seeking refuge. The newly elected British government refused. In November 1945, an Anglo-American Committee of Inquiry, composed of representatives appointed by their respective governments, was charged with studying the question of Jewish immigration to Palestine and the future of the

THE IRGUN

In part in response to anti-Jewish riots in 1929, the newly formed Revisionist Zionist movement developed its own militia. The Irgun (short for Irgun Zvai Leumi, or National Military Organization, also known by its Hebrew acronym, Etzel) was a clandestine defense organization founded in 1931 by militant members of the defense forces, the Haganah, and others who believed that the Haganah was not sufficiently responsive to Palestinian Arab violence against the Jews in the mandate. In 1936, the Irgun formally became the armed wing of the Revisionist movement. In 1937, an agreement with the Haganah for the merger of the two defense bodies led to a split in Etzel in April 1937. Until May 1939, the Irgun's activities were limited to retaliation against Arab attacks. After the publication of the British White Paper of 1939, the British mandatory authorities became the Irgun's target.

With the outbreak of World War II, the Irgun announced the cessation of anti-British action and offered its cooperation in the common struggle against Nazi Germany. The Stern Gang (Lohamei Herut Yisrael—Lehi—Fighters for the Freedom of Israel) was then formed due to disagreement within the Irgun over anti-British actions. Founder Avraham Stern and his followers sought continued anti-British action despite World War II.

Menachem Begin was the Irgun's commander from December 1943 to 1948. In January 1944, the Irgun declared that the truce with the British was over and renewed the state of war. The Irgun demanded the liberation of Palestine from British occupation. Its attacks were directed against government institutions such as immigration, land

British mandate. After numerous meetings and hearings in the region and elsewhere, it issued a report on April 20, 1946. Among the recommendations was the immediate issuing of 100,000 immigration certificates for Palestine to Jewish victims of Nazi and Fascist persecution. Truman accepted much of the report; the British government did not and refused to increase the limits on Jewish immigration to Palestine.

Faced with continued British opposition, the Yishuv decided to commence illegal Jewish immigration to Palestine. The goal was to move secretly, and primarily by ship, Jews from European camps for displaced persons to Palestine's ports. The Yishuv sought to evade the British navy and land in Palestine where the arriving immigrants were granted refuge among the Jewish community in Palestine. This alterna-

registry, and income tax offices and police and radio stations. Limited cooperation was established in the late fall of 1945 among the Irgun, Lehi, and Haganah and lasted, with occasional setbacks, until August 1946. On July 22 of that year, Etzel blew up the British army headquarters and the secretariat of the Palestine government, housed in the King David Hotel in Jerusalem.

After the United Nations adopted the Palestine partition plan on November 29, 1947, organized Arab bands launched anti-Jewish attacks; the Irgun vigorously counterattacked. One of these was the capture, on April 9, 1948, of the village of Deir Yassin by the Irgun-Lehi forces, which resulted in a large number of Arab civilian casualties.

When the State of Israel was proclaimed on May 14, 1948, the Irgun announced that it would disband and transfer its men to the Israel Defense Forces. For several weeks, however, until full integration was completed, the Irgun formations continued to function as separate units, especially in Jerusalem which the UN had declared to be an international city. On June 20, 1948, a cargo ship, the *Altalena*, purchased and equipped in Europe by the Irgun and its sympathizers and carrying 800 volunteers and large quantities of arms and ammunition, reached Israel's shores. The Irgun demanded that 20 percent of the arms be allocated to its still independent units in Jerusalem, but the Israeli government under David Ben-Gurion ordered the surrender of all arms and of the ship. When the order was not complied with, government troops opened fire on the ship, which consequently went up in flames off Tel Aviv. On September 1, 1948, the remaining Irgun units disbanded and joined the IDF.

tive immigration was referred to as Aliya Bet (Immigration B). More than 70,000 Jews arrived in Palestine on more than 100 ships of various sizes between the end of World War II and the independence of Israel in May 1948.

The End of the Mandate and the Partition Plan

The enormous drain on human and economic resources of the Allied powers during and immediately after World War II forced significant rethinking of political and strategic policies for the postwar era in most of the major states of the world. In Britain, the crucial decision was taken to reexamine the empire and reevaluate positions "east of Suez."

The British position in Palestine became increasingly untenable, and it soon became an obvious choice for British withdrawal: The costs of continuing the mandate far outweighed the benefits to Britain of

EXODUS

The *Exodus* was the best known of the many ships loaded with refugees that Zionist activists sought to bring to Palestine, in defiance of the British authorities. Originally known as the *President Warfield,* the *Exodus* was purchased by the Haganah expressly to transport immigrants to Palestine. It departed from France in July 1947 with a shipload of 4,500 Holocaust survivors who sought entrance to Palestine. As the *Exodus* sailed across the Mediterranean, it was trailed by a British warship and became the subject of international media attention. When it approached Palestine on July 18, it was intercepted by the British navy. International controversy intensified when the British, instead of deporting the refugees to Cyprus, shipped them back to France; however, all but a handful of the passengers refused to disembark. Then on August 22, the British ordered the refugees sent to the British zone of occupied Germany. Media coverage of the struggle further galvanized international criticism of Great Britain's policies. The passengers of the *Exodus* finally reached Israel in late 1948, following the establishment of the State of Israel.

The Haganah ship Exodus *carried thousands of Jewish refugees to Palestine.*
(Courtesy Embassy of Israel, Washington, D.C.)

remaining there, especially with the growing pressures accelerated by the war and its subsequent effects on the regional and external players. The British, reflecting on their inability over the previous decades to find a solution to the Palestine issue that would satisfy the conflicting views of the Jews and the Arabs, and reconsidering the cost in men and pounds sterling of their continuation as the mandatory power, made a decision to relinquish their control over the Palestine mandate.

On February 15, 1947, Great Britain turned the issue of the Palestine mandate over to the United Nations. In effect, the British gave up on the issues affecting Palestine and, rather than suggesting a serious resolution of the issue, chose to place the problem on the agenda of the international community. The United Nations Special Committee on Palestine (UNSCOP) was created to investigate the issue and suggest appropriate measures to be taken.

As part of the Zionist lobbying effort, WZO president Chaim Weizmann met with U.S. president Truman. These meetings were crucial to generate American support for the creation of a Jewish state in Palestine along the lines preferred by the Zionist movement. Direct and significant U.S. involvement in the Palestine question had developed since the shift of the Zionist movement from Europe to the United States during World War II. Toward the end of the hostilities, the United States was also involved in the question of the future of the displaced persons in the concentration camps liberated by the U.S. and Allied forces. Truman's interest and concern with this issue was among the earliest of the U.S. involvement in the Palestine matter.

After considerable deliberation, the UNSCOP proposed a plan that called for the partition of the British mandate of Palestine into an Arab state and a Jewish state, with an international regime (*corpus separatum*) for the city of Jerusalem and its environs, as the city was deemed too holy to be accorded to either. The partition plan proposed boundaries for a 4,500-square-mile Arab state that would be home to about 800,000 Arabs and 10,000 Jews. The Jewish state was to consist of some 5,500 square miles where some 498,000 Jews and 468,000 Arabs would live. The Jewish state was located in the coastal plain along the Mediterranean Sea from about Ashkelon to Acre, the eastern area of the Galilee, and much of the Negev desert. The Arab state included the remainder of the territory of the mandate west of the Jordan River, except for Jerusalem and the immediate area around it, which were included in the internationalized zone. All would be linked in an economic union. On November 29, 1947, the UN General Assembly, by a vote of 33 to 13, with 10 abstentions and one member absent, adopted

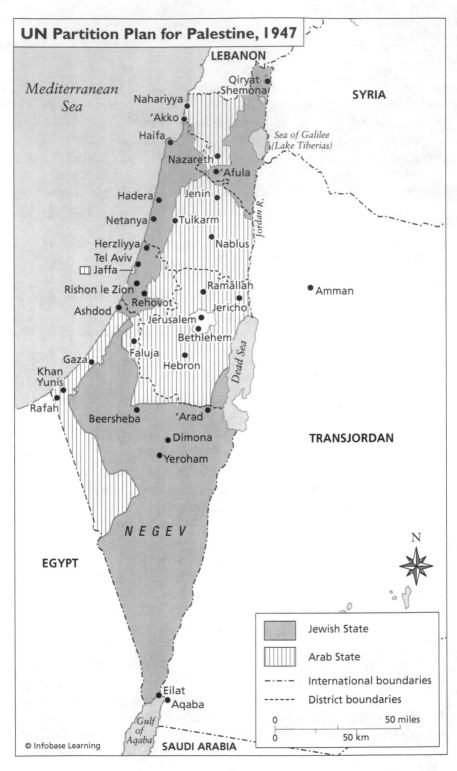

UN Partition Plan for Palestine, 1947

Mediterranean Sea

LEBANON

SYRIA

Qiryat Shemona

Nahariyya

'Akko

Haifa

Sea of Galilee (Lake Tiberias)

Nazareth

'Afula

Hadera

Jenin

Netanya

Tulkarm

Herzliyya

Nablus

Tel Aviv

Jaffa

Rishon le Zion

Ramallah

Amman

Rehovot

Jericho

Ashdod

Jerusalem

Bethlehem

Gaza

Faluja

Hebron

Khan Yunis

Rafah

Beersheba

'Arad

Dead Sea

TRANSJORDAN

Dimona

Yeroham

N E G E V

EGYPT

N

Eilat

Aqaba

Gulf of Aqaba

SAUDI ARABIA

© Infobase Learning

	Jewish State
	Arab State
—··—	International boundaries
- - - -	District boundaries

0 — 50 miles

0 — 50 km

Jordan R.

42

Resolution 181 (II), the plan of partition for Palestine. Thus, the international system created a Jewish state of Israel, within the territory of the Palestine mandate.

The Zionist movement and other Jews were divided concerning the United Nations decision. Among the Zionist groups in Palestine and the Diaspora there were essentially two perspectives. Both believed that they had been offered less than they wanted, but the left-of-center Labor Zionists adopted a practical stance and believed that acceptance of the partition was the most logical and appropriate step. The right wing of the Zionists, primarily the Revisionists, believed that they should have been awarded all of the land west of the Jordan River as well as the territory east of the river that the British had severed from the original League of Nations mandate for Palestine to create the state of Transjordan. Nevertheless, there was little that could be done. Thus, the Yishuv, though unhappy with the exclusion of Jerusalem, and the Jewish Agency accepted the decision of the General Assembly as an important step toward independent statehood and a practical necessity for providing refuge for survivors of the Holocaust. When the new state

ARAB OPPOSITION TO THE PARTITION OF PALESTINE
(NOVEMBER 29, 1947)

After the adoption of Resolution 181 (II) by the United Nations General Assembly, Saudi Arabia's chief delegate, Emir Faisal al-Saud, declared:

> [T]oday's resolution has destroyed the Charter and all the convenants preceding it.
>
> We have felt, like many others, the pressure exerted on various representatives of this Organisation by some of the big Powers in order that the vote should be in favour of partition. For these reasons, the Government of Saudi Arabia registers, on this historic occasion, the fact that it does not consider itself bound by the resolution adopted today by the General Assembly. Furthermore, it reserves to itself the full right to act freely in whatever way it deems fit, in accordance with the principles of right and justice. My Government holds responsible those parties that hampered all means of cooperation and understanding.

of Israel declared its independence in May 1948, it was within the lines drawn by the United Nations.

Meanwhile, the Arab leadership in Palestine and the League of Arab States unconditionally rejected the UN partition plan on the grounds that all of Palestine should be awarded to a Palestinian Arab state. The Arab rejection was based on the position that the United Nations had no right to give away approximately half of Palestine to the Zionists and that Palestinian Arabs should not be made to pay for Europe's crimes against the Jews. The latter argument was advanced despite the fact that the Balfour Declaration had been issued before the Nazis rose to power in Germany.

These clashing perspectives provided a basis for the ongoing Arab-Israeli conflict. The partition plan was supported by the United States and the Soviet Union, both of whom seemed to be courting the new Jewish state as an ally in the east-west struggle for regional mastery.

Fighting erupted in Palestine after adoption of the partition plan; the first Jewish buses were attacked the next morning; six passengers were killed, and many others were wounded. Armed Palestinian Arabs aided by volunteers smuggled in from neighboring Arab countries launched attacks on Jewish settlements and facilities. The forces of the Yishuv, especially the Haganah, were able to deal effectively with this threat in many areas. The civil war between the communities in Palestine was the prelude to full-scale hostilities after the British mandate ended on May 15, 1948.

3

POLITICAL, ECONOMIC, AND MILITARY CONSOLIDATION (1948–1967)

Israel's Declaration of Independence

The United Nations partition plan of November 1947 provided for the establishment of a Jewish state in Palestine, and the date of the termination of the British mandate was set for May 15, 1948. The Zionist leadership decided that an independent Jewish state would issue a declaration of independence. The British mandatory authority and its military forces withdrew from the mandate, as scheduled, on May 14, 1948 (corresponding to 5 Iyar 5708 in the Jewish calendar), and the new Jewish state declared its independence in Tel Aviv. David Ben-Gurion read the Declaration of the Establishment of the State of Israel. The declaration provided for a Jewish state in the Land of Israel and recalled the religious and spiritual connection of the Jewish people to Eretz Yisrael, but it did not mention boundaries. It specified that "it will guarantee freedom of religion and conscience, of language, education, and culture." The document did not address the meaning of a Jewish state or the roles that would be played by religious factors in such an entity.

Israel's declaration of independence was and remains something of a unique document. Israel's founding elite expressed their views of the nature of the state, its historical connection to the Land of Israel, and the main components of its view of the principles that should guide the state. It set out the framework for governing concepts and spoke of the need for peace with its neighbors.

Israel's declaration was greeted with jubilation among Jews in Palestine and Jewish communities worldwide. It was seen by some as the fulfillment of biblical prophecy and by others as a logical outcome

David Ben-Gurion delivers Israel's Declaration of Independence, May 1948. (Courtesy Embassy of Israel, Washington, D.C.)

of history. It provided a haven for persecuted Jews and a refuge for those displaced by the Holocaust. For the Zionist movement the creation of the state was the successful result of five decades of Zionist efforts. For the anti-Zionists, this result was unfortunate. Some ultra-Orthodox Jews opposed the creation of a state as blasphemous, because the Messiah had not yet come, and refused to abide by its laws and regulations. Some still do.

In the Arab world, the United Nations's decision and Israel's declaration of independence were greeted with negative reactions ranging from dismay to outrage and with a general view that the presence of a Jewish state in Palestine displaced the Arabs of Palestine and that this was unacceptable. The Arab League had expressed its dismay and disapproval of the Jewish state in the United Nations debates and in its reaction to the partition plan and vote. The secretary-general of the Arab League officially informed the secretary-general of the United Nations on May 15, 1948, that Arab armies would enter Palestine to restore the rights of the Palestinian Arabs in the territories of the Palestine mandate.

DECLARATION OF THE ESTABLISHMENT OF THE STATE OF ISRAEL
(MAY 14, 1948)

ERETZ YISRAEL was the birthplace of the Jewish people. Here their spiritual, religious and political identity was shaped. Here they first attained to statehood, created cultural values of national and universal significance and gave to the world the eternal Book of Books.

After being forcibly exiled from their land, the people kept faith with it throughout their Dispersion and never ceased to pray and hope for their return to it and for the restoration in it of their political freedom.

Impelled by this historic and traditional attachment, Jews strove in every successive generation to re-establish themselves in their ancient homeland. In recent decades they returned in their masses. Pioneers, *ma'pilim* [immigrants coming to Eretz Yisrael (Israel) in defiance of restrictive legislation] and defenders, they made deserts bloom, revived the Hebrew language, built villages and towns, and created a thriving community, controlling its own economy and culture, loving peace but knowing how to defend itself, bringing the blessings of progress to all the country's inhabitants, and aspiring towards independent nationhood.

In the year 5657 (1897), at the summons of the spiritual father of the Jewish State, Theodor Herzl, the First Zionist Congress convened and proclaimed the right of the Jewish people to national rebirth in its own country.

This right was recognized in the Balfour Declaration of the 2nd November, 1917, and re-affirmed in the Mandate of the League of Nations which, in particular, gave international sanction to the historic connection between the Jewish people and Eretz-Israel and to the right of the Jewish people to rebuild its National Home.

The catastrophe which recently befell the Jewish people—the massacre of millions of Jews in Europe—was another clear demonstration of the urgency of solving the problem of its homelessness by re-establishing in Eretz-Israel the Jewish State, which would open the gates of the homeland wide to every Jew and confer upon the Jewish people the status of a fully-privileged member of the comity of nations.

Survivors of the Nazi holocaust in Europe, as well as Jews from other parts of the world, continued to migrate to Eretz-Israel, undaunted by

(continues)

47

DECLARATION *(continued)*

difficulties, restrictions and dangers, and never ceased to assert their right to a life of dignity, freedom and honest toil in their national homeland.

In the Second World War, the Jewish community of this country contributed its full share to the struggle of the freedom- and peace-loving nations against the forces of Nazi wickedness and, by the blood of its soldiers and its war effort, gained the right to be reckoned among the peoples who founded the United Nations.

On the 29th November, 1947, the United Nations General Assembly passed a resolution calling for the establishment of a Jewish State in Eretz-Israel; the General Assembly required the inhabitants of Eretz-Israel to take such steps as were necessary on their part for the implementation of that resolution. This recognition by the United Nations of the right of the Jewish people to establish their State is irrevocable.

This right is the natural right of the Jewish people to be masters of their own fate, like all other nations, in their own sovereign State.

ACCORDINGLY WE, MEMBERS OF THE PEOPLE'S COUNCIL, REPRESENTATIVES OF THE JEWISH COMMUNITY OF ERETZ-ISRAEL AND OF THE ZIONIST MOVEMENT, ARE HERE ASSEMBLED ON THE DAY OF THE TERMINATION OF THE BRITISH MANDATE OVER ERETZ-ISRAEL AND, BY VIRTUE OF OUR NATURAL AND HISTORIC RIGHT AND ON THE STRENGTH OF THE RESOLUTION OF THE UNITED NATIONS GENERAL ASSEMBLY, HEREBY DECLARE THE ESTABLISHMENT OF A JEWISH STATE IN ERETZ-ISRAEL, TO BE KNOWN AS THE STATE OF ISRAEL.

WE DECLARE that, with effect from the moment of the termination of the Mandate, being tonight, the eve of Sabbath, the 6th Iyar, 5708 (15th May, 1948), until the establishment of the elected, regular authorities of the State in accordance with the Constitution which shall be adopted by the Elected Constituent Assembly not later than the 1st October, 1948, the People's Council shall act as a Provisional Council of State, and its executive organ, the People's Administration, shall be the Provisional Government of the Jewish State, to be called "Israel."

THE STATE OF ISRAEL will be open for Jewish immigration and for the Ingathering of the Exiles; it will foster the development

War of Independence

Although the fighting between the Jews and Arabs of Palestine had escalated after the adoption of the partition plan, full-scale war followed Israel's declaration of independence. This war is known in Israel

of the country for the benefit of all its inhabitants; it will be based on freedom, justice and peace as envisaged by the prophets of Israel; it will ensure complete equality of social and political rights to all its inhabitants irrespective of religion, race or sex; it will guarantee freedom of religion, conscience, language, education and culture; it will safeguard the Holy Places of all religions; and it will be faithful to the principles of the Charter of the United Nations.

THE STATE OF ISRAEL is prepared to cooperate with the agencies and representatives of the United Nations in implementing the resolution of the General Assembly of the 29th November, 1947, and will take steps to bring about the economic union of the whole of Eretz-Israel.

WE APPEAL to the United Nations to assist the Jewish people in the building-up of its State and to receive the State of Israel into the comity of nations.

WE APPEAL—in the very midst of the onslaught launched against us now for months—to the Arab inhabitants of the State of Israel to preserve peace and participate in the upbuilding of the State on the basis of full and equal citizenship and due representation in all its provisional and permanent institutions.

WE EXTEND our hand to all neighbouring states and their peoples in an offer of peace and good neighbourliness, and appeal to them to establish bonds of cooperation and mutual help with the sovereign Jewish people settled in its own land. The State of Israel is prepared to do its share in a common effort for the advancement of the entire Middle East.

WE APPEAL to the Jewish people throughout the Diaspora to rally round the Jews of Eretz-Israel in the tasks of immigration and upbuilding and to stand by them in the great struggle for the realization of the age-old dream—the redemption of Israel.

PLACING OUR TRUST IN THE ALMIGHTY, WE AFFIX OUR SIGNATURES TO THIS PROCLAMATION AT THIS SESSION OF THE PROVISIONAL COUNCIL OF STATE, ON THE SOIL OF THE HOMELAND, IN THE CITY OF TEL-AVIV, ON THIS SABBATH EVE, THE 5TH DAY OF IYAR, 5708 (14 MAY, 1948).

as the War of Independence, while the Arab world has referred to it as al-Nakba (the disaster or catastrophe). For Israel, the war affirmed its independence as a Jewish state in the Middle East, but it did not alleviate Arab opposition, nor did it guarantee Israel's existence. The Arab

This Government has been informed that a Jewish
state has been proclaimed in Palestine, and recognition
has been requested by the *provisional* Government thereof.

The United States recognizes the provisional gov-
ernment as the de facto authority of the ~~new Jewish~~ new *State of* ~~state.~~ *Israel.*

Harry Truman

Approved,
May 14, 1948.

6:11

U.S. recognition of Israel, corrected by hand, signed by President Truman (Courtesy National Archives and Records Administration)

world refused to accept Israel's presence and instead focused on the destruction and removal of the Jewish state and the establishment of a Palestinian Arab state in all of Palestine west of the Jordan River.

Armies of the Arab states entered Palestine and engaged in open warfare with the defense forces of the new state, with the stated goals of preventing the establishment of a Jewish state and of assuring that all of Palestine would be in Arab hands. This first Arab-Israeli war involved troops from Egypt, Syria, Jordan, Iraq, and Lebanon, with assistance from other Arab quarters, against Israel. The war was long and costly: Israel lost some 4,000 soldiers and 2,000 civilians—about 1 percent of the Jewish population.

The War of Independence had a substantial effect on the future state as well as on its neighbors and was formally ended by a cease-fire followed by a series of armistice agreements. Overall, Israel was victorious in that first major war with the Arabs. It survived the substantial Arab

ARAB STATES AND WAR AGAINST ISRAEL
(MAY 15, 1948)

The following statement was issued by the governments of the Arab League States on the occasion of the entry of the Arab armies into Palestine, on May 15, 1948, the day after Israel's declaration of independence.

When the General Assembly of the United Nations issued, on November 29, 1947, its recommendation concerning the solution of the Palestine problem, on the basis of the establishment of an Arab state and of another Jewish (state) in (Palestine) together with placing the City of Jerusalem under the trusteeship of the United Nations, the Arab States drew attention to the injustice implied in this solution (affecting) the right of the people of Palestine to immediate independence, as well as democratic principles and the provisions of the Covenant of the League of Nations and (the Charter) of the United Nations. (These States also) declared the Arabs' rejection of (that solution) and that it would not be possible to carry it out by peaceful means, and that its forcible imposition would constitute a threat to peace and security in this area . . .

Now that the British mandate over Palestine has come to an end, without there being a legitimate constitutional authority in the country, which would safeguard the maintenance of security and respect for Law and which would protect the lives and properties of the inhabitants, the Governments of the Arab States declare the following:

First: That the rule of Palestine should revert to its inhabitants, in accordance with the provisions of the Covenant of the League of Nations and (the Charter) of the United Nations, and that (the Palestinians) should alone have the right to determine their future.

Second: Security and order in Palestine have become disrupted. The Zionist aggression resulted in the exodus of more than a quarter of a million of its Arab inhabitants from their homes and in their taking refuge in the neighbouring Arab countries.

The events which have taken place in Palestine have unmasked the aggressive intentions and the imperialistic designs of the Zionists . . .

(continues)

ARAB STATE AND WAR *(continued)*

Sixth: *Therefore, as security in Palestine is a sacred trust in the hands of the Arab States, and in order to put an end to this state of affairs and to prevent it from becoming aggravated or from turning into (a state of) chaos, the extent of which no one can foretell; in order to stop the spreading of disturbances and disorder in Palestine to the neighbouring Arab countries; in order to fill the gap brought about in the governmental machinery in Palestine as a result of the termination of the mandate and the non-establishment of a lawful successor authority, the Governments of the Arab States have found themselves compelled to intervene in Palestine solely in order to help its inhabitants restore peace and security and the rule of justice and law to their country, and in order to prevent bloodshed . . .*

The Governments of the Arab States emphasize, on this occasion, what they have already declared before the London Conference and the United Nations, that the only just solution of the Palestine problem is the establishment of a unitary Palestinian State, in accordance with democratic principles, whereby its inhabitants will enjoy complete equality before the law, (and whereby) minorities will be assured of all the guarantees recognized in democratic constitutional countries, and (whereby) the holy places will be preserved and the right of access thereto guaranteed.

---

forces arrayed against it and added to its territory through a defeat of Arab armies and irregular forces. The armistice agreements between Israel and Egypt (February 24, 1949), Israel and Lebanon (March 23, 1949), Israel and Jordan (April 3, 1949), and Israel and Syria (July 20, 1949) established lines that incorporated thousands of square miles that had been allocated to the Arab state of Palestine by the partition plan. Territories that were now, for the first time, called the Gaza Strip and the West Bank came under Egyptian and Jordanian control.

During the armistice talks between Israel and Egypt, which began on January 13, 1949, on the island of Rhodes, the United Nations mediator and his staff occupied one wing of the hotel, the Israeli delegation occupied a floor in the opposite wing, and the Egyptian delegation resided in the floor above the Israeli delegation. Because of the presence of the UN mediator, the Egyptians considered the talks "not direct." The Israelis, however, claimed them "direct" because the parties were under one roof and at times spoke directly, despite the presence of a mediator. The daily activities were kept secret, which enhanced the success

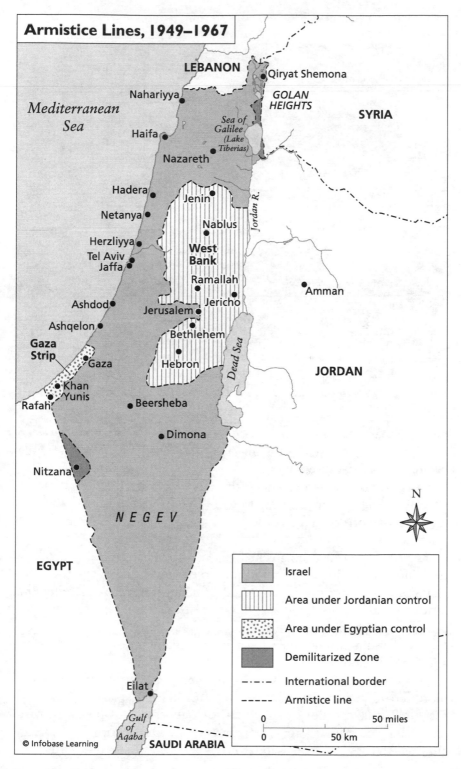

Armistice Lines, 1949–1967

LEBANON

Qiryat Shemona

Mediterranean Sea

Nahariyya

GOLAN HEIGHTS

SYRIA

Haifa

Sea of Galilee (Lake Tiberias)

Nazareth

Hadera

Jenin

Netanya

Nablus

Herzliyya

West Bank

Tel Aviv

Jaffa

Ramallah

Ashdod

Jerusalem

Jericho

Amman

Ashqelon

Bethlehem

Jordan R.

Gaza Strip

Gaza

Hebron

Dead Sea

JORDAN

Khan Yunis

Rafah

Beersheba

Dimona

Nitzana

N E G E V

N

EGYPT

Israel

Area under Jordanian control

Area under Egyptian control

Demilitarized Zone

International border

Armistice line

Eilat

Gulf of Aqaba

SAUDI ARABIA

© Infobase Learning

0   50 miles

0   50 km

53

A wall in Jerusalem marking the division of the city between Jordan and Israel from 1949 to 1967 (Courtesy Embassy of Israel, Washington, D.C.)

of the process. The Rhodes precedent of indirect negotiations between Israel and the Arab states was insisted upon by the Arab states as the prototype for later discussions.

Iraq, although a participant in the conflict, refused to negotiate an armistice. The agreements were to end the hostilities and pave the way for peace negotiations to lead to peace treaties that would replace the armistice agreements, but the latter did not occur.

Each of the armistice agreements was based on several principles: no military or political advantage should be gained under the truce, no changes in military positions should be made by either side after the armistice, and the provisions of the armistices were a consequence of purely military considerations and temporary, pending the negotiation of more binding arrangements. Each agreement set up a mixed armistice commission to observe and maintain the cease-fire.

As a consequence of the War of Independence, Israel encompassed more territory than that allocated to it by the UN partition plan. At the same time, portions of the territory allocated to the Palestinian Arab state came under Egyptian control (the Gaza Strip), and Jordan annexed the area that came to be known as the West Bank. Jerusalem was divided between Israel and Jordan. The 1949 armistice agreements between Israel and the neighboring Arab states also created four demilitarized zones (DMZs)—one on the border with Syria, a second at al-Auja on the border with Egypt, and two in the Jerusalem area including the Hebrew University and Hadassah Hospital and near the high commissioner's palace. A large number of Arabs fled the area of hostilities for more secure areas in the Gaza Strip and West Bank and in neighboring Arab states. By the end of hostilities, the number of refugees reached into the hundreds of thousands (variously estimated between 200,000 and 700,000). Of the original Arab population in Palestine, estimated at 600,000 in 1914, only some 160,000 remained in the territory that was now Israel. A United Nations Relief and Works Agency (UNRWA) was created to help care for the Palestinian refugees, whose status remains a major element of controversy.

The Government

On independence and while fighting the war, Israel began to focus on the need to develop its polity. Social, economic, political, and administrative needs had to be met, and a new state had to be developed. The outline of Israel's system, contained in the declaration of independence, had to be converted into reality. Several issues were crucial and required immediate action: What was to be done about the remnants of European Jewry and the Jews in Arab countries who fled from there to Israel? What should be done about a constitution for the state, and what type and form of political system should be created?

A provisional government formed upon declaring independence was responsible for the administration of the new state. This provisional government was in fact new only in title and name. It had actually begun functioning after the adoption of the UN partition plan and was based on the institutions created by the Yishuv to administer the affairs of the Jewish community under the British mandate and drew on that experience. As early as March 1948, a temporary State Council, chosen from the National Council and the executive committee of the Jewish Agency, had assumed control in many areas. On May 14, this government officially repealed the British mandatory restrictions on immigration and the sale of land.

The provisional government was made up of three elements: the State Council of 38 members, which acted as parliament; a cabinet of 13 ministers, elected by the State Council from among its members; and a president elected by the State Council. Ben-Gurion, chairman of the

Jewish Agency and leader of the dominant political party, Mapai (Israel Workers Party), was elected prime minister (the leader of the new government) and minister of defense; Weizmann was elected president (head of state and essentially a figurehead). The National Council of the mandate period formed the basis of the State Council; the executive committee of the National Council became the cabinet; the presidency was entirely new.

Among the initial actions was to convert the Haganah into the Israel Defense Forces (IDF). After the Arab invasion, Israel's provisional government issued an order that established the IDF (Zvah Hagana Leyisrael) and outlawed all other military forces in the country. The Irgun and the Stern Gang were reluctant to disband and merge into the IDF, but soon afterward Irgun members were successfully incorporated. The *Altalena* incident (SEE sidebar, pages 36–37) made it clear that the government would not tolerate challenges to its authority or the existence of armed forces competing with the IDF. It also contributed to the personal animosity between Menachem Begin, leader of the Revisionist Zionists and of the Irgun, and Ben-Gurion, the new prime minister, that characterized Israeli politics in subsequent decades.

The provisional government directed the war with the Arab states, levied taxes, established administrative agencies, and conducted essential public services. It functioned from May 14, 1948 until early 1949. At its last session prior to the national elections of January 25, 1949, the State Council adopted a transition ordinance transferring its authority to a Constituent Assembly and extending its own life until that body was convened. The functions of the provisional State Council ceased when the Constituent Assembly convened on February 14, 1949.

This assembly, which later declared itself the first Knesset, was a unicameral parliament composed of 120 members representing 12 of the 24 parties that contested the January 1949 elections. Nearly 85 percent of eligible voters cast their ballots in the election.

The institutions of the new state and the individuals who ran them were charged with a series of responsibilities whose cumulative effect was to create a functioning Jewish state in the territory allocated by the United Nations. Israel became the 59th member of the United Nations on May 11, 1949.

The First Election

The first Knesset elections were held on January 25, 1949, in all areas then under the jurisdiction of the State of Israel. It was a test of the state and its ability to establish and sustain a democratic structure. The

President Chaim Weizmann casts his ballot in the first Knesset election, January 1949.
(Courtesy Embassy of Israel, Washington, D.C.)

Declaration of the Establishment of the State of Israel called for elections to create a Constituent Assembly, and the existing leadership soon created the procedures for Israel's first parliamentary election. Before this could be done a census was required so that a list of eligible voters could be compiled. The census was taken on November 8, 1948, in the territory under Israeli control as of October 14. This included immigrants who arrived that day. The census identified a population of 712,000 Jews and 69,000 Arabs. The elections were then set for January 25, 1949.

The election campaign was relatively quiet by subsequent Israeli standards, in part because so many Israelis were serving in the army and because there was no expectation of great political changes given the prominence of the prestatehood groups and leaders. Ben-Gurion was associated with and widely given credit for the political and military triumphs of the Jewish community in Palestine and with the postindependence state. Challenging him and his Mapai Party would prove a daunting task. New political groups were established, but it was difficult for them to develop quickly a substantial constituency under existing conditions in the short period since independence.

The elections reflected an orderly democratic process, and a large number of political parties contested the 120 seats in the parliament. There were no major disturbances and no complaints of election fraud. Officially, there were 506,567 eligible voters and 440,095 of them (86.9 percent) voted. (For each election, the Knesset specifies/defines voting eligibility. The criteria are similar to those in the United States.) The results reflected a generally left-of-center, labor-oriented electorate. Mapai clearly emerged as the most powerful party, gaining 46 of the 120 seats in the Knesset.

Significantly, this first election took place while the country was still at war with its Arab neighbors, armistice agreements had not yet been negotiated, and its place in the region and the world had not been assured. In addition, many of the voters were recent immigrants who had come to the Palestine mandate or to Israel only since the end of World War II, and some were Holocaust survivors. Many had never voted before, and some had little experience with democratic processes or orderly governmental change. So the experience of the first election was important in convincing Israelis that the democratic process and the parliamentary system not only worked but allowed expression of their views for the orderly functioning and changing of government.

The first election led to the establishment of a coalition government, a pattern that has been followed ever since, because no single party won a majority of the seats in parliament. The coalition was composed primarily of the left-of-center parties and the religious parties, a pattern that also became rather commonplace in subsequent decades. But there were religious differences and discord that soon led to the need for a second parliamentary election, which took place in 1951.

The Second Knesset Election

The second election did not show any significant shift in the composition of the Knesset with the exception of an increase in votes for the General Zionists. More than 75 percent of the eligible voters participated in the second election on July 30, 1951, but again did not give a majority to any one party. Mapai again emerged as the dominant party and again formed the government with religious party participation. The majority of its members were the old guard followed by officials of the Histadrut and its numerous bodies.

Constitutional Consensus

Israel is a republic based on an unwritten constitution. The first act of the Constituent Assembly in February 1949 was to enact the Transition Law (Small Constitution) that became the basis of constitutional life in the state. Administrative and executive procedures were based on a combination of past experience in self-government, elements adapted from the former mandatory structure, and new legislation. According to the Small Constitution, Israel was established as a republic with a weak president and a strong cabinet and parliament. It was anticipated that this document would be replaced in due course by a more extensive one, and the first Knesset devoted much time to a profound discussion of the constitutional issue. The main poles of the debate were between those who favored a written constitution and those who believed that the time was not appropriate for imposing rigid constitutional limitations on the country. The latter group argued that a written constitution could not be framed because of constantly changing social conditions resulting from mass immigration and lack of experience with independent governmental institutions. There was also concern about the relationship between state and religion and the method of incorporating the precepts and ideals of Judaism into the proposed document. The discussion of these issues continued for more than a year. On June 13, 1950, it was decided that a written constitution would ultimately be adopted, but that for the time being there would not be a formal and comprehensive document. Instead, a number of fundamental or basic laws would be passed dealing with specific subjects, which might in time form chapters in a consolidated constitution.

Nevertheless, there are areas of general consensus, which together with the fundamental laws form the parameters of Israel's system. Israel's "Jewishness" is perhaps the most significant area of agreement, although there is a divergence of views on some of its tenets and their interpretation. This general agreement centers on what are sometimes termed the goals or purposes of Israel such as the "ingathering of the exiles" (the return of the Jewish people from the Diaspora to their ancient homeland in Eretz Yisrael) and the establishment of a state based on "Jewish" principles. Consensus is similarly applied to the view that Israel should be a welfare state, although there are conflicting views regarding the specific scope and method of implementation of this principle. Foreign and security policy constitutes another area enjoying wide consensus because of its overriding importance in light of the continuing Israel-Arab dispute. The IDF enjoys an enviable military reputation despite occasional criticism of its actions. It remains outside politics and under civilian control and is identified with the state rather than with any particular group or party but has served as an incubator for future political leaders. Its role in internal cohesion is increased by universal military service and the great awareness of the security situation.

Political Institutions

The president, the government (cabinet), and the parliament (Knesset) perform the basic political functions of the state within the framework delineated by Israel's constitutional consensus. The president is elected by parliament. He is head of state, and his powers and functions are essentially of a representative character.

The member of parliament entrusted with the task of forming the government establishes a cabinet, generally with himself as prime minister and a number of ministers. The government is constitutionally instituted upon obtaining a vote of confidence from the parliament. The cabinet is collectively responsible to parliament, reports to it, and remains in office as long as it enjoys the confidence of that body. A government's tenure may also be terminated by ending the parliament's tenure, by the resignation of the government on its own initiative, or by the resignation of the prime minister.

The Knesset is the supreme authority in the state. It is a unicameral parliament of 120 members elected by national, general, secret, direct, equal, and proportional suffrage for a term not to exceed four years. The main functions of the Knesset are similar to those of most modern parliaments. They include expressing a vote of confidence or no-confidence in the government, legislating, participating in the formation of national policy, and supervising the activities of the governmental administration. The Knesset must also approve the budget and taxation, elect the president, recommend the appointment of the state comptroller, and participate in the appointment of judges.

Law of Return

Zionism as a political solution to anti-Semitism was enshrined in Israel's declaration of independence. Israel faced the practical issue of what to do about Jewish remnants in Europe and Jews elsewhere who saw Israel as a refuge from their problems in their respective states.

LAW OF RETURN
(1950)

1. Every Jew has the right to come to this country as an *oleh* [Jew immigrating to Israel].
2. (a) *Aliyah* [immigration of Jews to Israel] shall be by *oleh*'s visa.
   (b) An *oleh*'s visa shall be granted to every Jew who has expressed his desire to settle in Israel, unless the Minister of Immigration is satisfied that the applicant-
   (1) is engaged in an activity directed against the Jewish people; or
   (2) is likely to endanger public health or the security of the state.
3. (a) A Jew who has come to Israel and subsequent to his arrival has expressed his desire to settle in Israel may, while still in Israel, receive an *oleh*'s certificate.
   (b) The restrictions specified in section 2(b) shall apply also to the grant of an *oleh*'s certificate, but a person shall not be regarded as endangering public health on account of an illness contracted after his arrival in Israel.
4. Every Jew who has immigrated into this country before the coming into force of this Law, every Jew who was born in this country, whether before or after the coming into force of this Law, shall be deemed to be a person who has come to this country as an *oleh* under this Law.
5. The Minister of Immigration is charged with the implementation of this Law and may make regulations as to any matter relating to such implementation and also as to the grant of *oleh*'s visas and *oleh*'s certificates to minors up to the age of 18 years.

Upon independence, Israel reversed the British restrictions on Jewish immigration to Palestine, affirmed the right of every Jew to live in Israel, and allowed essentially unfettered immigration in the Law of Return (1950). In the first four months of independence, some 50,000

The prickly pear cactus (in Hebrew tzabar) that grows in Israel. It characterizes the native-born Israeli, or sabra, whose nickname is derived from the plant. (Courtesy Embassy of Israel, Washington, D.C.)

newcomers, mainly Holocaust survivors, arrived in Israel; by the end of 1951, a total of 687,000 had arrived, more than 300,000 of them from Arab states, thus doubling the Jewish population.

Israel's Early Years

In Israel's early years, the economic strain caused by the War of Independence and the need to provide for a rapidly growing, primarily immigrant population required austerity and rationing at home and financial aid from abroad. Assistance extended by the U.S. government, loans from U.S. banks, contributions of Diaspora Jews, and postwar German reparations were all used to build housing, mechanize agriculture, set up a merchant fleet and a national airline, exploit available minerals, develop industries, and expand roads, telecommunications, and electricity networks.

Toward the end of Israel's first decade, the output of industry had doubled, as did the number of employed persons, with industrial exports increasing fourfold. The vast expansion of agriculture had brought about self-sufficiency in the supply of basic food products except meat and grains, and the area under cultivation increased dramatically. During this time, native-born Israelis began to use the nickname *sabra* (literally, "prickly pear" in Hebrew)—tough on the outside (enabling survival in a harsh environment against enemies sworn to their demise) and soft and sweet on the inside.

The educational system was greatly expanded. School attendance became free and compulsory for all children between the ages of five and 14. Cultural and artistic activity flourished, blending Middle Eastern and Western elements, as immigrant Jews arriving from all parts of the world brought with them the unique traditions of their own communities as well as those of the culture prevailing in the countries where they had lived for generations.

When Chaim Weizmann, Israel's first president died in 1952, he was replaced by Itzhak Ben-Zvi, who served until his death in 1963. David Ben-Gurion remained prime minister until December 1953, when he temporarily retired to a kibbutz in the Negev desert area to serve as an example to Israeli youth. Foreign minister Moshe Sharett then became prime minister. Ben-Gurion returned to the government as defense minister in February 1955 and eight months later regained the post of prime minister, which he continued to hold until 1963. Despite crises in the governing coalition and frequent political party splits and mergers, Israel's political system and government were remarkably stable.

Tension and Conflict with the Arabs

The armistice agreements of 1949 were not followed by comprehensive peace as intended. In general, the Arab states refused to accept their defeat, continued to regard the establishment of Israel as an injustice to

ASHKENAZI, SEPHARDI, AND ORIENTAL JEWS

Although Israel is a Jewish state and the overwhelming majority of its citizens are Jews, they are of diverse backgrounds and customs, as a consequence of the worldwide dispersion of the Jews over the centuries. Among Jews, there are three general divisions.

Ashkenazi Jews (Ashkenazim) are predominantly Jews of eastern and central European origin and descent, although they have migrated to various other areas. Ashkenazi Jews immigrated to Palestine and Israel in large numbers late in the 19th century and during the first half of the 20th century where they shaped the prestate society in the British mandate and became the leaders of the Yishuv and the state in its earliest years.

Sephardi Jews (Sephardim) are descendants of Jews who were expelled from Spain and Portugal at the end of the 15th century and settled in other European countries such as Holland, Bulgaria, Greece, and Turkey. Sephardi immigration to Israel was dramatic after independence was declared.

Oriental, or Eastern, Jews (sometimes erroneously grouped with Sephardim) have their origins in the ancient Jewish communities of the Islamic countries of North Africa and the Middle East. Some went to Israel centuries before the founding of the state, others in the late 19th and 20th centuries. The largest numbers, however, went to Israel in the 1950s.

In Israel's first years, Holocaust survivors and others from Europe and entire Jewish communities in North Africa and the Middle East arrived in large numbers. Israel's society was thus composed of a "first Israel" of Ashkenazim, both veterans and newcomers primarily from Europe, and some longtime residents of the Holy Land of Sephardic background, and a "Second Israel" of Oriental immigrants who were unfamiliar with the democratic process and the nature and requirements of a modern, industrialized society. Initially, the two groups did not meld.

Second Israel did not readily adopt or adapt to Western mores but rather tended to adhere to traditional Judaism and the values generally inherent in Eastern societies. They also tended to be less educated

be corrected, and sustained a political and economic boycott of Israel. While Israel was engaged in state-building, these efforts were overshadowed by growing and serious security problems. The armistice agreements often were violated by the Arab states, as was a United Nations

Jewish immigrants to Israel (olim) from Yemen, 1949 (Courtesy Embassy of Israel, Washington, D.C.)

than Ashkenazim. The result was a great difference in socioeconomic status. Second Israel was involved in antigovernment demonstrations and support in elections for opposition parties (as occurred in the 1977 political "earthquake" that brought the right-wing Likud bloc to power).

By the 1980s, there were advances on all levels for those of Second Israel, and by the 1990s, members of the Oriental Jewish communities held senior positions in the government, reached high ranks in the military, and made achievements in all facets of economic and cultural life. Consequently, references to Second Israel had virtually disappeared by the beginning of the 21st century. The term increasingly was used for second-, third-, even fourth-generation Israelis whose backgrounds were in Islamic countries. Moshe Katsav, a first-generation member of Second Israel was the first to represent it as president of Israel. When he was elected president in July 2000, the term was suddenly and briefly resurrected.

Security Council resolution of September 1, 1951, that called for Israeli and Israel-bound shipping to pass through the Suez Canal connecting the Gulf of Suez and the Mediterranean Sea. An Egyptian blockade of the Strait of Tiran was sustained, thus preventing shipping to and from Israel's port city of Eilat, the country's gateway to East Africa and the Far East. Terrorist groups engaged in sabotage and murder and launched raids into Israel from neighboring Arab states.

Following the signing of the armistice agreements in 1949, the Arab states maintained a policy of isolating Israel and of focusing their rhetoric on a "second round" of war. There was an increase in attacks against Israel, leading in 1951 to more than 150 Israelis killed or wounded, the worst attacks originating in the Gaza Strip. Israel adopted an active strategy, including a campaign of reprisal raids. These raids had early failures, and reprisals helped little in reducing the threat of infiltrating terrorists. But planning continued, and the Israelis contemplated the occupation of Gaza, which would deny the Arabs a launching pad from which to attack Israeli population centers. The IDF created an elite force of paratroop commandos, known as Unit 101, to launch a campaign of reprisal raids into enemy territory in an effort to halt the attacks on Israel. Ariel Sharon became the commander of these special forces.

Tensions rose on Israel's borders as Palestinians, often accompanied by other Arabs, began infiltrating into Israel from the West Bank and the Gaza Strip and attacking people and property. Israel held the Arab governments responsible and launched retaliatory raids. The ensuing cycle of violence, in which Israeli and Arab civilians and soldiers were killed, escalated and encompassed Syria as well. Conflicts also arose over control of DMZs along the frontiers and over projects to divert the Jordan River water for use in Israel's more arid sectors.

In the years immediately following the 1952 Egyptian revolution, which overthrew King Farouk and brought Gamal Abdul Nasser to power, the new government continued its opposition to Israel's existence and built its military capability. The threat to Israel grew as the Arab states established military alliances and linkages. Tensions continued to increase, and the situation was exacerbated by external arms supplies. On February 28, 1955, Israeli forces launched a raid against an Egyptian army base in the Gaza Strip. President Nasser later argued that this raid prompted him to organize Palestinian fedayeen (Arab commando) operations against Israel. He also intensified efforts to build a strong military and to acquire arms from outside sources. Egypt concluded an arms deal with Czechoslovakia (acting for the Soviet Union) to enhance its military strength that was announced on September 27, 1955. Israel found these developments, along with Nasser's emergence as the leader of an Arab nationalist movement, threatening.

As the fedayeen actions became bolder and more Israelis were killed, Israel sought to negatively affect Egypt's relations with the United States and Great Britain by bombing U.S. installations in Egypt in 1954 and trying to place the blame on Egypt. This would later become known as the Lavon Affair, when it was uncovered during a 1960 investigation. Israel also contemplated striking deeper into Egypt than Gaza, using a force large enough to deny the Egyptians their base of operations in the Sinai Peninsula as a whole.

By mid-1955, with the return of Ben-Gurion to the cabinet and the decline in fortunes of Prime Minister Moshe Sharett, who advocated a more restrained Israeli retaliatory policy, the Israeli government moved toward war. Ben-Gurion had already decided that a war was inevitable, and on October 2, 1955, ordered the IDF chief of staff, Moshe Dayan, to prepare for a major military action. The first step was to test new tactics in an operation against Egyptian forces that had occupied the al-Auja DMZ. Unit 101, the commando/paratroops unit under Sharon, operated in coordination with regular army forces to attack and evict Egyptian forces with minimal casualties.

Nasser, nevertheless, continued to pose a threat to Israel, as well as to European nations such as Great Britain—whose presence in Egypt, especially in the Suez Canal Zone, he hoped to bring to an end—and France, which had colonies in North Africa. In July 1956, Egypt nationalized the Suez Canal and other British and French properties in Egypt creating a congruence of interests between Israel and these two European states.

By October 1956, fedayeen raids had reached an all-time high in both violence and intensity, and the Israeli reprisals had not succeeded in preventing new ones. The Israeli objectives thus became to relieve the Egyptian stranglehold over Israel's sea routes via the Suez Canal and the Strait of Tiran to Israel and to counter Egypt's threat by fedayeen and rearmed Egyptian forces against it on its western borders in both the Gaza Strip and the Sinai Peninsula. A regime change in Egypt that would bring a less bellicose neighbor was also a desired objective.

By late October, Britain and France had agreed with Israel to launch a coordinated action against Nasser's Egypt. The arrangement was that Israeli forces would invade the Sinai Peninsula, followed by an Anglo-French ultimatum to both Israel and Egypt to agree immediately to a cease-fire while Anglo-French troops seized the canal, ostensibly to protect it. It was anticipated that this would ensure the safety of the Suez Canal, lead to the ouster of Nasser, and reduce the threat to Israel from the largest Arab state.

MOSHE DAYAN
(MAY 20, 1915–OCTOBER 16, 1981)

Moshe Dayan was born in Kibbutz Degania in 1915 but grew up in Nahalal. Dayan was one of the first to join the Palmach (the domestic defense force) when it was established, on May 18, 1941, and served under Orde Wingate in his "night squads" (mobile bands of fighters created to deter nighttime Arab attacks on isolated Jewish settlements). From 1939 to 1941, Dayan was imprisoned by the British in Acre on charges of possession of illegal firearms but was released in order to take part in an Allied venture against Vichy France in Syria and Lebanon in 1941. On June 7, Dayan headed a squad of Haganah members who joined the British in an operation intended to destroy bridges in Syria. During an assault on a police station he lost his left eye. He wore an eye patch from then on, and it became his distinguishing trademark. In July 1948, he was made the commanding officer of Jerusalem while it was under siege. In that capacity he took part in informal negotiations with King Abdullah of Jordan and later served as a member of the Israeli delegation to the armistice negotiations in Rhodes. Between 1950 and 1953, Dayan served as commander of the southern and northern commands of the Israel Defense Forces (IDF) and later head of the General Branch of Operations in the General Staff. In December 1953, he was appointed chief of staff after a stormy cabinet defense committee meeting and with David Ben-Gurion's support.

Dayan led the IDF during the Sinai Campaign of 1956 then left the army in January 1958. In November 1959, he was elected as a member of the Knesset on the Mapai list and became minister of agriculture in Prime Minister Ben-Gurion's government. In 1963, Ben-Gurion left Mapai over the Lavon Affair and established Rafi. Dayan joined Ben-Gurion and Shimon Peres, who served during this period as deputy defense minister, but continued to serve as minister of agriculture under Prime Minister Levi Eshkol. Dayan resigned from the cabinet on November 4, 1964, when Eshkol tried to prevent him from participating in the formulation of defense policy. In 1965, he was elected to the sixth Knesset on the Rafi list.

Sinai Campaign, 1956

On October 29, 1956, Israel's campaign began with a daring paratroop drop deep into the central area of the Sinai Peninsula at the eastern

Chief of Staff Moshe Dayan with IDF soldiers at Sharm el-Sheikh in the Sinai Peninsula, 1956 (Courtesy Embassy of Israel, Washington D.C.)

In June 1967, by popular demand, Prime Minister Eshkol was forced to appoint Dayan as minister of defense. This appointment inspired the country with confidence. When Eshkol was succeeded by Golda Meir, Dayan remained as minister of defense. He was among those blamed by the public for the delay in the mobilization of Israel's reserve forces at the time of the Yom Kippur War but continued to serve under Meir's leadership after the elections of December 31, 1973.

When Meir resigned in April 1974, however, the new prime minister, Yitzhak Rabin, did not include Dayan in the cabinet. Between 1974 and 1977, Dayan served as a member of the Knesset and actively pursued his interests in archaeological excavation. When Menachem Begin became prime minister in 1977, Dayan joined the government as foreign minister and in that capacity played a crucial role in the negotiations that led to the Camp David Accords and the Egypt-Israel Peace Treaty. Dayan resigned in 1979 over differences of viewpoint and policy with Begin. On April 4, 1981, Dayan established a new political party, Telem, which secured two mandates in the 1981 Knesset elections. Dayan died later that year.

entrance to the Mitla Pass, some 150 miles from Israel and 50 miles from the Suez Canal. At this key line of communication at the western end of the Sinai Peninsula, paratroopers would sever communications with Egypt's forces in the Sinai. This was to pave the way for the Anglo-French intervention to protect the canal and ensure it would remain open. One day after the drop, on October 30, the French and British issued an ultimatum calling on both sides to cease fire and withdraw to positions 10 miles on either side of the canal. The Egyptians refused the ultimatum on October 30, allowing Israel to continue fighting and consolidate its control over the peninsula and remove the threat of the Egyptian army. Israeli forces reached the Suez Canal and gained control of the Sinai Peninsula.

Israeli army General Headquarters issued a communiqué:

> Units of the Israeli defense forces have penetrated and attacked fedayeen bases . . . and have taken up positions . . . toward the Suez Canal. This operation was necessitated by the continuous Egyptian military attacks on citizens and on Israel land and sea communications, the purpose of which was to cause destruction and to deprive the people of Israel of the possibility of peaceful existence.

After the commencement of hostilities, the United States took the matter to the United Nations Security Council, and President Dwight Eisenhower made a national radio and television address on October 31, 1956, in which he stated that the action Israel took was wrong. President Eisenhower wrote to Ben-Gurion and pressured Israel to withdraw from Sinai. In its efforts to secure Israel's withdrawal, the United States sought to reassure Israel with regard to the passage of Israeli shipping through the Strait of Tiran and in the Gulf of Aqaba.

As part of that process, U.S. secretary of state John Foster Dulles handed to the Israeli ambassador to the United States, Abba Eban, an aide-mémoire on February 11, 1957, seeking to assure Israel that the Gulf of Aqaba "comprehends" international waters and that no state had the right to prevent free and innocent passage in the gulf and "through the Straits giving access thereto." He said that the United States, "in the absence of some overriding decision to the contrary, as by the International Court of Justice," was prepared to exercise the right of free and innocent passage and to "join with others to secure general recognition of this right."

Eventually Israel withdrew from all of the captured Egyptian territory and the Gaza Strip to the prewar frontiers under the weight of UN resolutions, but especially the Eisenhower administration's pressure. The United Nations Emergency Force (UNEF) was created to patrol the Egyptian side of the armistice line, which it did until the days immediately preceding the 1967 Six-Day War. The UN force was also to have deployed in the Gaza Strip to keep that area demilitarized and end the threat of further fedayeen raids, but this provision was never implemented. The sea lanes through the Strait of Tiran from the Red Sea to the Israeli port of Eilat were opened, for the first time, to Israeli shipping. But the hope that peace talks might follow was not realized. Although the other Arab states did not join in the hostilities they made no effort to reach a peace agreement with Israel, and the territories of those states that shared a frontier with Israel, often became bases for attacks across the border into Israel. Israel maintained and strengthened its defensive posture and capability to deal with the Arab threat.

Israel, 1957–1967

Israel's conflict with the Arabs receded into the background for much of the next decade as its frontier with Egypt remained quiet, although sporadic border incidents continued on other fronts, mainly with Syria. Industrial and agricultural development allowed the government to end its austerity measures, unemployment almost disappeared, and living standards improved.

During the country's second decade, emphasis was placed on relations with the rest of the world. Foreign relations expanded steadily as close ties were developed with the United States, the British Commonwealth countries, most Western European and Asian states, and nearly all the countries of Latin America and Africa. The decade was marked by extensive programs of cooperation, as hundreds of Israeli physicians, engineers, teachers, agronomists, irrigation experts, and youth organizers shared their expertise with the populations of the developing countries in Africa, Asia, and Latin America. Exports doubled and the gross national product (GNP) increased significantly. Israel now manufactured such items as paper, tires, radios, and refrigerators, but the most rapid growth took place in the areas of metals, machinery, chemicals, and electronics. As the domestic market for locally grown food was reaching the saturation point, the agricultural sector began to grow a variety of crops for the food-processing industry as well as for export. To handle the greatly increased volume of trade, a deep-water port was constructed on the Mediterranean coast at Ashdod, in addition to the existing one at Haifa.

ISRAEL AND
THE DEVELOPING WORLD

Israel's response to the emergence from colonial control of the new states of Africa and Asia in the 1950s and 1960s focused on helping them develop and prosper. Israel sought to befriend less-developed states by pursuing a policy in keeping with its own aspirations for economic development and modernization. Israel's policy constituted an important area of its overall foreign policy and involved exchange and training programs, technical assistance, joint economic enterprises, loans, and trade.

Students and civil servants were trained in Israel, where university scholarships enabled them to acquire specialized education. The initial decade involved thousands of young people from countries in Africa, Asia, the Mediterranean basin, Latin America, and the Caribbean. They came to Israel to study methods of agricultural settlement, the labor movement, youth education in the Nahal and Gadna programs, vocational training and cooperation, and various branches of science at the Hebrew University in Jerusalem, the Technion in Haifa, and the Weizmann Institute of Science in Rehovot. At the same time, thousands of Israeli experts were active in Asian, African, and Latin American countries. Israeli professors and instructors were provided to overseas educational institutions, where they taught subjects ranging from eye surgery to ship navigation. Israeli technicians and specialists in various fields, including city planning, union organization, tourism, irrigation, and water supply, were sent to developing countries, as well as a large number of Israeli advisers in the fields of agriculture, agricultural planning, and cooperative arrangements. Other major fields of assistance included doctors and medical technicians, educators, armed forces instructors, and youth corps leaders.

A number of economic enterprises jointly owned by Israeli organizations and foreign governments or agencies were established. The basic idea was to train local personnel so that the home country could take over complete control of the company after a specified period.

Israeli trade with these states was on a small scale, but both sides profited by it. Israel was able to gain markets for its manufactured goods, while the trading partners supplied raw materials for Israeli processing and manufacturing industries.

Water pipes for Israel's National Water Carrier (Courtesy Embassy of Israel, Washington D.C.)

Israel's efforts to "make the desert bloom" and to provide adequate water supplies for its citizens reached an important milestone when the National Water Carrier was put into operation in 1964. It was to bring water from Lake Tiberias (the Sea of Galilee) to various parts of the country, including the northern arid Negev, through a series of aqueducts, canals, pipes, reservoirs, dams, tunnels, and pumping stations.

In 1965, a permanent building for the Knesset was built in Jerusalem, and facilities for the Hadassah Medical Center and the Hebrew University were constructed on alternate sites to replace the original buildings on Mount Scopus, which had to be abandoned after the War of Independence. The Israel Museum was established with the aim of collecting, conserving, studying, and exhibiting the cultural and artistic treasures of the Jewish people.

Domestic Politics

David Ben-Gurion resigned as prime minister in 1963 and two years later led his supporters, including Minister of Agriculture Moshe Dayan and Deputy Defense Minister Shimon Peres, out of Mapai and into his

73

The candelabrum, symbol of Israel, stands opposite the entrance to the Knesset compound. It has seven branches decorated with relief panels that depict figures and events in Jewish history. (Courtesy Bernard Reich)

new political party, the Israel Labor List (Rafi). Levi Eshkol of Mapai took Ben-Gurion's place as prime minister from 1963 until his death in 1969, when former Foreign Minister Golda Meir replaced him.

An economic recession began in 1965 and unemployment grew. These led to domestic distress and a declining economic and social status for much of Israel's population. As a consequence of this and security issues, emigration from Israel rose.

Perhaps the most noteworthy event of this period was the Eichmann trial, which generated extensive worldwide attention. Adolf Eichmann was brought to Israel on May 23, 1960, to stand trial under the Nazis and Nazi Collaborators (Punishment) Law of 1950. Eichmann was born in Solingen, Germany, in 1906. He became an SS officer and under the Nazi regime was one of the main organizers of Adolf Hitler's "final solution," the extermination of European Jews, during World War II. At the end of the war, he escaped to Argentina where he was captured by Israeli agents in 1960 and brought to Israel. His trial opened in April 1961 and eventually he was found guilty of war crimes against humanity and the Jewish people and was sentenced to death. After the rejection of his appeal to the Supreme Court, he was hanged on May 31, 1962. It was the only time that the death penalty has been carried out under Israeli law.

Israel and Germany

In 1965, Israel exchanged ambassadors with the Federal Republic of Germany (West Germany), a move that had been delayed until then because of the bitter memories of the Holocaust. Vehement opposition and public debate in Israel preceded normalization of relations.

West Germany's approach to Israel had its origins in the views and policies of its first postwar chancellor, Konrad Adenauer, who believed that there should be reconciliation between Germany and the Jewish people. Adenauer admitted to crimes committed by Germany against the Jewish people and argued that the rehabilitation of the Jews through moral and material reparations by Germany was essential. After negotiations, which began in the early 1950s, a restitution agreement (known as the Luxembourg Agreement) was signed by representatives of Israel and West Germany, and a second agreement was signed by West Germany with the Conference on Jewish Material Claims against Germany in September 1952, despite strong Arab opposition. The agreements were of great importance to Israel as they provided substantial economic support at a crucial time for the young state. West

Adolf Eichmann on trial in Jerusalem for Nazi-era war crimes, 1961 (Courtesy Embassy of Israel, Washington D.C.)

Germany subsequently became a supplier of military equipment to the Jewish state. Nevertheless and despite the significance of these agreements for Israel, there was strong opposition in Israel to any arrangement with West Germany, the successor state to Nazi Germany. A number of issues that precluded substantial movement toward a diplomatic relationship between Israel and West Germany included the trial of Adolf Eichmann, which rekindled old memories, and the activities of German scientists in assisting in the development of Arab military capabilities. Diplomatic relations between the two states were achieved only in 1965. For West Germany, the agreements were crucial in helping to reestablish its international position and to help prepare the way for its reintegration into the Western European alliance structure. West Germany became a major trading partner with Israel, and its aid to Israel was indispensable to the economic growth of the state.

Growing Arab-Israeli Tension and Progression

The decade after the Sinai Campaign of 1956 was one of relative tranquility for Israel. Although no appreciable progress was made toward resolving the issues of the Arab-Israeli conflict, no major hostilities took place. The Egypt-Israel frontier remained calm but tense, and there were exchanges along Israel's frontiers with Jordan and Syria, including a growing number of terrorist raids into Israel.

As Israel put its National Water Carrier into operation in 1964, and began to divert water from the Jordan River for use by the growing population in its heartland, the situation deteriorated. Syria responded with efforts to divert the Jordan River to reduce its flow to Israel. Tensions between Israel and Syria over water and the use of the DMZs between them led to numerous border incidents. This war over water had its origins in the Arab Summit in Cairo in 1964, when the Arab leaders made it a matter of policy to divert the waters of the Jordan River. Funds were allocated for this purpose, and both Syria and Lebanon began work on projects to shunt the waters of the Hasbani and Banias Rivers away from the Jordan River, where Israel could not utilize it. Israel noted that such actions would be considered acts of war. Israel used artillery and tank fire and aircraft to stop these projects. The Israelis proved successful, and the Arab efforts were halted.

On February 22, 1966, a coup d'état brought a radical military regime to power in Syria. The new Syrian government noted its desire to make common cause with progressive and leftist elements of the Arab world to confront imperialist moves and alliances. The new regime's policy focused on the Palestine problem and the necessity of a war to secure the liberation of the usurped Arab land. It called for the unification of popular forces to face the Zionist enemy and expel it from Palestine.

In a speech on February 22, 1966, President Nasser of Egypt (then known as the United Arab Republic, or UAR, because of a short-lived union between Egypt and Syria) articulated his view that the forces of Arab unity and Arab nationalism were divided by imperialism and reaction. Nasser argued that Israel was planted in the heart of the Arab nation to prevent cooperation among the Arab states by sowing seeds of sedition, discord, and division.

On November 4, Egypt and Syria signed a mutual-defense agreement known as the Cairo-Damascus Defense Pact. It provided for the establishment of joint command over the armed forces of the two states. Each state would regard armed aggression against the other as an attack against itself and would come to the aid of its defense partner by taking all necessary measures, including the use of armed force, to defeat the aggressor.

On November 13, Israel launched a retaliatory raid against the Jordanian village of Samua. Two days prior, three soldiers had been killed by a mine planted by Fatah, a group within the Palestine Liberation Organization (PLO). Fighting between the Israeli army and

THE PALESTINE LIBERATION ORGANIZATION

The Palestine Liberation Organization (known popularly as the PLO) was originally created and established by the Arab League in 1964 to represent the Palestinian people wherever they may live and to help coordinate Arab military efforts against Israel. It soon became an umbrella organization for a number of Palestinian groups and entities generally committed to the replacement of Israel by a Palestinian state. In 1965 Palestinians began armed attacks from the bordering Arab states against Israel, to which the latter responded with reprisal raids against Syria and Jordan.

Within the PLO was Fatah (the acronym in reverse of Harakat al-Tahrir al-Filistin or Movement for the Liberation of Palestine). (*Al-Fatah* also is "the conquest" in Arabic.) Fatah was founded in the late 1950s by a group of Palestinian students that included Yasser Arafat. Its objective was the liberation of Palestine, and its first armed attack took place on January 1, 1965, against the Israeli National Water Carrier. After the Six-Day War and the substantial Israeli victory, Arafat took over the leadership of Fatah, by then the largest faction in the PLO, and subsequently of the PLO itself. Arafat remained its chairman until his death in late 2004 and was the international representative and symbol of the Palestinian cause and of the PLO. He gave voice to its demands and guided its overall direction and policy.

Israel's relationship with the PLO was slow to develop inasmuch as it was viewed by most Israelis as a terrorist organization pledged to Israel's destruction. Until 1993, it was illegal for an Israeli to have any contact with anyone suspected of membership in the PLO.

The Palestine National Covenant was adopted by the PLO in 1964 as its charter and was modified in 1968. Its central theme was the elimination of Israel and its replacement by a Palestinian state in all of Palestine. Article 1 provides that "Palestine is the homeland of the Arab Palestinian people." At the core of the covenant is Article 20, which declares that the "Balfour Declaration, the Mandate for Palestine and everything that has been based upon them, are deemed null and void." Although various Palestinian leaders have suggested that the covenant has been superseded in part by subsequent statements and declarations, the covenant remained formally unchanged as the guide to Palestinian objectives until December 14, 1998, when the PLO Central Council, meeting in Gaza, voted to revoke the specific clauses of the covenant that called for Israel's destruction, as referred to in a letter from Arafat to U.S. president Bill Clinton pledging to repeal those provisions.

a Jordanian legion unit ensued, leading to the deaths of 15 Jordanian soldiers. Palestinians rioted, complaining that Jordan's King Hussein was not doing enough to defend them.

On April 7, 1967, Syrian military units fired on an Israeli tractor in the DMZ south of Galilee, and mortar, tank, and artillery shellings were concentrated on three Israeli villages in the area. Israel sent planes to destroy the artillery positions and engaged Syrian jets. Israel reported that six MiG-21 aircraft of the Syrian air force were shot down and no Israeli planes lost, while the Syrians claimed victory in the air battle.

Border skirmishes with Jordan and Syria culminated on May 8, 1967, when forces emanating from Syrian territory infiltrated five miles into Israel, planted an explosive charge on the main highway north of the Sea of Galilee, waited for a military vehicle to pass, and then detonated the charge under the vehicle. The deep penetration into Israel, the choice of a major highway, the decision to wait for an appropriate target, and the use of comparatively sophisticated equipment clearly indicated to Israel that the Arab terrorists were able to act in Israel almost with impunity. Israeli prime minister Levi Eshkol indicated that Israel reserved the right of action and that continued acts of terrorism would be responded to by Israel at a time, place, and method of its own choosing.

Northern Israel as seen from pre–Six-Day War (1967) Syrian military positions on the Golan Heights (Courtesy Embassy of Israel, Washington D.C.)

LEVI ESHKOL
(OCTOBER 25, 1895–FEBRUARY 6, 1969)

Levi Eshkol was born in Oratovo in the Kiev district of the Ukraine, in 1895. In January 1914, he set out as part of a contingent representing the Zionist youth organization Hapoel Hatzair (The Young Worker) to the port of Trieste, where he sailed for Jaffa. At first, he served as a common farm laborer and watchman but soon became involved in the building of a pumping station and was elected to the Workers' Agricultural Council of Petah Tikva. He entered military service in the Jewish Legion, and upon demobilization in 1920, he helped to create Kibbutz Degania Bet. When the Histadrut was created in 1920, Eshkol joined the Executive Board, and when the Mapai political party was founded in 1930, he was elected to its Central Council. David Ben-Gurion became a powerful figure in the party, and with him Eshkol was drawn into the party leadership. Eshkol increasingly was seen as a political appendage to Ben-Gurion because of the parallels in their careers and their friendship.

After Israel's independence, Eshkol was appointed director-general of the Ministry of Defense. He was appointed head of the Land Settlement Department of the Jewish Agency in 1949. In 1951, he became minister of agriculture and development and the following year minister of finance. Eshkol replaced Ben-Gurion as prime minister in June 1963 and served in that position until his death in early 1969. He and Ben-Gurion split over the Lavon Affair, which led to the defection of Ben-Gurion from Mapai and the creation of another party, Rafi. Eshkol was known for his contributions to Israel's economic development in a crucial period and for his skills as a compromiser. He led Israel through the Six-Day War and the crisis that preceded it. He was considered one of the more dovish of Israel's leaders and did not wish to formally annex areas inhabited by large numbers of Arabs. Nevertheless, on June 27, 1967, he issued an administrative order to apply Israeli law and administration to East Jerusalem.

Syria reacted by alerting its military, announcing the movement of forces to the Israeli border, and calling for the activation of the Cairo-Damascus Defense Pact. A state of emergency was proclaimed in Egypt on May 16, and consultations were reported in progress between Cairo and Damascus on implementation of their defense pact.

On May 17, Cairo and Damascus announced that the UAR and Syria were combat-ready and alleged that a strong Israeli military buildup on the borders of both countries was taking place. In fact, this was not true; there was no such Israeli buildup. On May 18, Jordan, Iraq, and Kuwait proclaimed that their forces had been mobilized and were ready to take part in the battle against the common enemy. Yemen's support was also pledged to the UAR. Israel announced it was taking appropriate measures in view of the concentration of Arab forces on its borders. The following day, the United Nations Emergency Force was officially withdrawn from the Israeli-Egyptian border at Egypt's request, and its positions were filled by contingents of the PLO and the UAR armed forces. Egypt's Ministry of Religious Affairs ordered the country's religious leaders to preach a jihad (holy war) to regain Palestine for the Arabs. Vitriolic radio attacks were made against Israel, Zionism, and imperialism. Field Marshal Abdul Hakim Amer indicated that UAR armed forces had taken up positions from which they could deliver massive retaliation against Israeli aggression. Troop buildups continued throughout the ensuing period.

On May 21, both Israel and Egypt announced the calling up of reserves, and Cairo spoke of the continued eastward movement of Egyptian armed forces. Ahmed Shukairi, leader of the PLO, announced that some 8,000 of his troops had been placed under the military commands of the UAR, Syria, and Iraq. He declared that Israel would be completely annihilated if war broke out and that the PLO would continue its raids on Israel. In addition, Shukairi called on the Jordanian people to overthrow King Hussein. Syrian defense minister Hafez al-Assad stated that his country's armed forces were ready to repel Israeli aggression and to take the initiative in liberating Palestine and destroying the Zionist presence in the Arab homeland.

On May 23, the UAR announced not only the closing of the Strait of Tiran to Israeli shipping but also the blockade of the Gulf of Aqaba. Such actions effectively blockaded the Israeli port of Eilat at the head of the gulf, Israel's only outlet to the Red Sea. The Cairo announcement said that the blockade applied to vessels flying the Israeli flag and to ships of any other country carrying strategic goods to Eilat. Nasser knew that this would be regarded by Israel as an act of aggression (casus belli) and would almost certainly lead to an armed clash. Israel described this action as a gross infringement of international law and an aggressive act against Israel. It was logical to assume that the United States would concur in Israel's view since it was on record as supporting freedom of passage through the Strait of Tiran.

On May 23, Eshkol spelled out the dangers resulting from the blockade of the strait and called on the United Nations and the major powers to act without delay in maintaining the right of free navigation through the Strait of Tiran and in the gulf. The importance of the Gulf of Aqaba and of Israel's willingness to use military action in support of its claim to freedom of passage was emphasized by Eshkol on May 29, 1967: "Members of the Knesset, the Government of Israel has repeatedly stated its determination to exercise its freedom of passage in the Strait of Tiran and the Gulf of Aqaba and defend it in case of need. This is a supreme national interest on which no concession is possible and no compromise is admissible."

U.S. president Lyndon Johnson stated that the United States considered the Gulf of Aqaba to be an international waterway and that the blockade of Israeli shipping in the gulf was illegal and potentially dangerous to peace. He also expressed dismay at the hurried withdrawal of the United Nations Emergency Force from the Gaza Strip and the Sinai Peninsula and noted that the United States remained firmly committed to the support of the political independence and territorial integrity of all the nations of the Middle East.

On May 26, Nasser stated that if war with Israel should come, the battle would be a general one and "our basic objective will be to destroy Israel." This was based on his assessment of the combined weight of Egypt, Syria, Algeria, Iraq, and Kuwait against Israel. He referred to the United States as the chief defender of Israel and an enemy of the Arabs, described Britain as "America's lackey," and noted that France had "remained impartial" on the question of Aqaba and did not toe the U.S. or British line. In Jerusalem, Israeli officials warned that Israel would not wait indefinitely for an end to the Egyptian blockade of Aqaba and stressed that it would be entirely within its rights in breaking the blockade as an act of self-defense if the United Nations or the maritime powers did not do so.

On May 30, Egypt and Jordan entered into a defense pact in which both states committed themselves to "immediately take all measures and employ all means at their disposal, including the use of the armed forces." On June 4, King Hussein announced that the Egyptian-Jordanian Mutual Defense Treaty had been extended to include Iraq. With Iraq's acquiescence, Egypt could include Syria, Iraq, and Jordan in its defense system.

In June 1967, Israel was surrounded by Arab states dedicated to its eradication. The objective was referred to as "politicide," the destruction of a state. Between 1949 and 1967, many Israelis had been hopeful that peace with the Arab states could be established based on the 1949 armistice agreements. Now, the crisis of 1967 convinced many Israelis that politicide was the goal of the Arab world. Egypt was ruled by Nasser, a nationalist whose army was the strongest in the Arab Middle East. Syria was governed by the radical Baathist Party, constantly issuing threats to push Israel into the sea. The PLO focused on replacing Israel with Palestine.

As the crisis developed, Israel sent Foreign Minister Abba Eban to the United States to inquire into its position. En route he met with President Charles de Gaulle of France and Prime Minister Harold Wilson of Great Britain. During his discussions with U.S. president Johnson, Eban noted that Israel was ready, willing, and able to utilize military force in support of its position concerning the Gulf of Aqaba. Johnson urged restraint and suggested that Israel wait for the exhaustion of diplomatic efforts.

Once the United States and Great Britain had attempted to ensure freedom of navigation and were seemingly making little headway, public pressures in Israel were exerted to include former chief of staff of the IDF Moshe Dayan in the government as minister of defense. It was reported that on the evening of May 30, Eshkol was confronted by his cabinet, who suggested that for the sake of stability either Dayan or Yigal Allon, former commander of the Palmach, had to be co-opted. Eshkol's initial opposition to the inclusion of either man stemmed from long-standing political arguments, as both were critics of Eshkol and opponents of his policies. Dayan, widely admired in Israel because of his role in the establishment of the IDF's commando units and for an aggressive retaliatory doctrine that culminated in the Sinai Campaign, felt that the appropriate and immediate response should be essentially military, not political. His co-option to the government as minister of defense indicated that the time left for diplomacy to prevent war was short. Israel established a national unity government, with a "wall-to-wall" coalition to deal with the crisis.

4

FROM THE SIX-DAY WAR
TO THE YOM KIPPUR WAR
AND ITS AFTERMATH
(1967–1975)

The Six-Day War of June 1967 was a major watershed in the history of Israel, of the Arab-Israeli conflict, and of the Middle East. It altered the geography of the region, changed military and political perceptions, and triggered an intensified international effort to resolve the Arab-Israeli conflict with expanded U.S. involvement.

Throughout the period between the Six-Day War and the Yom Kippur War of 1973, the focal point was the effort to achieve a settlement of the Arab-Israeli conflict and to secure a just and lasting peace based on UN Security Council Resolution 242. Although some of the efforts were promising, peace was not achieved and there was little movement in that direction. The 1969–70 War of Attrition, formally launched by Egypt against Israel along the Suez Canal in April 1969, and the 1973 Yom Kippur War marked the fourth and fifth rounds of conflict between Israel and the Arabs. It was also in this period that a restructured PLO emerged under the leadership of Yasser Arafat and posed new challenges to Israel.

The Six-Day War
On June 5, 1967, war broke out between Israel and Egypt and was followed shortly by a general Arab-Israeli confrontation. Israel launched a preemptive strike against Egypt on the morning of June 5. The Israeli action was taken in the context of a crisis situation that included assertions of belligerent intent on the part of Israel's Arab neighbors. In the weeks leading up to June 5, Israel found itself surrounded by large

Israeli paratroopers at the Western Wall during the Six-Day War, June 1967 (Courtesy Embassy of Israel, Washington, D.C.)

armies mobilizing in Syria, Jordan, and Egypt. The combined military forces on these three fronts gave Israel a distinct disadvantage in military readiness. In the face of these overwhelming odds, Israel planned to strike the Egyptian air force while still on the ground: On the morning of June 5, it destroyed Egypt's air force in hours. Later that morning, the ground war began. Columns of Israeli tanks and artillery blasted into the Sinai, and Egypt's army soon crumbled. In the Arab world, however, the story told by the state-controlled media was quite different. Arab sources spoke of Arab successes and Israeli defeats.

Despite Egypt's losses, Nasser convinced King Hussein of Jordan to join in the defense of Arab allies. Jordanian forces began shelling Israeli positions in Jerusalem. Israelis responded by surrounding and taking the Old City of Jerusalem and made gains elsewhere in Jerusalem and in the West Bank, which had been under Jordan's control under the terms of the 1949 Israel-Jordan armistice agreement.

Israel sought to avoid conflict with Jordan. Prime Minister Eshkol sent King Hussein a message stating that Israel would take no actions against him if he ceased hostile activities. Jordan, however, received misinformation of Arab victories emanating from Cairo and pressed forward. Israeli paratroopers entered the old city through the Lion Gate and took control of the Temple Mount. The entire city of Jerusalem has been in Israeli hands ever since.

Midway through the war, Egypt's Nasser sought to excuse its poor position by claiming that the United States had entered the war on the side of Israel. On day four, the Israeli air force mistakenly attacked a U.S. intelligence ship near its coast, the *Liberty*, killing 34 Americans and wounding 171. The next day hostilities broke out with Syria, and on the last day, June 10, the Israeli army captured the Golan Heights. In six days, Israel's defense forces had successfully pushed back the Egyptians in Sinai, the Jordanians in Jerusalem and the West Bank, and the Syrians on the Golan Heights.

After the Six-Day War

Israel's victory in the Six-Day War inaugurated a period of security, euphoria, and economic growth and prosperity in Israel. The Six-Day War substantially modified the content of the issues central to the Arab-Israeli dispute. The realities of Arab hostility, the nature of the Arab threat, and the difficulties of achieving a settlement became more obvious. The issues of the conflict changed with the extent of the Israeli victory: Israel occupied the Sinai Peninsula, the Gaza Strip, the West

Before the Six-Day War, there was limited access to the Western Wall, as can be seen in this 1965 photo (top). After Israel took control of Jerusalem in 1967, Israel expanded the area in front of the wall to allow access for Jews to visit the area and engage in prayer at Judaism's holiest site. (Courtesy Bernard Reich)

Bank, East Jerusalem, and the Golan Heights. Israel adopted the position that it would not withdraw from those territories until there were negotiations with the Arab states leading to peace agreements that recognized Israel's right to exist and accepted Israel's permanent position and borders. U.S. president Lyndon B. Johnson supported this policy.

On November 22, 1967, the UN Security Council adopted Resolution 242, which called for peace between Israel and the Arabs and for Israel's withdrawal from territories occupied in the conflict. The British-sponsored resolution was left deliberately vague to allow the negotiators to seek compromise among the parties on the exact content of a settlement. In the deliberations preceding the adoption of the resolution, the Soviet Union and the Arab states sought to secure total Israeli withdrawal from the territories they had taken in the hostilities. The United States, Great Britain, and Israel, however, sought, and achieved, a resolution that was somewhat imprecise and called for Israeli withdrawal to negotiated lines but not necessarily to the armistice lines that existed on the day before the hostilities began. Thus, Resolution 242 calls only for "withdrawal from territories," not "*the* territories," that is, Israeli withdrawal from some of the newly occupied territories to negotiated final borders. The resolution also contains no mention of the Palestinians, per se, although several of the elements refer to them. Finally, on the matter of refugees, the resolution simply called for a "just settlement of the refugee problem" without indicating which refugees were intended nor what "just" would entail.

Resolution 242 established the mandate and the framework for a mission entrusted to Ambassador Gunnar Jarring, the purpose of which was to achieve a working arrangement that would lead to an Arab-Israeli settlement. At the time of his appointment Jarring was serving as ambassador of Sweden to the Soviet Union.

Foreign Minister Abba Eban articulated Israel's position at the United Nations. He rejected the idea that the status quo ante could be restored and suggested that the time had come for the Arab world to accept the existence of Israel and to live in peace with it: "The Middle East, tired of wars, is ripe for a new emergence of human vitality. Let the opportunity not fall again from our hands."

The Six-Day War of 1967 was of such magnitude and character that it brought into being conditions vastly different than those prevailing before the conflict; those new conditions had a clear and far-reaching effect on Israel's political system and its economic and social infrastructure. The war increased Israel's territorial size and improved its defense posture by providing Israel, for the first time, with "strategic depth," or

UNITED NATIONS SECURITY COUNCIL RESOLUTION 242
(NOVEMBER 22, 1967)

The Security Council,

Expressing its continuing concern with the grave situation in the Middle East,

Emphasizing the inadmissibility of the acquisition of territory by war and the need to work for a just and lasting peace in which every State in the area can live in security,

Emphasizing further that all Member States in their acceptance of the Charter of the United Nations have undertaken a commitment to act in accordance with Article 2 of the Charter,

1. Affirms that the fulfillment of Charter principles requires the establishment of a just and lasting peace in the Middle East which should include the application of both the following principles:
   (i) Withdrawal of Israeli armed forces from territories occupied in the recent conflict;
   (ii) Termination of all claims or states of belligerency and respect for and acknowledgment of the sovereignty, territorial integrity and political independence of every State in the area and their right to live in peace within secure and recognized boundaries free from threats or acts of force;
2. Affirms further the necessity
   (a) For guaranteeing freedom of navigation through international waterways in the area;
   (b) For achieving a just settlement of the refugee problem;
   (c) For guaranteeing the territorial inviolability and political independence of every State in the area, through measures including the establishment of demilitarized zones;
3. Requests the Secretary-General to designate a Special Representative to proceed to the Middle East to establish and maintain contacts with the States concerned in order to promote agreement and assist efforts to achieve a peaceful and accepted settlement in accordance with the provisions and principles in this resolution;
4. Requests the Secretary-General to report to the Security Council on the progress of the efforts of the Special Representative as soon as possible.

a buffer zone. It also significantly affected politics in the Arab states and the course of inter-Arab relations. The euphoria in Israel that followed the termination of hostilities combined with, and in part resulting from, the extent of changes wrought by the war led many to suggest that peace between Israel and the Arab states might be attainable. This was an important factor in the changed U.S. approach to the Arab-Israeli conflict in which, since 1967, it has actively sought the achievement of peace.

The congruence of U.S. and Israeli policies toward achieving peace contrasted sharply with the Arab and Soviet view widely expressed at conferences and meetings, such as the Arab League's Khartoum summit (August 29–September 1, 1967). At that conference the Arab heads of state reassessed the Arab position in the wake of the debacle of the Six-Day War. Overall, the main focus of the conference was negative: The leaders pledged joint military, political, and diplomatic activity to achieve Israeli withdrawal from occupied Arab territory and articulated the "three no's" in which they pledged "no peace with Israel, no recognition of Israel, no negotiation with it" while seeking to secure the rights of the Palestinians.

The Arab refusal to negotiate with Israel, the activities of the Palestinian terrorist and guerrilla groups, and the hostilities between Israel and the Arabs that followed the war quickly diminished the prospects for a dramatic change in the Arab-Israeli relationship and continued to focus the attention of most Israelis on "war and peace" rather than on domestic economic and social issues.

KHARTOUM ARAB SUMMIT COMMUNIQUÉ
(SEPTEMBER 1, 1967)

...The Arab heads of state have agreed to unite their political efforts on the international and diplomatic level to eliminate the effects of the aggression and to ensure the withdrawal of the aggressive Israeli forces from the Arab lands which have been occupied since the 5 June aggression. This will be done within the framework of the main principle to which the Arab states adhere, namely: no peace with Israel, no recognition of Israel, no negotiations with it, and adherence to the rights of the Palestinian people in their country.

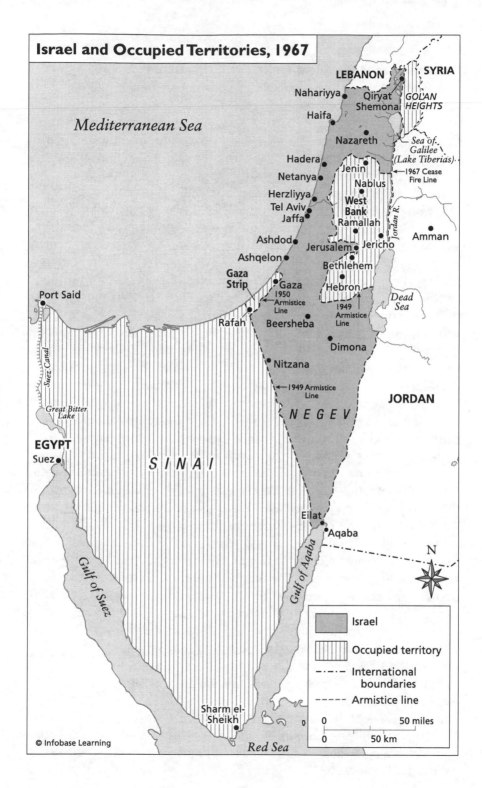

Israel and Occupied Territories, 1967

LEBANON
SYRIA

Mediterranean Sea

Nahariyya
Qiryat
Shemona
GOLAN
HEIGHTS

Haifa

Nazareth
Sea of
Galilee
(Lake Tiberias)

Hadera
Jenin
1967 Cease
Fire Line

Netanya
Nablus

Herzliyya
**West
Bank**

Tel Aviv
Ramallah

Jaffa

Ashdod
Jerusalem
Jericho
Amman

Ashqelon
Bethlehem

**Gaza
Strip**
Gaza
Hebron
Dead
Sea

1950
Armistice
Line
1949
Armistice
Line

Rafah
Beersheba

Dimona

Port Said
Nitzana

Suez Canal

1949 Armistice
Line

JORDAN

Great Bitter
Lake

NEGEV

EGYPT
Suez

S I N A I

Gulf of Suez

Eilat
Aqaba

Gulf of Aqaba

N

Israel

Occupied territory

International
boundaries

Armistice line

Sharm el-
Sheikh

0   50 miles

0   50 km

Red Sea

© Infobase Learning

Domestic Factors and Political Consensus

Israel's domestic problems receded from the forefront of public attention and of governmental concern, planning, and expenditure. The focus on national defense was ensured by continued Arab hostility and by the improvement of economic and social conditions in Israel following the war. Shortly thereafter, the recession that had characterized the economy before the war became an economic boom, with full employment. Building construction developed rapidly and exports grew. The slackening immigration rate reversed itself. The demand for foreign currency (especially U.S. dollars) for military equipment was positively assisted by the increasing influx of tourists and an increase in contributions from world Jewry. Israel's lifestyle materially improved, and increased prosperity characterized the postconflict period.

National security considerations had a catalytic effect on domestic politics and the political consensus. The crisis of May 1967 and the war in June helped to coalesce Israeli thinking (particularly about the danger of the situation) and to draw Israel's political factions closer together despite diverse political ideologies and contending politicians. The crisis was ultimately confronted by a national unity government (NUG), a specially created coalition of all political parties but Israel's two communist parties, which survived the vicissitudes of political life until the withdrawal of Menachem Begin's Gahal bloc in summer 1970.

The NUG was united on the need for peace and security, the concept of danger and threat, and the view that a return to the pre–June 5, 1967 armistice lines was unacceptable. The basic government position was that peace had to be achieved through direct negotiations with the Arabs and that captured Arab territory should not be relinquished until that time. The period of stress fostered the merger and alliance of the major left-of-center socialist political parties, which had been political rivals of some intensity despite the relative similarity of their positions on most issues. The desirability of cooperation to present a united front concerning the Arab-Israeli conflict contributed to the creation of a climate suitable for the consummation of the merger.

On January 21, 1968, Mapai, which had been the predominant political party in Israel and was the major political force in the preindependence Jewish quasi-government in mandatary Palestine, merged with two other labor parties—Ahdut Ha'avodah–Poalei Zion (the United Labor–Workers of Zion) and Rafi (Israel Labor List)—to form the Israel Labor Party (Mifleget Ha'avodah HaIsraelit). In November 1968, Labor and Mapam, a socialist Zionist workers' party, submitted a joint list of candidates for the 1969 Knesset elections. The Labor-Mapam Alignment,

GOLDA MEIR
(MAY 3, 1898–DECEMBER 8, 1978)

Golda Meir was born Golda Mabovitch in 1898 in Kiev, Russia. In 1903, her family moved to Pinsk and three years later settled in Milwaukee, Wisconsin, where she graduated from high school and attended the Milwaukee Normal School for Teachers. At age 17, she joined the Poalei Zion (Workers of Zion) Party. She married Morris Meyerson in December 1917, and in 1921 they moved to Palestine. They settled in Kibbutz Merhaviah, but later moved to Tel Aviv and then to Jerusalem. In 1928, she became secretary of the Women's Labor Council of the Histadrut in Tel Aviv. When Mapai was formed in 1930 by the merger of Ahdut Ha'avodah and Hapoel Hatzair, she quickly became a major figure in the new party.

In 1934, she was invited to join the executive committee of the Histadrut (General Federation of Labor) and became head of its political department. In 1946, when the British mandatory authorities arrested virtually all the members of the Jewish Agency Executive and of the National Council (Vaad Leumi) that they could find in Palestine, she became acting head of the political department of the Jewish Agency, replacing Moshe Sharett, who was imprisoned in Latrun. In the months immediately preceding Israel's declaration of independence, she met secretly with King Abdullah of Transjordan to dissuade him from joining the Arab League in attacking Jewish Palestine, but her efforts failed. In early June 1948, she was appointed Israel's first minister to Moscow but returned to Israel in April 1949. She was elected to the first Knesset in 1949 on the Mapai ticket and became minister of labor, a post she held until 1956, when she became foreign minister for a decade under Prime Ministers David Ben-Gurion and Levi Eshkol. As minister of labor, her principal function was the absorption of hundreds of thousands of immigrants who arrived in Israel in the first years after independence. She initiated large-scale housing and road-building programs and strongly supported unlimited immigration, and she helped provide employment and medical care for the immigrants.

When she succeeded Sharett as foreign minister in 1956, she Hebraized her name and became known as Golda Meir. As foreign minister, she concentrated on Israel's aid to African and other developing nations as a means of strengthening Israel's international position. She resigned as foreign minister in January 1966 and was succeeded

(continues)

GOLDA MEIR *(continued)*

by Abba Eban. Because of her enormous popularity in Mapai, she was prevailed on to accept appointment as general secretary of the party and in that position was Prime Minister Levi Eshkol's closest adviser. In January 1968, she was instrumental in facilitating the union of Mapai, Rafi, and Ahdut Ha'avodah as the Israel Labor Party. After serving for two years as secretary-general, she retired from public life.

Following Eshkol's death in February 1969, party leaders prevailed on her to succeed Eshkol. She became Israel's fourth prime minister in March 1969 and only the second woman worldwide to be elected prime minister. She retained the national unity government that Eshkol had constructed at the time of the Six-Day War. In the Knesset election at the end of October 1969, the Labor Party won 56 seats, and Meir once again became prime minister. She led Israel through the trauma of the Yom Kippur War and its aftermath. Following the 1973 election, which was postponed until December 31, she had great difficulty in forming a government with Dayan as minister of defense. In April 1974, she resigned.

Golda Meir was affectionately referred to as "Golda" despite holding senior positions in Zionist and Israeli institutions for more than half a century. She died in 1978.

like the formation of the national unity government in 1967, did not eliminate differences among the politicians or their parties but rather shifted the quarrels to the intragovernmental and intraparty spheres.

Despite the merger of the three major left-of-center socialist labor parties, coalition governments remained an essential part of the Israeli political dynamic. In such a situation, political leadership and succession became important factors. Prime Minister Golda Meir, who took office in March 1969 following the death of Eshkol, continued to maintain firm control over the political reins, but she indicated that her retirement was not too far in the future.

War of Attrition

At the end of the Six-Day War, Israeli troops were situated on the east bank of the Suez Canal and were occupying a large portion of Egyptian territory: the Sinai Peninsula and the formerly Egyptian-occupied Gaza Strip. France adopted an arms embargo against Israel, reversing its role as Israel's main arms supplier. U.S. Phantom jets began to replace

French-supplied Mirage aircraft. In spring 1969, Nasser launched the War of Attrition, shelling targets along the canal. Israeli casualties soon mounted, and Israel constructed the Bar-Lev line (a defensive system of fortifications and strong points) along the Suez Canal. After the arrival of the Phantom jets in fall 1969, Israel began to launch deep penetration air raids into Egypt. Soon after the Israeli raids began, Nasser went to Moscow where he requested and received Soviet aid and support including surface-to-air (SAM) missiles, other advanced equipment, pledges of training for the Egyptian military, and assistance by Soviet troops and pilots. By June 1970, the situation had significantly escalated. Israeli pilots shot down a number of Egyptian aircraft flown by Soviet pilots over the Suez Canal Zone.

1969 Election

On October 28, 1969, Israel held its seventh parliamentary election since independence. The election was overshadowed by the international situation and by the defense requirements of the War of Attrition. The usually raucous political campaign was more subdued than previous ones, in part because of the national unity government in place since 1967 that continued to function and to blunt the often public acrimonious debates that generally characterized political life in Israel. The future of the territories captured during the war and their administration in the interim were widely considered. Israel now held a large amount of territory with a substantial and growing Arab population. On one hand this meant the availability of manpower and markets for the economy, but there were also the economic costs of administering the territories. The defense budget grew dramatically as well. The United States increasingly emerged as an important factor in Israel's quest for peace as well as a strategic partner and provisioner for Israel's military.

The mood of the people reflected the changes in circumstances and was mixed. The euphoria of the significant victory following the Six-Day War was soon replaced by dismay over the increasing hostilities during the ongoing War of Attrition. In the months prior to the election, the number of Israeli casualties grew, although the air force had become increasingly active and effective along the Suez Canal.

Sixteen lists contested in the 1969 election, and 13 received at least one seat in the Knesset. The most successful electoral list was that of the Labor-Mapam Alignment, which won 46.2 percent of the votes and gained 56 seats in the Knesset. The leadership and institutions now combined in the alignment had dominated Israeli politics and the political

Israeli soldiers in a bunker on the Suez Canal, 1970 (Courtesy Embassy of Israel, Washington, D.C.)

scene since the establishment of the Yishuv during the mandate and since independence. It remained a left-of-center, labor-oriented party, with a leadership that included the most prominent of Israeli political and historical figures, such as Golda Meir, Shimon Peres, Yitzhak Rabin, Yigal Allon, Moshe Dayan, and Abba Eban. Clearly Labor continued to prevail, although it did not win an absolute majority of the seats and thus still required coalition partners to form the government.

Gahal, a joint list of Herut and the Liberal Party on the right side of the political spectrum and led by Menachem Begin, its original founder, won 26 seats. The National Religious Party (NRP) was the third largest party winning 12 seats in parliament. The remaining seats were distributed among the other parties that achieved the 1 percent minimum threshold for a seat. The outcome of the election suggested no major changes in the political situation in Israel nor in the policies of the government and the state.

Black September
After the Six-Day War, the PLO had established its major base of operations for attacks against Israel in Jordan. PLO attacks into and against

Israel were followed by Israeli retaliatory attacks in Jordan, some of which caused extensive damage.

In September 1970, factions of the PLO hijacked aircraft of several international airlines and landed them in Jordan. The Jordanian military and King Hussein chose to act and began to use military force against the PLO to force its removal from Jordan. The civil war in Jordan, in turn, led to an escalation of Jordanian-Syrian tensions as the latter moved to support the PLO and its fighters. At U.S. president Richard Nixon's request, Israeli prime minister Golda Meir mobilized a small number of Israeli forces along the Jordan River. This appeared to convince Syria that an invasion of Jordan was not a viable strategy. Nixon saw this as a positive sign, and Israel's position in Nixon's perspective grew. PLO forces moved northward from Jordan to Syria and, later, to Lebanon.

The Search for an Interim Agreement

On June 25, 1970, U.S. secretary of state William Rogers announced a new political initiative in the Middle East, "the objective of which is to encourage the parties to stop shooting and start talking under the auspices of [UN special envoy] Ambassador Jarring . . . " The June 1970 effort was primarily a result of the increased Soviet military presence in Egypt. Egypt had acquired a new Soviet air defense missile system to deal with Israeli aircraft, and Soviet pilots were flying planes in Egypt. There was growing concern about the deteriorating situation along the Suez Canal. It provided the first serious challenge to the political cohesiveness and relative domestic tranquility that seemed to have developed in Israel in the wake of the Six-Day War. But the debate and discussion that accompanied it, as well as the resumed mediation effort of Jarring and the search for an interim settlement, also reaffirmed the centrality of national security in the Israeli system.

Israel's initial reaction was to reject a temporary cease-fire because it would facilitate Arab preparations for resuming hostilities against Israel. While the government was discussing the proposal, Egyptian president Nasser announced his conditional acceptance of the cease-fire on July 23, 1970. On August 4, 1970, Meir announced Israel's affirmative decision in the Knesset, and the reply was transmitted to the United States. Israel's response emphasized the importance of the U.S. assurances that had facilitated the initiative. The decision to accept the proposal led to the breakup of the government of national unity when

Gahal voted to withdraw from the coalition. Gahal had agreed to the concept of a limited cease-fire but objected to the idea of withdrawal from occupied Arab territory implicit in the U.S. proposal. Begin, Gahal's leader, described the coalition as "a government of national surrender to a Middle East Munich."

The cease-fire formally went into effect along the Suez Canal on August 7, 1970, but was immediately followed by reports of Egyptian military deployments, especially SAMs along the Suez Canal, in violation of the agreements. Indirect talks between Israel, Jordan, and the UAR, held under the auspices of UN ambassador Jarring, began on August 25, but after the initial round, Israel's ambassador to the United Nations was called home. The Egyptian violations had caused consternation in Israel, and the initial United States reaction, which minimized the problem, did not allay Israel's fears. By early September, the Israeli cabinet had decided that it would not participate in the talks so long as the agreement was not respected in its entirety and if the original situation was not restored. After a lengthy process of discussion and clarification between the United States and Israel during which Israel received political, economic, and military support to "rectify" the imbalance resulting from the Egyptian missile movements and to allow Israel to reenter the talks in a position of confidence, Israel's cabinet on December 28, 1970, unanimously decided to resume peace talks with the UAR and Jordan, under the auspices of Ambassador Jarring.

On the central question of withdrawal, Israel said it would undertake "withdrawal of Israel armed forces from the Israel-UAR cease-fire line to the secure, recognized and agreed boundaries to be established in the peace agreement. Israel will not withdraw to the pre–June 5, 1967 lines." On numerous occasions, Israeli spokesmen had noted the strategic benefits to Israel of the 1967 cease-fire lines compared to the ones that existed from 1949. After the Six-Day War, Israel gained natural defense positions, advance warning time in the event of enemy attacks, and strategic depth that did not characterize the armistice lines established in 1949. Israel's chief of staff, General Haim Bar-Lev, stated that the security position resulting from the Six-Day War provided Israel with greater flexibility and a greater number of alternative strategic military options. Furthermore, the new lines removed the Arab threat from Israel's centers of population, industry, and government. The threat to Israel's survival was significantly reduced even though the conflict remained unresolved.

Yom Kippur War

President Nasser died of a heart attack in September 1970, as he concluded the negotiations designed to terminate the Black September developments. Anwar Sadat succeeded Nasser as president and developed a focus on Egypt's domestic, economic, and social problems rather than on the conflict with Israel. Peace with Israel seemed to be his long-range objective, although this was not clear until after the Yom Kippur War.

The U.S.-initiated Middle East cease-fire of August 1970 was shattered by a coordinated Egyptian and Syrian attack on Israeli positions on the Suez Canal and the Golan Heights on October 6, 1973. The Yom Kippur War, which lasted 19 days, ended the efforts to achieve an Arab-Israeli settlement associated with the Six-Day War of 1967. Israel was at first shaken but then fought back aggressively. Neither Egypt nor Syria regained the territories each had sought, but the armies of both states performed far better than Israeli intelligence had expected. Egypt inflicted heavy losses on the Israelis in the Sinai; Syria's thrust into the Golan Heights in the first days looked unstoppable. Israel recovered, but its army did not appear to be invincible. In the last days of the war, tensions peaked between Washington

Temporary bridge across the Suez Canal allowing Israeli troops to cross to the western side during the Yom Kippur War (Courtesy Embassy of Israel, Washington, D.C.)

and Moscow, the chief backer of Egypt and Syria, which brought all U.S. military forces to a DEFCON 3 alert. A cease-fire and the passage of UN Security Council Resolutions 338, 339, and 340 marked the end of hostilities. The cease-fire finally took effect on October 25, 1973, and was soon followed by a meeting between Israeli and Egyptian officers at Kilometer 101 on the Cairo-Suez road to discuss implementation. The war ended with Israel still in control of the Golan Heights and most of the Sinai, but the military balance had shifted. The unusual configuration of the initial cease-fire lines provided the opportunity and need to negotiate a disengagement of military forces on both the Egyptian and Syrian fronts. The discussions between Israel and Egypt soon gave way to a peace conference in Geneva, Switzerland, that involved representatives from Egypt, Jordan, and Israel under UN auspices and with the United States and the Soviet Union as cochairs.

In January 1974, U.S. secretary of state Henry Kissinger began his first "shuttle diplomacy" and achieved an Egypt-Israel Disengagement of Forces Agreement. Later in the spring of 1974, Kissinger conducted another round of shuttle diplomacy, this time between Israel and Syria. The disengagement agreement in this instance was signed in Geneva and called for Israel to relinquish its forward positions on the Golan Heights and to withdraw from the city of Kuneitra and return it to

---

UNITED NATIONS SECURITY COUNCIL RESOLUTION 338
(OCTOBER 22, 1973)

The Security Council
1. *Calls upon* all parties to the present fighting to cease all firing and terminate all military activity immediately, no later than 12 hours after the moment of the adoption of this decision, in the positions they now occupy;
2. *Calls upon* the parties concerned to start immediately after the cease-fire the implementation of Security Council resolution 242 (1964) in all of its parts;
3. *Decides* that, immediately and concurrently with the cease-fire, negotiations start between the parties concerned under appropriate auspices aimed at establishing a just and durable peace in the Middle East.

KILOMETER 101

It was at Kilometer 101 along the Cairo-Suez road where, beginning on October 28, 1973, Israeli and Egyptian military officials met for negotiations toward implementing the conditions of United Nations Security Council Resolution 338. The talks, mediated by U.S. secretary of state Henry Kissinger, resulted in a six-point agreement, signed by Egyptian general Abdul Ghani Gamassy and Israeli general Aharon Yariv, on November 11. This was the first bilateral accord between the two parties since the 1949 armistice agreements and augured well for future progress. The Kilometer 101 talks set the stage for the Egypt-Israel Disengagement of Forces Agreement of January 1974, which was signed at Kilometer 101.

Israelis and Egyptians meeting at Kilometer 101 on the Suez-Cairo road after the Yom Kippur War, 1973 (Courtesy Embassy of Israel, Washington, D.C.)

Syria. A DMZ was then monitored by a United Nations Disengagement Observer Force (UNDOF).

The cease-fires of October did not end the hostilities. A semi-war atmosphere, with the attendant mobilization of large numbers of reservists and tensions on the home front and at forward positions, continued for months after the war. Tension contributed to Israeli uncertainties and further affected the orderly pursuit of change. Only with the implementation of the disengagement accords was Israel able to concentrate fully on the reorganization and redeployment of the military, the acquisition of equipment, the reinfusion of morale, and the restructuring of the political environment.

Aftermath of the Yom Kippur War

The 1973 Yom Kippur War wrought substantial change in Israel. The war stunned a population that had believed that the Arabs would not dare attack. Also, Israel had lionized its military: In the popular view, the IDF's capability for combat reached near legendary levels. Its intelligence services were regarded as among the finest in the world. At the same time, Arab military capabilities had been underestimated, and senior Israeli decision makers had talked about the absence of war in the Middle East for the next 10 to 15 years.

Israel's confident optimism was eroded by the war, and the subsequent reevaluation tended to breed a feeling of uncertainty. There was a mixture of anger and frustration engendered by political and military factors associated with the conduct of the war. Despite significant military accomplishments, Israel, under international pressure, was unable to achieve its desired goals. In purely tangible terms, the war had perhaps the most far-reaching effect of any of the conflicts to that date. Manpower losses for the period October 6 to October 24 were announced as 1,854 Israeli soldiers killed in battle, but this figure rose as severely wounded soldiers died and as those who were killed in the cease-fire period were added to the totals. The number of wounded was about double this. The total of about 5,000 casualties was high for a country with a total population just over 3 million. The war shook morale and confidence.

Deteriorating economic conditions contributed to the unsettling circumstances. The prewar economic boom was replaced by increasingly stringent conditions in the postwar period. The mobilization of the largest part of the civilian reserve army of several hundred thousand caused dislocations in agriculture and industrial production despite the large number of volunteers, from within Israel and other countries, who replaced the mobilized reserves. Tourism and diamond sales, major and important sources of foreign currency, fell during the war. The port of Eilat, at the southern tip of Israel on the Gulf of Aqaba, a major oil terminus, was cut off by an Arab blockade at the Bab el Mandeb Strait between the Arabian Peninsula and the Horn of Africa at the entrance to the Red Sea, thus affecting the flow to Israel of oil from Iran and trade with East Africa and Asia. The material losses were large and included important and expensive elements of Israel's air force and armor (most notably Phantom and Skyhawk aircraft and tanks). The mobilization of civilian trucks severely affected the transportation sector, and this, in turn, further hampered the recovery of the economy.

The cost of the war—including tanks, planes, guns, fuel, and ammunition—was estimated to exceed $5 billion, higher than the annual state budget. Military expenditure, lost production, and damage to civilian and military installations on the Golan Heights were part of the cost.

Increased taxes and war-related levies were introduced, and a high rate of inflation (approximating 40 percent) began to have its effect. Initially, the economy was slowed by the mobilization of much of the country's able-bodied manpower, not only during the war but in the period that followed. The replacement of military equipment lost in battle, the servicing of the prewar debt, and the acquisition of new matériel to meet current and future defense needs added to the burden. But there was also the realization that Israel could not readily reduce nondefense expenditures. There were the requirements of immigrant absorption and the need to continue development programs and to deal with social and economic gaps. In a partial effort to improve the situation, the Israeli pound was devalued by 43 percent and a broad-scale austerity program was instituted. These measures were announced on November 10, 1974.

International Isolation

Israel's position in the international community deteriorated with the outbreak of fighting. Although Israel had not initiated the war, Israel was widely condemned, and numerous states broke diplomatic relations with it.

Prior to the war, Israel's international position had been declining. The propaganda war had been turning in favor of the Arabs, and Israel had been losing world sympathy. This could be traced in most instances to Israel's continued refusal to withdraw from occupied Arab territories and its responses to Arab terrorism, which increasingly came under international condemnation. Since the break in relations with Uganda in the spring of 1972, prompted by Arab (especially Libyan) financial and technical assistance, several states in Africa severed relations, and in September 1973, Cuba took a similar action. Immediately prior to the outbreak of the Yom Kippur War, Israel had come into sharp dispute with Austria over the refusal of Austria to continue to provide facilities for Russian Jewish emigrants on their way to Israel.

"ZIONISM IS RACISM"

On November 10, 1975, the UN General Assembly, by a vote of 72 in favor and 35 against, with 32 abstentions, adopted Resolution 3379, which "*Determines* that Zionism is a form of racism and racial discrimination." This resolution has subsequently been the basis for further condemnations in different agencies and at various meetings of the United Nations. The votes in favor of the resolution did not represent a united or equally committed opposition to Israel, per se. The majority had no direct stake in the Arab-Israeli conflict. The sponsorship was a combined effort of the Arab states and their associates, pursuing an anti-Israeli policy, and the Soviet bloc, pursuing its general effort against the West, its institutions, and its friends. The motivation for the Arab sponsors was in keeping with their consistent position on Israel to question Israel's right to exist. The objective in linking Zionism with racism was to delegitimize Israel.

On December 16, 1991, the General Assembly, with 111 countries voting in the affirmative and 25 against, with 13 abstentions and 17 absences, repealed its November 10, 1975, resolution equating Zionism with racism. The repeal was opposed by most Arab states, which either voted against it or were absent from the chamber when the vote was taken. U.S. deputy secretary of state Lawrence Eagleburger introduced the one-sentence resolution: "The General Assembly decides to revoke the determination contained in its resolution 3379 (XXX) of 10 November 1975." The Soviet Union was among the 85 cosponsors of the resolution. Israel welcomed the decision and saw it as correcting a historic distortion. Although most of the Arab states voted against the repeal measure, some—including Egypt, Kuwait, Bahrain, Oman, Morocco, and Tunisia—decided not to vote on the issue.

Increasingly, international and regional organizations called on Israel to withdraw from the occupied territories.

During the course of the war and immediately afterward, Israel's ties with most of the states of Africa were broken. Many of them linked the rupture of relations with Israel's refusal to withdraw from territories occupied since the Six-Day War. Except for South Africa, no major African state publicly backed Israel or offered assistance. To most Israelis, this not only symbolized the injustice of the international community but also the success of Arab oil blackmail and the failure of

Israel's program of international cooperation. Israel had provided many of these African states with technical assistance, which they had lauded publicly for its importance in promoting African development.

A shift in the attitudes and policies of the European states was more significant. Israel's international isolation was compounded by the unwillingness of the European allies of the United States to allow the use of their facilities and/or airspace for the shipment and transfer of supplies to Israel during the war. On November 6, 1973, the nine members of the European Community (EC) called on Israel to withdraw from occupied Arab territories and recognize the rights of the Palestinians. Japan, which had hitherto adopted and maintained a posture of neutrality in the Arab-Israeli conflict, now shifted to a more pronounced pro-Arab position. Japan called for implementation of the UN Resolution 242 (1967) and stressed the Arab interpretation of the resolution, calling on Israel to withdraw from all Arab territories.

The war also increased Israel's dependence on the United States. No other country could or was prepared to provide Israel with the vast quantities of modern and sophisticated arms required for war or for the political and moral support necessary to negotiate peace. Many members of the U.S. Congress went on record in support of the Israeli position and the U.S. military resupply effort. On October 19, 1973, President Richard Nixon asked Congress to authorize $2.2 billion in emergency security assistance for Israel in order "to prevent the emergence of a substantial imbalance resulting from a large-scale resupply of Syria and Egypt by the Soviet Union." The United States also alerted its armed forces when there was an indication that the Soviet Union might become involved militarily in the area.

A year later, on October 14, 1974, the General Assembly of the United Nations invited, by a vote of 105 to 4 (with 20 abstentions and seven absences), the PLO to participate in the General Assembly debate on the Palestine question. This was a further setback for Israel's position. It emphasized Israel's international isolation and its dependence on the United States (which, with Israel, had provided two of the four votes against the UN decision). In addition, it complicated Israel's negotiating stance. The decision of the Arab summit meeting in Rabat (October 26–29, 1974) to recognize the PLO as "the sole legitimate representative of the Palestinian people" and to call for the creation of an independent Palestinian state on any occupied "Palestinian land" that Israel may relinquish created a new factor. Prime Minister Yitzhak Rabin responded, "Well, I don't believe that Israel can negotiate with those that first declare that their purpose is the destruction of Israel.

After all, these leaders are committed to the destruction of Israel as a Jewish independent state. Second, they try to carry it out by murderous activities, the kind that were carried into Qiryat Shemona, Ma'alot and other places." On November 5, 1974, Rabin reiterated that Israel would not negotiate with the PLO.

The Wars of the Jews

The cease-fire of October 22, 1973, was followed by what Israelis often refer to as the "wars of the Jews"—internal political conflicts and disagreements. The initial impact of the Yom Kippur War on Israeli politics was to bring about the postponement of the elections, originally scheduled for October 30, to December 31, and the suspension of political campaigning and electioneering for the duration of the conflict.

The war interrupted the campaign for the Knesset election and provided new issues for the opposition to raise, namely the conduct of the war and the "mistakes" that preceded it. A new word entered Israel's political lexicon: *mechdal*. The word, meaning "omission" or "failure," was used to refer to the failures of the government and of the military to be fully prepared for the outbreak of the war and to respond to the initial attacks. Prior to the war, a right-wing opposition bloc, Likud (Union), composed of several parties and groups including Gahal, Free Center, State List, and the Land of Israel Movement was formed. The basic campaign theme was, it is "time for a change." Although Likud seemed to falter prior to the war, the conflict allowed its resurgence. General Ariel "Arik" Sharon, who had retired from the army and had been a major force in the consolidation of Likud, was mobilized in the war and emerged as a popular hero for leading Israeli forces to the west bank of the Suez Canal. Menachem Begin, the leader of Gahal, criticized the government for accepting the cease-fire, saying it was detrimental to national security and would invite rather than prevent further Arab aggression. He also criticized the failure of the government to meet the Egyptian-Syrian threat at the outbreak of the Yom Kippur War and called on Prime Minister Meir to resign. General Sharon was critical of the Israeli high command for their delay in crossing the canal and subsequently in reinforcing his troops and their advanced positions on the west bank of the canal, a delay that he felt cost Israel some important military accomplishments. Sharon was also critical of the military posture that allowed the initial Egyptian crossing of the canal.

Within the government there were also voices of dissatisfaction. There were challenges within the Labor Party to Prime Minister Meir

Chief of Staff Haim Bar-Lev (left) with Major General Ariel Sharon during the Yom Kippur War, 1973 (Courtesy Embassy of Israel, Washington, D.C.)

and in particular to two of her closest advisers—Israel Galili and Moshe Dayan—on the questions of defense, security, and the occupied territories. There were demands that the election be postponed, that the party revise its platform, and that the election lists be reopened for the addition of new candidates. There were clear indications in the weeks following the war that Labor had lost an element of popular support and that this would be reflected in the polls. Partly to quiet internal political complaints, the cabinet decided on November 18, 1973, to establish a commission of inquiry to investigate the events leading up to the war (including information concerning enemy moves and intentions), the assessments and decisions of military and civilian bodies in regard to this information, and the IDF's deployment and preparedness for battle and its actions in the first phase of the fighting. The commission of inquiry consisted of the president of the Supreme Court, Justice Shimon Agranat; the state comptroller, Yitzhak Nebenzahl; Supreme Court justice Moshe Landau; and two former chiefs of staff, Yigael Yadin and Haim Laskov. All were widely respected and enjoyed public confidence.

Political Change

The war accelerated the momentum for political change, which was only partly reflected in the election held at the end of December 1973 for the Eighth Knesset. Despite last-minute preelection polls that suggested important shifts in voting patterns, the results seemed to indicate that nothing had changed significantly. The Labor-led Alignment lost six of its 57 seats, while the Likud increased its strength by eight seats, to 39. The religious parties lost two of their 17 mandates. There were also shifts within the parties, as younger elements began to assert themselves and sought to affect political positions.

After initial difficulties, Golda Meir was able to form a coalition cabinet very similar to the previous cabinet. The new government was confirmed by the Knesset on March 10, 1974, by a vote of 62 to 46 (with nine abstentions). But on April 10, Meir resigned, in large measure because of the debates within the Labor Party on the political responsibility for Israel's lapses at the outset of the Yom Kippur War. Her resignation set the stage for the selection of a new Labor Party leader and prime minister and the formation of a new coalition. The major member of the Alignment, the Labor Party, had to choose a successor to be nominated by the president to form a new government. The choice was between General Yitzhak Rabin, the IDF chief of staff during the

Six-Day War who later served as ambassador to the United States and subsequently as minister of labor in Meir's cabinet, and Shimon Peres, who was then minister of information but who for a long time had run the Defense Ministry. Rabin and Peres were relatively young (in their 50s) and belonged to the new generation, not the group of pioneers who came to Israel at the beginning of the 20th century and had controlled Israeli politics since.

Rabin was chosen, but it was not clear that the coalition could achieve sufficient strength to endure. Rabin's qualifications were also questioned. There was the so-called Weizman document, in which former general Ezer Weizman (now a member of the opposition) argued that in 1967, Rabin had been unfit to make important decisions at a critical juncture. Rabin's experience was questioned because his major posts prior to 1973 were that of a general in the army, chief of staff, and ambassador to the United States, positions that hardly prepared him for the rough and tumble of Israeli politics. He was also called to task for accepting speaking fees while serving as ambassador to the United States.

In Rabin's government, Yigal Allon replaced Abba Eban as foreign minister, Shimon Peres replaced Moshe Dayan as defense minister, and Yehoshua Rabinowitz replaced Pinhas Sapir as finance minister. The coalition that supported Rabin in the Knesset had a new composition. The National Religious Party (NRP) did not participate and was replaced by the Citizens' Rights Movement (CRM), which had campaigned in part against the special position of religion in the state. However, by the first anniversary of the Yom Kippur War, the internally split NRP agreed to join the coalition while the CRM withdrew. Despite Rabin's slim margin, his government showed a remarkable stability during its initial months in office.

5

THE BEGIN EARTHQUAKE
AND PEACE WITH EGYPT
(1975–1979)

The Yom Kippur War did not end the Arab-Israeli conflict although it created the conditions to achieve a settlement, including new efforts by the United States, led by Secretary of State Henry Kissinger. Developments within Israel were not as tranquil as after the Six-Day War; economic problems and political uncertainties characterized the immediate postwar period.

Sinai II and After (1975–1977)

After achieving disengagement agreements between Israel and Egypt in January 1974 and between Israel and Syria in May 1974, Kissinger secured the Sinai II Accords between Israel and Egypt in September 1975. These accords were not a simple disengagement of military forces. The parties agreed that "the conflict between them and in the Middle East shall not be resolved by military force but by peaceful means." It therefore moved the parties closer to a peace agreement.

The Sinai II agreements of September 1975 marked the beginning of a period of relative tranquility for Israel, providing a respite from the pressures of the Yom Kippur War and its aftermath. Tensions between Israel and Egypt were reduced, and Israel believed, and many Arabs agreed, that Egypt had been effectively neutralized in the military conflict. Underlying this view was the feeling that Arab military prospects vis-à-vis Israel were significantly reduced without Egyptian participation.

In the north, Israel's relations with its neighbors also improved. The civil war in Lebanon, which broke out in 1975 between the country's Islamic and Christian factions and would last 15 years, brought a reduction in terrorist actions against Israel and a general calm along the frontier. Later, tacit links developed between Israel and Lebanon, when Lebanese civilians in need of medical attention came to the border for Israeli medical care. Israel also purchased Lebanese commodities (for example, tobacco), gave permission to some Lebanese to work in Israel, and permitted some family reunions across the frontier. Israelis hoped that this "open fence" policy would have a positive influence. Furthermore, there were reports that Israel was providing military equipment to Lebanese Christian forces, especially in the southern Lebanon sector known as "Fatahland" owing to its control by Arafat's Fatah organization. Meanwhile, peace was maintained along the Israeli-Jordanian border, and civilian crossings of the Jordan River continued.

Some openings along Israel's border with Syria were also reported, as Druze families (members of a religious sect of Muslim origins) separated by the frontier line were permitted limited and controlled meetings under an arrangement involving Israel, Syria, and the United Nations. Military clashes were replaced by limited peaceful encounters along Israel's borders with each neighboring Arab state.

Domestic Factors

The calm regional and international environment was not reflected inside Israel. Despite some respite from the intense antigovernment protests on the Arab-Israeli situation that had become a hallmark of negotiations leading to the Sinai II Accords, tranquility did not prevail in the domestic political, economic, and social sectors.

Israel continued to face severe economic pressures. Defense expenditures remained at a high level after the Yom Kippur War. Austerity budgets were adopted. A program of continuous small devaluations ("mini devaluations") of the Israeli currency was established to make imports more expensive and hopefully less attractive in an effort to reduce foreign currency drains and imbalances in the balance of payments. Taxes were raised and restructured to increase government revenues and to maintain individual incentive. At the same time, the government reduced subsidies on basic foodstuffs, such as bread, milk, and eggs, which led to increased costs of goods and services for most consumers and an increased cost of living. Inflation continued at a high rate, estimated to be as much as 30 percent in 1976, although unemployment remained low, about 3 percent.

Israel also faced a reduction in the population growth rate and diminished immigration. It was reported that in 1975 emigration nearly matched immigration; government figures indicated that 18,500

Israelis had left the country and 20,000 newcomers had arrived, of whom about 8,500 were from the Soviet Union (compared to 58,886 in 1973 and 31,970 immigrants in 1974).

Israelis became worried about the country's increasingly politicized Arab minority. Israel's Arab population of 450,000 had long enjoyed legal equality, participated in parliamentary elections and in local government, and had its own state-supported educational and religious institutions. But below the surface equanimity, Israeli Arabs felt discontent with a perceived second-class status resulting from various forms of subtle discrimination.

In spring 1976, Israeli Arabs participated in their first general protest and staged the most violent demonstrations in Israel's history. The riots, whose extent and ferocity were surprising to Israel's Arab and Jewish communities alike, grew out of a general strike, centered in Nazareth, that was called to protest land expropriations in Israel's northern section. The government had recently adopted a five-year plan to increase the number of Jewish settlers in the Galilee and had expropriated lands for that purpose, some of which were Arab owned. The Arabs protested that although they were compensated, their land should not be expropriated to provide land for Jewish settlers. The expropriation served as a catalyst; the initial demonstrations escalated and eventually became broader and more general in their focus, incorporating complaints about Arab second-class status. In the ensuing violent clashes with Israeli security forces, some demonstrators were killed.

Meanwhile, the coalition under Prime Minister Yitzhak Rabin continued to control the government by a narrow margin. The weakness of the Rabin government encouraged rivalry and bickering on a host of matters among Rabin, Defense Minister Shimon Peres, and Foreign Minister Yigal Allon, although the three constituted the government's negotiating team in foreign affairs.

In time, Rabin's hand and the position of his government grew stronger. The accession of the National Religious Party (NRP) to the government in the fall of 1974 was an important factor in solidifying it, despite the withdrawal of the Citizens' Rights Movement. Rabin also gained public support when he responded positively to Kissinger's Sinai II initiative and secured important political and diplomatic support, economic aid, and arms for Israel from the United States. In addition, Peres and Allon tended to check each other; the opposition Likud was stalemated; and no alternative candidates seemed to emerge.

The debates on Israel's political future between the parties and within the Labor Party became more intense as external issues became

GUSH EMUNIM

The Gush Emunim (Bloc of the Faithful) movement was founded after the Six-Day War to promote the establishment of Jewish settlements in Judea and Samaria (the West Bank), and Gaza as a means of retaining these areas, especially the West Bank. Gush Emunim combines religious fundamentalism and secular Zionism to create a new political force. Its leaders assert a biblically based Jewish claim to Judea and Samaria but profess a belief that peaceful and productive coexistence with the Arabs is both possible and desirable. It was not until after the Yom Kippur War that it organized politically in order to oppose further territorial concessions and to promote the extension of Israeli sovereignty over and settlement in the occupied territories. Its official founding meeting took place in March 1974 at Kfar Etzion, a West Bank kibbutz that had been seized by the Arabs in Israel's War of Independence and recovered by Israel in the Six-Day War.

Gush Emunim's primary commitment is to settlement beyond the 1949 armistice agreement demarcation lines, which had served as the de facto borders between Israel and the Jordanian-annexed West Bank and between Israel and the Egyptian-administered Gaza Strip and Sinai Peninsula from 1949 to 1967. Gush Emunim continues to advocate for settlements in all parts of Eretz Yisrael.

less pressing. Among the more significant issues was the debate over the future of Jewish settlements in the occupied territories, especially in the West Bank. This became a political-religious question, and the settlers were backed by the religious parties, the Gush Emunim militants, and others with a strong nationalistic bent. Cabinet and popular debates on the future of the settlements tended to split political parties and the governing coalition and further exacerbated the so-called hawk-dove split within the Israeli system.

Despite the importance of political, economic and social issues, a new feeling of optimism and security was generated in Israel by the relative tranquility on Israel's borders. Contributing to this was the improved position of the IDF and its restored status. After the war, the IDF began to reinvigorate its forces and to modify its organization and tactics to reflect Israel's new situation. Within a short time after the conflict, the IDF and its senior officers learned the lessons of 1973 and incorporated the appropriate responses into the training, equipment,

SETTLEMENTS

The status and disposition of Jewish settlements in the West Bank (and to a different degree in the Gaza Strip until the evacuation of 2005) remain one of the most complex issues affecting the Israeli-Palestinian conflict. Historically, Jews have lived in Judea and Samaria (the present-day West Bank) since ancient times. The Jewish community in Hebron existed throughout the centuries of Ottoman rule, while such settlements as Neve Ya'acov and the Gush Etzion (Etzion Bloc) were established under the British mandatory administration. Beginning in the second half of the 19th century, Jewish immigrants began to establish new settlements throughout Palestine.

From 1920 to 1948, Great Britain administered the areas as part of the League of Nations mandate for Palestine. The mandate not only legitimized Jewish immigration to Palestine, it instructed the mandatory authority to encourage and facilitate Jewish settlement throughout the territory. It was partly on this basis that new Jewish communities were established in the West Bank during the mandatory period, often near ancient religious sites. The Arab repudiation of the United Nations Partition Plan (General Assembly Resolution 181 of November 1947), combined with the termination of the mandate on May 14, 1948, left the West Bank and Gaza in a legal limbo. Though Israeli sovereignty was applied to areas under Jewish control at the end of the War of Independence, no legal regime was instituted in Arab-controlled areas to replace mandatory law. From 1948 to 1967, no Jews resided in the Egyptian-occupied Gaza Strip, and Jordanian law prohibited Jews from living in the West Bank. But Egypt did not incorporate Gaza, nor was Jordan's 1950 annexation of the West Bank and eastern Jerusalem recognized internationally.

Several of the early settlements were destroyed or evacuated in the War of Independence. Many of them, especially Gush Etzion and Hebron, were reestablished immediately after the 1967 Six-Day War, while new settlements were established in the Sinai, Gaza Strip, and Golan Heights.

A great deal of settlement activity occurred between 1967 and 1977 under Labor-led governments, but the emphasis in that period tended to be on using settlements to reinforce Israel's strategic interests in the occupied territories and around Jerusalem. Under Labor, most settlement activity was state sponsored and funded; however, in some cases (such as the small settlement established by Rabbi Moshe Levinger in Hebron on the eve of Passover 1968), settlements were established as a result of private initiatives and against government wishes. The pace and scope of settlement activity increased substantially with the ascendance of Likud to power in 1977, with an emphasis on encouraging maximum Jewish presence in all parts of the occupied territories. Nevertheless, it was under Likud that Israeli settlements in the Sinai Desert (such as Yamit) were evacuated in the early 1980s in fulfillment of the peace treaty with Egypt. After 1967, no Israeli government formally introduced as policy the prospect of disbanding and evacuating settlements in the West Bank until Ariel Sharon became prime minister. Sharon evacuated all Israelis from the Gaza Strip and four small settlements in the West Bank in 2005. Sharon's Kadima Party, under Ehud Olmert's leadership, suggested further unilateral dismantling of settlements and withdrawal from parts of the West Bank as part of its 2006 election platform and government program.

The Oslo Accords of September 1993 stipulated that discussion of the final disposition of the settlements question should be deferred until the last phase of Israeli-Palestinian peace talks. The Oslo II agreement of September 1995 incorporated all settlements in "Area C" which includes areas of the West Bank and Gaza over which Israel retained exclusive control during the period of interim autonomy and from which it would undertake a phased, partial redeployment before the conclusion of permanent status talks. Nevertheless, the settlements issue was a source of controversy between Israeli and Palestinian negotiators from the outset.

Since 1967, official Palestinian policy (backed by widespread international opinion) has argued that all Jewish settlement activity in the West Bank and Gaza is illegal under international law and must be withdrawn as a precondition for peace. This policy is based primarily on a narrow interpretation of the Fourth Geneva Convention, which prohibits the "occupying power" from altering the status of territories taken in war.

Israel rejects the Palestinian perspective. It disputes the applicability of the Fourth Geneva Convention to the West Bank and Gaza Strip, inasmuch as the convention relates explicitly to the responsibilities of a foreign power in belligerent occupation of another country as the consequence of an aggressive war, whereas Israel came into possession of the disputed areas in 1967 as the result of a purely defensive war. With specific reference to settlement activity, Israel discounts the Arab interpretation of Article 49 of the Fourth Geneva Convention, arguing that the reference was clearly to the forced transfer of civilian populations whereas settlement activity in the West Bank and Gaza is entirely voluntary.

and doctrine of the Israeli armed forces. Israel's general officers believed that the army was stronger than ever.

A galvanizing event was inadvertently provided by Palestinian and other terrorists who hijacked a plane to Uganda in late June 1976. IDF troops raided the airport at Entebbe, Uganda, on July 4 and freed the hostages with little loss of life. The raid served an important morale-building purpose for Israel and tended to restructure the Israel-Arab psychological balance, which had been upset by the Yom Kippur War. Israel was once again proud and confident, some suggested even euphoric, and others asserted that the Yom Kippur War ended in Entebbe. The raid provided a political boost for Rabin and redefined his image into a forceful decision maker willing to take risks and make hard decisions.

Some areas of contention between Israel and the United States began to emerge during this time. Shortly after Sinai II was signed, the Arab states sought PLO participation in the United Nations Security Council debate on the Middle East, while Israel urged a U.S. veto to bar a Palestinian role. The United States refused to bar the PLO and voiced criticism of some Israeli policies and actions during the UN debate. The United States and Israel also disagreed about Israel's policy in the occupied territories and particularly the establishment of settlements in those areas, and maintained opposing positions on the status of Jerusalem. While Israel reunited the city in 1967 and considers the united city to be the capital of the Jewish state, the Palestinians claim a portion as theirs and seek it as a capital. In general much of the world does not support the Israeli position and periodically the future of the eastern portion of the city has become a matter of major controversy. Conflict also existed over U.S. military aid to Israel and the supply of military equipment to several Arab States. In early 1976, the issue revolved around military aid to Saudi Arabia, the proposed sale of C-130 transport aircraft to Egypt, and the training of Egyptian airmen in U.S. military schools.

The divergence of U.S. and Israeli positions, despite the reiteration of American support during the presidential election campaigns and the continued flow of economic and military assistance, seemed to foreshadow a period of crucial decision. In the last analysis, the time of tranquility Israel enjoyed after Sinai II became only a brief respite from the forces and pressures unleashed by the Yom Kippur War.

"Political Earthquake" of 1977

In May 1977, Israel's parliamentary election resulted in the victory of Menachem Begin and the right-wing Likud bloc, replacing the Labor

MENACHEM BEGIN
(AUGUST 16, 1913–MARCH 9, 1992)

Menachem Begin was born the son of Ze'ev-Dov and Hasia Begin in Brest-Litovsk, Russia (now Poland), in 1913. He was educated in Brest-Litovsk at the Mizrachi Hebrew School and later studied law at the University of Warsaw. At the age of 16, he joined Betar, the youth movement affiliated with Revisionist Zionism, and in 1932, he became the head of the Organization Department of Betar in Poland. Upon the outbreak of World War II, he was arrested by the Russian authorities and confined in concentration camps in Siberia and elsewhere. After his release in 1941, he joined the Polish army and was dispatched to the Middle East. After demobilization in 1943, he remained in Palestine and assumed command of the Irgun Zvai Leumi. For his activities against the British authorities as head of that organization, he was placed on their "most wanted" list but managed to evade capture by living underground in Tel Aviv.

With the independence of Israel in 1948 and the dissolution of the Irgun, Begin founded the Herut (Freedom) Party and represented it in the Knesset since its first meetings in 1949. Begin led the party's protest campaign against the reparations agreement with West Germany in 1952. He was instrumental in establishing the Gahal faction (a merger of Herut and the Liberal Party) in the Knesset in 1965. He developed a reputation as a gifted orator, writer, and political leader. He remained in opposition in parliament until the eve of the Six-Day War, when he joined the Government of National Unity. He and his Gahal colleagues resigned from the government in August 1970 over opposition to its acceptance of the peace initiative of U.S. secretary of state William Rogers, which implied the evacuation by Israel of territories occupied in the Six-Day War. Later, Gahal joined in forming the Likud bloc in opposition to the governing Labor-Mapam Alignment, and Begin became its leader.

In June 1977, Begin became Israel's first nonsocialist prime minister when the Likud bloc secured the mandate to form the government after the Knesset election. He also became the first Israeli prime minister to meet officially and publicly with an Arab head of state when he welcomed Egyptian president Anwar Sadat to Jerusalem in November 1977. He led Israel's delegations to the ensuing peace negotiations and signed, with Sadat and U.S. president Jimmy Carter, the Camp David Accords in September 1978. In March 1979, he and Sadat signed the

(continues)

MENACHEM BEGIN *(continued)*

Egypt-Israel Peace Treaty, with Carter witnessing the event, on the White House lawn. Begin and Sadat shared the 1978 Nobel Peace Prize for their efforts. For Begin and Israel, the treaty with Egypt was a momentous but difficult accomplishment: It brought peace with Israel's most populous and most significant military adversary, but it was traumatic given the extensive tangible concessions required of Israel, especially the uprooting of Jewish settlements in the Sinai Peninsula.

The Knesset election of June 30, 1981, returned a Likud-led coalition government to power in Israel, and Begin again became prime minister. Prior to that, he had served as minister of foreign affairs in 1979–80 and as minister of defense from May 1980 to August 1981. The 1982 war in Lebanon was a factor in Begin's decision to step down from the prime minister's office a year after taking office. He resigned on September 16, 1983, and thereafter led a secluded life until his death in 1992.

Begin's political skills were considerable and apparent. Despite his European origins and courtly manner, he was able, through his powerful oratorical skills, charismatic personality, and political and economic policies, to secure and maintain a substantial margin of popularity over other major political figures. At the time of his resignation, he was the most popular and highly regarded of Israeli politicians, as public opinion polls regularly indicated.

Party, which had been in power since Israel's independence and had dominated the political system. This change was regarded as a "political earthquake." The establishment of a government by Begin marked the first time that a non-Labor, non-Mapai government ruled the State of Israel.

Initially, 28 political parties contested the 1977 election, and eventually 22 proposed candidates. Those 22 political parties represented all points on the political spectrum on most significant domestic and foreign policy issues. Thirteen parties secured seats in the Knesset, in which some 80 percent of those eligible voted.

Three main perspectives concerning the Arab-Israeli conflict and appropriate Israeli policy emerged. The "annexationist" position was represented primarily by General Ariel Sharon and his Shlomzion Party, which argued that, for all practical purposes, Israel should annex the territories occupied in 1967 and that the appropriate strategy in dealing with the Arab states was to maintain maximum military might as a deterrent to conflict. On the left were the doves, which included a combination of communist parties and noncommunist individuals, such as Arieh Eliav, Matityahu Peled, Meir Pail, and Uri Avnery. The doves argued that there was an independent Palestinian people with whom Israel should negotiate, including the PLO if necessary, that there should be almost total withdrawal from the occupied territories, and that a Palestinian state should be created alongside Israel. This viewpoint was conditioned by the belief that within the Arab world there was a moderate and realistic school of thought and there were statesmen who, for the return of the territories occupied by Israel since 1967, with some adjustments by both sides, were ready to end the conflict and live in peace with Israel.

More to the center of the political spectrum, the Labor-Mapam Alignment (under Rabin and Peres) basically restated its existing positions, which argued for the return of some of the occupied territory, the creation of defensible borders, and planned settlements in the occupied territories. It opposed the creation of a third state between the Mediterranean and Iraq and opposed dealing with the PLO. The Democratic Movement for Change (DMC), under Yigael Yadin, articulated a similar view. Likud supported many of these positions, but on the issue of territory it stood, as its campaign literature stated, for "Israeli sovereignty between the Mediterranean and the Jordan; *Eretz Yisrael* for the Jewish people."

The voters focused on the centrist parties. The dovish position, represented by the Democratic Front for Peace and Equality (primarily the communists) and Peace for Israel, or Shelli, received about 9 percent of the vote, most of which went to the Democratic Front and came from Israeli Arabs protesting a series of issues, not just Israel's position concerning the conflict. Of those 9 percent, Peace for Israel, whose platform contained no other significant elements beyond a lenient approach to the Arab-Israeli conflict, received only 1.5 percent of the votes cast. Shlomzion at the other end of the spectrum also received only 2 percent of the vote. The NRP, which represented both a religious perspective and a hawkish position on the Arab-Israeli conflict, received approximately 9 percent of the vote. The mainstream parties that argued for consensus positions received the largest proportion (between 60 and 70 percent) of the vote. The Israeli electorate provided a clear mandate for the centrist position on the Arab-Israeli conflict.

The new government was composed of center and religious parties; Labor moved to the opposition. Prime Minister Begin reiterated the commitment of all previous prime ministers to work for permanent peace in the region and called upon the Arab leaders to come to the negotiating table.

The Carter Administration

Jimmy Carter came to office in January 1977, and his administration believed that the Arab-Israeli conflict called for a new approach that would replace the step-by-step process utilized by Secretary of State Henry Kissinger under Presidents Richard Nixon and Gerald Ford. A reconvened Geneva conference was now regarded as an appropriate beginning, and the United States sought to establish a set of principles that might serve as the basis for negotiations among the parties.

Begin's election raised doubts about the efficacy of the U.S. policy, so the Carter administration decided to wait and see what Begin would do once in power. When Begin came to Washington, D.C., in mid-July 1977, both he and Carter sought to allay suspicions of fundamental disagreement over the peace process. Although no substantial changes in the position of either side resulted, a foundation of personal rapport and mutual confidence was established between them. Nonetheless, various actions of the Begin government clashed with the views of the U.S. administration; for example, the Begin government authorized further Jewish settlements in the West Bank although Secretary of State Cyrus Vance regarded them as illegal.

By the end of September 1977, Israel agreed to a U.S. proposal that Palestinian representatives constitute part of a unified Arab delegation at the opening session of a reconvened Geneva peace conference. Then, on October 1, 1977, the United States and the Soviet Union issued a joint statement on the Middle East that brought the Soviets back into the forefront of the peace process, to the dismay of both Israel and Egypt.

The intensity of opposition to this joint statement was not expected by the White House, which tried to diffuse the situation through a series of statements and in meetings reaffirming the support of the United States and Carter for Israel. A series of meetings in New York between Carter, Vance, and Dayan, Israel's foreign minister under Begin, moderated Israeli concerns and resulted in a working paper whose purpose was not only to avoid a crisis in U.S.-Israel relations but also to clear procedural obstacles on the path to reconvening the

Geneva conference. The working paper was accepted by the Israeli cabinet on October 11 but was flatly rejected by the PLO and was unacceptable to most Arab states. The basic objection of the Arabs was over the form of representation of the Palestinians at the Geneva conference, who were to be represented in a proposed unified Arab delegation, but not by the PLO.

Sadat Initiative

It was in this context that Egypt's president Anwar Sadat changed everything when he announced, on November 9, 1977, to the Egyptian National Assembly that he was prepared to go to Jerusalem to discuss the situation face-to-face with the Israelis: "I am ready to go to the Israeli Parliament itself to discuss [going to Geneva] with them." He asserted that he regarded the Geneva conference as a means for recovering lands lost by the Arabs in 1967 and for obtaining recognition of the right of the Palestinians to a homeland.

Begin welcomed Sadat's offer and invited him to Israel. On November 19, Sadat debarked from his plane at Ben-Gurion International Airport

November 19, 1977: President Anwar Sadat (center) arrives in Israel, where he is greeted by President Ephraim Katzir (right) and Prime Minister Menachem Begin (left) to begin negotiations for peace. (Courtesy Embassy of Israel, Washington, D.C.)

in Israel, and the next day, after meetings with Israeli political leaders, he addressed the Knesset. Although in his Knesset speech Sadat made no policy concessions to Israel and reiterated his demands as a basis for peace, the fact that he came to Israel and was willing to meet with Israeli leaders had a fundamental effect on all parties to the conflict. For Egypt and Israel, the process of moving toward peace through direct negotiation had begun. In the Arab world, reactions to Sadat's trip ranged from concern (Jordan and Saudi Arabia) to outrage (Libya and Iraq); only three states (Morocco, Sudan, and Oman) of the 22 members of the Arab League supported Sadat's actions.

Sadat apparently felt that the military option was no longer a viable one. Since Israel could not be defeated militarily and the cost of continued conflict was becoming unbearable to Egypt, he undertook his "sacred mission" to Jerusalem to bridge the gap between the two sides with a single, dramatic action.

On November 26, Sadat invited all parties to the Arab-Israeli conflict, plus the Soviet Union, the United States, and the United Nations, to send representatives to Cairo to discuss the obstacles to reconvening the Geneva peace conference. The invitation was accepted by Israel, the United States, and the United Nations and rejected by all Arab states and the Soviet Union. Sadat, in the meantime, announced that he was willing to negotiate with Israel alone, if necessary. The Cairo Conference opened on December 14. Various meetings took place, and negotiations continued over the following month.

The United States tried to persuade the parties to reduce the public recriminations and to continue private negotiations. As a part of this process, Sadat conferred with Carter at Camp David, in Maryland, on February 3, 1978, and announced that the United States was no longer a "go-between" but a "full partner in the establishment of peace" and that Israel's policy of building new settlements in the occupied territories was a barrier to negotiations. After Sadat's visit, U.S. spokesmen criticized Israel's settlements policy and announced that the administration intended to sell military aircraft to Egypt and to Saudi Arabia, as well as to Israel, in part to encourage prospects for a resolution of the problem.

Spring 1978 Plane Sales

The announced aircraft sale quickly escalated into a major bone of contention between the United States and Israel. Israel's objection was not so much over the sale of planes to Egypt but over the sale of

F-15s to Saudi Arabia, which Israel viewed as a threat to its security. Although the Carter administration insisted that these planes would not be used against Israel and were to protect Saudi and U.S. interests in the increasingly destabilized Persian Gulf area, Israel and its supporters in the United States brought great pressure on the administration to cancel this sale. On February 24, Vance announced that the proposed sale of planes was a package plan, and it either was to be approved by the Senate as a whole, or the administration would withdraw the proposed sale.

The debate over the sale lasted into the spring, but on May 15, the Senate failed to disapprove the administration's proposal to sell the planes to all three nations by a vote of 54-44. This led to a further strain in U.S.-Israel relations. Despite the administration's efforts to reassure Israel that the package was not meant to adversely affect Israel's security situation, Israel perceived this sale as another indication of the Carter administration's tilt toward the Arabs and away from Israel.

Begin and Peace Now

During the early phases of the debate over the aircraft sales, the Begin government, to the consternation of both the United States and Egypt but in response to domestic pressures, announced a proposed plan for the creation of 31 new settlements in the territories. Begin also shocked the Carter administration by asserting that in his view UN Security Council Resolution 242 did not apply to the West Bank and therefore did not require Israeli withdrawal. This interpretation of Resolution 242 had not been taken by any previous Israeli government and prompted Carter, on March 9, 1978, to state that if the Israeli government maintained such a position, it would constitute a very serious blow to the prospects of peace in the Middle East.

The actions by Begin not only caused a great deal of concern in the United States and Egypt, but also an uproar in Israel. Defense Minister Ezer Weizman, while visiting the United States, reportedly told Begin that if construction of new settlements commenced, he would terminate his visit and resign his defense portfolio. On March 7, 1978, 350 reserve officers and soldiers sent a letter to Begin asking him to choose peace with the Arabs over territory. On April 1, the Peace Now movement staged a large rally in Tel Aviv in support of a more flexible negotiating position on the part of the Israeli government. A petition in support of the Peace Now movement was signed by 360 Israeli academics and intellectuals.

Operation Litani

Begin's pronouncements and Israel's actions, as well as the peacemaking process, were soon overshadowed by other developments in the region. On March 11, 1978, a PLO terrorist unit landed on a beach in Israel and attacked and seized a bus filled with Israelis. The resulting firefight left 37 Israelis killed and more than 75 injured. It was against this background that 15,000–20,000 Israeli troops in a combined air, sea, and ground assault, entered Lebanon on March 14. The declared objective of the operation was to direct blows at the terrorist organizations and to eliminate PLO bases and staging areas south of the Litani River. After initially securing a strip along the border between its territory and that of Lebanon, Israel continued to move northward and eventually occupied much of Lebanon south of the Litani River.

U.S.-sponsored United Nations Security Council Resolutions 425 and 426 were adopted on March 19. They called for an immediate Israeli withdrawal and the establishment of a United Nations Interim Force in Lebanon (UNIFIL) for the purpose of confirming the Israeli withdrawal. Israel began a phased withdrawal from southern Lebanon on April 11, after a UN peacekeeping force entered the area to prevent infiltration by hostile forces from Lebanon into Israel. On June 13, the last Israeli troops withdrew.

Negotiations between Egypt and Israel, meanwhile, continued, but progress was minimal. The foreign ministers met at Leeds Castle, in England, in July 1978, with no significant advances. On July 23, Sadat asked for Israel to return portions of the Sinai to Egypt as a symbolic gesture. Begin refused, adding that "Nobody can get anything for nothing." Sadat's reaction was angry. In a series of moves, he publicly denounced Begin, demanded evidence of greater Israeli flexibility, expelled the Israeli military delegation from Cairo, and declared that the peace talks could not resume until Israel provided some new element.

In August, Carter sent handwritten invitations to the leaders of Israel and Egypt to come to the United States to meet with him at Camp David in early September. Both Begin and Sadat gave immediate and unconditional affirmative responses.

Camp David

The Camp David Summit was referred to by Sadat as a last chance for a peaceful settlement. No time limit was set for the duration of the meetings, and it was agreed that the three leaders, along with a small number of aides and advisers, would be isolated from the rest of the

UNITED NATIONS SECURITY COUNCIL RESOLUTION 425
(MARCH 19, 1978)

The Security Council,

Taking note of the letters of the Permanent Representative of Lebanon (S/12600 and S/12606) and the Permanent Representative of Israel (S/12607),

Having heard the statements of the Permanent Representatives of Lebanon and Israel,

Gravely concerned at the deterioration of the situation in the Middle East, and its consequences to the maintenance of international peace,

Convinced that the present situation impedes the achievement of a just peace in the Middle East,

1. *Calls for* strict respect for the territorial integrity, sovereignty and political independence of Lebanon within its internationally recognized boundaries;
2. *Calls upon* Israel immediately to cease its military action against Lebanese territorial integrity and withdraw forthwith its forces from all Lebanese territory;
3. *Decides,* in the light of the request of the Government of Lebanon, to establish immediately under its authority a United Nations interim force for southern Lebanon for the purpose of confirming the withdrawal of Israeli forces, restoring international peace and security and assisting the Government of Lebanon in ensuring the return of its effective authority in the area, the force to be composed of personnel drawn from States Members of the United Nations;
4. *Requests* the Secretary-General to report to the Council within twenty-four hours on the implementation of this resolution.

world (especially the press), to prevent the political posturing from interfering with the negotiation process. Therefore, only brief, general statements noting some progress, some disagreement, and the need for greater flexibility in negotiating positions was all the information the world was given on the progress of the summit.

On September 17, 1978, after 13 days at the summit, the three leaders appeared at the White House to announce the conclusion of two agreements. President Carter, President Sadat and Prime Minister Begin

Seated from left to right: President Anwar Sadat, President Jimmy Carter, and Prime Minister Menachem Begin sign the Camp David Accords, 1978. (Courtesy Embassy of Israel, Washington, D.C.)

signed a Framework for Peace in the Middle East Agreed at Camp David and a Framework for the Conclusion of a Peace Treaty Between Egypt and Israel. Taken together, the two documents provided the basis for continuing negotiations leading to agreements between Israel and the Arab states. The Middle East framework set forth general principles and some specifics that would govern a comprehensive peace settlement between Israel and its Arab neighbors.

Although Israel agreed to withdraw from all of the Sinai Peninsula, the ultimate fate of Israeli settlements in the Sinai was not determined. It was agreed that the matter would be submitted to the Knesset, where it voted to remove Israeli settlers from Sinai. All peace plans prior to this had envisaged Israel keeping a strip of land, at minimum, along the east coast of the Sinai, connecting Eilat and Sharm el-Sheikh.

The Camp David Accords, although supported by an overwhelming majority in both Egypt and Israel, were not greeted with the euphoria that had greeted Sadat's journey to Jerusalem 10 months before, but rather with a more cautious optimism and some skepticism. In Egypt, although internal opposition was not significant, the positive official reaction was tempered by the reaction of the Arab world, which was initially overwhelmingly negative. (Oman was the only Arab state to provide a positive comment.) Arab opposition to Sadat, which had begun during his trip to Jerusalem, intensified as a result of the Camp David Accords.

Begin began to face growing internal opposition to the Camp David Accords, mostly from members of his own party and from within his ruling coalition. Nevertheless, on September 24, 1978, the Israeli cabinet endorsed the Camp David Accords, and four days later the Knesset approved it by an 84-19 vote, with 17 abstentions, after a 17-hour debate. The dissenting votes and abstentions were mostly from members of Begin's coalition.

The Camp David Accords provided frameworks for peace between Israel and Egypt and for a comprehensive settlement of the broader issues of the Arab-Israeli conflict. The focal point of post–Camp David activity was therefore to convert these documents into peace treaties through a process of continuing and broadened negotiations. After substantial negotiation, a draft treaty was devised. Despite agreement on this draft document, however, various points remained contentious between Egypt and Israel. As regional events began to have an effect on the negotiations, additional demands, especially by President Sadat, further complicated the process.

Generally, Egypt sought to achieve the maximum connection between the bilateral Egypt-Israel peace process and the overall, comprehensive peace process. Israel sought to reach agreement with Egypt on bilateral questions while reducing the connection between that agreement and the overall settlement of the Arab-Israeli conflict. For Sadat, movement toward Palestinian autonomy was crucial, for it would serve to reduce Arab criticism that he had made a separate peace with Israel. For Begin, any movement toward Palestinian autonomy on the West Bank and Gaza would draw additional opposition from right-wing elements of his party and the religious parties, which were important elements of support for his government. Israel also feared that if the peace treaty were linked to a timetable for Palestinian autonomy, it could give the Palestinians an effective veto over an Egypt-Israel peace treaty merely by refusing to participate in any autonomy discussions and arrangements, thereby preventing the timetable from being met. The Egyptian demand for linkage between the two Camp David Accords, including a detailed timetable for Israel's relinquishing of its military rule over the West Bank and Gaza and a fixed date for the election of a Palestinian parliamentary council, was rejected by the Israeli cabinet.

President Carter (second from right) and Prime Minister Begin (second from left) and their aides during consultations on Egypt-Israel peace in March 1979 (Courtesy Embassy of Israel, Washington, D.C.)

Along with these controversial issues, two other factors directly affected the negotiating process, although they were only indirectly related to it. One was the periodic Israeli announcements concerning the expansion of existing Israeli settlements on the West Bank and/or setting up new settlements in the area. These pronouncements were obviously made by the government as an attempt to soothe right-wing and religious opposition to the draft treaty. Nevertheless, they placed both Sadat and the United States in an awkward position and raised questions as to Israel's sincerity in regard to the proposed negotiations on Palestinian autonomy. The other factor was the continuing strain in relations between the United States and Israel, in no small part caused by Israeli settlement policies. Israel perceived the United States as siding with Egypt on all major disputes and felt the United States was being one sided and unjust in its criticism of Israel's negotiating position. While the first of these factors tended to foster a harder Egyptian line in negotiations over the remaining issues, the latter had the same effect on Israel.

The areas of controversy and discord promoted substantial recrimination between the drafting of the treaty in the fall of 1978 and its signature in March 1979. The December 17, 1978 deadline for conclusion of the Egypt-Israel treaty was not met despite a last-minute effort at shuttle diplomacy by Secretary of State Cyrus Vance. Israel's cabinet rejected the terms Vance brought from Cairo in mid-December and blamed the failure to reach agreement on Egypt. The United States labeled this a "deliberate distortion" since it regarded the terms as fair and reasonable.

Discussions continued, and in late February 1979, Carter decided to reconvene a variation of the Camp David Summit; this time Sadat would remain in Egypt and be represented by his prime minister, Mustafa Khalil. Sadat had noted that he had made all the compromises he intended to make, and the Israeli cabinet vetoed Prime Minister Begin's participation, partly because of the anticipation that the only purpose such a meeting could serve would be to focus pressure on Israel for further concessions. Carter then invited Begin for private talks without Khalil, and Begin accepted. Disagreements over the treaty's content were accompanied by differences in perspective concerning the issues in dispute. Carter believed that the differences that required reconciliation were insignificant. Begin demurred; he characterized the differences as great issues relating to Israel's future and security.

On March 4, Carter submitted a new set of compromise proposals to Begin, who characterized them as "interesting," and the next day the Israeli cabinet approved them. Carter decided to go to Cairo, hoping that the weight of his office would convince Sadat to accept these suggestions. Carter arrived in Cairo on March 8, and after Sadat accepted some of the new proposals and rejected or modified others, Carter flew to Israel on March 10 to secure Israeli cabinet acceptance of these changes. In Israel, Carter met with Begin and the Israeli cabinet to pressure them to make the last few concessions needed for an agreement. Carter found Begin initially unwilling to do so, but just when it appeared that the negotiations would stall, Begin made a few final concessions. With these in hand, Carter returned to Cairo. At a meeting on March 13, Carter informed Sadat of Begin's concessions and was able to get modifications in Sadat's position, which were conveyed to Begin. Carter returned to the United States with an agreement essentially in hand. The next day, Begin telephoned and informed Carter that the Israeli cabinet had approved the concessions made by both Begin and Sadat. The Egypt-Israel Peace Treaty was thus concluded.

The peace treaty, signed at the White House on March 26, 1979, ended the state of war between Egypt and Israel and was a significant step toward achieving a comprehensive settlement of the Arab-Israeli

From left to right: President Sadat, President Carter, and Prime Minister Begin after signing the Egypt-Israel Peace Treaty on the White House lawn, 1979 (Courtesy Embassy of Israel, Washington, D.C.)

conflict. Egypt, by entering into a treaty with Israel, acknowledged the fact that Israel was a state; both parties agreed to recognize and respect each other's sovereignty over their respective territories. For the first time in history, an Arab state had accepted Israel as a legitimate state in the Middle East. President Sadat and Prime Minister Begin were jointly awarded the Nobel Peace Prize for their accomplishments.

Ultimately, the two states exchanged territory for peace. Israel withdrew from all of the Sinai Peninsula, which was returned to Egypt; and Israel and Egypt established diplomatic relations and began a process of normalization of their ties. They also agreed to discuss the question of autonomy for Palestinians.

The process of normalization of relations moved ahead on schedule and without major disturbances. "Normal relations" between Egypt and Israel began officially on January 26, 1980. By that date Israel had completed its withdrawal from two-thirds of Sinai, as called for in the peace treaty, and land, air, and sea borders between the two states were opened. Holders of valid visas were able to travel from one country to the other through air and sea ports as well as at the Sinai crossing point at El Arish. Direct communication links by telephone, telex, and post

MENACHEM BEGIN'S ADDRESS DELIVERED AT THE TREATY-SIGNING CEREMONY ON THE WHITE HOUSE LAWN
(MARCH 26, 1979)

I have come from the Land of Israel, the land of Zion and Jerusalem, and here I stand in humility and with pride, as a son of the Jewish people, as one of the generation of the Holocaust and Redemption.

The ancient Jewish people gave the world the vision of eternal peace, of universal disarmament, of abolishing the teaching and learning of war. Two prophets, Yeshayahu Ben Amotz and Micha HaMorashti, having foreseen the spiritual unity of man under God—with His word coming forth from Jerusalem—gave the nations of the world the following vision expressed in identical terms.

> *"And they shall beat their swords into ploughshares and their spears into pruning hooks. Nation shall not lift up sword against nation; neither shall they know war anymore."*

It is a great day in the annals of two ancient nations, Egypt and Israel, whose sons met in our generation five times on the battlefield, fighting and falling. Let us turn our hearts to our heroes and pay tribute to their eternal memory; it is thanks to them that we could have reached this day. . . .

It is, of course, a great day in your life, Mr. President of the Arab Republic of Egypt. . . . But now is the time, for all of us, to show civil courage in order to proclaim to our peoples, and to others: no more war, no more bloodshed, no more bereavement—peace unto you, Shalom, Salaam—forever.

And it is, ladies and gentlemen, the third greatest day in my life. The first was May the Fourteenth 1948 when our flag was hoisted, our independence in our ancestor's land was proclaimed after one thousand eight hundred and seventy-eight years of dispersion, persecution, and physical destruction. We fought for our liberation—alone—and won the day. That was spring; such a spring we can never have again.

(continues)

BEGIN'S ADDRESS *(continued)*

The second day was when Jerusalem became one city, and our brave, perhaps most hardened soldiers, the parachutists, embraced with tears and kissed the ancient stones of the remnants of the Western Wall destined to protect the chosen place of God's glory. Our hearts wept with them—in remembrance.

"Omdot hayu ragleinu b'sha'arayich Yerushalayim; Yerushalayim hab-nuya ke'ir shechubrah la yachdav." (Psalm 122)

This is the third day in my life, I have signed a treaty of peace with our neighbor, with Egypt. The heart is full and overflowing. God gave me the strength to survive the horrors of Nazism and of a Stalinist concentration camp, to persevere, to endure, not to waiver in, or flinch from, my duty, to accept abuse from foreigners and, what is more painful, from my own people, and from my close friends. This effort too bore some fruit.

---

were inaugurated. Embassies were opened in Cairo and Tel Aviv, and on February 26, 1980, Ambassadors Eliahu Ben-Elisar of Israel and Saad Mortada of Egypt presented their credentials.

The peace treaty with Egypt eliminated the threat from Israel's primary Arab adversary with the largest military capacity. It also led to increased U.S. economic and military assistance to both Israel and Egypt. Despite this peace treaty with Egypt and its implementation, a comprehensive peace was not achieved, and Israel's other borders remained tense. The Arab League condemned Egypt for its separate peace with Israel, and Egypt was suspended from the Arab League. Their successes were not followed by additional achievements of consequence.

6

FROM PEACE WITH EGYPT TO THE PALESTINIAN INTIFADA (1979–1990)

Autonomy Negotiations

On May 25, 1979, in keeping with the previously agreed timetable, Egypt and Israel opened negotiations in Beersheba, Israel, to discuss the West Bank and Gaza Strip. The goal was full autonomy for the people in the West Bank and Gaza under a freely elected self-governing authority that would serve for a transitional period of not more than five years. The final status was reserved for a second stage of negotiations to begin as soon as possible but not later than three years after the self-governing authority was inaugurated.

In 1980, representatives of the parties met at several locations to continue the discussions. The issues were complex, and there were constant breakdowns. Despite some progress, President Sadat suspended Egyptian participation in the talks in mid-May 1980, ostensibly because an Israeli parliamentary resolution declared that Jerusalem was the eternal capital of the Jewish state. After some U.S. efforts, the negotiations were resumed in mid-July, but on August 3, Sadat informed Begin that the talks would be postponed. The stated reason was the final passage by Israel's parliament of a law confirming Jerusalem's status as Israel's "complete and united" capital.

The bill had been proposed by Geula Cohen, a right-wing member of the Knesset seeking to undermine the Camp David process and to embarrass Begin. Despite strong criticism of the bill as unnecessary, meaningless, and harmful, no real opposition to it could be expected, and the Basic Law was passed by a vote of 69 to 15 on July 30. The failure to reach agreement by the May 1980 deadline and the May and

BASIC LAW: JERUSALEM, CAPITAL OF ISRAEL
(JULY 30, 1980)

1. Jerusalem, complete and united, is the capital of Israel.
2. Jerusalem is the seat of the President of the State, the Knesset, the Government and the Supreme Court.
3. The Holy Places shall be protected from desecration and any other violation and from anything likely to violate the freedom of access of the members of the different religions to the places sacred to them or their feelings towards those places.
4. (a) The Government shall provide for the development and prosperity of Jerusalem and the well-being of its inhabitants by allocating special funds, including a special annual grant to the Municipality of Jerusalem (Capital City Grant) with the approval of the Finance Committee of the Knesset.
   (b) Jerusalem shall be given special priority in the activities of the authorities of the State so as to further its development in economic and other matters.
   (c) The Government shall set up a special body or special bodies for the implementation of the section.

August suspensions reflected the complex nature of the issues and the widely divergent positions of the two states.

The autonomy talks resumed in Washington, D.C., in mid-October 1980. Although the initial rounds indicated that stubborn issues remained, the talks augured well for the future. The earlier suspension had been followed by a period of tension and recriminations. The Egyptian media launched personal attacks on Begin, and Israel was accused of putting obstacles in the way of peace. But for the three involved parties, the resumption represented a more important policy objective: Egypt and Israel clearly saw the value of the peace effort and were motivated by their respective needs for peace, although their visions of its content and of their own requirements were dissimilar. For Carter, suspension of the talks called into question his Middle East policy and his image as peacemaker.

The Lebanese Missile Crisis

The Lebanese missile crisis developed in late April 1981 but had a long and complex background. The Lebanese civil war between Muslims and Christians had erupted in 1975, and Syria had become involved as early as 1976. In performing its "peacekeeping" role, with Arab League sanction, Syria was subject to limitations, among them that it would not deploy ground-to-air missiles in Lebanon. Israel provided support for Christian forces, especially those of Major Saad Haddad in the south, flew reconnaissance missions over Lebanon, and periodically attacked Palestinian positions in retaliation for strikes in Israel. The relatively quiescent situation began to collapse early in 1981 when Phalangist (a Lebanese Christian political party) militia clashed with Syrian and Palestinian elements. In the escalated conflict, Syria used helicopters against the Phalangists, and Israeli Phantom jets eventually shot down two of them on April 28, 1981. Syria subsequently moved SAM-3 and SAM-6 missiles into the Bekaa Valley of Lebanon, and Israel warned that the missiles should be removed, or its air force would eliminate them. Syria's response was to increase its missile and troop concentrations in Lebanon. Tensions rose.

Israel accepted a mediation effort by U.S. special envoy Philip Habib. Begin was willing to give diplomacy a chance but indicated that Israel would not indefinitely tolerate the missiles in Lebanon. The Lebanese-Syrian missile crisis became a theme in Israel's ongoing election campaign. The opposition charged that Begin sought to use it for political advantage, and the matter was debated both in the Knesset and at election rallies. Begin sought to focus on the security factor and on Israel's need for unimpeded access to Lebanon's skies for surveillance and for air strikes against Palestinians in Lebanon. The Likud complained that the opposition acted irresponsibly in attacking Begin on this issue at a time when Israel should present a united front to the enemy.

1981 Election

The 1981 election campaign was a long one, extending nearly six months, and featured some new techniques adapted from the United States by the two main blocs' consultants. Labor sought to focus the voters' attention on the failures of the Begin government, especially the weak economy and triple-digit inflation. Security and foreign policy issues seemed to benefit the Likud, which trumpeted its peace efforts and the treaty with Egypt.

Likud's campaign highlighted Begin's abilities. Begin projected a charismatic appeal to large segments of the electorate and made skillful use of his incumbency. Likud stressed that it was not the party of war, as it had been portrayed by the Labor Alignment, but rather a party that brought Israel both peace and security. It also campaigned on a platform that hailed Jerusalem as the undivided capital of Israel. Likud emphasized its policy of establishing settlements with the slogan "We are on the map" (anachnu al hamapa). In its first four years in office, the Likud government had established 155 new settlements, of which 55 were in Judea and Samaria (the West Bank); it argued that every one of them strengthened Israel's security, and it pledged to continue its settlements in those areas.

The Labor Alignment, on the other hand, supported Shimon Peres's Jordan option, which suggested that Israel negotiate with Jordan instead of the Palestinians to determine the future of the West Bank and Gaza. Likud maintained that this position sought to return 70 percent of Judea and Samaria (the West Bank) to Jordan, which in turn would hand these territories over to Yasser Arafat, who would establish a Palestinian state. The Likud suggested that voters were therefore required to choose between the security of Israel or a Palestinian state.

On May 7, Begin spoke at the West Bank settlement of Ariel before a crowd of 35,000. He vowed no withdrawal from the territories: "I, Menahem, the son of Ze'ev and Hasia Begin do solemnly swear that as long as I serve the nation as prime minister, we will not leave any part of Judea, Samaria, the Gaza Strip and the Golan Heights." (Kieval 1983, p. 165) He warned that the Jordan option proposed by Peres meant surrendering to the terrorists (and to "Arafatism") the Samarian mountain ridge on which Ariel was situated.

Labor, under the leadership of Peres, focused instead on the urgency of assuring Israel's future as a Jewish state that is democratic and secure within defensible borders. Labor argued that the permanent absorption of 1.25 million Palestinian Arabs, as advocated by Begin, would eventually turn Israel into a second Lebanon, while his autonomy program would lead to a Palestinian state. Labor supported the concept of territorial compromise. The Jordan option was based on the assumption that there is an integral connection between the Palestinians in the West Bank and the Gaza Strip and the Palestinians in Jordan. Labor opposed both the Likud policy of annexation of the West Bank and Gaza Strip and the PLO policy of establishing an independent and sovereign Palestinian state in those areas. It offered instead a policy of compromise. The Jordan option was seen as the solution to the West Bank

SHIMON PERES
(AUGUST 15, 1923–   )

Shimon Persky was born in 1923, in Vishneva, Poland (now Belarus), to Isaac and Sarah Persky. His father immigrated to Palestine in 1931, and the family joined him there in 1934. In his youth, Peres became involved in Hashomer Hatzair (Young Guard) and later joined Hanoar Haoved (Working Youth). Peres rose to the rank of commander in the Haganah by his late teens and was active in the procurement and manufacture of arms for the Israel Defense Forces. His success in developing and acquiring arms both at home and abroad gained him recognition as one of the pioneers of Israel's defense industry. In February 1952, he was appointed to serve as deputy director general of the Defense Ministry and in October became acting director general of the ministry. Peres spent much of his time fostering Franco-Israeli relations, and France remained Israel's primary supplier of major weapons systems until after the Six-Day War of 1967. Peres was instrumental in the creation of Bedek, which later came to be known as Israel Aircraft Industries (IAI) and then as Israel Aeorospace Industries.

Peres's Knesset career began in 1959 when he was elected as a member of the Mapai Party, although he continued to serve as deputy minister of defense. In 1965, Peres joined David Ben-Gurion's Rafi party and became its secretary-general. In 1968, Rafi joined with Mapai and Ahdut Ha'avodah to form the Israel Labor Party. Between 1969 and 1973, Peres held a variety of cabinet posts.

When Golda Meir resigned as prime minister in 1974, her possible successors were Peres and Yitzhak Rabin. Rabin, the preferred choice of the party establishment, won a close vote over Peres in the Labor Party's central committee. The new government was established in June with Rabin as prime minister and Peres as minister of defense.

Peres unsuccessfully challenged Rabin for party leadership at the Labor convention in February 1977. A series of scandals, however, led Rabin to resign in April 1977, so Peres became the party's new leader and candidate for prime minister. But, Likud won a plurality of Knesset seats in both the 1977 and 1981 elections and formed a government headed by Menachem Begin. Then in the 1984 election, Labor secured 44 seats to Likud's 41, and although Peres received the mandate to form the government, he was unable to establish a majority coalition. This led to the formation of a national unity government (NUG), a new experiment in Israeli politics. A rotation agreement was adopted that called

(continues)

SHIMON PERES *(continued)*

for Peres to serve as prime minister for the first half of the 50-month term while the Likud's Yitzhak Shamir served as foreign minister. After 25 months, the two rotated positions for the balance of the term. During his tenure as prime minister, Peres presided over Israel's withdrawal from Lebanon and confronted the economic problems with austerity measures. He also actively sought to establish diplomatic contacts with Arab leaders such as King Hassan II of Morocco and King Hussein of Jordan, and tried to improve relations with the United States that had become strained under Begin and Shamir. The 1988 Knesset election again did not produce a clear victory for either Labor or Likud, and the Government of National Unity was reformed, this time with Shamir as prime minister for the duration of the government. Peres accepted the position of finance minister.

In 1990, Peres and the other Labor ministers forced a vote of confidence in the Knesset that the Shamir-led government lost. However, Peres was unable to form a coalition government, and he reverted to the role of leader of the opposition in the Knesset.

After several tries, Rabin ousted Peres as Labor Party chairman in early 1992 and led his party to victory in the elections to the 13th Knesset. Peres served as foreign minister in the new governing coalition. To the surprise of many, Peres and Rabin achieved a modus vivendi, and together they set Israel on a course that resulted in a series of interim agreements with the PLO, the 1994 peace treaty with Jordan, and the

and the Gaza Strip problem, and Peres made clear his opposition to the PLO as a terrorist organization committed to the destruction of Israel.

Likud and Labor overshadowed the other parties and dominated the campaign. The other parties devoted their attention primarily to religious matters (particularly the NRP and the ultra-Orthodox Ashkenazi Agudat Israel Party), to ethnic and personal appeals (especially the Traditional Movement of Israel, or Tami), and to more specific concerns such as the revocation of income tax, Arab issues, and so forth. Telem (Movement for National Renewal) and Tehiya (Israel Renaissance Party) headed by Moshe Dayan and Yuval Ne'eman, respectively, included foreign policy and security themes as important segments of their public appeals, as did the NRP. Telem argued that it was necessary to reinforce the process of active peacemaking with Israel's neighbors, and its leader, Dayan, suggested that his position was closer to Labor

opening of commercial relations and substantive diplomatic discussions with a number of other Arab countries, including Syria. For their efforts, Peres, Rabin, and the PLO's Yasser Arafat received the 1994 Nobel Peace Prize. Peres actively promoted the vision of "a new Middle East," one premised on the completion of formal peace agreements and the full political, social, and economic integration of Israel into the Middle East.

He became interim prime minister and defense minister following the November 1995 assassination of Rabin. Seeking a mandate of his own, he opted for early elections in the spring of 1996; he lost by less than 1 percent of the popular vote for the direct election of the prime minister to Likud's Benjamin Netanyahu. Peres subsequently relinquished the chairmanship of the Labor Party and was succeeded by Ehud Barak. He was named regional cooperation minister, in the coalition government formed by Barak and deputy prime minister and minister of foreign affairs in Israel's 29th government (until November 2, 2002). He served in the Knesset on behalf of the Labor Party and as vice prime minister in Israel's 30th government in 2005. He was defeated for the Labor Party leadership, resigned from the party, and joined Sharon's Kadima Party in November 2005. He was reelected to the Knesset on the Kadima list in March 2006 and became vice prime minister in the 31st government established by Ehud Olmert in May 2006. He was elected Israel's ninth president, capping a six-decade career In which he held every senior government post. He was sworn into office on July 15, 2007, for a seven-year term.

---

than to Likud. Tehiya focused its concern on the land of Israel. The party was established after the signing of the Camp David Accords and the Egypt-Israel Peace Treaty primarily by defectors from the Likud who believed that Begin had sold them out and that Israel needed to retain full possession of all the territories occupied in the Six-Day War.

The foreign policy sections of the NRP's political platform called for making it possible for the settlements in Sinai to remain in Israel's hands; it proposed legislation to prevent the removal of settlements from Judea, Samaria, Gaza, and the Golan Heights and recommended that suitable conditions be found for extending Israeli law to the Golan. On the issue of the autonomy negotiations, at which NRP leader Yosef Burg led the Israeli team, the NRP noted that Israel must insist that responsibility for security—both internal and external—remain in Israeli hands in Judea, Samaria, and Gaza and that the existence, expansion, and development of the Israeli settlements, as well as the right to set up more settlements, be safeguarded.

Regional Developments

In early June 1981, Egyptian president Sadat held a meeting with Begin (at the latter's invitation) for the first time in almost a year and a half at Sharm el-Sheikh, Egypt. The summit meeting boosted Begin's position, especially among voters committed to neither Labor nor Likud, but contributed little to the Egyptian-Israeli peace process. Later that year, in October 1981, President Sadat was assassinated in Cairo. Despite his past role as a warrior against Israel, at the time of his death he was eulogized by Israel as the first Arab leader to recognize, negotiate with, and make peace with Israel. Israelis also expressed the hope that his commitment to peace would be sustained by his successors.

On June 8, 1981, Israel announced that the Israeli air force had attacked and destroyed the Osirak nuclear reactor, near Baghdad, in Iraq. Israel justified the strike with the argument that the reactor was meant to produce nuclear weapons, posing a danger to its existence. Preventing Iraq from acquiring nuclear weapons was seen as essential for Israel's survival. A negative reaction worldwide followed. The United States condemned the attack, temporarily suspended the delivery of F-16 aircraft to Israel, and joined in a United Nations Security Council resolution strongly condemning the raid.

Despite international criticism, the destruction of the reactor had an electrifying effect on the Israeli voters as it conjured up images of regional threats and of Israeli capability. Although the circumstances and the timing were debated, few Israelis questioned the raid itself. Begin and his supporters declared the raid to be in the national interest and insisted that it had been necessary for Israel to act how and when it did.

Begin's Second Government

The election of June 30, 1981 returned a Likud-led coalition government to power—contrary to early predictions of a significant Labor victory—but it was different from its predecessor in party composition, participating personalities, and policy perspectives. For the first time, the two major parties emerged approximately equal in parliamentary strength, and the small parties in parliament lost votes and seats.

Between them, Likud and Labor won nearly 100 of the 120 seats in the Knesset. Begin put together a coalition of four parties controlling a slim majority of 61 seats in the Knesset. This coalition, consisting of Likud, the NRP, Agudat Israel, and Tami, was approved by the Knesset on August 5, 1981, after substantial bargaining that culminated in an 83-clause agreement.

The government's program submitted to and approved by the Knesset on August 5 was general in nature and not too dissimilar from those of its predecessors. It spoke of the right of the Jewish people to the Land of Israel. Among other points, it noted, "The autonomy agreed upon at Camp David means neither sovereignty nor self-determination. The autonomy agreements set down at Camp David are guarantees that under no conditions will a Palestinian state emerge in the territory of Western 'Eretz Yisrael.'" Begin continued to see autonomy as primarily administrative in nature with Israel responsible for security. Specifying that "settlement in the Land of Israel is a right and an integral part of the nation's security," the government reiterated its position regarding Jewish settlements, promising to "strengthen, expand, and develop settlements." It also noted, "Equality of rights for all residents will continue to exist in the Land of Israel, with no distinction (on the basis) of religion, race, nationality, sex, or ethnic community." Begin also foreshadowed future action concerning the Golan Heights in the program: "Israel will not descend from the Golan Heights, nor will it remove any settlements established there. It is the Government that will decide on the appropriate timing for the application of Israeli Law, jurisdiction, and administration of the Golan Heights." Finally, the government program reiterated the long-standing policy of Israel concerning Jerusalem: "Jerusalem is the eternal capital of Israel, indivisible, entirely under Israeli sovereignty. Free access to their holy places has been and will be guaranteed to followers of all faiths."

Begin's 1981 government was narrower and less pragmatic in nature than his previous government but also more firmly under his control. It presented a harder line concerning the West Bank and related negotiations. Although willing to include Jordan and representatives of the Palestinians in future negotiations, as called for in the Camp David Accords, Begin continued to rule out any dealings with the PLO on the grounds that it was a terrorist organization committed to the destruction of Israel. On the other hand, the new Begin government saw the renewal of the autonomy talks and the expansion of the peace and normalization process with Egypt as important elements of policy.

Relations with the United States

In 1980, Ronald Reagan was elected president of the United States. Relations between the Begin and Reagan administrations were complex. Israel and the United States continued to clash over divergent interpretations of the regional situation, the peace process, and Israel's security needs. Israel struck at the Iraqi reactor and at PLO bases in Beirut during summer 1981 and took action on other issues when it believed that its national interest was at stake even though it expected U.S. opposition on these issues. There were disputes about settlements and Israel's concern about a perceived pro-Saudi tendency in U.S. policy, manifest in part by arms supplied to Saudi Arabia (including F-15 enhancements and Airborne Warning and Control System [AWACS] aircraft).

Israeli anxiety was heightened when the Reagan administration seemed to suggest that a peace plan put forward in August 1981 by Crown Prince Fahd of Saudi Arabia and opposed by Israel had some merit. The U.S. administration's stand lent credence to the Israeli perspective of a tilt toward Saudi Arabia in U.S. policy.

In an effort to mitigate the effects of the AWACS sale, Reagan sought to reassure Israel that the United States remained committed to helping Israel retain its military and technological advantages. On November 30, the United States and Israel signed a Memorandum of Understanding on Strategic Cooperation in which the two countries recognized the need to enhance strategic cooperation. The agreement called for cooperation in response to Soviet or Soviet-controlled threats and was not directed against any Middle Eastern state or group of states. Bilateral working groups were to negotiate the details of implementation. For the Begin government, the agreement constituted an important milestone, suggesting improved relations with the United States. However, the thaw in relations was short lived.

A month later, the government of Israel, in keeping with its campaign themes, decided to alter the status of the Golan Heights. On a number of occasions, Begin and other spokesmen for Likud had made clear that Israel was prepared to negotiate with Syria but would not agree to withdraw ("come down") from the Golan Heights or to remove any settlement from it.

On December 14, the government presented to the Knesset the Golan Heights Law, whose operative clause applied the law, jurisdiction, and administration of Israel to the area. The rationales were many but centered on historical and security factors and on the refusal of Syria to recognize Israel's existence and to negotiate with Israel for peace. The Knesset subsequently endorsed the government's proposal, the government gaining some support from the ranks of the Labor opposition. U.S. spokesmen stressed that the United States had been given no advance warning and opposed the decision to change the status of the Golan through unilateral action. Statements of displeasure and condemnation were accompanied by U.S. support for a UN Security Council resolution of condemnation and by U.S. suspension of the Agreement of Understanding on Strategic Cooperation. Israel was stunned by the extent of the U.S. response, and Israel's strongly negative reaction included Begin's castigation of the U.S. ambassador.

Operation Peace for Galilee

On June 3, 1982, gunmen from the Abu Nidal Palestinian terrorist group shot the Israeli ambassador to Britain, Shlomo Argov, and paralyzed him in an assassination attempt. He died in February 2003. This was a factor in Israel's decision to launch military strikes against Palestinian positions in Lebanon. The operation was described as a major response to years of PLO terror attacks against Israel and its people. After the expulsion of the PLO from Jordan in September 1970, the PLO shifted its infrastructure to Lebanon and established a massive presence there—a state within a state—from which it launched terrorist operations against Israel. Over the years these attacks grew in number, intensity, and sophistication, despite various efforts by Israel and the international community (including an unofficial cease-fire arranged by U.S. ambassador Philip Habib) to defuse the situation and establish a quiet border.

On June 6, Israel launched a major military action against the PLO called Operation Peace for Galilee. The military objective was to ensure security for northern Israel; to destroy the PLO's infrastructure, which had established a state within a state in Lebanon; and to eliminate a center of international terrorism and a base of operations from which Israel was threatened. The objective of the IDF was to ensure that the civilian population of the Galilee was beyond the range of terrorist fire from Lebanon. Prime Minister Begin conveyed to the United States that the operation would be limited to a distance of about 25 miles (some 40 kilometers) from its borders, but it soon went beyond this self-imposed limit. Israel also noted its aspiration to sign a peace treaty with Lebanon after PLO and Syrian influence had been eliminated. But the political objectives were not as precise, and in many respects the results were ambiguous.

In the first few weeks of the invasion, Israeli forces gained control of all southern Lebanon up to Beirut, most of the southern Beqa Valley in the east, and most of the Beirut-Damascus highway. The war occasioned major debate and numerous demonstrations within Israel and resulted in substantial casualties. The PLO infrastructure and the Palestinian camps in the south, which had taken almost 12 years to build, were systematically destroyed, and more than 10,000 Palestinians and Lebanese suspected of PLO sympathies were sent off to a detention camp. Significant numbers of Syrian missiles, aircraft, and tanks were either hit or captured, and Syrian soldiers were killed. Then, Israel laid siege to Beirut, which came to an end with the PLO's departure from Beirut and the entry of a small multinational force. The United States played the crucial role of mediating among the parties and guaranteeing the safety of Palestinian civilians remaining in Beirut.

The hostilities in Lebanon were terminated by a brokered cease-fire achieved by U.S. envoy Philip Habib. The PLO was forced to withdraw its forces from Lebanon in August 1982. Israel's northern border was consequently more secure and northern Galilee was safer, but southern Lebanon had been transformed into an area of growing Shiite influence and control. The PLO was weakened, but its more radical elements had taken effective control over Lebanon's Palestinians. The Israeli troops that remained in Lebanon until the summer of 1985 became targets of terrorists and others, and numerous casualties resulted.

After the end of hostilities, Phalange leader Bashir Gemayel became president-elect of Lebanon but was assassinated on September 14, 1982 before he could take office. Immediately Israel ordered its army into Beirut to restore order but with the stipulation that no troops were to enter the camps. Gemayel's brother, Amin, was then elected in his place. Although the Israelis controlled Beirut and the camps were closed and surrounded, right-wing Lebanese Christian (Phalangist) militia entered the camps of Sabra and Shatila on September 16 and massacred hundreds of Palestinians. The two camps were basically residential areas with a population exceeding 50,000 people. Israel established a commission of inquiry to ascertain events pertaining to the massacre and to determine Israeli responsibility, if any. The Kahan report was issued in the spring of 1983 and determined that there was no direct Israeli responsibility. The massacre was the direct result of Phalangist action. Nevertheless, the report suggested indirect culpability on the part of some Israelis and recommended a number of important changes. Among these was the resignation of Ariel Sharon as minister of defense.

After the war in Lebanon in 1982, Israel engaged in negotiations with the Gemayel government in Lebanon under the auspices of the United States, concerning the withdrawal of foreign forces from Lebanon and

KAHAN COMMISSION OF INQUIRY (1982–1983)

Toward the end of the war in Lebanon, Christian Phalangist forces massacred Palestinians at the Sabra and Shatila refugee camps in the Beirut area. Some alleged that the Israeli army knew about and could have prevented the massacres since the camps were within the army's range of control. The resultant anguish within Israel led to the decision, taken by the cabinet on September 28, 1982, to create a commission of inquiry whose terms of reference were described this way: "The matter which will be subjected to inquiry is: all the facts and factors connected with the atrocity carried out by a unit of the Lebanese Forces against the civilian population in the Shatila and Sabra camps." The commission of inquiry consisted of Yitzhak Kahan, president of the Supreme Court, who served as commission chairman; Aharon Barak, justice of the Supreme Court; and Yona Efrat, a reserve major general in the Israel Defense Forces (IDF). Its final report was issued in February 1983. Among its recommendations, was that Major General Yehoshua Saguy no longer continue as director of military intelligence, that division commander Brigadier General Amos Yaron not serve in the capacity of an IDF field commander, and that Ariel Sharon resign as minister of defense.

related arrangements. After months of negotiations that included the extensive involvement of U.S. secretary of state George Shultz, an agreement was reached and signed on May 17, 1983.

The Israel-Lebanon agreement was not a peace treaty; rather the two states agreed "to respect the sovereignty, political independence and territorial integrity of each other" and to "confirm that the state of war between Israel and Lebanon has been terminated and no longer exists." The existing international boundary between Israel and Lebanon was to remain the border, and Israel undertook to withdraw all its armed forces from Lebanon. Syrian forces and the PLO were also to withdraw.

Syria rejected the agreement, and Palestinian leaders, meeting in Damascus, also opposed it. Syria objected to the Israeli security presence in southern Lebanon, claiming that it infringed on Lebanese sovereignty and Syrian security. Meanwhile, the Soviet Union's reaction was multifaceted. It charged that the United States and Israel were grossly violating Lebanese territory, and it demanded the unconditional withdrawal of Israeli troops from Lebanon as the first and foremost condition for bringing peace to that country. Although signed and ratified by both states, Lebanon abrogated the agreement in March 1984, yielding to heavy pressure from Syria and the Soviet Union. Israeli forces remained in Lebanon.

The war in Lebanon also led to tensions and verbal clashes between Israel and the United States. The initial U.S. effort to secure the PLO's evacuation was soon supplemented by the decision to return U.S. forces to Beirut after the massacres at the Shatila and Sabra camps. The war also led to the Reagan administration's "fresh-start initiative," which sought to reinvigorate the Arab-Israeli peace process. Israel saw the U.S. proposals as detrimental to its policies and rejected them. That action, coupled with the massacres at the Shatila and Sabra camps, resulted in a sharp deterioration in Israel's standing in U.S. public opinion and further disagreements with the U.S. administration. Relations appeared to have come full circle by summer 1983, when the two states benefited from a congruence of policy that included recognition of Israel's strategic anti-Soviet value and its desire for peaceful resolution of the Arab-Israeli conflict as well as parallel views concerning Lebanon. This development comported with Reagan's initial perceptions of Israel and received explicit expression in a December 1983 agreement on closer strategic cooperation between Reagan and the new prime minister of Israel, Yitzhak Shamir.

Yitzhak Shamir as Prime Minister

On September 16, 1983, Prime Minister Begin resigned from office and retired from public life, ending a major era in Israeli history and politics. He was clearly affected by the death of his wife and by the costs to Israel of the war in Lebanon. Shamir won Likud's leadership in an internal party election in which he defeated David Levy by a two-to-one margin.

On October 10, the Knesset, by a vote of 60 to 53, endorsed the Shamir-led government and its programs. The government was essentially the same as its predecessor, and Shamir retained the foreign affairs portfolio. Israel and the Shamir government faced a range of foreign policy issues that focused on the Arab-Israeli conflict and relations with the United States. Although Israel's military position in Lebanon improved with the IDF's redeployment from the Shuf Mountains to the Awali River, it did not guarantee the security and safety of Israeli forces. Israel's major goals in Lebanon had not been fully achieved, and even the May 17 agreement had not been implemented.

The involvement of the United States in Lebanon, and the attacks on U.S. forces and positions in Lebanon and elsewhere in the region, provided the context for improved relations between the United States and Israel after Shamir took office. Reagan and Shamir agreed on the need to reinforce the Gemayel government and rebuild Lebanon as a free, independent, and sovereign state, with a reconstructed economic infrastructure; to force the withdrawal of all foreign forces; and to provide an army capable of supporting the government's position. They identified Syria and the Soviet Union as threats to peace and stability. This coincidence of perspective and objective led Israel and the United States to achieve wide-ranging agreement on closer coordination and policy. At the same time, there were issues of discord that focused on the West Bank and Gaza and on the Reagan fresh-start initiative.

The National Unity Government

In July 1984, Israeli voters went to the polls to select members of the Eleventh Knesset. Likud's Shamir and the Labor Alignment's Peres led their party blocs in the contest. Labor was unable to capitalize on Likud's various misfortunes, including the retirement of Begin, the continued presence of Israeli forces in Lebanon, and the economic problems reflected in hyperinflation. Shamir proved able to retain much of Likud's electoral support, avoiding what many thought, and public opinion polls had earlier predicted, would be a substantial Labor victory.

Fifteen of the 26 political parties that contested the election secured the necessary 1 percent of the valid votes cast to obtain a parliamentary seat. Overall, the election results were inconclusive. The two major blocs were relatively close in size: the Labor alignment secured 44 seats, and the Likud, 41. The remaining seats were not distributed in any clear pattern that would facilitate the formation of a new government.

The division in the Israeli body politic proved to be the main factor leading to the complicated formation of a national unity government (NUG) that was approved by the Knesset in September. The coalition negotiations were lengthy and complex, and at their foundation were an intricate and involved series of compromises, including the rotation of the prime minister's position between Shimon Peres for the first 25 months of the coalition's life and Yitzhak Shamir for the second 25-month period. This formation of a two-headed national unity government was a new experiment in Israeli politics and brought about a virtual paralysis of decision making in all but areas of broad consensus.

Israelis were divided on key foreign policy as well as political, economic, social, and religious issues facing the country. This situation was compounded by a lack of dynamic and charismatic leadership. A consequence was that little was accomplished in matters requiring a bold initiative, including the peace process. This paralysis was accompanied by much popular cynicism and scathing criticism of blunders, cover-ups, and scandals such as the Pollard Affair (involving a U.S. civilian Navy intelligence analyst, Jonathan Jay Pollard, who gave secrets to the Israeli government) and its aftermath.

Nevertheless, the forced marriage of Labor and Likud survived a turbulent and challenging two years of major and minor crises as a consequence of conflicting styles and substantive differences. The dominant question was whether the coalition would endure and whether or not Labor would honor the agreement to rotate the posts of prime minister and foreign minister.

When Peres resigned his post on October 10, 1986, he was popular in public opinion polls. Ironically, in turning over the prime minister's position to Shamir, Peres added to his credibility and overcame doubts about his trustworthiness, a long-persistent criticism of his political style. He emerged as something of a statesman, with an image as a patient, skilled politician able to keep together his fractious government and to achieve important policy goals. Peres was credited with the withdrawal of Israeli troops from Lebanon (and the attendant drop in Israeli casualties) and the reduction of high levels of inflation; Israel's currency since 1980, the shekel, which replaced the Israeli pound, was rehabilitated and renamed the new Israeli shekel (NIS); the balance of payments had improved; and exports had increased.

Peres established a popular style at home and was given relatively high marks for his role in the otherwise stalemated Arab-Israeli peace process as a consequence of some movement on the part of King Hussein of Jordan and a meeting with King Hassan in Morocco. The resumption of dialogue with Egypt that led to an agreement to arbitrate the Taba dispute (a small enclave on the Egypt-Israel border that remained in dispute when the international border was established between the two counties following their peace treaty of 1979) and culminated in a summit with Egyptian president Hosni Mubarak. All were deemed successes for Peres. He seemed to be constantly on the move,

FREE TRADE AREA
BETWEEN ISRAEL AND
THE UNITED STATES

The U.S. Congress, in October 1984, authorized the president to negotiate a free trade area agreement with Israel. Israel became the first country in the world to enjoy such an arrangement with the United States. It allowed Israel access to its largest single trading partner on substantially improved terms, thereby aiding its export capability. Israel eventually would gain virtually complete and permanent duty-free access to the world's largest market.

and his visits with world leaders, at home and abroad, enhanced his image. He presided over the establishment of diplomatic relations with Spain in January 1986, the renewal of relations with the Ivory Coast and Cameroon, and the unprecedented visit to Israel of British prime minister Margaret Thatcher. The August 1986 Soviet-Israeli meeting in Helsinki, Finland, and Peres's meeting with Soviet foreign minister Eduard Shevardnadze at the United Nations in fall 1986 were important if not immediately productive events.

Israel's special relationship with the United States remained central and reached new levels of cooperation and euphoria during the NUG through strategic cooperation and broad agreement on political themes and issues. The United States and Israel entered an era of good feeling that became pervasive in both the U.S. legislative and executive branches, the latter under the leadership of President Ronald Reagan and Secretary of State George Shultz.

The concept of the Jordan option, central to the Peres perspective on the peace process, was a crucial element in the Reagan peace plan announced in September 1982. In addition, while Begin and his government had rejected the Reagan plan, Peres and the Labor Party were more open-minded. The United States saw the Peres tenure as one that contributed to the peace process. The culmination of his term in office was Peres's visit to Washington in mid-September 1986, at a high point in U.S.-Israel relations. In addition, the United States–Israel Free Trade Area agreement was adopted, and wide-ranging political and strategic cooperation was sustained.

Economic Problems

Peres's greatest achievement was in the economic sector. Economic problems had beset Israel since its independence, but their nature varied over time. The dominant economic issues facing the NUG were high inflation and slow growth rates that had been characteristic of the economy since the 1973 war. The standard of living of the average Israeli was stagnant.

In July 1985, Israel adopted a new program to deal with the several ills of the economy, notably, the problem of hyperinflation. The budget deficit was cut, the shekel was devalued, then pegged to the U.S. dollar, prices and wages were frozen for three months, and the indexing of wages to prices was suspended. The latter had the effect of a 20 percent drop in real wages, and a dramatic rise in unemployment was prevented. The wage and price freeze was gradually lifted. High interest rates tightened credit. The program met its basic objectives. The annual inflation rate of more than 400 percent declined to a rate less than 20 percent by 1987. The change was accomplished without the usual side effect of unemployment, which remained at about 7 percent at the end of 1986 and dropped to less than 6 percent in 1987. A recession was avoided, too. The country's balance of payments improved, and foreign currency reserves doubled. The shekel remained relatively stable against the dollar. The state budget, which was about $24 billion, was virtually in balance, partly through the cutting of food and transportation subsidies and the imposition of new taxes on such luxury items as foreign travel and cars.

Peres and the NUG were prepared to take the difficult measures necessary to make the program, which attacked all sectors of the problem—manufacture, labor unions, the state budget, and the exchange rate—work. Facilitating the effort was the fact that crude oil prices and commodity prices were down and worldwide interest rates had declined. The worldwide decline in oil prices was important to Israel's energy-importing economy and reduced its expenditures for oil by about 35 percent between 1985 and 1986.

These factors enabled Israel to save a substantial amount of foreign currency during the initial two years of the austerity period. The United States proved particularly helpful. During 1985 and 1986, it provided Israel with an additional $750 million per year over and above the regular aid program of some $3 billion a year in economic and military assistance. The extra U.S. aid was crucial; it made it possible for Israel to take risks that otherwise might not have been adopted. The United States was also instrumental in offering advice from Secretary of State Shultz and his economic team.

The NUG under Shamir

As stipulated in the 1984 coalition agreement, after stepping down as prime minister, Peres became foreign minister and Shamir returned to the post of prime minister. The 25-member Shamir government was almost identical to the Peres government, although there were disputes over subcabinet appointments, including the post of the Israeli ambassador to the United States. With his shift to the foreign ministry, Peres took with him many of his advisers and replaced the ministry's two most senior professionals, Director General David Kimche and Deputy Director General Hanan Bar-On. Compromises averted a major crisis and permitted a relatively smooth transition. On October 20, 1986, the Knesset approved the new government by a vote of 82 to 17, with three abstentions.

The new prime minister was very different from his predecessor and even from his political mentor, Begin. Nevertheless, Shamir noted that he was presenting a government of continuity, the second term of the national unity government. "The government will continue to place the aspiration for peace at the top of its concerns, will act to continue the peace process according to the framework agreed upon in Camp David, and will call on Jordan to open peace negotiations." The government's official guidelines also stated that Israel would object to the establishment of another Palestinian state in the Gaza Strip and in the area between Israel and Jordan and that Israel would not negotiate with the PLO.

To consolidate the previous government's economic achievements, the Shamir-led government had to restrain spending, while trying to generate real growth. In January 1987, the NUG adopted a series of measures that, in effect, constituted the second stage of the 1985 emergency efforts. The government sought to lower inflation to an annual one-digit rate, improve further the balance of payments, increase exports and their profits, create a climate and condition for business growth while reducing government involvement in the economy (that is, to reduce the size and significance of the public sector), and cut the budget. The government devalued the shekel by 10 percent (from 1.5 to 1.65 to the dollar), increased prices on some subsidized goods (for example, bread, milk, frozen chicken), extended some price controls, instituted tax reform, and postponed payment of part of the cost of living allowances, as well as other measures. The programs proved successful.

Under pressure from the United States, the Israeli cabinet decided at the end of August 1987, by a vote of 12 to 11, with one abstention, to terminate an important military project, construction of the Lavi jet fighter. The Lavi had been designed specifically to meet Israel's military needs, and there had been some hope that it would make

Intifada, 1989: Young Palestinians throw stones at Israeli soldiers in Ramallah. (Courtesy Embassy of Israel, Washington, D.C.)

Israel less dependent on foreign military supply. The project was canceled because of its cost and the economic burden it placed on Israel, the U.S. Department of Defense's displeasure with the program, and division within the IDF general staff over the utility and importance of the project, especially when other programs were competing for scarce resources. The Israeli government was concerned that, unless it canceled the project, U.S. aid and, potentially, the overall relationship would be negatively affected, since much of the development funding came from the United States. The United States argued that Israel would be better off buying advanced American fighter jets.

Although many Israelis accepted the apparent logic of the decision, there was substantial anger and dismay in Israel, particularly among the workers at Israel Aircraft Industries and their supporters. Moshe Arens, generally considered to be the "father of the Lavi," resigned from the government in protest.

The Palestinian Intifada

The relative quiet in the West Bank and Gaza Strip that had followed the war in Lebanon was shattered in December 1987. The Palestinian Intifada (literally, "shaking off" in Arabic) began after an accident on

December 8, in which a truck driver at a Gaza Strip military checkpoint crashed into a car in which four Gaza residents were killed. The next day protests and violent demonstrations took place in the Gaza Strip and soon spread to the West Bank and later to Israel, especially Jerusalem. Many of the protesters were young Palestinians who used rocks and rubble to confront Israeli authorities. The efforts continued for months and violence continued to escalate. Israel was confronted with the need to stop the uprising and restore order. As the Intifada expanded, Israel, under the direction of Defense Minister Yitzhak Rabin, responded with an effort to terminate the riots and demonstrations.

The Intifada helped to generate a new effort by U.S. secretary of state George Shultz to offer a peace plan and pursue negotiations to end the conflict, but little progress was made. Demonstrations, riots, and violence increasingly characterized the area.

The 1988 Election

The occupied territories and their future had been a core issue in the peace process since Israel took control of them in the Six-Day War, but their status took on new immediacy with the onset of the Intifada. Israel's initial, somewhat uncertain interpretation of the Intifada soon gave way to the view that it was an indigenous and authentic, if somewhat amorphous movement that would not "go away" but could be "managed," albeit at some cost. Under this management policy, some Israelis refused military service in anti-Intifada operations, and some actions of the IDF had a negative effect on Israel's international image.

The Intifada loomed over the 1988 election, forcing attention to the immediate and urgent problem of tranquility and public safety and to the long-term issue of the disposition of the territories and their inhabitants. The use of force, including the IDF, against the Intifada was supported strongly by a clear majority of Israel. Israelis appeared more supportive of a policy to quell the Palestinian uprising and restore order than they were of permanent retention of the places and peoples of the West Bank and Gaza.

Israelis went to the polls on November 1, 1988, to elect the 12th Knesset. Voters continued to be divided on the key foreign policy, political, economic, social, and religious issues facing the country. This disunity had led to and complicated the formation of the national unity government of September 1984; it ultimately also contributed to the virtual paralysis of decision making on some of the key issues facing the country. The 1988 election required Israelis to reassess the consequences of the 1984 vote but did not result in a more clear-cut outcome.

As in previous elections, there were important economic issues, including a downturn connected to the Intifada and its disruption of normal patterns of economic activity in tourism and other service sectors and in manufacturing and construction. However, no matter their significance, economic concerns such as unemployment and inflation did not play a central and determining role in electoral decisions. The focus of interest and public debate was, as usual, on the issues of security, defense, and the peace process that related to the Arab-Israeli conflict, and, more narrowly, to the Intifada and Israel's reaction.

Israelis, whatever their perspective of the nature and content of the peace process, concluded that peace was not at hand. Thus, the continuing Arab-Israeli conflict remained a central test of Israeli diplomacy with peace and security as the elusive but sought-after prizes. Peace, and arguably a fragile one, existed only with Egypt.

Prime Minister Shamir represented those who argued that only direct, independent, open-ended, face-to-face negotiations with Israel's Arab neighbors could provide the unpressured atmosphere that was vital for reaching agreements. He believed that Israel should not negotiate with the PLO; that Judea and Samaria (the West Bank), and Gaza were part of the Land of Israel; and that an independent sovereign state between Jordan and Israel made no sense politically, could not be viable economically, and would only serve as a terrorist, irredentist base from which Israel (and Jordan) would be threatened as Palestinian groups tried to regain control of the land.

Foreign Minister Peres of the Labor Alignment reflected a different view, and while he saw the need for peace through direct negotiations, he believed that an international conference would be of utility and that it could not impose a solution unacceptable to Israel. Unlike Shamir he supported territorial compromise in the West Bank, a trade of land for peace, within limits required for security.

The ultimate solution to the Arab-Israeli conflict was complicated further, especially for Peres and those who had argued for the Jordan option, by King Hussein's decision, announced in July 1988, to separate his kingdom's future from that of the West Bank. At the same time, a policy supported by some of the right of the political spectrum, to retain the territory, while arranging for the transfer of the Arab population, seemed to gain adherents, and the subject became part of the public policy debate. The policy was promoted by Rabbi Meir Kahane, leader of the Kach Party. The Central Election Committee declared

RABBI MEIR KAHANE, KACH, AND KAHANE CHAI

Meir Kahane was born in Brooklyn, New York, in 1932, the son of an Orthodox rabbi, and became an ordained rabbi in the 1950s. He founded the Jewish Defense League in 1968 in response to vicious outbreaks of anti-Semitism in New York and a perceived need to change the Jewish image. The Jewish Defense League became known for its violent methods, especially those designed to call attention to the plight of Soviet Jewry. He moved to Israel in 1971. In Israel, he was arrested numerous times and served some months in prison in 1981 under preventive detention for threatening violence against Palestinian protesters in the West Bank. He headed the Kach (Thus) Party, which he had founded, and was elected to the Knesset in 1984.

Kahane had campaigned on a theme of "making Israel Jewish again" by seeking the expulsion of the Arabs from Israel, as well as from the West Bank and Gaza Strip. Initially, the Kach Party was banned from participation in the election by the Central Elections Committee, but the ruling was reversed by the Supreme Court, a move that gained the party additional publicity and probably facilitated its efforts to secure a Knesset seat. Despite Kahane's success in the 1984 elections, he was considered an extremist, even by many on the right, and his political ideology and programs remained marginal in Israel. He was ruled out as a political ally and coalition partner by all the major factions in the Knesset. Kach was banned from participation in the 1988 Knesset election by the Central Elections Committee on the grounds that the party was racist; similar grounds were cited for banning it from participating in the 1992 and 1996 elections.

A prolific author, Kahane advocated the necessity of retaining Israel's Jewish character as its first priority. Thus, he proposed that the Arabs leave Israel and go elsewhere in the Arab world because of the violence they had perpetrated against the Jews and because their growing numbers threatened the Jewish nature of Israel. Kahane was assassinated while on a speaking engagement in New York City in fall 1990.

Disputes over tactics and personal rivalries within Kach led to the formation of a breakaway faction called Kahane Chai (Kahane Lives) and headed by Benjamin Kahane, the rabbi's son. Both Kach and Kahane Chai were outlawed and disarmed after the February 1994 massacre of Arab worshipers in Hebron by Baruch Goldstein, a Kach activist. Benjamin Kahane and his followers continued to operate underground until Kahane was killed on December 31, 2000.

Kahane's Kach Party ineligible to contest the election because it advocated a racist policy in violation of a law specifically devised for the purpose of restricting Kahane's ability to promote such ideas.

The 1988 Israeli parliamentary elections were inconclusive concerning the trend in Israeli thinking on both domestic and foreign policy issues, as both Labor and Likud secured virtually the same one-third of public support in the balloting. After weeks of maneuvering, Shamir was able to establish another national unity government in which he would remain as prime minister through its tenure. Peres became finance minister, a post in which he would have little international visibility and little opportunity to pursue his foreign policy agenda or to generate popular support within Israel. Peres's primary Labor Party rival, Rabin, retained the post of defense minister. Moshe Arens became foreign minister.

Foreign Policy and a No-Confidence Vote

In December 1988, Yasser Arafat announced the PLO's acceptance of UN Security Council Resolutions 242 and 338 and Israel's right to exist and renounced terrorism, statements that the United States had established as the conditions for dialogue. The Reagan administration instituted a formal dialogue with the PLO through the U.S. ambassador to Tunisia (the PLO had been headquartered there since its expulsion from Lebanon in 1982) that lasted until June 1990 when Arafat refused to condemn an abortive Palestinian terrorist raid against Israel on the beach at Tel Aviv and the United States suspended the talks.

A new peace effort was launched during the first months of the administration of George H. W. Bush, who was elected president in November 1988. In the spring of 1989, the Shamir government proposed an initiative calling for the termination of the state of war with the Arab states; a solution for the Palestinian Arabs of the West Bank and Gaza, to be negotiated with freely elected representatives of the Palestinian Arab inhabitants of these areas; peace with Jordan; and the resolution of the problem of Palestinian refugee camp residents in the West Bank and Gaza Strip through international efforts. Various efforts were made to implement this idea and foster negotiations between Israel and Palestinians, with U.S. secretary of state James Baker as the main protagonist, but eventually they foundered.

Labor believed that Shamir was obstructing Baker's efforts and preventing Israeli negotiations with Palestinians resident in the West Bank and Gaza. The Labor members decided to withdraw from the

NUG and bring the government down in a vote of no confidence. Shamir's plan to substantially increase the number of Jewish settlements provided the mechanism to end the government's tenure. As minister of finance, Labor leader Peres refused to provide the money to build new settlements. On March 15, 1990, Labor left the coalition and Shamir was defeated in the Knesset by a vote of no-confidence (the first such successful vote in Israel's history). This gave Peres and Labor an opportunity to secure a mandate to form a successor coalition and run the government, but Peres was unable to construct a viable coalition government. Shamir was then given a mandate to form a government, and he succeeded in presenting it to the Knesset in early June.

In the debates over the peace process and the proposals made by U.S. secretary of state Baker in early 1990, more right-wing members of Likud sought assurances that Shamir would not give in on the issues of participation in the Palestinian representation election process by East Jerusalem residents and by other nonresidents of the territories (for example, deportees). The far right insisted that Palestinians in East Jerusalem should be excluded from the roster of those eligible to represent the Palestinians. They argued that since Israel regards Jerusalem as united and under Israeli sovereignty, allowing residents of East Jerusalem to represent the Palestinians would call into question Israel's control of the city. Former defense minister Ariel Sharon, meanwhile, was responsible for increasing settlements in Judea and Samaria (as well as in pre-1967 Israel). He did so with great energy and initiative and argued that settlements in the West Bank area were primarily designed to serve Israel's security needs. Sharon regarded the establishment of settlements in the territories as logical and also sought to enlarge existing ones. He believed that the retention of the Golan Heights and the West Bank and Gaza were all essential to his security concept, as was continued Israeli settlement in these areas. He also appeared to believe that the peace agreement with Egypt would have to be scrupulously maintained with no erosion of either the diplomatic normalization process or the postpeace military status quo.

During the Likud convention in 1990, Sharon and his supporters challenged Shamir on the peace process, charging that Shamir was prepared to give in to the United States on key points. These concessions, they argued, could affect the unity of Jerusalem and lead to the potential inclusion of the PLO in the peace process and to the establishment of a Palestinian state in the territories. Sharon tried to portray himself as a strong leader who could solve the immediate problems and establish a base that would ensure long-term success. After the convention, Sharon resigned from his position as minister of industry and trade in the government and started a campaign to gain control of the party in the branch units of Likud. Despite internal opposition and challenges, Shamir emerged as the Likud's candidate to form the next government. Shamir was concerned about the role of the PLO in the peace process and there was a crisis of confidence with the U.S. administration over statements and positions on such issues as terrorism and the status of East Jerusalem.

Shamir's Government, 1990

Shamir's government, approved by the Knesset on June 11, 1990 by a vote of 62 to 57, with one abstention, was relatively narrow in scope (Labor would not join) and potentially fragile. The coalition was vulnerable to threats from small parties or even individuals with their own agendas. The delicate balancing of competing demands and the quest for the funds to pursue specific policies at times of budget constraints complicated the issues for the prime minister and made coalition bargaining a continuous and more complex process. Nevertheless, the relative stability of the government was assured in the short term, barring a major international challenge relating either to the prospects for war or peace or to a major domestic challenge that would be more politically focused on particular policies, political maneuvering, or patronage-related issues.

In the presentation of the government, Shamir reiterated some standard themes but also stressed the need for action in the areas of immigrant absorption and socioeconomic policy. In foreign policy, he restated some of Likud's central perspectives (shared by parties to its right on the political spectrum) in ways not previously stated in formal government guidelines. For example, his government program stated, "The eternal right of the Jewish people to *Eretz Yisrael* is not subject to question and is intertwined with its right to security and peace." It also asserted, "Settlement in all parts of *Eretz Yisrael* is the right of our people and an integral part of national security; the government will act to strengthen settlement, to broaden and develop it." Shamir restated the refusal to negotiate with the PLO, reiterated the view that Jerusalem is the eternal capital of Israel, and added that Jerusalem would not be included in the framework of autonomy for the Arab residents of Judea and Samaria (the West Bank) and the Gaza Strip. In a general sense, the overriding goal was the security of Israel within a relatively peaceful environment that reduced the prospects for full-scale war with the Arab states.

In the wake of the formation of the new Shamir government, the peace process was suspended. Within Labor, questions about Peres's role as party leader reemerged, and his position would be tested within the party hierarchy in July 1990. Peres succeeded in retaining his position, despite a challenge from Rabin.

7

THE PERSIAN GULF WAR
AND THE MIDDLE EAST
PEACE PROCESS
(1990–1996)

Yitzhak Shamir's government was installed and the Arab-Israeli peace process was moribund by the time Iraq invaded Kuwait on August 2, 1990. The subsequent war further delayed efforts to seek an Arab-Israeli peace, and the United States deliberately excluded Israel from the international coalition established to respond to Iraq's aggression, which included several Arab states that opposed Iraq, in an effort to avoid splitting the group. Soon after the inauguration of the hostilities in January 1991, Iraq fired 39 Scud missiles at Israel, seeking to divide the coalition by diverting Arab attention away from its anti-Iraqi stance to renewed opposition to Israel. Israel acceded to U.S. requests and refrained from responding to the missile attacks.

Israel's Position during the Gulf War
Israel's reaction to the crisis must be seen against the background and within the framework of the Arab-Israeli conflict. Israel remained technically at war with Iraq since the first Arab-Israeli war when it participated in hostilities against Israel. Iraq was the only major participant in that conflict that refused to sign an armistice agreement. It also fought against Israel in the Six-Day War and the Yom Kippur War. Iraq was among those Arab states that took the lead against Egyptian president Sadat's peace overtures to Israel in 1977 and 1978, and Iraq opposed the Egypt-Israel Peace Treaty of 1979. It supported and gave sanctuary to Palestinian terrorist groups. During the Iran-Iraq War (1980–88), Israel grew increasingly concerned about Iraq's growing military strength

and capability and its potential threat to Israel after the end of hostilities. The worry took a dramatic turn in spring 1990 when Iraqi leader Saddam Hussein threatened to "burn half of Israel" and it became an open secret that he was developing a nuclear-biological-chemical capability. There was also concern that much of the international community did not take Hussein's threats as seriously as Israel did.

Nevertheless, Israel was preoccupied during much of the year and a half before Iraq's invasion of Kuwait with other issues, especially the peace process and the usual political maneuvering among and within the political parties and the political elite. In the spring of 1990, the national unity government collapsed. This crisis coincided with a large influx of Soviet Jewish immigrants that had begun earlier but gained dramatic momentum in 1990, leading Israelis to focus on the massive requirements of immigrant absorption. The collapse of the Soviet bloc in Eastern Europe and the end of the cold war led Israel to rethink its position in the international system and especially its relations with the two superpowers, as well as the implications of these developments for the Arab-Israeli conflict and for the Middle East as a whole. The Intifada that had begun in December 1987 was continuing in the West Bank and Gaza Strip and affected Israeli politics, economics, and society. It was a growing security threat as the level of violence increased and more murders were committed by Palestinians against Israelis.

Strategic and intelligence cooperation that focused on a Soviet bloc threat had become a visible part of the special relationship between the United States and Israel in the Reagan administration. With the end of the cold war, there developed a perspective that Israel's role as a strategic asset had diminished and a widespread view that Israel was not relevant for potential actions in the Arabian Peninsula and the Persian Gulf. The Iraqi invasion of Kuwait tested this perspective.

Israel did not serve as a staging area for U.S. forces, nor as a storage depot for military materiel, nor was it utilized for medical emergencies. From the outset, the United States made a conscious effort to build a broad-based international force that included an Arab component to oppose Saddam Hussein; it was also a diligent effort to distance Israel from such activity. The obvious and stated objective of the United States was to avoid giving Saddam Hussein the opportunity to recast his aggression in terms of the Arab-Israeli conflict and to avoid giving credence to Iraqi arguments that the U.S. military buildup in the region was to serve Israeli interests and that Israelis were directly involved. Iraq accused Israel of joining with U.S. forces in Saudi Arabia and of making combat planes and pilots available to the United States. Saddam

Hussein tried to draw the Israelis into the crisis and thereby mobilize opinion in Arab and Islamic and developing nations against the United States. He argued that he would not withdraw from Kuwait until all issues of occupation were resolved, including the Israeli presence in the occupied territories, that is the West Bank and Gaza Strip. Although the charge of Israeli-U.S. cooperation in the Arabian Peninsula was patently absurd, it struck a responsive chord in much of the Arab and Muslim world. Israel was determined not to be used as a tool to break the coalition. Nevertheless, Israel was concerned that it was not a full partner with the United States in the crisis and that it was not part of the coalition. Israel sought to prove its utility, if not value, but was precluded by Washington, D.C.

In the short term, U.S. government attention was directed to such matters as reversing the Iraqi invasion, assuring the dependable supply of oil at reasonable prices, guaranteeing the security of Saudi Arabia, ensuring the safety of U.S. and other hostages in Kuwait and Iraq, establishing an embargo of Iraq, and creating the necessary international force on the Arabian Peninsula and in the waters around it to achieve these objectives. These goals did not include a publicly identified role for Israel. Israel did, however, endorse the firm and rapid U.S. reaction to Iraq. It opposed the aggression against Kuwait as a practical matter as well as on moral principle. It also adopted a clear position to deter Iraq from moving west. Israel established a "red line" in Jordan, making clear that the movement of Iraqi troops into Jordan, by invitation or not, would be regarded as an act of war, to which Israel would respond.

The Relationship with the United States

Until the Persian Gulf War, the Bush-Shamir relationship had been one of political disagreement on various issues with a personal relationship characterized by a lack of positive chemistry. In addition, the United States had criticized curfews in the West Bank and Gaza, the deportation of Palestinians, travel restrictions, and the establishment of settlements, and had focused attention on the other issues that had been the subject of discord between the two states in the Bush administration.

In a meeting in December 1990, Bush and Shamir accentuated the support of Israel for the U.S. response to Saddam Hussein, and Israel was assured that there would be no Persian Gulf solution at its expense. The positive meetings and the congruence of the policies of Israel and the United States during the crisis helped to allay Israeli fears about the postwar situation.

Politically, Israel benefited from the fact that Palestinians in the West Bank and Gaza Strip generally applauded the Iraqi takeover of Kuwait, identified Saddam Hussein as a hero, and showed little sympathy for the occupied Kuwaitis. The PLO voted against the Arab League resolution opposing Iraq's action, and Arafat openly supported and embraced Saddam Hussein. The articulation of terrorist threats against American targets by Baghdad-based and Iraqi-supported Palestinian groups (some of which were PLO constituents) gave credence to Israel's arguments about the lack of appropriate Palestinian negotiation partners.

Iraq's Scud Missile Attacks

During the 1991 Persian Gulf War, Iraq fired 39 Scud missiles with conventional warheads in 18 attacks on Israel. These missiles caused extensive damage but few casualties. These were the first strikes of consequence at Israel's population and civilian centers since its War of Independence, and Israel did not respond. The military impact on Israel was not significant. While Israel's existence was never threatened, there were important psychological, economic, and political consequences. The Scud missiles created a new and more somber situation in Israel and tested Shamir's leadership. They also helped to confirm Israeli attitudes about Saddam Hussein; reaction in the Arab world further confirmed Arab hostility toward Israel. The factors that ultimately swayed Israel against a military response to the Scuds was the arrival of Patriot missiles—a tangible way to assure that Israel would be protected—and even more significant, the request and cajoling of President Bush in a crucial telephone conversation with Shamir. Shamir in turn was able to hold sway within the cabinet and prevailed against the political arguments and military perspectives suggesting a response was imperative. The visit of U.S. deputy secretary of state Lawrence Eagleburger was especially important in Israeli confidence in its restraint. In January 1991, both the U.S. Senate and House of Representatives unanimously approved a resolution condemning Iraq's attack on Israel and commending the government of Israel for its restraint and perseverance. The Senate also reaffirmed the U.S. commitment to provide Israel with the means to maintain its freedom and security, and the House of Representatives explicitly recognized Israel's right to defend itself.

Israelis with gas masks in a sealed room during Iraqi missile attacks on Israel during the Persian Gulf War, 1991 (Courtesy Embassy of Israel, Washington, D.C.)

After the War

During the period of hostilities the Israeli government moved further to the right when the Moledet (Homeland) Party, represented by Rehavam (Gandhi) Ze'evi, joined the cabinet. Shamir's domestic political approval rating and popularity increased during the war, particularly because of the decision not to respond to the Scud missile attacks. Israeli doves who were disheartened, dispirited, or disappointed by developments during the diplomatic-political phase of the crisis were effectively neutralized during the hostilities as the situation did not support their perspectives and arguments.

In the immediate aftermath of the hostilities Israel's military situation improved. Saddam Hussein had been vanquished and humiliated. Iraq's massive offensive war machine was virtually destroyed, and its ability to wage war against Israel was significantly reduced. This altered the Arab-Israeli, as well as the regional, military balance to Israel's advantage. Despite these accomplishments, the ability of Saddam Hussein to survive and to reassert his authority in Baghdad was of major concern to Israel.

After the war, the Bush administration decided to make a major effort to resolve the Arab-Israeli conflict. Secretary of State Baker, in testimony before the U.S. Congress on February 6, 1991, outlined the administration's conception of a "new world order" in which the United States would "resume the search for a just peace and real reconciliation for Israel, the Arab states, and Palestinians." In a speech to a joint session of Congress on March 6, President Bush noted:

> We must do all that we can to close the gap between Israel and the Arab states and between Israelis and Palestinians. . . . A comprehensive peace must be grounded in United Nations Security Council Resolutions 242 and 338 and the principle of territory for peace. This principle must be elaborated to provide for Israel's security and recognition, and at the same time for legitimate Palestinian political rights . . . The time has come to put an end to the Arab-Israeli conflict.

Within months of the Gulf War cease-fire, the U.S.-Israel relationship was again characterized by discord and tension, with much of the goodwill built up during the gulf crisis dissipated by disagreements over the modalities and substance of the peace process and other matters. Tensions developed as the Bush administration appeared to link proposed housing loan guarantees essential to settle Soviet Jews in Israel with actions concerning settlements in the West Bank and Gaza Strip and responsiveness on the peace process.

The Madrid Conference

U.S. secretary of state Baker's visits to the Middle East in the spring and early summer of 1991 made it clear that there was no agreement to convene a conference that would lead to bilateral negotiations; there was discord on both procedural and substantive issues. The issues in contention included the venue of a conference (whether in the region or elsewhere), what powers and authority it would have (for example, primarily ceremonial in nature), under whose auspices it should be conducted (whether the United Nations would be a factor), which Palestinians and other Arabs could and would attend, and what prior commitments had to be made by the participants. But, following months of shuttle diplomacy by Baker, a Middle East peace conference was convened in Madrid, Spain, on October 30, under American and Soviet cosponsorship, with the participation of Israel, Lebanon, and Syria and a joint Jordanian-Palestinian delegation.

The Madrid conference did not achieve a substantive breakthrough, although it broke the procedural and psychological barriers to direct bilateral negotiations between Israel and its immediate neighbors: The

Prime Minister Yitzhak Shamir addresses the Madrid Peace Conference, October 1991.
(Courtesy Embassy of Israel, Washington, D.C.)

Israeli, Syrian, Egyptian, Lebanese, and Jordanian-Palestinian delegations met at an open, public, and official plenary session and delivered speeches and responses. These formal proceedings were followed by bilateral negotiations in Washington, D.C. between the parties in December 1991 and in 1992, 1993, and 1994, and by multilateral talks addressing regional concerns.

The Madrid Peace Conference seemed to resolve the problem of Palestinian representation, at least in the immediate context of the bilateral discussions. The Palestinian representatives were not formally part of the PLO, not from the areas outside the West Bank and Gaza, and not from East Jerusalem.

The first rounds of talks achieved accord on nonsubstantive matters, and progress was measured primarily by the continuation of the process rather than by significant achievements. The United States adhered to its role as a facilitator and sought not to intervene on substantive matters. It was not a party to the bilateral talks, and its representatives were not in the room or at the negotiating table, although it did meet separately with the parties and heard their views and perspectives.

The Madrid-inaugurated process included multilateral discussions on several broader regional issues: refugees, economic development, water resources, environment, and arms control. An initial organizing conference met in Moscow in January 1992. The goal was to achieve progress on these issues, even without a political solution, and to rein-force the bilateral negotiations. The five permanent members of the Security Council and a number of other important powers (including the European Community and Japan) were represented in Moscow; the sessions were boycotted by the Palestinians because Palestinians from outside the West Bank and Gaza Strip were prevented from par-ticipating.

Despite the achievements symbolized by the Madrid conference and the subsequent bilateral and multilateral discussions, by the time of the hiatus for the Israeli elections in June 1992 and the U.S. elections in November 1992, no breakthrough of substance had occurred and no specific achievement, beyond continuation of the process, had been recorded.

Election 1992, the Second "Earthquake"

In January 1992, after three rounds of Arab-Israeli bilateral talks, the right-wing Tehiya and Moledet Parties resigned from the Shamir gov-ernment because of its willingness to discuss an interim agreement on Palestinian self-rule in the West Bank and Gaza Strip. The defection of the two parties deprived the coalition of a majority in parliament, and Likud and Labor subsequently agreed to schedule a national election for June 23, 1992.

Israel's Knesset election campaign in the spring of 1992 slowed the Arab-Israeli peace process, but the outcome of the election was widely heralded as a significant and positive factor that would alter the regional situation, the prospects for progress in the Arab-Israeli peace process, and the nature of the U.S.-Israeli relationship. Within Labor, the election provided a new opportunity for Yitzhak Rabin to try to unseat Shimon Peres as Labor Party leader. Since Rabin's unsuccessful challenge in July 1990, the party had adopted a primary election system for choosing its leader, and in a dramatic showdown in February 1992, Rabin won the internal primary election for party leader. The subse-quent election to select the party's slate of Knesset candidates resulted in a list that included many new faces and was generally younger and more dovish than previous Labor Party electoral lists.

The election of June 1992 for the 13th Knesset was contested by 25 political parties, representing virtually all points of the political spec-trum. Five additional parties, including the two successor groups to Meir Kahane's political legacy, were banned from participation because the electoral commission determined that they advocated racist and

YITZHAK RABIN
(MARCH 1, 1922–NOVEMBER 4, 1995)

Yitzhak Rabin was born in Jerusalem on March 1, 1922, to Russian immigrants to Palestine. He entered the prestigious Kadourie Agricultural School in the Galilee in 1937, and after graduation in 1940, he moved to Kibbutz Ramat Yohanan. He joined the Haganah in May 1941 and subsequently served in the Palmach. Later, he was arrested in a massive sweep by British mandatory authorities and he spent a brief period in a British prison. In October 1947, he was appointed deputy commander of the Palmach. A month before Israel declared its independence on May 14, 1948, he was put in charge of the Palmach's Harel Brigade and was assigned the task of eliminating Arab strongholds along the Tel Aviv–Jerusalem road.

Rabin's military career included a variety of positions in the Israel Defense Forces (IDF) during Israel's formative years, including head of the army's tactical operations division from 1950 to 1952, head of the training branch from 1954 to 1956, and commanding officer of the Northern Command from 1956 to 1959. He was then appointed army chief of operations and came into conflict with then deputy defense minister Shimon Peres over the question of who should determine the priorities in the acquisition and manufacture of arms. Rabin believed that the decision should be made by professional soldiers rather than by civilians in the Defense Ministry. The political rivalry with Peres developed into a bitter personal feud.

Rabin was appointed chief of staff of the IDF in January 1964 and during his tenure focused on the restructuring of the army and on acquiring more advanced weaponry. In the Six-Day War, Rabin's army won a decisive victory over its Arab adversaries in less than a week, radically transforming the situation in the Middle East. In February 1968, he became Israel's ambassador to the United States; in March 1973, he returned to Israel.

After the Knesset election of December 1973, Rabin was invited by Golda Meir to join the new cabinet as defense minister because of Moshe Dayan's refusal to serve in the new government. When Dayan suddenly announced his willingness to join, Rabin became minister of labor. Then Meir resigned as prime minister following publication of the Agranat Commission's interim report. On April 22, 1974, Rabin was chosen by the Labor Party Central Committee to succeed Meir. Shimon Peres's strong showing in the vote earned him the post of defense minister, from which he tried to undermine Rabin's authority at almost every turn in the hope of replacing him. Rabin served as prime minister from June 1974 to May 1977, during which time he concentrated on rebuilding the IDF. The successful raid and freeing of hostages at the airport in Entebbe, Uganda, in July 1976 contributed to restoring the army's and nation's self-confidence. Rabin successfully negotiated with Egypt a second disengagement of forces agreement, brokered by the United States.

Rabin's term as prime minister ended prematurely in 1977 after a cabinet dispute led to the scheduling of early elections. A month before the election, Rabin was forced to step down after admitting that his wife had maintained an illegal bank account in the United States. Peres was designated to head the Labor Party list in the election, but Labor was defeated at the polls. For the next four years, Rabin found himself in Peres's political shadow, and the relationship between the two was highly contentious. Rabin challenged Peres for the party's leadership at its national convention in December 1980 but lost. In 1984, Rabin became minister of defense in the national unity government that was formed following the July election. He once again became minister of defense in the government established in December 1988. As defense minister in the early phases of the Intifada, he was responsible for quelling the demonstrations and restoring order. He left the government with the other Labor ministers in spring 1990. Rabin failed in his challenge to Peres in summer 1990 for the leadership of the party.

In early 1992, Rabin finally succeeded in ousting Peres as Labor Party chairman. Exploiting his reputation as "Mr. Security," Rabin led his party to victory in the election to the Knesset. In the new government, he served as both prime minister and defense minister and appointed Peres as foreign minister. Though skeptical about dealing with the PLO, Rabin approved transforming the secret private discussions in Oslo between Israelis and Palestinians into formal negotiations culminating in the Israeli-PLO Declaration of Principles of September 1993. Unlike his contact with the PLO's chairman, Yasser Arafat, which remained cool and formal, Rabin's relationship with King Hussein of Jordan, with whom he also negotiated a peace treaty, was warm and personal. During his tenure, important progress was also reported in achieving commercial and/or diplomatic contacts with Arab countries, including Syria. In 1994, Rabin received the Nobel Peace Prize, along with Peres and Arafat. On November 4, 1995, at the conclusion of a mass peace rally in Tel Aviv, Rabin was assassinated by Yigal Amir, a Jewish extremist. The social and political implications of his murder were significant in Israel and throughout the Middle East.

antidemocratic programs. A number of new parties or coalitions were created, such as Meretz—the union of Shinui (a party established as a protest movement after the Yom Kippur War), CRM, and Mapam—and United Torah Judaism—a combination of Agudat Israel, Degel HaTorah (an ultra-orthodox party), and Moriah. Some parties were constructed by individuals or groups that split from major parties, including the New Liberal Party, led by Yitzhak Moda'i. At the same time, a number of new parties formed to reflect specific concerns and interest groups. Democracy and Aliyah (DA), for example, was created by and for Soviet immigrants. Among the more than 3.4 million Israelis eligible to vote in the June 1992 Knesset elections were some 300,000 recent immigrants, the overwhelming majority of whom came from the former Soviet Union (some 340,000 immigrants from the former Soviet Union arrived in Israel between 1989 and 1991).

The 1992 elections marked the second time in Israel's political history that there was a significant transfer of power from one side of the political spectrum to the other and a reordering of the country's national priorities. Political commentators called the outcome of the 1992 election another "earthquake," or *mahapach,* in the sense of revolutionary change as had occurred in 1977. This time Labor was the victor, winning more than 900,000 votes and 44 Knesset seats—an increase of more than 200,000 votes and five seats—and ending a decade and a half of Likud-led administrations. Likud lost eight mandates, falling to 32. Meretz emerged as the third-largest political bloc, with 12 seats. The secular-nationalist Tzomet increased its parliamentary representation from two to eight seats. The religious parties dropped from 18 to 16 seats.

Ultimately, 10 parties were able to secure the 1.5 percent of the valid vote that was now required to secure a seat in parliament. The crucial element in the outcome was the creation of a "blocking majority" of 61 parliamentary seats composed of Labor, Meretz, and the Arab parties, which meant that Shamir would not be able to reconstruct a Likud–right-wing–religious party coalition. The election result was a classic case of voters' punishing the incumbent party for years of bad or ineffectual government. It also reflected in part the effect on the electoral system of new immigrants from the former Soviet Union, who were voting for the first time. The *olim* (immigrants), who generally supported the left-of-center parties, contributed significantly to the ability of Labor and Meretz to gain five critical mandates without which their victory would not have been possible. Forty-seven percent of the immigrants voted for Labor and 13 percent voted for Meretz. In contrast, 35

SOVIET JEWRY

Immigrants have played a central role in the political and social life of Israel before and after its 1948 independence. Israel's commitment to unlimited and virtually unrestricted Jewish immigration was enshrined in the country's Declaration of Independence and the Law of Return, and it has been reinforced by successive governments with overwhelming popular support.

Immediately after independence, Holocaust survivors arrived in large numbers and soon were followed by hundreds of thousands of other Jews, mostly from Arab countries. By the mid-1970s, Orientals composed the majority of Israel's Jewish population. After the 1967 war, there was an increase in emigration from the West, as well as tens of thousands of Jews from the Soviet Union. With the disintegration of the Soviet system and its ultimate collapse, hundreds of thousands of Jews began immigrating to Israel in the fall of 1989.

These immigrants were different from earlier Soviet immigrants in various respects, including their origins within the former Soviet Union, level of education, age distribution, and degree of Jewish identity. Perhaps the most outstanding feature was their level of

(continues)

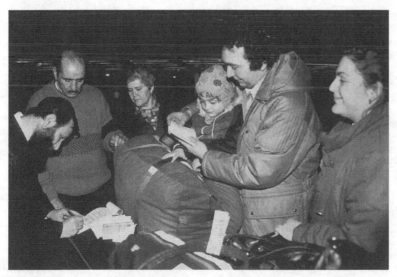

Emigrants from the Soviet Union arrive in Israel, 1991. (Courtesy Embassy of Israel, Washington, D.C.)

SOVIET JEWRY *(continued)*

education. Within that group, more than 42 percent had scientific and academic professional educations, a figure four times the Israeli average. They added significantly to the number of both medical doctors and holders of doctorate degrees in Israel. While an overwhelming majority said that both their parents are or were Jewish, more than 50 percent of the immigrants indicated that their level of Jewish identity was either cultural or a result of family ties. Only a very small percentage identified themselves as belonging to the category of a "practicing religious believer." When asked about their Jewish identity, 5 percent replied "Zionist."

This wave of migration can be characterized more as emigration from the Soviet Union than as immigration to Israel. It consisted overwhelmingly of people who chose to leave the Soviet Union because of various social, political, or economic factors that were primarily of a negative nature. Thus, rather than immigrating to Israel for reasons such as ideology or religion, they had opted to leave the Soviet Union, not necessarily by choice, but for survival; it was not a "Jewish" or "Zionist" immigration in the traditional or usual sense of those terms. Most of the immigrants listed Israel as their first choice of residence even when given the option of choosing any other location. Nearly 90 percent responded that they were very likely to remain in Israel for at least the next few years, thus discrediting the idea that most Soviet Jews would prefer to settle elsewhere if given the opportunity to do so.

Ethnic political parties based on a constituency of immigrants from the former Soviet Union developed in the 1990s. Initial polls and surveys of the new Soviet immigrants indicated that in the 1992 elections, they would vote for Likud and other right-wing parties. These analyses, together with the widely held perception of much of the political leadership that Soviet Jews would not support a socialist party—such

percent of the general Israeli population voted for Labor (an increase over previous years) and 10 percent for Meretz; the immigrants contributed four seats to Labor and one to Meretz.

The immigrant vote was, above all, an economically motivated protest directed at Likud by an electorate with generally right-of-center foreign policy positions. Likud's failure at immigrant absorption, as perceived by the immigrants, as well as Labor's and Meretz's effective campaigns on these and related issues, were among the central factors

as Labor or the United Workers Party (Mapam)—reinforced the view that in the 1992 elections Likud would emerge victorious. Other polls offered further support for such views, depicting the immigrants as a relatively hawkish group, unwilling to compromise on issues of peace and security.

For Israel's political parties, the large number of Soviet immigrants presented a challenge and an opportunity because of voting power and potential to alter the political balance. The parties' activities were based on two general and widely held yet contradictory expectations: Either anticommunist and antisocialist sentiments dominated among Soviet voters, and, thus, they would tilt toward the Right; or, since they were a highly educated and cultured group, similar in many respects to the Israeli voters who support the Left, they too would lean Left.

Initially, the new immigrants supported existing political parties especially Rabin and Labor in 1992. But, by the 1996 election, a new party, Yisrael B'Aliya, was formed by Natan Sharansky, who argued that the existing parties were not doing enough for the new immigrants and the problems they faced in Israel. Sharansky suggested that the party would enter into a governing coalition with whichever party would address those needs. In 1996, Yisrael B'Aliya joined in the Likud-led coalition.

By 1999, the Soviet immigrants were concerned about their situation and there was discord with Shas (an ultra-orthodox religious party that became part of the government in 1992), which had serious concerns about whether or not the immigrants were in fact Jewish. This led Soviet voters to support Labor because of the link of Shas with Likud. Yisrael B'Aliya joined in the Barak-led government coalition. A second Russian-based party, Israel Beiteinu, developed on the right. After the 1999 elections, Democratic Choice split from Yisrael B'Aliya, thus providing a further option and three Soviet immigrant parties in the Knesset.

behind the success of the left-of-center parties. Most of the immigrants were consumed by immediate personal problems, such as employment and housing.

Yitzhak Rabin moved quickly to forge a coalition that included Meretz and Shas, though his original plan was to form a broad-based coalition, balancing left and right, and secular and religious, with Labor at the center. The new government was presented to the Knesset on July 13, 1992, and won its approval by a vote of 67 to 53. Rabin noted that he would set the policy in any coalition government. He pledged to promote immediately the peace process, stop massive government investment in the settlements in the territories and put those funds into programs to strengthen the economy, and improve the relationship with the United States. He said that he would advance the peace talks with the Palestinian delegation from the territories within the Madrid framework and reiterated the policy of not negotiating with the PLO. Labor's return to control of the Knesset and government portended changes in politics, policies, and patronage. While Labor's victory generated an initial euphoria among many in Israel, external observers, especially in the United States, were especially hopeful that the peace process might be reinvigorated.

Restarting the Arab-Israeli Peace Process

Bill Clinton's defeat of George H. W. Bush in the 1992 U.S. presidential election generated questions about whether continuity or change would be the dominant theme in the U.S. approach to the Middle East, especially to the Arab-Israeli peace process, and to bilateral relations with Israel. The Clinton administration entered office with no coherent view of the post–cold war world and no overall conception of the foreign and national security policy essential for the post–Persian Gulf War and post–Madrid Conference Middle East.

During the election campaign, Clinton pledged to guarantee loans for Israel to help settle Soviet Jews, to recognize Jerusalem as the capital of Israel, to oppose the creation of an independent Palestinian state, and to modify foreign aid programs to promote democracy. Clinton also made clear that he wanted to keep the peace process on track. He suggested a focus on the Arab-Israeli conflict and a desire to move the peace process to some resolution in 1993. He made clear his perception of the U.S. role as a "full partner" that served as an honest broker and, at times, a catalyst. Consultation with Israel was a feature of the process, especially since Clinton had suggested that he would treat the Arab-Israeli conflict as one in which the survival of Israel is at stake and had made clear that the United States must maintain its special commitment to its democratic partner, Israel, and its overall security.

The Oslo Accords

The new secretary of state Warren Christopher's first foreign trip was to the Middle East primarily to reinvigorate and restart the Arab-

Prime Minister Yitzhak Rabin of Israel and PLO chairman Yasser Arafat shake hands as U.S. president Bill Clinton looks on, at the Declaration of Principles signing ceremony on the White House lawn, September 13, 1993. (Courtesy Embassy of Israel, Washington, D.C.)

Israeli peace negotiations. Christopher prepared the way for his visit with a flurry of personal diplomacy to neutralize the obstacles to the peace process caused by the deportation of more than 400 Palestinian militants to Lebanon by Israel in December 1992. He persuaded Prime Minister Rabin to agree to a complicated formula under which Israel would take back some of the deportees and then the UN Security Council would endorse the compromise and urge the Palestinians to return to the peace negotiations. He also issued invitations, with the Russian foreign minister Andrei Kozyrev, for a ninth round of post-Madrid bilateral Arab-Israeli negotiations to be held in Washington, D.C., in April 1993.

Concurrent with the highly publicized bilateral Arab-Israeli negotiations in Washington and the multilateral talks in other world capitals, there were other covert negotiations. Secret talks in Oslo, Norway, between Israeli and PLO representatives in the spring and summer of 1993 resulted in historic agreements: an exchange of mutual recognition, soon followed by the formal signing on September 13, 1993, of the Declaration of Principles (DOP) on Interim Self-Government Arrangements. Israeli foreign minister Peres and PLO Executive Committee member Mahmoud Abbas (Abu Mazen) signed the DOP in a ceremony on the White House lawn, witnessed by U.S. secretary of state Christopher and Russian foreign minister Andrei Kozyrev and in the presence of U.S. president Clinton, Israeli prime minister Rabin and PLO chairman Arafat. The PLO recognized Israel's right to exist in peace and security, and Israel recognized the PLO as the representative of the Palestinian people. The PLO also renounced the use of terrorism and other forms of violence and committed itself to resolve the conflict with Israel through peaceful negotiations. The DOP outlined the proposed interim self-government arrangements for the Palestinians as a first step toward resolving the dispute between the two parties. This agreement focused on Gaza and Jericho first and set the stage for the establishment in those territories of the Palestinian Authority (PA) under the leadership of Arafat.

The signing ushered in a new era in Israel's history and changed the nature of the Arab-Israeli conflict and of other factors so inextricably linked to it. The symbolism of the event and the euphoric and optimistic mood it created overshadowed the difficulties in implementing and expanding the agreements that were to follow.

After the Oslo Accords

Israel began formal public negotiations with the Palestinians in the fall of 1993. Within months, the two parties had reached an agreement regarding implementing elements of the DOP that Arafat and Rabin signed in Cairo on May 4, 1994. The agreement formally initiated Israel's withdrawal from the Gaza Strip and the Jericho area and granted the Palestinians a measure of self-rule. It provided for negotiations to resolve the problem of the territories, including how much Israel would return to the Palestinians, within a relatively short period. The parties gave themselves five years, with a deadline of May 4, 1999, to negotiate the permanent or final status of the Israeli-Palestinian problem, including the difficult issues of Jerusalem, refugees, settlements, security arrangements, borders, regional neighborly arrangements, and others of common interest.

A second agreement was initiated in Cairo in August 1994 and signed at the Erez crossing between Israel and the Gaza Strip on August 29. It dealt with the transfer of powers concerning education, culture, health, social welfare, taxation, and tourism in the remainder of the West Bank from Israel to the PA. On September 25, 1995, Israel and the PLO signed the Israel-Palestinian Interim Agreement, commonly referred to as Oslo II. Oslo II focused on Israeli withdrawals from the major towns and cities in the West Bank and the election of a Palestinian Council. The agreement noted that permanent status negotiations between the parties would commence as soon as possible, but not later than May 4, 1996, and would focus on remaining issues. On October 6, the Knesset squeezed through a vote in support of the agreement and a vote of confidence in the government with 61 votes out of 120.

Jordan: A "Warm Peace"

In the immediate aftermath of the signing of the DOP, Israel and Jordan established a "common agenda" to facilitate negotiations that led to the Washington Declaration, issued in summer 1994, and the subsequent signing of a peace treaty between Israel and Jordan in fall 1994. Israel and Jordan exchanged ambassadors in early 1995.

Jordan's kings had been secretly meeting with the leaders of Israel since 1947. King Abdullah had met with Golda Meir, representative of the Labor Party that led the prestate Yishuv government, in the desert between the two countries, and dozens of secret meetings had taken place at the highest levels of both governments from that point forward. But when Israel and the PLO reached an arrangement to negotiate in 1993, King Hussein made the decision to commence public discussions for peace between his country and Israel.

During Israel's War of Independence, Jordan occupied (and later annexed) a portion of the territory of the Palestine mandate that had been allocated to the Arab state of Palestine and came to be known as the West Bank. In 1949, Jordan and Israel signed an armistice agreement that established the de facto frontier between the two states that existed until the Six-Day War (1967). The frontier was generally peaceful, but there were periodic raids and reprisals. Jordan joined in the Arab fighting against Israel in the Six-Day War, during which Israel took control of the West Bank and East Jerusalem from Jordan. Jordan abstained from participating in the Suez War (1956) and the War of Attrition (1969–70). During the Yom Kippur War (1973), King Hussein committed only token forces to the battle against Israel, and these fought alongside Syrian troops in the Golan Heights. The Israel-Jordan frontier remained quiet.

On September 14, 1993, the day after the signing of the DOP, Israel and Jordan signed the substantive Common Agenda outlining their approach to achieving peace between them. On October 1, Jordan's crown prince Hassan and Israel's foreign minister Peres met at the White House with U.S. president Clinton. They agreed to set up a bilateral economic committee and a U.S.-Israeli-Jordanian trilateral economic committee. The first meeting of the trilateral committee was held on November 4, in Paris, and a second was held in Washington on November 30. As Israel and the PLO continued their efforts to implement the DOP, Israel and Jordan conducted negotiations to achieve peace along the lines of their agreed Common Agenda. On July 25, 1994, Prime Minister Rabin of Israel and King Hussein of Jordan signed, on the White House lawn, the Washington Declaration, formally ending their state of belligerence, and just over a year after they began the process, Israel and Jordan signed a peace treaty in the desert between the two countries, where they formally put in place the border that had been created by the British after World War I, when Transjordan was created.

The Israel-Jordan Peace Treaty, signed on October 26, 1994, covered all of the usual ground but incorporated some innovative arrangements to deal with sensitive issues such as border demarcation and water resources. Provisions for economic cooperation included a commitment to terminate economic boycotts, essentially a reference to Arab boycotts of Israel. On the matter of Jerusalem, whose eastern portion, including the old walled city, Jordan had controlled between 1949 and 1967, Israel stated that it "respects the present special role of ... Jordan in Muslim Holy shrines in Jerusalem." Israel also noted that "when negotiations on the permanent status will take place, Israel will give high priority to the Jordanian historic role in these shrines."

The Israel-Jordan peace was remarkable in several respects, most notably, the speed with which it was negotiated and implemented, the ingenuity and creativity by which thorny problems were dealt with if not fully resolved, and the warmth between senior Israeli and Jordanian figures involved in the negotiation and implementation. It was overwhelmingly accepted by the Knesset, in sharp contrast not only to the narrow vote margins on the several Israel-PLO agreements but also to the vote on the 1979 peace treaty with Egypt, despite the fact that the latter was shepherded through the parliament by Menachem Begin. The actions and statements of King Hussein, the crown prince, and other Jordanian officials at home and abroad, were extraordinary in conveying the positive sentiments of the leadership of Jordan.

Jordan and Israel established a close and warm peace that went beyond formal peace and normalizing relations, although there was opposition within the Jordanian populace and even within the government there were those who were more cautious than the king and his closest advisors.

The Israel-Jordan Peace Treaty signing ceremony, 1994. Seated from left to right: Israeli prime minister Yitzhak Rabin, U.S. president Bill Clinton, and Jordanian prime minister Abdul Salam al-Majali. Standing behind them: U.S. secretary of state Warren Christopher, an unidentified aide, Israeli president Ezer Weizman, and Jordanian king Hussein (Courtesy Embassy of Israel, Washington, D.C.)

The Israeli agreement with Jordan was without built-in security arrangements, and there was no international force separating the two countries. Third-party observers and supervision were also omitted. Instead, cooperation between the military forces of the two states was enhanced. King Hussein made a number of visits to Israel. Israelis developed a very positive view of King Hussein and of the peace he made with them.

Rabin and Syria, 1995

After Madrid, negotiations between Israel and Syria focusing on the exchange of land for peace continued sporadically. The central issue was the Golan Heights, territory that Israel had seized from Syria in the 1967 Six-Day War. For Syrian president Hafez al-Assad, the issue was clear. He seemed interested only in a total and unilateral withdrawal by Israel from the Golan Heights to the line that had existed on July 4, 1967, in exchange for minor concessions that would follow the withdrawal.

For Israel, the issue was peace, security, and the guaranteed flow of water, Israel insisted that the Golan Heights be demilitarized, the intelligence from it be made available to Israel, the water that originates on it flow safely, and that no Syrian army encamp on the shores of the Sea of Galilee, which ultimately controls about a third of the waters of the Jordan River. The issues of determining the Syrian-Israeli border and water security were linked: Syria insisted on withdrawal by Israel from the Golan Heights to the pre–Six-Day War line; Israel insisted on the border that had been established during the British mandate, leaving the entire shore of the Sea of Galilee in Israel's control.

It was this latter line that had formed the basis of the armistice agreement between Israel and Syria in 1949. On the northeastern shore of the Sea of Galilee, the line ran about 33 feet (approximately 10 meters) from the water's edge. This line, however, was soon altered as both Israel and Syria took land in subsequent sporadic fighting between the two states. Although U.S. secretary of state Kissinger had managed to negotiate a Syrian-Israeli military disengagement agreement that was signed in Geneva at the end of May 1974, no serious peace negotiations took place until the Rabin administration in 1995.

During the negotiations, Rabin was concerned that Israeli security considerations be given priority, recognizing both the strategic and political imperatives. Rabin needed to reassure Israelis that giving up the Golan Heights would not gravely affect Israeli security, and thereby, he would be able to attain the measure of domestic support essential to make the deal and, later, to win reelection. Rabin was not prepared for unilateral Israeli actions and pledged that he would submit the Golan issue to an Israeli referendum prior to a final agreement.

In June 1995, a new round of American-mediated security talks concentrated on security arrangements on and near the Golan Heights, with the area around the Sea of Galilee becoming the major point of contention. Plans were made for talks to continue in Washington, D.C., later that year.

The Assassination of Rabin

On November 4, 1995, Yigal Amir fired three bullets, killing Prime Minister Rabin. Amir had been waiting patiently, unbothered by police who believed him to be a plain clothes agent, in the Kings of Israel parking lot in Tel Aviv for 40 minutes until the prime minister returned to his waiting vehicle after participating in a well-attended peace rally. Rabin descended the stairs into the parking lot and was shot at point

Foreign Minister Peres (left) and Prime Minister Rabin (center) join in a "Song for Peace" at a peace rally in Tel Aviv, November 4, 1995, minutes before Rabin's assassination. (Courtesy Embassy of Israel, Washington, D.C.)

blank range as he approached the door of his car, two bullets hitting him in the chest. Rabin was pronounced dead at 11:10 P.M., an hour and 20 minutes later. After his arrest, Amir complained that "a Palestinian state is starting to be established" because "Rabin wants to give our country to the Arabs."

The assassination of Rabin threw Israel and the peace process into turmoil. It was uncertain whether Peres, who became acting prime minister, would be able to convince Israelis that making concessions and turning over land to the Palestinians would not jeopardize the country's security. While Rabin had been seen as "Mr. Security," Peres was seen as too much of a politician and did not generate the same trust and respect among Israelis as Rabin had. Rabin also brought unparalleled military credentials to the peace process; Peres was seen as more visionary but less realistic.

Israelis were shaken and sobered by the assassination but major opinion shifts did not follow. Nevertheless, they soon returned to the raucous debates typical of Israeli public life and politics. The assassination did not substantially alter the views of those who believed in a "Greater Israel," which includes the West Bank and Gaza Strip, and who opposed a Palestinian state. In the short term, Peres gained support, in part as a sympathy factor, from among those young and new Israeli voters who appeared to be the most affected by the assassination.

Killing the Peacemaker but Not the Peace Process

In retrospect, although Amir sought to abort the peace process by killing Rabin, he succeeded only in killing a peacemaker. In the weeks immediately following the assassination, the peace effort gained new vigor and proceeded with a new intensity toward implementation of the agreements Rabin had signed and toward a renewed Israel-Syria dialogue.

Prime Minister Peres's government was approved by the Knesset in a vote of confidence 62 to 8, with 32 abstentions, on November 22, 1995. In announcing the new government, Peres noted that his main objective would be to arrive at a comprehensive peace in the Middle East, if possible by the end of the 20th century. To achieve this, he suggested beginning with Damascus and appealed to the president of Syria suggesting that the differences that remained could be resolved through negotiations based on mutual respect.

The interim agreement (Oslo II) signed between Israel and the Palestinians was carried out with relative dispatch. At the time of the assassination, Israel had already begun to redeploy its forces from the major West Bank cities, except Hebron, and to turn them over to the Palestinian Authority and Palestinian self-rule. This process now continued: Jericho had been turned over earlier; Jenin, Tulkarm, Nablus, Qalqilya, and, just prior to Christmas Day, Bethlehem followed. On December 27, 1995, Israeli troops withdrew from Ramallah (and the neighboring El Birah), completing the withdrawal from six West Bank cities and more than 400 towns and villages, as scheduled, and in preparation for Palestinian elections in January 1996. This essentially ended Israeli control over most of the Palestinians and much of the West Bank. Virtually all Palestinians were now accountable to the PA. The only major West Bank city left in Israeli hands was Hebron, which was to be turned over in March 1996, albeit leaving Israeli settlers in the center of the city and Israeli soldiers to provide for their security.

For the Palestinians, this marked self-rule in much of the West Bank and Gaza Strip for the first time and included much of what is normally seen as the characteristics of an independent sovereign state. The PA, at the beginning of 1996, governed much of the West Bank as well as the Gaza Strip and Jericho.

In the Palestinian elections held on January 20, 1996, more than 700 candidates competed for 88 seats on the Palestinian self-governing council. Despite this large number of candidates, the process was not truly diverse and was not truly democratic. It was dominated by Arafat and Fatah, which supplied the candidates; Hamas (the Islamic Resistance Movement, which seeks to establish an Islamic Palestinian state in place of Israel) and like-minded groups and individuals failed to participate, and their perspectives were absent from the choices available. In a separate contest, the Palestinians elected a *rais* (the formal term for what the Israelis call a chairman or head and the Palestinians call a president) of the PA. In that vote, Arafat was challenged by only one candidate, Samiha Khalil, an opponent of the accords with Israel.

Renewed Talks with Syria

In the months preceding Rabin's assassination, the chances of achieving an agreement between Israel and Syria in 1996 were appraised as virtually nonexistent. Rabin had retained full control over the Syrian negotiating track, even keeping his foreign minister (Shimon Peres) only partially informed, and had seemed determined not to rush toward a deal with Assad at the expense of Israel's security interests.

After his endorsement as prime minister, Peres acted quickly to assume control of the process and the policy. Peres believed that the Golan Heights were of limited strategic utility but could be a bargaining chip for peace. He believed it possible for Israel to withdraw from the Golan Heights to the international border established in the mandate period. Syria, meanwhile, sought an Israeli withdrawal to the lines that existed on June 4, 1967, and withdrawal from key areas such as the shoreline of the Sea of Galilee and the area of Hamat Gader.

Peres sought to accelerate the pace of negotiations and conclude them by the spring of 1996. He would hold parallel discussions, in public or in private, on different issues and raise them to the foreign ministerial level. Peres suggested that a summit meeting with Assad would be an appropriate way to open negotiations, without preconditions, concerning the Golan Heights.

Peres retained the defense portfolio and appointed Ehud Barak, former chief of staff of the IDF, as foreign minister. He initially chose not to seek an early parliamentary election, thus allowing time for an approach to Syria to mature. He hoped that the process would lead to an agreement with Syria and the election could then serve as a referendum on the peace process and specifically on the Golan Heights.

Further, Peres sought to portray a peace agreement with Syria and the relinquishing of the Golan Heights as a means of creating a broad peace in the Middle East rather than a narrow one involving only Israel and Syria.

Everything depended on Assad. In Israel-Syria relations, as well as in the overall peace process, Assad had clearly been the dominating and manipulating element. Assad, in control of Syria for a quarter of a century, had survived by developing extraordinary political skills that helped to sustain his position and posture. Within weeks of the assassination of Rabin, there was a growing view that the Syrians seemed ready to deal. While Peres visited Washington, D.C., in December 1995, U.S. president Clinton telephoned Assad, and after a subsequent visit by U.S. secretary of state Christopher to Damascus, agreement was reached for meetings near the U.S. capital between Israeli and Syrian representatives.

At the end of December 1995, and continuing into 1996, negotiations between Israel and Syria were resumed at the Wye Plantation in Maryland. The United States sponsored the talks and participated at the table, partly because the Syrians opposed direct contact with their Israeli counterparts without an American presence. The atmosphere was designed to be off the record with no news leaks; the meetings were to be intense and unstructured.

The issues included security, water rights, and regional development. Talk of full withdrawal revolved around territorial definitions and the lines to which the Israelis would withdraw. Talk of full peace was more complicated. Israel saw a broad interpretation of the term—open borders; exchanges of ambassadors, tourists, and businesspeople; in effect, an opening of a closed society. Among the specifics to be determined was the question of how to assure Israeli security once the Golan Heights were returned to Syria. Other matters were the timetable for Israeli withdrawal, demilitarization of the Golan Heights and possibly other sectors, and access to water.

In the spring of 1996, Israel launched Operation Grapes of Wrath in response to Hizballah (a radical Shiite terrorist group) attacks on northern Israel. Peres had been under pressure to take action to improve security after Palestinian rocket attacks and suicide bombings in Israel claimed more than 50 victims in February and March 1996. In April, Israel fired artillery and missiles and launched air strikes on bases of Hizballah and of the Popular Front for the Liberation of Palestine–General Command in southern Lebanon. The operation was ended by a cease-fire on April 26, 1996.

8

THE NETANYAHU AND BARAK GOVERNMENTS (1996-2000)

The assassination of Rabin and the tension and conflict that followed inaugurated a new period in Israel's domestic as well as in its international relations. Continuity was not the central characteristic of the transition from Rabin to Peres to Netanyahu to Barak. The Israeli electorate shifted its voting patterns and its policy perspectives. At the same time progress on Israeli-Palestinian negotiations slowed dramatically.

The 1996 Election

Shimon Peres called for elections in May 1996. Preelection polls indicated a close race for prime minister but also suggested that the configuration and membership of parliament might prove unusual. The election of May 29 was the 14th since Israeli independence but differed from those previously conducted in its format and structure, as well as in its outcome and portent. This was the first direct election of the prime minister utilizing a new electoral system introduced in 1992 in which voters chose both a prime minister and members of parliament in separate ballots cast at the same time.

As usual, the campaign was relatively brief but intense, and the turnout was relatively high. When Israelis went to the polls they were faced with two ballots, and this allowed them to split their vote. In the 1996 elections, the prime ministerial ballot was seen as a vote on the peace process, while the ballot for the Knesset allowed voters to focus on more specific issues, individuals, or interests. Thus, for example, ultra-Orthodox Jewish voters could still vote for their preferred religious party (e.g., Shas or NRP), as they traditionally had, and at the same time vote for one of the candidates of the two major parties to express their views on the peace process.

Peres, the incumbent prime minister who campaigned on a theme of continuity and expansion of the peace process, was defeated by Benjamin (Bibi) Netanyahu, who focused on the need for security as the first imperative during the peace process. Netanyahu's victory was narrow, a margin of less than 1 percent. The election results may have been in part due to a fateful decision by Peres, made soon after the assassination of Rabin in 1995, not to call for early elections. The reason, apparently suggested by the United States and conforming to Peres's view, was that a deal between Israel and Syria could be achieved in time for both Clinton and Peres to run for election in November 1996 with a Syrian-Israeli agreement as part of an overall theme of their foreign policy successes. But Peres thereby also allowed time for terrorists to remind Israelis of the security issue and to question the speed with which the existing peace arrangements had been achieved. His decision to make Ehud Barak, the former chief of staff of the IDF, minister of foreign affairs, and to keep the defense portfolio for himself, did little to enhance Peres's security credentials, essential for a prime minister seeking peace with security.

In the period between the 1992 and 1996 elections, Israel had negotiated and reached several agreements with the PLO and a peace treaty with the Hashemite Kingdom of Jordan. On the other hand, a string of gruesome bombings in Jerusalem and Tel Aviv in February and March 1996 left numerous Israelis wounded and killed. Terrorism had become the main threat to Israelis' security. A resumption of bomb attacks by Islamic fundamentalists before the elections would almost certainly result in Peres's defeat. Because terrorism would facilitate a Likud victory, Peres, in a theme used by Labor since Rabin was assassinated, urged Israelis not to let terror determine the government. At the same time, the public was reminded by the political Right that more Israelis had been killed in terror attacks since the signing of the Oslo Accords than were killed in the same period before the signing.

The election campaign was, in a sense, a referendum on Peres's and Netanyahu's approaches to peace and security. The incumbent Labor Party employed the legacy of assassinated prime minister Rabin to evoke sympathy for its cause. Likud used the memory of those killed in suicide bombings to inspire distrust of the Labor government's position on security. External influences such as the broad threat of terrorism and the strong pro-Labor stance of the Clinton administration also had a role. Economic policy and social problems remained in the background.

The peace process included other issues that were central to Israeli concerns, such as the status of Jerusalem and the Golan Heights. Peres suggested that compromises would be necessary in either one or both of these areas, and not all Israelis were ready to make such concessions. In response, Peres assured voters that he would hold a referendum before any permanent deals were struck. Netanyahu interpreted this pledge as a suggestion that Peres was deceiving the public and avoiding the issues. Netanyahu declared the election a referendum to force the public to define their beliefs.

Israeli Arab voters retained a strong interest in the success of the peace process and, generally, the creation of a Palestinian state. For this reason, they had supported Labor consistently, but their support wavered in 1996. They felt betrayed by the Israeli military action in Lebanon in April 1996 and by the strict closure of the occupied territories preventing Palestinians from crossing into Israel following Hamas terrorist bombings. Likud, aware of the sentiments, sought to sway some of this constituency by pointing to the harsh measures employed by the Peres government.

The 1996 elections also marked the first time immigrants from the former Soviet Union had the opportunity to vote for their own party, Yisrael B'Aliya, led by Natan Sharansky. Aware of his constituency's focus on security and the peace process and in the interest of his party's success, Sharansky did not demand that his voters choose a particular position on the peace process. He told his supporters to follow their conscience in their choice of a prime minister and to vote for Yisrael B'Aliya, in support of immigrant issues, for parliament.

The ultra-Orthodox camp supported Netanyahu. One reason was a shared hard-line view of the peace process. Perhaps more important, however, was the religious parties' loathing of the stridently secularist Meretz Party (a coalition of left-wing Zionist parties formed in 1992), which had been Labor's junior partner in the outgoing government, and of the secularists within Labor, who also were seen as threatening the Jewishness of the state.

The May 29, 1996, election outcome was important in several ways. Clearly Netanyahu defeated Peres because of two significant factors: the Arab vote, which did not turn out to support Peres, and the religious party vote, which did turn out in very high proportions to support the less secular and more nationalist Netanyahu. This created a narrow but sufficient victory for Netanyahu over Peres.

In the end, the religious parties received their largest-ever vote totals and seats in the Knesset, and 11 new parties proved able to secure enough votes to gain seats in parliament. The results thus portended changes in government personnel and policies, and the large parties were the big "losers" in the Knesset vote. Labor went down from 44 to 34 seats and Likud from 40 to 32. Despite forecasts to the contrary, Shas posted the most significant improvement, increasing its share to 10 seats and becoming the third-largest party in the Knesset. The NRP increased its share to nine seats. The left-of-center parties, Meretz especially, lost the most. Yisrael B'Aliya, with the support of Soviet immigrants, obtained seven seats. The Third Way, a political party that offered an alternative to Labor and Likud, sought to assure the role of the Golan Heights in Israel's future and obtained four seats.

The outcome of the election was also atypical in that although Netanyahu defeated Peres by a very slim margin (50.49 percent to 49.51 percent) in the vote for prime minister, the Labor Party outpolled the Likud by a margin of 34 seats to 32 in parliament. Netanyahu thus faced the challenge of forming a government despite the small size of his own party in the Knesset.

Netanyahu cobbled together a government that was endorsed by the Knesset on June 18, by a vote of 62 to 50. Netanyahu spoke of a new government that would introduce fundamental changes in the country and would lead Israel into the 21st century. In reference to particularly the presidents of Syria and Lebanon but also other Arab leaders, he called for direct negotiations for peace that would be sustainable and stable. And, he reminded the country of the relationship with the United States, which would continue to be the cornerstone of Israel's foreign policy. He also noted the government's commitment to encourage settlement throughout Israel, Judea and Samaria (the West Bank), and Gaza.

Netanyahu pointed out that he was the first prime minister to have been born after the establishment of the state. He stressed that the government would follow a new path, new in its approach to security and to the quest for peace. He believed that genuine peace with Israel's neighbors could be attained; nevertheless, the political parties opposed to the Oslo peace process were considerably strengthened in the election, as were the religious parties. Netanyahu was able to form a coalition government that included the religious parties (Shas and NRP), Yisrael B'Aliya, and the Third Way. His cabinet included some of the most prominent and well-known figures in Israel: David Levy as foreign minister, Yitzhak Mordechai as minister of defense, and Dan Meridor as minister of finance. Natan Sharansky became minister of industry and trade, an important post for the representative of immigrants from the former Soviet Union, and Eli Suissa of the Shas Party held the interior portfolio, an important post for that party.

Netanyahu as Prime Minister

Netanyahu's rhetoric during the campaign and his record as Likud leader suggested that he would modify Israel's approach to the peace process. Netanyahu promised Israeli voters that he would achieve a "secure peace" and that while he accepted the reality of the Oslo framework for Israeli-Palestinian negotiations, he would never accept a Palestinian state. The prospects for peace with the Palestinians appeared bleak as Netanyahu assumed the premiership, and the Arab-Israeli conflict remained the country's most important problem.

Managing a coalition composed of diverse personalities and competing interests proved to be a difficult task for Netanyahu. From the outset, issues relating to the peace process—in particular, U.S. pressure on Israel to abide by the timetable of the Oslo agreements for implementing IDF redeployments in the West Bank—proved to be a source of significant internal strain for the Netanyahu government.

Prime Minister Benjamin Netanyahu of Israel (right) shakes hands with Palestinian Authority chair-man Yasser Arafat at the White House on the first day of the Wye Plantation Summit. U.S. vice president Al Gore and U.S. secretary of state Madeleine Albright look on. (Israel National Photo Collection ; Photographer: Ya'acov Sa'ar)

BENJAMIN NETANYAHU
(OCTOBER 21, 1942–   )

Benjamin (Bibi) Netanyahu was born in 1942 in Tel Aviv and raised partly in the United States, where his father, Professor Benzion Netanyahu, a strong supporter of Vladimir Ze'ev Jabotinsky and Revisionist Zionism, taught medieval Jewish history. From 1967 to 1972, Benjamin Netanyahu served in the elite Sayeret Matkal anti-terrorism unit of the Israel Defense Forces. He graduated from the Massachusetts Institute of Technology with degrees in architecture and business administration and was pursuing a business career in the United States when his older brother, Jonathan (Yoni), was killed in the Israeli raid on a hijacked airplane in Entebbe, Uganda (Operation Entebbe), in July 1976.

Netanyahu returned to Israel and established the Jonathan Institute, a foundation devoted to studying international terrorism. In 1982, he was recruited to serve as deputy chief of mission at Israel's embassy to the United States. From 1984 to 1988, he served as Israel's permanent representative to the United Nations. First elected, on the Likud list, to the 12th Knesset in 1988, he served as deputy foreign minister from 1988 to 1991 and as deputy minister in the prime minister's office from 1991 to 1992.

On March 25, 1993, Netanyahu was elected to succeed Yitzhak Shamir as Likud Party leader, defeating David Levy. In June 1996,

The Netanyahu period was marked primarily by limited activity concerning the Arab-Israeli conflict. Negotiations were focused on the territorial components of the Oslo Accords, and the pace was essentially dictated by Netanyahu's and Likud's preferences rather than those of the outgoing Labor government. The Wye and Hebron accords were emblematic of the process.

In January 1997, Israel and the PLO concluded an agreement, the Protocol Concerning the Redeployment in Hebron, to transfer control of 80 percent of the city to the Palestinian Authority, with the IDF remaining in the other 20 percent to protect Hebron's Jewish population. In a Note for the Record dated January 15, Netanyahu and Arafat agreed that "the Oslo peace process must move forward to succeed" and thus they reaffirmed their commitment to implement the agreements already reached. The agreement to redeploy from Hebron led

he defeated Israel Labor Party leader Shimon Peres by less than 1 percent of the popular vote in the first direct election of the prime minister. The first prime minister to be born in Israel since independence, Netanyahu was generally viewed as representative of the new generation of Israeli politicians. Although it was marked by a series of missteps and scandals, Netanyahu's government did achieve significant diplomatic agreements.

On May 17, 1999, Netanyahu was defeated in the direct election for prime minister, receiving 43.92 percent of the popular vote compared to the 56.08 percent won by One Israel leader Ehud Barak. Netanyahu immediately resigned as Likud leader and subsequently relinquished his seat in the Knesset. He agreed in November 2002 to serve as foreign minister under Ariel Sharon, a position he held until his reelection to the 16th Knesset in January 2003. In February 2003, Netanyahu was appointed finance minister.

On August 7, 2005, Netanyahu resigned from the government in protest of Sharon's Gaza disengagement plan.

On December 19, 2005, he was elected to once again lead the Likud Party, but it won only 12 seats in the March 28, 2006 Knesset elections.

Netanyahu's control of the Likud Party was overwhelmingly reaffirmed in a leadership primary held on August 14, 2007. In the 2009 election, his party won 28 seats, and Netanyahu became prime minister, forming a government approved by the Knesset on March 31, 2009.

to the resignation of Science Minister Benjamin Begin (son of former Likud prime minister Menachem Begin). A year later, in January 1998, Foreign Minister David Levy resigned from the cabinet, in part over the pace of negotiations with the Palestinians and Levy's role in those negotiations.

The Wye River Memorandum was signed in Washington, D.C., on October 23, 1998, by Israel and the PLO following a nine-day summit meeting hosted by U.S. president Bill Clinton at the Wye Plantation in Maryland. The agreements spelled out specific steps to facilitate the earlier accords between Israel and the PLO. The memorandum effectively provided for the implementation of the terms of the Oslo II accords of September 1995 and the Hebron protocol of January 1997. The Wye River Memorandum was a further problem for Netanyahu who sought "political cover" for himself by appointing Ariel Sharon as foreign minister. Netanyahu also elicited additional commitments from Arafat and Clinton regarding Palestinian compliance with its obligations, in particular the combating of Hamas terrorism, in return for further IDF redeployments in the West Bank. But this did not last very long. Faced with the prospect of being abandoned by much of his own coalition in a Knesset vote of no confidence over his handling of the peace process, Netanyahu on December 21, 1998, supported a bill to dissolve the Knesset for early elections. An agreement was eventually reached to hold new prime ministerial elections and elections to the 15th Knesset on May 17, 1999.

The 1999 Elections

The 1999 elections took place during a relatively placid period in Israel's history. The debate focused more on how to make peace than on immediate questions of security and the danger of war. Five candidates initially contested the prime ministerial election; eventually the race narrowed to two, Ehud Barak and Netanyahu. Yitzhak Mordechai, the newly formed Center Party's candidate for prime minister, offering a middle ground between Likud and Labor, faced substantial pressure to drop out of the race and join forces with Barak, the front runner. Benjamin Begin, on the right, similarly withdrew. Azmi Bishara, the first Israeli Arab to run for prime minister, also pulled out of the race.

The 1999 elections were among the most fateful in Israeli history. The populace faced a choice between continuity by keeping Netanyahu in office or selecting a change in direction, symbolized by Barak, newly chosen leader of the Labor Party in place of Shimon Peres. Barak won by a wide margin over Netanyahu in the direct election for prime minister. The Knesset election produced a less clear outcome, although Likud lost seats in parliament. Netanyahu resigned as party leader soon thereafter, and Sharon was chosen as his successor.

Barak's election focus was on peace and security, suggesting that his career in the IDF would be a crucial factor in his ability to lead Israel toward the two goals. Despite a significant margin of victory over Netanyahu (Barak gained 56.08 percent of the vote compared with 43.92 percent for Netanyahu), Barak was faced with the most fractionalized Knesset in Israel's history, in which 15 parties shared 120 seats. Nevertheless, Barak succeeded in pulling together a broad-based coalition of these diverse political units that included parties on the right and left and virtually all points on the social and religious spectrums. His bloc, composed of Labor, Gesher (a breakaway from Likud formed by David Levy), and Meimad (a moderate Orthodox party), emerged as the largest party in the Knesset but was able to obtain only 26 seats. Besides One Israel, his government, presented to the Knesset for a confidence vote on July 6, included the ultra-Orthodox Shas Party (which had 17 seats), the leftist Meretz party (10 seats), the Russian immigrant Yisrael B'Aliya Party (six seats), the Center Party (six seats), the NRP (five seats), and the ultra-Orthodox United Torah Judaism Party (five seats). Once he succeeded in merging and meshing the divergent perspectives and personalities of the parties, Barak was able to embark on the efforts to implement his major goals and objectives.

Barak as Prime Minister

Barak's election was as much a vote for "anyone but Bibi" as it was a choice of Barak. Although he had only a short and not very impressive track record as a political figure, Barak had a military record of distinction and was widely seen as Rabin's disciple. Thus, he was the new "Mr. Security."

Barak embarked on an ambitious agenda as prime minister seeking to establish a broad government that could implement important changes at home while achieving peace with Israel's neighbors, especially the Palestinians and Syrians. Domestically, he was faced with a series of challenges on social and religious matters.

Withdrawal from Lebanon, 2000

On March 5, 2000, the government adopted a resolution that "the Israel Defense Forces will deploy on the border with Lebanon by July 2000 and from there will secure the safety of the northern towns and villages."

Israel's 18-year-long military presence in Lebanon came to an end in May 2000 as Israel evacuated its remaining outposts in the security zone. Barak believed that it would end Israel's tragedy in Lebanon, would contribute to Israel's security, and might help facilitate peace with Lebanon and perhaps Syria. Barak focused on bringing the boys home and defending Israel from inside Israel. Some on the Israeli Right called the turmoil and the "sudden" withdrawal ahead of the planned schedule a "humiliation" for Israel.

Hizballah and its allies regarded the IDF withdrawal as a victory and vowed to continue the military process of regaining territory along the Lebanese border, in the Golan Heights, and, later, Israel itself. They called the Israeli decision to withdraw a historic defeat for Israel and

POPE JOHN PAUL II
VISITS ISRAEL (2000)

In March 2000, Pope John Paul II became the first pope to make an official visit to Israel, in significant contrast to the visit of Pope Paul VI to the Holy Land (specifically not referred to as Israel) in 1964, which was both unofficial and low key. On his arrival, John Paul II said in a ceremony held at the airport, "Today, it is with profound emotion that I set foot in the land where God chose to pitch his tent." He concluded his airport remarks with the traditional Hebrew greeting, "shalom" (peace). President Ezer Weizman greeted him but reminded him of the differences between Israel and the Vatican over the status of Jerusalem. Weizman referred to Jerusalem as a city that "had been reunified" by Israel's capture and subsequent control over the eastern portion of the city during the 1967 war. The Vatican has referred to Israel's occupation of East Jerusalem as "illegal."

At Yad Vashem, the Pope paid homage to the 6 million Jewish victims of the Holocaust and called anti-Semitism a sin "against God and man." In the political arena, his visit to Israel was an effort to build a relationship between Israel and the Vatican, yet a major disappointment for Israelis was his neglecting to explicitly recognize the failure of the Vatican to confront the Holocaust. The visit was the culmination of a series of earlier efforts. In June 1994, Israel and the Vatican had announced agreement on opening full diplomatic relations.

In addition, the pope spent time in territory controlled by Yasser Arafat and the Palestinian Authority and expressed his empathy with the suffering refugees. He noted that the Palestinians had a natural right to a homeland.

---

claimed the Zionists' routing from Lebanon was achieved by Hizballah with the strong backing of Arab Syria and Islamic Iran.

On May 25, Israel announced that the withdrawal from Lebanon was complete. The IDF deployed along the international border in accordance with UN Security Council Resolution 425 with the objective of defending Israel's northern communities from there. Despite its intention to achieve peace and security, the unilateral withdrawal of the IDF was accompanied by the disintegration of the Israeli-backed South Lebanese Army (SLA) and the return of hostile elements to the area that had been a buffer between Israel and Hizballah.

Israelis generally were pleased with the decision to withdraw from Lebanon, to help minimize casualties, although there were mixed reactions to the "hurried" nature of the withdrawal ahead of the announced and self-imposed schedule and to the perception in the Arab world, where the early withdrawal was seen as a defeat for Israel.

Clinton and Barak

Throughout his tenure as prime minister Barak paid careful attention to and continued the cultivation of Israel's relationship with the United States and particularly President Bill Clinton. Barak understood the importance of the United States and appreciated the role that Clinton might play in making progress toward resolution of the Arab-Israeli conflict. Clinton and Barak established a relationship on both personal and political levels that was facilitated by the fact that Barak was seen as the successor to Rabin. Barak's election and his desire to make substantial progress in the peace process coincided with Clinton's final 18 months in office as a lame duck seeking a foreign-policy legacy. Nevertheless, agreement on all aspects of the peace process did not exist. Clinton seemed impatient about implementing the already agreed-upon arrangements. Barak suggested that he wanted to postpone implementation of the Wye accord and instead include discussions about a broader final settlement.

Focusing on Peace with Syria

The Syrian peace track was soon identified as the more important one. Syria presented a significant military threat given the size, armaments, and capability of its military forces, and peace with Syria was seen as existential. The status of the Golan Heights remained the central issue. Barak decided to withdraw from Lebanon, which he saw as having limited security value and causing a growing number of Israeli casualties, and because he believed that withdrawal from Lebanon might facilitate negotiations and agreement with Syria.

Assad continued to insist that regaining all of the Golan Heights meant the inclusion of the northeastern shore of the Sea of Galilee. Assad's demand was that Israel had to withdraw totally from the Golan Heights to the line that existed on June 4, 1967, the day before the Six-Day War began. Israel's position was that the international frontier, demarcated by Britain and France in 1923, should be reestablished as the international boundary. When negotiations were resumed, the

Syrians claimed that Rabin had given them a firm commitment, through American intermediaries, that withdrawal from the Golan Heights meant to the line of June 4, 1967. Barak suggested that he would be prepared to withdraw to the prewar line along most of the frontier, but not on the shore of the Sea of Galilee. Under Barak, high-level talks between Israel and Syria were resumed in Washington, D.C., toward the end of 1999, and shortly after the beginning of 2000 Clinton, Barak, and Syrian foreign minister Farouk al-Shara met in Shepherdstown, West Virginia. They did not reach an agreement.

On March 26, 2000, Assad and Clinton met in Geneva where each side seemed convinced that it could emerge from the talks with its position victorious. Clinton apparently believed that he could negotiate the deal without Israel relinquishing the sliver of land on the shore of the Sea of Galilee, and Assad apparently believed that Clinton would be bringing the concession Syria sought from Barak. These perceptions proved erroneous, and the summit failed. The sudden death of Assad in June and the accession of his son Bashar al-Assad to the presidency effectively halted the ability to pursue that track of diplomacy until such time as the new president established his regime and determined the course of his administration.

On May 19, 2000, Barak, summing up his first year as prime minister, noted:

> We are not closing the door on the possibility of renewing talks with Syria, but we see issues of water, sovereignty over the Kinneret, and control over the Jordan river north of the Kinneret as Israel's vital interests. We also see early warning, security arrangements, normalization first, and changes in the atmosphere and style of the diplomatic and public dialogue between ourselves and the Syrian people as additional vital interests.

Israel and the PLO

Barak shifted his attention from the stalled process with Syria to a new effort focused on the Palestinians and began to prepare the Israeli public for both negotiations with the Palestinians and potential concessions to them.

Barak's election as prime minister had revived hopes for advances in the peace process and was followed by substantial optimistic talk. Barak continued to reiterate his government's promise to stand by the Wye River Memorandum of October 1998. Nevertheless, he soon suggested that he would prefer to delay implementation of the agreement and move directly into final status discussions to arrive at settlement of all outstanding issues and potentially lay foundations for an independent Palestinian state. The negotiations began soon after Barak's formation of his government. His travel to Washington, D.C., in July 1999, the establishment of new negotiating teams for Israel, and his indefatigable efforts to move the process forward became commonplace. The expired deadline of May 4, 1999, was replaced by various new target dates established by Barak and Arafat. Some progress was made, although it was usually followed by regression.

By the summer of 2000, a year after Barak's accession to power, the process had reached a critical juncture. It was with that in mind that Barak and Clinton agreed that a summit meeting at Camp David, in the United States, might be an appropriate next step toward an accord.

The Palestinians wanted all the territory that Jordan and Egypt had lost to Israel in the Gaza Strip and West Bank in the Six-Day War, Jerusalem as their capital, the right of return of refugees, and full sovereignty. A majority of the Israeli government and a majority of Israelis believed that Jerusalem was not negotiable. Most Israelis also did not foresee the return to Israel of any sizable number of Arab refugees. And many Israelis believed that a Palestinian state would eventually exist, but that it should be restricted in its powers.

Barak was apparently pleased by the decision to convene the summit, since he had sought the meeting for some time and believed that it could serve to hold his divided government together. He thought that it could also revive the momentum of the negotiating process and that the time was appropriate to convene such a meeting.

U.S. secretary of state Madeleine Albright traveled to the Middle East in June 2000 and reported that Barak and Arafat remained too far apart on the core issues for a summit to be successful. Nevertheless, in early July 2000, Clinton called for a summit. Recognizing that this move would carry with it various perils, Clinton wrote in a guest essay in *Newsweek,* that "while Israeli and Palestinian negotiators have made real progress, the most complex and sensitive issues are still unresolved. Success now depends on decisions only the two leaders can make. . . . If the parties do not seize this moment to make more progress, there will be more hostility and more bitterness—perhaps even more violence." Barak and Arafat accepted Clinton's summit invitation, and the talks were to be held in the secluded presidential retreat (Camp David) in the Catoctin Mountains of Maryland, beginning on July 11.

Barak's position was tenuous. In the days preceding his departure for the summit, Barak's coalition partners deserted him and then sought to obtain a Knesset vote of no confidence in his government because they feared he might make unacceptable, far-reaching concessions to the Palestinians. Shas, his biggest coalition partner, with 17 seats in the Knesset, withdrew along with the NRP. Interior Minister Natan Sharansky resigned, and Barak thereby lost four more seats. In total, nearly half of his ministers resigned.

The opposition failed to achieve a no-confidence vote of 61 needed to topple his government even though the motion gained 54 votes to 52 for Barak. Seven Knesset members abstained, and seven were absent. A second attempt was postponed. The government did not fall, although the coalition had collapsed, and Barak left the country with only about one-third of the Knesset's support.

Another test for Barak came when President Ezer Weizman resigned on July 10, a day before the summit was to begin. In early April, Israeli police had announced that an investigation of the president concluded that he had committed fraud and breach of trust by accepting unreported funds and favors from two private businessmen, but Weizman could not be indicted because of the statute of limitations.

Barak sought to allay fears about concessions. At a predeparture airport ceremony on July 10, he suggested, "The choice is between a peace of the brave and, heaven forbid, a violent confrontation that will cause suffering and will not solve anything." He added:

> If there is an agreement, it will only be one that will comply with the principles to which I have committed myself before I was elected, and principles that I have consistently and repeatedly stressed: a united Jerusalem under Israeli sovereignty; the '67 borders will be amended; the overwhelming majority of the settlers in Judea, Samaria and the Gaza Strip will be in settlement blocs under Israeli sovereignty; no foreign army in the entire area west of the Jordan River; and a solution of the problem of refugees outside Israeli sovereign territory.

Camp David II

The summit at Camp David was a significant attempt to achieve an Israeli-Palestinian agreement through lengthy, detailed, and substantial talks. Barak made far-reaching concessions and altered long-held Israeli positions. Barak apparently offered the idea of recognizing a Palestinian state, accepting 100,000 Palestinian refugees in Israel, and granting broad autonomy to Palestinians in East Jerusalem. His position remained, however, that there would not be full withdrawal to the 1967 lines, no recognition of a right of return for Palestinian refugees, no removal of all settlements beyond the 1967 lines, no remilitarization of the West Bank and Gaza, and no return of parts of East Jerusalem. As the talks proceeded, it looked as though Barak was ready to go further than anyone could have imagined to reach an agreement. At one point,

From left to right: Israeli prime minister Ehud Barak with U.S. president Bill Clinton and Palestinian leader Yasser Arafat at Camp David, Maryland, during the summit of 2000 (Israel National Photo Collection; Photographer: Avi Ohayon)

he put as much as 90–95 percent of the West Bank and Gaza on the table to be returned to Palestinian control and even went so far as to put Jerusalem on the table.

In the end, the talks collapsed, and the parties went home. Clinton told reporters at the White House on July 25: "After 14 days of intensive negotiations between Israelis and Palestinians, I have concluded with regret that they will not be able to reach an agreement at this time." Clinton went out of his way to praise Barak for his efforts at Camp David. "I think it is fair to say that at this moment in time … the prime minister moved forward more from his initial position than Chairman Arafat, particularly on the questions of Jerusalem." Clinton's assessment was widely shared by the media and public opinion in the United States and elsewhere. Barak came to the talks at tangible political risk to himself but ready to make serious compromises. He found Arafat unprepared to make the hard compromises needed to reach an accord. Clinton's gamble at Camp David had failed, and no deal was made. Each side blamed the other.

Barak had convinced himself that his proposals could not be refused and was shocked by Arafat's reaction. Arafat did not realize that Barak gave him the best offer ever made by Israel, and he did not suggest a counter offer. By simply opposing each idea, Arafat missed a historic opportunity to move forward and reconfirmed the generally held view that he was inflexible and unwilling to take serious risks in exchange for peace.

Arafat was not satisfied with Barak's offer. For him, full Israeli withdrawal from all the occupied territories, including all of East Jerusalem with the Haram al-Sharif (Temple Mount), was the only acceptable solution. A Palestinian state would need to be established and recognized with East Jerusalem as its capital. Refugees would need to have the right to return to their homes or would need to receive compensation for their loss. To Arafat, what was offered was inadequate: The refugee problem was only vaguely mentioned, land exchange was not balanced, and both the Haram al-Sharif and parts of Arab Jerusalem were to stay under Israeli sovereignty.

Clinton vented his frustrations over the collapse of the peace process and directed his anger at Arafat. Clinton believed that Arafat turned down the best peace deal he ever was going to get and was guaranteeing the election of the more hawkish Ariel Sharon. Clinton also revealed that in his perspective, the key issue that prevented accord was not the division of Jerusalem and the role of the Israelis and Palestinians there but the "right of return" of Palestinian refugees to locations inside

Israel. Arafat continued to insist on the right of return of large numbers of refugees from the 1948 and Six-Day Wars, and these numbers were unacceptable to Israel.

Barak's Deteriorating Political Position

Arafat was greeted in Gaza with acclaim for having refused to abandon his core demand for a sovereign East Jerusalem as the capital of a Palestinian state. Barak returned to a more somber and sober homecoming where he faced protests and demonstrations and the potential disintegration and fall of his government in a vote of no confidence. In addition to the ministers who had resigned just before he went to Camp David, Foreign Minister David Levy resigned after his return on the grounds that Barak had broken the agreements under which his government had been established by offering the Palestinians control of parts of Jerusalem. Levy argued that he could not explain things with which he did not agree. With the resignations from his cabinet, Barak's government was reduced from a total of 75 of the Knesset's 120 seats in July 1999 to only 30 seats as of August 2000, although the prime minister could rely on some support from outside the government for retention of power.

At the end of July, the Knesset passed the first reading of a law concerning Jerusalem, by a vote of 71 to 27. It would amend the Basic Law: Jerusalem the Capital of Israel and fix the boundaries of Jerusalem. Any subsequent transfer of any neighborhoods or quarters then included within the city's municipal boundaries to the Palestinian Authority or another non-Israeli entity would now require a majority of 61 votes in the Knesset for approval. Barak's government noted that the law was superfluous, as there was already one on the statute books from 1998 that determined that a majority of 61 members of the Knesset was required to relinquish any sovereign Israeli territory. Nonetheless, the argument lost, and Barak was further embarrassed as his proposals at Camp David were clearly the target of the proposed law.

Also awaiting Barak upon return from Camp David was the election for the post of president, which had been vacated with Weizman's resignation the day before the summit began. Barak proposed that Shimon Peres be elected in the hope that Peres would represent the state well in the international community and would be able to use the platform of the largely ceremonial presidency to support peace efforts. Opposing him was Moshe Katsav, a relatively unknown Israeli

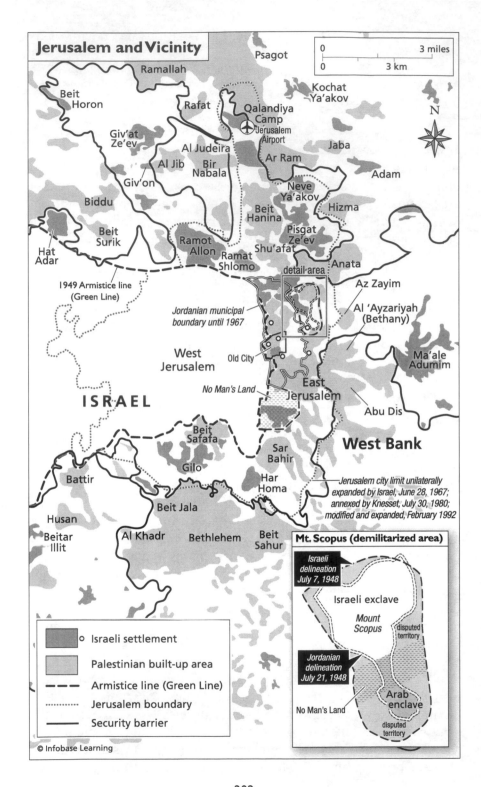

Jerusalem and Vicinity

| 0 | 3 miles |
| 0 | 3 km |

N

Psagot

Ramallah

Beit Horon

Rafat

Kochat Ya'akov

Qalandiya Camp
Jerusalem Airport

Giv'at Ze'ev

Al Judeira

Jaba

Al Jib

Bir Nabala

Ar Ram

Giv'on

Adam

Biddu

Neve Ya'akov

Hizma

Beit Hanina

Beit Surik

Ramot Allon

Pisgat Ze'ev

Hat Adar

Ramat Shlomo

Shu'afat

Anata

1949 Armistice line (Green Line)

Az Zayim

Jordanian municipal boundary until 1967

detail area

Al 'Ayzariyah (Bethany)

West Jerusalem

Old City

Ma'ale Adumim

ISRAEL

No Man's Land

East Jerusalem

Abu Dis

Beit Safafa

West Bank

Sar Bahir

Gilo

Battir

Har Homa

Jerusalem city limit unilaterally expanded by Israel, June 28, 1967; annexed by Knesset, July 30, 1980; modified and expanded, February 1992

Beit Jala

Husan

Beitar Illit

Al Khadr

Bethlehem

Beit Sahur

Mt. Scopus (demilitarized area)

Israeli delineation July 7, 1948

Israeli exclave

Mount Scopus

disputed territory

Jordanian delineation July 21, 1948

Arab enclave

No Man's Land

disputed territory

⊙	Israeli settlement
	Palestinian built-up area
– – –	Armistice line (Green Line)
··········	Jerusalem boundary
——	Security barrier

© Infobase Learning

202

Prime Minister Ehud Barak (left) congratulates newly elected (July 2000) president Moshe Katsav (right). Knesset Speaker Avraham Burg is in the center. (Israel National Photo Collection; Photographer: Ya'acov Sa'ar)

political figure nominated by the Likud Party. His views were more reflective of and representative of Israel's majority population, the Sephardim, and the Second Israel, but the conventional wisdom was that Peres would win by a significant margin because he was a public favorite and Katsav was barely recognizable. In a stunning upset, however, Katsav won in a second round of Knesset voting by a margin of 63 to 57.

Katsav's victory marked what appeared to be a humiliating end to Peres's political career and was another blow to Barak. Katsav was one of the first of Israel's political leaders to rise to prominence from a poor, new-immigrant town on the nation's socioeconomic and geographic periphery. Iranian born, Katsav started his political career as Israel's youngest mayor of Kiryat Malachi in 1969, when he was but 24. He was elected to parliament in 1977 and became tourism minister and deputy prime minister.

Within this setting, after the summit's collapse, there was a general realization of the need to regain some momentum in the peace process and to sustain some of the positive achievements of the summit.

Senior negotiators sought to move forward from the compromises that were achieved on such issues as security, borders, refugees, and settlements. But the Palestinians were talking about unilaterally declaring a Palestinian state if no agreement was reached by September 13. Clinton, in turn, suggested that the United States might move its embassy to Jerusalem, thereby giving recognition to Jerusalem as the capital of Israel.

9

THE AL-AQSA INTIFADA
AND SHARON'S ASCENT
TO POWER
(2000–2002)

The failure of the Camp David summit marked the formal end of the Oslo process, the hope that the Arab-Israeli conflict might end, and the hope of Israel's acceptance by its neighbors as a legitimate Jewish state in the Middle East. For Israel, it also ushered in a period of violence, without security for Israel and Israelis. Ultimately, the intifada and the accompanying violence paved the way for Ariel Sharon to be elected prime minister of Israel and to institute new policies designed to ensure the security of Israel.

Sharon's Visit to the Temple Mount

On September 28, 2000, opposition leader Ariel Sharon visited the Temple Mount, Judaism's holiest area. The mount is the site of the biblical First and Second Temples and a touchstone of the faith. The elevated platform, known to Muslims as Haram al-Sharif, or Noble Sanctuary, is revered as Islam's third holiest site.

The visit, on which Sharon was accompanied by more than 1,000 police officers, infuriated Palestinians, other Arabs, and some Israelis, who saw the visit as a provocation. Barak regarded it as a domestic political act and a security issue but did not anticipate the levels of violence and the lethality that followed; he refused to prohibit the visit.

The visit spurred serious clashes that day that continued into Friday, September 29, when a large number of unarmed Palestinian demonstrators and a large Israeli police contingent confronted each other. Palestinians threw stones at police and Jewish worshippers in the vicinity

The Western Wall, also known as the Wailing Wall and, in Hebrew, Hakotel (The Wall), Judaism's holiest site, with the Dome of the Rock situated above it on the Temple Mount (Courtesy Bernard Reich)

of the Western Wall where Jews had gathered to pray. By day's end, four Palestinian demonstrators were killed on the Temple Mount, and more than 200 were injured. Others were killed and injured elsewhere.

Violence spread across the West Bank and the Gaza Strip and within Israel for several days. At first, the violence was limited to Palestinian youngsters throwing rocks at Israeli civilians to which the IDF responded with gunfire. Soon, however, there was a growing use of gunfire by armed Palestinians against the IDF and Israeli settlers and settlements, leading to Israeli counterattacks that included the use of nonlethal weapons, heavy weaponry, and snipers targeting Palestinian gunmen. Palestinian calls to continue and expand the uprising became general and constant, and the term *intifada* came back into general use. Calls for Palestinian resistance came from individual figures and movements as well as from the media controlled by the PA. School was suspended on the third day, releasing students for participation in demonstrations, and sporadic efforts by Palestinian security officers to control the crowds were gradually abandoned. Public support for continuing the intifada remained high.

Once the violence had begun, Israel's countermeasures became an additional source of grievances among Palestinians. The policy of closure of the territories and the establishment of hundreds of roadblocks made Palestinian movement between towns almost impossible. As a result, Palestinian life came to a virtual standstill.

The al-Aqsa Intifada

The outbreak of a new uprising, dubbed the al-Aqsa Intifada, came as a major shock to most Israelis. Although the Camp David summit had failed to achieve a major breakthrough, the ensuing violence was not widely anticipated or expected. It reminded many of the Intifada of the late 1980s and early 1990s, which was formally terminated with the signing of the Oslo Accords in 1993. Clearly the outbreak of another intifada suggested that the chasm between Israel and the Palestinians was greater than had been believed or anticipated.

Earlier violence, as in 1996, after the Israeli government allowed the opening of a tunnel alongside the Western Wall in Jerusalem despite protests by Palestinians, had been quelled quickly by an Arafat order to stop the violence. Why not this time? In September 2000, Arafat clearly controlled the Palestinian populace, and in the view of many Israelis and others, this time he helped foment, escalate, supply, fund, and otherwise facilitate the acts of violence and terrorism.

Palestinians and some Israelis, especially on the liberal Left, argued that Sharon's highly publicized, heavily guarded visit to the Temple Mount had ignited the Palestinian violence. Sharon remained unapologetic and asserted his right and the right of every Jew to visit Jerusalem's Jewish holy places. Sharon instead put the blame for the demonstrations and riots on Arafat. The police had not anticipated major disturbances after the visit, and Israel had received assurances from the Palestinian security chief in the West Bank that as long as Sharon did not enter Muslim shrines, there was no cause for concern.

To the Palestinians, however, Sharon was not just any Jew or Israeli; he was a hated figure, the architect of Israel's invasion of Lebanon in 1982 when Christian militia allied with Israel massacred hundreds of Palestinians in the Beirut refugee camps of Sabra and Shatila. To many, Sharon had defiled the al-Aqsa Mosque and provoked the negative feelings of the entire Muslim world.

Nevertheless, to most Israelis, even those who saw Sharon's visit as a mistake and some among those who saw it as provocative, the visit was not what precipitated the armed conflict and its subsequent escalation. For many, rather, the Sharon visit was seen as a pretext for a planned escalation of Palestinian violence to generate increased attention to the Israeli occupation and efforts for a solution to the Israeli-Palestinian conflict favorable to the Palestinian position. And there was evidence indicating Palestinian leadership preparations for the second intifada, including the releasing of militants from Palestinian custody and detention, the military training of Palestinian children in summer camps, an increase in hostile propaganda, the failure to confiscate illegal weapons, and the stockpiling of medical supplies and of food, among other factors. There were also indicators in various Palestinian media and other public statements that anticipated the violence. Once the intifada began, the Israelis noted the active involvement of Palestinian security personnel in the killing of Israelis.

Substantial violence developed. For Israelis, the intifada that began in September 2000 confirmed some of their worst concerns and created an environment of fear, anxiety, and uncertainty that had rarely been that negative since the early days of independence. Despite the positive atmosphere in the years that followed Oslo, the second intifada marked a new period of concern. Many Israelis were convinced that there was no Palestinian partner for peace. The Israelis, to varying degrees, believed that Arafat legitimized terror and had never reconciled himself to Israel's existence. Rather, he repeated the old myths and policies, which had led the Palestinians to their current situation.

Crisis Management, Fall 2000

After the failure to reach agreement at Camp David and with the deteriorating situation in the fall of 2000, efforts were made to achieve some form of crisis management. On October 4, in Paris, the United States brokered attempts to mediate between the parties and end the violence. The talks failed when Arafat did not sign an accord reached verbally between the parties that their respective commanders be given orders to withdraw troops and restore calm to flash points under their control.

The Israeli-Palestinian crisis threatened to spread across Israel's other borders. On October 7, Hizballah members abducted three Israeli soldiers on the Israeli side of the border with Lebanon. Under immense pressure to respond, Barak issued a 48-hour ultimatum for the Palestinians to halt their assaults on Israeli military outposts and civilian settlements and threatened to direct the IDF and the security forces to use all means at their disposal to halt the violence if the PA failed to comply. Tensions came to a peak on October 10 when two Israeli army reservists, apparently having taken a wrong turn in their car, were lynched by a mob in Ramallah, with the complicity of the Palestinian police. The lynching, caught on camera by an Italian film crew and subsequently televised internationally, led the IDF to retaliate by attacking five targets associated with the Palestinian Security Services.

An emergency summit meeting was held on October 16–17 at Sharm el-Sheikh, Egypt, hosted by Egyptian president Hosni Mubarak. But, although a general cease-fire understanding was reached, the meeting also demonstrated the overall erosion of the peace process. Israel and the Palestinians, who had been talking in the summer about final status issues, were now unable even to sign a formal agreement to end the violence that began in September. Direct Israeli-Palestinian talks generally gave way to a process in which Clinton acted as intermediary. At the end of the summit, Clinton summarized its results. He noted that the primary objective had been to end the violence so that the parties could again resume their efforts toward peace. To achieve that goal, the parties agreed to issue public statements unequivocally calling for an end to violence. They also agreed to take immediate concrete measures to end the confrontation, eliminate points of friction, and maintain calm. To accomplish this, Israel and the Palestinians agreed to return to the situation that existed prior to the current crisis. The United States agreed to create, with the parties and in consultation with the UN secretary-general, a fact-finding committee on the events of the past weeks and on how to prevent their recurrence. The commission, led by former U.S. senator George Mitchell, began its inquiries on December 11.

On October 20, the UN General Assembly, in an "emergency special session on illegal Israeli actions in occupied East Jerusalem and the rest of the occupied Palestinian territory," condemned the violence that had taken place in Jerusalem, the West Bank, and Gaza, since September 28, especially the "excessive use of force by Israeli forces against Palestinian citizens." This resolution followed a similar Security Council Resolution 1322 adopted on October 7.

On October 22, after a two-day meeting of Arab heads of state in Cairo, a communiqué announced support for the Palestinian uprising and encouraged the suspension of further political and economic links with Israel, while failing to endorse the U.S.-brokered Sharm el-Sheikh cease-fire. The Arab leaders also called upon the UN Security Council to "assume responsibility of providing the necessary protection for the Palestinian people . . . by considering the establishment of an international force or presence for this purpose."

Israel, in response, issued a statement rejecting the threats emanating from the summit and condemned "the call for continued violence." It called on the Palestinians to honor their commitments to halt the violence and incitement and to restore calm and order immediately.

On November 1, hopes for an end to the violence briefly rose when Peres met Arafat at the Gaza-Israel border. Despite the meeting, Arafat did not order an end to the violence. During November, shooting incidents directed at the IDF as well as against Israeli civilians, especially in the Gilo area on the outskirts of Jerusalem, increased, with the Israeli army retaliating. The situation seemed to escalate further when on November 22, a car bomb detonated near a bus in the coastal city of Hadera, killing two Israelis and wounding 60. The IDF chose not to retaliate.

In late November, Barak made new proposals in which he seemed to abandon his quest for an all-inclusive end-of-conflict agreement between Israel and the Palestinians, such as was discussed at Camp David, opting instead for an interim agreement based on the declaration of a Palestinian state. Violence continued, with gun battles between Israelis and Palestinians becoming a frequent occurrence. Israel adopted a policy of systematic targeted assassination of Palestinian instigators of violence, although it refrained from eliminating leaders within the higher political echelons. Israel described its strategy as striking at those who are "leading the shooting cells and their deputies"; the Palestinians referred to it as "state terrorism."

In mid-December, efforts to revive peace talks between the Palestinians and the Israelis were renewed. Foreign Minister Shlomo Ben-Ami indicated that Israel had dropped its precondition for restarting talks with the Palestinians and would now be willing to negotiate as long as it saw an effort on the Palestinian side to rearrest Islamic militants, clamp down on gunmen, and halt incitement against Israel. Initial meetings in Gaza between Ben-Ami; Gilad Sher, Barak's chief of staff; and Arafat were fruitless, but a new round of talks was arranged.

On December 23, a five-day discussion at Bolling Air Force Base in Washington, D.C., between Israeli and Palestinian negotiators ended. Although the sides failed to close a deal, Clinton put forward a comprehensive framework and asked the parties to respond by December 27. Reportedly, this plan included a trade-off: Palestinian sovereignty on the Temple Mount/Haram al-Sharif for giving up the demand that Palestinian refugees could return to Israel. While Israel accepted the Clinton proposals as a basis for discussion "provided that they become the basis for discussion also for the Palestinians," the Palestinians failed to provide the United States with an unequivocal answer.

The so-called Clinton Plan was essentially a proposal to bridge the gap between the positions of Israel and of the Palestinians. Barak's most serious reservation concerned Clinton's proposal of transferring the Temple Mount plaza and mosques to the Palestinian state that would be established under the final accord. In a cabinet meeting, Barak repeated his pledge "not to sign a document that transfers the Temple Mount to Palestinian sovereignty." Foreign Minister Ben-Ami, on the other hand, enthusiastically endorsed the U.S. proposal. There were additional concerns relating primarily to the security aspects of the proposal and particularly the important requirement that the Palestinian state be demilitarized.

Barak Resigns

Under increasing domestic criticism, and feeling his prospects were better in a race for prime minister without parliamentary elections, Barak decided on a bold gambit. On December 9, he unexpectedly announced his resignation (it took effect on December 12), thus setting the stage for new direct elections for prime minister, but not for parliament, within 60 days. Barak remained in office as head of a caretaker government.

Election 2001

Under the existing legislation, only sitting members of parliament could run for the prime minister's position. Former prime minister Benjamin Netanyahu had resigned from parliament after his 1999

ARIEL SHARON
(FEBRUARY 27, 1928-)

Ariel (Arik) Sharon was born in 1928 in Kfar Malal, a farm village not far from present-day Tel Aviv. At the age of 14, he joined the Haganah, was wounded during the War of Independence in 1948, and subsequently rose swiftly in the ranks of the Israel Defense Forces (IDF). He participated in all of Israel's six major wars from 1948 to 1982. In 1953, he established the 101 Unit for special operations (a commando force known for its daring counterterrorist operations behind enemy lines), and in 1956, he commanded a paratroop brigade, units of which parachuted into the Mitla Pass to mark the beginning of the Sinai Campaign. He then studied at the British Staff College in Camberley and upon his return, was appointed head of the IDF School of Infantry. In 1962, he became director of military training of the IDF, and that same year, he graduated from the law school of Hebrew University. In the Six-Day War of 1967, he commanded an armored division that fought in the Sinai Peninsula and in 1969, became commanding officer of the Southern Command.

In June 1973, Sharon resigned from the IDF, joined the Liberal Party, and was instrumental in bringing about the alignment of Herut, the Free Center, the State List, and the Liberal Party within the framework of the Likud bloc. The Yom Kippur War brought him back to active military service as a reserve officer in command of an armored division, units of which were the first to cross the Suez Canal and establish an Israeli bridgehead on the Egyptian side. In December 1973, he stood for election to the Knesset and was elected on behalf of the Liberal Party faction of the Likud bloc. In December 1974, Sharon resigned from the Knesset in order that his reserve commission with the IDF might be reinstated. In June 1975, he was appointed adviser to Prime Minister Yitzhak Rabin on security affairs and held that position until April 1976, when he resigned to form the Shlomzion Party, which gained two seats in the elections to the ninth Knesset in May 1977. Immediately following the elections, the Shlomzion Party merged with the Herut Party faction of the Likud bloc, and it was on this ticket that he was elected to the 10th Knesset on May 30, 1981.

Sharon was appointed minister of agriculture in June 1977. On August 5, 1981, he was sworn in as minister of defense but was forced to resign from this position in February 1983 after the Kahan

Commission of Inquiry report concerning the massacre at the Sabra and Shatila refugee camps in Lebanon was published. But he remained in the cabinet. He later became minister of industry and trade and in December 1988, was reappointed to that position. In June 1990, he became minister of construction and housing and in that capacity, instituted a plan to increase substantially the number of Jewish settlers in Judea and Samaria (the West Bank). Although he initially announced his intention to vie for the prime ministership in 1996, he subsequently withdrew and instead concentrated on unifying the center-right vote behind the Likud's prime ministerial candidate, Benjamin Netanyahu. Sharon played an important role in facilitating the formation of the joint "national camp" list for the 1996 Knesset election involving Likud, Gesher, and Tzomet. He was initially not included in the cabinet formed by Netanyahu, but after intense negotiations, he agreed to accept a new portfolio, that of minister of national infrastructure. He also was named a member of Netanyahu's kitchen cabinet on foreign and security policy and in that capacity formulated a model of "strategic interests" in the West Bank that helped to set the parameters for the internal debate in Israel over the future nature of relations with the Palestinians. Appointed foreign minister in October 1998, he joined Netanyahu in negotiations with the Palestinians that culminated with the Wye River Memorandum of October 23, 1998.

On May 17, 1999, Sharon was reelected to the Knesset on the Likud list. He was chosen temporary leader of the party after Netanyahu's resignation following his defeat by One Israel's candidate, Ehud Barak, in the direct election for prime minister and Likud's defeat in the Knesset election. On September 2, he was elected party leader, defeating Ehud Olmert and Meir Shitreet. A year later, in September 2000, he visited the Temple Mount—an action regarded by the Palestinians as a provocation—which was followed by the al-Aqsa Intifada. Sharon was elected prime minister of Israel in February 2001 and in March was sworn in.

After elections on January 28, 2003, Sharon was charged with forming a new government, and he presented it to the Knesset on February 27, 2003. He planned and executed the policy that led to the dismantling of all the Israeli settlements in the Gaza Strip and Israel's total withdrawal from the area. In November 2005, he left the Likud and established a new political party—Kadima—that he planned to lead in the 2006 election. However, he suffered an incapacitating stroke in January 2006, effectively terminating his role in Israel's national life.

defeat and thus was not eligible to contest the race. There was an effort to change the Basic Law to permit private citizens, who were not members of the Knesset, to run for prime minister. The amendment, referred to as the "Netanyahu Amendment," was passed by the Knesset on December 19. However, Netanyahu conditioned his candidacy for prime minister on general elections in which he assumed (as public opinion polls suggested) that right-wing parties, especially Likud, would gain seats in the Knesset. Thus, he reasoned, he could win and govern with a right-wing coalition majority. The Knesset voted against general elections, apparently because elections could jeopardize the status of the incumbent members. Netanyahu announced that he would not run, leaving Sharon as the sole Likud choice. Peres sought to challenge Barak as a center-left candidate but failed to gain the necessary support. Barak was left as the sole candidate of the center-left camp.

The stage was set for a face-off between Barak, who was to ask the nation for a new vote of confidence and a "referendum on peace," and Sharon the leader of Likud. It was a time to reassess the political/policy landscape and to identify a leader and direction for the state.

Two candidates with clear differences in policy and perception presented very different choices to Israeli voters. Many Israelis believed that Barak's credibility had deteriorated when he failed to act against the violence in the al-Aqsa Intifada and continued to offer further concessions under fire. Barak had failed to achieve any significant movement toward peace, despite substantial concessions to the Palestinian position. At the same time, Israel's Arab population was concerned about the apparent deterioration of its status. Israeli Arabs expressed their dismay and distress by demonstrating (and some were killed and wounded) and by voting in small numbers (primarily through absences and abstentions), rather than supporting Barak in substantial numbers as they had in 1999. Sharon made clear in his campaign that he considered the Oslo process "dead" and that security would be the central requirement and objective of his administration. He demanded that an end to Palestinian violence must precede a return to negotiations that would not be restricted by the Oslo process. Sharon understood Israeli concerns about security, especially personal security. Israelis sought, and Sharon promoted, "security and peace."

The political fortunes of Barak were also hurt by Israelis' recent pattern of voting against the incumbent, as well as a general view of Barak as a political neophyte and someone who had too much self-confidence or, perhaps, arrogance. He was attacked for constantly changing his mind and for consulting with few of his advisers. An effective campaign slogan against him was "Is he Dr. Zig or Mr. Zag?" referring to the fact that his positions could change from one day to the next, be it on domestic issues, foreign policy, or people with whom he worked or trusted.

The 2001 election had the lowest voter turnout in Israeli history. Generally about 80 percent of eligible voters participate; this time only about 62 percent of the eligible voters went to the polls. It was the first and, so far, the only election in Israel's history in which voters went to the polls to choose only a prime minister. The low overall voter turnout included a virtual boycott by Israel's Arab voters. The Israeli voters made a clear decision—Sharon defeated Barak by a margin of 63.3 percent to 37.7 percent of valid votes cast. Sharon won the election overwhelmingly, primarily because he suggested a different way to ensure personal security for the average Israeli. He became the sixth prime minister in a decade.

The focus of the campaign debate, the election itself, Sharon's victory speech, and the government's program was on security and peace. In his victory statement, Sharon noted that there was a public thirst to stand together to focus on the challenges facing Israel and thus he called "for the establishment of a national unity government, as wide as possible" to restore security to the citizens of Israel and achieve peace and stability in the region.

Soon after the election, Barak announced his resignation from the Knesset and from politics, setting off another internal search for a Labor Party leader. Knesset member Salah Tarif, grandson of Sheikh Amin Tarif who had been the spiritual leader of the Druze community, took Barak's seat in parliament. He was appointed as minister without portfolio in the government and became the first non-Jewish cabinet minister in the history of Israel. Reactions were widespread and varied. Tarif had served in the IDF and was mayor of Julis before joining the Knesset. Tarif resigned in January 2002 anticipating criminal charges in an alleged bribery scandal.

The Aftermath of the Election

Following Sharon's overwhelming victory, his first priority was to create a governing coalition, and his most urgent challenge was Palestinian violence. He took office with broad popular support from a population that believed that its security had deteriorated significantly during Barak's tenure. In a press conference on February 25, 2001, Sharon said:

> *I would like to emphasize that Israel's citizens have the full right to live in this country, tiny small country, the only democratic country in the region, that is the only place where the Jewish people have the right and the capabilities to defend themselves by themselves, and that is something that they have to preserve.*

Sharon focused on the need for the PA to take immediate action to stop acts of terror and violence and noted that he would conduct negotiations with the PA only following the cessation of hostilities.

On March 7, Israel's largest government ever to that point, with 26 ministers and 15 deputy ministers from eight parties, was installed. It was supported by the votes of Likud, Labor, Shas, Israel Beiteinu, National Union (a coalition of right-wing political parties), Yisrael B'Aliya, One Nation (a centrist party), and the New Way (the one-person faction led by Dalia Rabin-Pelossof, Rabin's daughter). But there was the potential for additional supporting votes from some of Sharon's natural allies who were not part of the cabinet, including the NRP, Gesher, United Torah Judaism, and ex-Likud members from the remnants of the Center Party. Despite the coalition's large size, there were outstanding issues, especially for *haredi* (ultra-Orthodox) parties, that made the coalition potentially fragile.

Sharon's government, approved by a Knesset vote of 72 to 21, was wide and broad-based, including both Likud and Labor as well as a number of smaller secular-nationalist and religious parties. Noteworthy was the inclusion of former Labor Party leader, prime minister, and Nobel laureate Shimon Peres as foreign minister and Labor's Benjamin Ben-Eliezer as minister of defense. The cabinet also included two well-known "hawks" on the Arab-Israeli issue, Rehavam Ze'evi and Avigdor Lieberman. Labor and Likud were joined by a wide-range of other parties and individuals from points across the political spectrum. Among them was Rabin-Pelossof, who joined Sharon's government as deputy defense minister because, as she noted, the issue of national unity was a top priority and she was willing to make compromises for it. The government reflected a broad Israeli consensus that the time was *not* ripe to achieve a peace treaty. Supporters and opponents of Oslo joined a cabinet whose first objective was to stop the violence and restore security to the average Israeli.

In his inaugural speech to the Knesset, Sharon stressed: "Citizens of Israel, the government, under my leadership, will act to restore security to the citizens of Israel, and to achieve genuine peace and stability in the area." Sharon's assessment of the situation was that "despite considerable concessions we made on the way to peace—by all governments of Israel—in the past few years, we still haven't found a willingness for reconciliation and true peace on the other side." Thus, "we will demand of the Palestinians that they renounce violence, terror, and incitement, and of the Palestinian Authority that they fulfill their obligations and combat terrorism directed against Israel, its citizens, and soldiers." With the end of violence would come negotiations. He noted:

> Jerusalem is the great dream, for which Jews yearned for and prayed for in every generation. . . . Jerusalem was and will be the eternal capital of the Jewish people. Israeli Prime Ministers have always reiterated this commitment in their inauguration speeches, including the late Yitzhak Rabin. So, too, in the words of the vow: "If I forget thee Jerusalem, let my right hand lose its cunning" . . .

He left room for potential compromises on portions of the city.

The Peace Process Restarted? Or, Violence Continued

The establishment of new administrations in Jerusalem and in Washington, D.C. (George W. Bush took office in January 2001), suggested that the peace process would take new form and have new content. The first objective was to reduce, or eliminate, terror and violence so that negotiations could resume. This had been stressed by Sharon during and after his election campaign and was noted by Colin Powell during his first visit to the region as U.S. secretary of state in late February 2001. Powell stressed continued U.S. support for direct negotiations between Israel and the PA based on UN Security Council Resolutions 242 and 338, a position of continuity in U.S. policy. Powell also stressed the traditionally close relationship of the United States and Israel.

The violence continued. On March 12, the Israeli army sealed off the city of Ramallah, the unofficial seat of government of the PA in the West Bank, blocking roads with trenches, mounds of earth, and checkpoints backed by tanks and armored troop carriers. Palestinians protested. Sharon denied that he was pursuing a new security policy and noted that it was directed "against those who attack and those behind them" while easing the situation for the majority of the population. Toward the end of March, Israeli helicopter gunships bombarded training camps and bases of Arafat's personal security forces after a Palestinian suicide bomber killed two Israeli teenagers.

Sharon came under mounting pressure to take decisive action against Palestinian attacks that had escalated since he took office. Israel adopted as policy the targeting of individuals directly responsible for violence and terrorism as deemed by the Shin Bet (General Security Service). If the PA did not act to prevent terrorism, the Israeli military would respond in "self-defense." Sharon's office stated: "The government's guiding principle is constant and persistent action against the terrorists, as well as against those who both dispatch and assist them."

The Bush administration spent much of the spring of 2001 determining its course of action on a number of Middle Eastern issues. President Bush conspicuously refused to meet with Arafat, focusing on the need for the violence to abate and trying to avoid the appearance of the constant meetings of Clinton with Arafat.

The Mitchell Report

In October 2000, President Clinton had asked former senator George Mitchell and four eminent international colleagues to investigate and write a report about the outbreak of violence after the failure of the Camp David summit "to determine what happened and how to avoid it recurring in the future." After visits to the region and consultation with regional leaders, the Sharm el-Sheikh Fact-Finding Committee Report (popularly known as the Mitchell Report) was sent to President Bush on April 30 and issued in May, immediately engendering a debate about its recommendations.

The report provided the first authoritative assessment of developments since the beginning of the Intifada. The basic conclusion was that Palestinians and Israelis had lost all confidence in each other and that Israeli and Palestinian leaders needed to take measures to break the cycle of violence. The report called on the PA to "make clear through concrete action to Palestinians and Israelis alike that terrorism is reprehensible, and unacceptable, and that the Palestinian Authority will make a 100 percent effort to prevent terrorism and to punish perpetrators." At the same time, it called on the Palestinians to "prevent gunmen from using Palestinian populated areas to fire upon" Israelis.

It called on the Israel Defense Forces to consider withdrawing to positions held before September 28, 2000, and to adopt policies encouraging nonlethal responses to unarmed demonstrators. Its conclusion was that in order to move ahead with Israeli-Palestinian negotiations, there had to be a cessation of all violence followed by confidence-building efforts. The report recommended that Israel freeze settlements, including natural growth, that Palestinians crack down on terrorism, and that both sides halt violence without condition. It apportioned responsibility for the situation to both sides. Israel expressed reservations about the recommendation calling for a freeze on building Jewish settlements in the West Bank and Gaza as an unwarranted concession on an issue that should be resolved only in peace talks, not in advance.

On May 21, the Bush administration endorsed the report and began diplomatic action in its support while stressing that the United States was not putting forward a peace plan but would work to implement a series of confidence-building measures that were contained in the report. Arafat accepted the report. Nonetheless, it was followed by a new round of violence.

Arafat Is "Engaged in Terrorist Activity"

On Saturday night, June 2, 2001, the Israeli political-security cabinet met and issued a communiqué concerning the previous night's terrorist attack in which 21 young Israelis at Tel Aviv's Dolphinarium disco were killed.

> The Government of Israel has determined that the Palestinian Authority (PA) and Chairman Arafat are engaged in terrorist activity, encourage it and are inciting to hatred and violence. The PA has not only violated all the obligations and agreements to fight the terrorist and incitement infrastructure, but its members are themselves engaged in terrorism and incitement. The PA has established in its territory a coalition of terror, and is attempting to disguise it with words of peace as lip service to the international community, while continuing to incite its people to hatred and violence. The violent Palestinian attack against Israel came after far-reaching Israeli proposals for peace were rejected.

The cycle of violence and terrorism by the Palestinians and Israel's retaliatory responses continued through the summer of 2001.

September 11, 2001, and After

The regional situation was overshadowed by the September 11, 2001, terrorist attacks on the United States. The Bush administration worked to create an international coalition to respond to terrorism focusing on Osama bin Laden and the Islamic fundamentalist al-Qaeda movement that he headed and sought Arab and Muslim participation in that effort. In a statement, bin Laden attributed the attacks in part to the plight of the Palestinians and the unequivocal U.S. support for Israel. Although these comments were widely discounted as efforts to split further the United States and the Muslim states, many in the Palestinian and the broader Arab worlds saw this as an accurate depiction of the situation.

In a press conference on October 11, President Bush noted that his administration would continue to focus on resolution of the Arab-Israeli conflict within the context of continued U.S.-Israeli friendship. At the same time, he noted,

> *I also stated the other day that if we ever get into the Mitchell process, where we can start discussing a political solution in the Middle East, that I believe there ought to be a Palestinian state, the boundaries of which will be negotiated by the parties so long as the Palestinian state recognizes the right of Israel to exist, and will treat Israel with respect, and will be peaceful on her borders.*

Powell elaborated on these themes in an address on November 19, where he noted a vision of a region in which Israelis and Arabs lived together in peace, security, and dignity. He stressed the need to stop terror and violence. But it continued.

The Assassination of Rehavam Ze'evi

The assassination of Tourism Minister Rehavam ("Gandhi") Ze'evi by Palestinian gunmen on October 17, 2001, outside his hotel room in Jerusalem was unprecedented. It was the first time that an Israeli cabinet minister was killed by a Palestinian since Israeli independence. The Popular Front for the Liberation of Palestine (PFLP), which had rejected the Oslo Accords and opposed the PA, claimed responsibility and said it was in retaliation for Israel's assassination of its leader, Abu Ali Mustafa, in August.

The Israeli reaction was immediate and significant. Prime Minister Sharon announced that, "everything has changed" as this was clear evidence that Arafat had failed to carry out his promise to prevent more violence. U.S. president Bush condemned the assassination "in the strongest terms" and called on the PA to act against those responsible. The U.S. State Department called it a "despicable act of terrorism" and called upon Arafat and the PA to find and arrest those responsible.

Ze'evi had been a prominent individual in Israel's military and political spheres. In prestate days, he was a Palmach commando. He served in Israel's War of Independence and in the Six-Day War. He had an illustrious military career, rising to the rank of general. Politically, he was outspoken on his belief of the need to transfer Arabs from lands claimed by Israel and reflected right-wing political attitudes and perspectives. Although Ze'evi was head of a right-wing political party (Moledet), his murder generated strong responses from both the Right and Left. The leader of the Meretz opposition at the opposite end of the political spectrum noted that the murder of Ze'evi put the PA to a test. He said the PA could not remain silent for long and would have to take strong measures to deal with the murderers.

Sharon v. Arafat

Violence and especially terrorism against Israelis escalated dramatically in early December 2001. Attacks in Jerusalem and Haifa elicited a special cabinet meeting on December 3 at which the cabinet determined that actions more wide ranging than those taken against Palestinian terrorism to that point were required:

> According to the decision by the Ministerial Committee for National Security of October 17, 2001, the Government has determined that the Palestinian Authority is an entity that supports terrorism, and must be dealt with accordingly. In the framework of this decision, the Ministerial Committee for National Security is authorized to decide on operational steps (military, diplomatic, information and economic). This determination is subject to change—by Cabinet decision—if the Palestinian Authority fulfills its commitments, according to the agreements, to prevent and foil terrorism, punish terrorists and dismantle the terrorism infrastructure. . . .
>
> By the authority of section 8 of the Anti-Terrorism Regulations, the government hereby declares that the Tanzim and Force 17 [Presidential Guard] are terrorist organizations, and will be acted against accordingly.

President Bush had issued a statement about the attacks on December 2:

> I was horrified and saddened to learn of the bombings that took place tonight in Jerusalem. I strongly condemn them as acts of murder that no person of conscience can tolerate and no cause can ever justify. . . . Chairman Arafat and the Palestinian Authority must immediately find and arrest those responsible for those hideous murders. They must also act swiftly and decisively against the organizations that support them. Now more than ever, Chairman Arafat and the Palestinian Authority must demonstrate through their actions, and not merely their words, their commitment to fight terror.

"ARAFAT IS IRRELEVANT"

Jerusalem, December 12, 2001
Security Cabinet Decision

1. The Government of Israel takes a grave view of the deadly attacks this evening (December 12).
2. The Government of Israel views Arafat as directly responsible for this series of attacks, and, in light of this, states that Arafat is no longer relevant from Israel's point of view, and there will be no more communication with him.
3. The Security Cabinet approves the military actions as presented by the Defense Minister and the Chief of Staff at the "kitchen cabinet" meeting this evening.
4. The IDF will deploy rapidly for action in the urban areas of the West Bank and the Gaza Strip, in order to carry out arrests and to confiscate weapons.
5. The defense establishment will present to the Cabinet as soon as possible the revised methods for combatting the Hamas, Islamic Jihad and other terrorist organizations in light of the increased severity of terrorist attacks.
6. The Government of Israel views the Palestinian Authority and its head as directly responsible for the difficult situation of the Palestinian population. The Government of Israel will continue to make every effort to assist this population.

Israel intensified its crackdown on PA territory in mid-December, a day after Palestinian extremists ambushed a bus in the West Bank, killing at least 10 Israeli civilians, and a day after Israel severed all ties with Arafat, blaming him for Palestinian violence against the Jewish state, including recent attacks that killed 44 people in 11 days. In retaliation, Israeli helicopters and F-16 fighter jets hit Palestinian security force targets in Gaza City, including a compound used by Arafat. Two Israeli missiles struck near a Palestinian mosque while the political and spiritual leaders of the militant Islamic group Hamas were inside. In Ramallah, helicopter gunships fired missiles at a Palestinian government building, and Israeli troops advanced on Arafat's headquarters, sending tanks to within 200 yards of it. Other troops seized the Voice of Palestine radio station compound, bulldozed several buildings, and forced the station off the air. Offices of Arafat's Fatah organization in Jenin were hit in a helicopter raid. Israel also moved against Arafat's senior aides, including Marwan Barghouti, the head of the Fatah faction in the West Bank and one of the most popular figures in the intifada who was linked to a large number of shooting attacks against Israelis. The Israeli security cabinet said that while Arafat would not be personally harmed he was "no longer relevant as far as Israel is concerned and there will be no more contact with him."

The *Karine-A* Affair: "Ship of Terror"

On January 3, 2002, Israel captured the *Karine-A,* a 4,000-ton freighter carrying more than 50 tons of arms destined for Arafat's PA in Gaza. It was the most substantial arms-smuggling incident connected to the Palestinians to date. The capture was a daring and complicated mission by Israeli navy commandos, air force pilots, and the intelligence community in the Red Sea between Sudan and Saudi Arabia about 500 kilometers from Israel's shores and was carried out in a professional, precise, coordinated operation without any casualties.

The inventory of the weapons suggested that most of the cargo was Iranian in origin and included both short- and long-range Katyusha rockets, Sagger guided antitank missiles, light antitank weapons (LAWs), mortars, mines, explosives, sniper rifles, bullets, and other weapons. The ship's captain identified himself as both a longtime member of Arafat's Fatah and a naval adviser to the Palestinian Authority's Ministry of Transport and disclosed his instructions were first to collect arms at a specified point off of Iran's coast and then to sail north through the Red Sea and Suez Canal and transfer them to three small boats that were supposed to "unload in Gaza." Israel noted that there was no doubt that the attempt to smuggle the arms was planned, financed, and carried out by the most senior echelons of the PA.

Israel regarded the smuggling attempt as part of a policy among senior officials in the PA and as confirmation of the PA's intention to continue its policy of terror and violence, to escalate it over time, and to make the attacks more deadly, as well as deeper inside Israel.

Colin Powell, in mid-February, said that Arafat had accepted responsibility for the shipment of arms. "He [Arafat] wrote me a letter three days ago on the *Karine-A,* accepting responsibility—not personal responsibility, but as chairman of the Palestinian Authority."

The Arab Peace Initiative

In February 2002, Saudi Arabia's Crown Prince Abdullah launched a peace initiative that quickly became a focus of discussion and diplomacy. Abdullah's plan was initially "leaked" in an interview and later presented to the Arab League at a summit meeting for its endorsement. The proposal gained the support of the Arab League but only after modifications of the original ideas. Abdullah suggested that the Arab states would be prepared to normalize relations with Israel if Israel met certain conditions. It called for Israel to withdraw to the 1967 lines, remove the remaining Israeli troops from Lebanon, and recognize the right of return of the Palestinian refugees and the establishment of a Palestinian state with East Jerusalem as its capital. It reiterated the Arab stand on UN Security Council Resolution 242 and related resolutions and proposals. The fact that it was Saudi Arabia that proposed it was innovative since the kingdom rarely made public policy initiatives of this ilk.

Israel was pressed to consider the Saudi initiative that was adopted by the Arab League, and subsequently referred to as the Arab Peace Initiative, even though Israel believed that the plan had many problems in that it demanded very tangible concessions from Israel but offered only vague promises of rewards. Nevertheless, Israel did not reject the Saudi plan, as it wanted to see negotiations resume and the Saudi initiative was a plausible starting point.

Negotiations did not resume, however, and the security situation remained unacceptable as Israeli casualties from the intifada continued to grow.

10

A NEW PERSPECTIVE
ON SECURITY
(2002–2006)

In early 2002, a new perspective on security began to emerge in the Israeli government that was informed by the post–September 11 reality. The intifada that had begun in 2000 was considered to be of a different nature from that in the late 1980s, which had terminated with the Oslo Accords in 1993. The first Intifada was seen in Israel as primarily a popular uprising through riots and demonstrations; the al-Aqsa Intifada, on the other hand, was seen as a "top down" conflict with direct connections to Arafat and those around him.

Large-Scale Military Operations Begin

On February 27, 2002, the IDF began a large-scale military operation in several cities and refugee camps in the West Bank and Gaza Strip. It ended about three weeks later with the withdrawal of Israeli troops from Bethlehem and Beit-Jalla on March 18. To that point, it was the largest-scale Israeli military response to the intifada, involving simultaneous actions in several locations in the West Bank and Gaza utilizing air, naval and ground forces. The operations included penetration into areas under full Palestinian control and into refugee camps that had hitherto been virtually off-limits to Israeli forces.

The Israelis struck at the terrorist infrastructure: people, weapons, tunnels for smuggling weapons from Egypt into Rafah in the Gaza Strip, weapons workshops and laboratories, and so on. This marked a shift, from the previous indirect Israeli effort of putting pressure on the PA to put pressure on the terrorists, to direct Israeli action against the terrorists. The Israeli operations had some tactical successes: Some rockets were captured, rocket producing workshops were destroyed, suicide bomber supplies were destroyed, various terrorists were arrested and some killed.

Operation Defensive Shield

The new Israeli policy became official under Operation Defensive Shield. It involved simultaneous actions in several locations in the West Bank and Gaza utilizing air, naval, and ground forces. Previous military incursions were narrowly focused and targeted limited areas. The decision to launch this operation was taken following the suicide bombing of the Passover seder at the Park Hotel in Netanya on March 27. It reflected the belief of Israel's government and public that Palestinian terrorism had reached intolerable levels and that Israel had to take drastic action to contain it because Arafat and the PA could not be induced to take real steps to stop terrorism and to promote that end. Israel could rely only on itself. The method adopted was the temporary reoccupation of population centers in the West Bank where the terrorism infrastructure was located.

The extensive military operations carried out by the IDF in Operation Defensive Shield had several goals included neutralizing the terrorist infrastructure in the West Bank and Gaza Strip, highlighting the PA's involvement with terrorism, and isolating Arafat, who was seen as the principal stimulator of violence. All of this was to be accomplished without escalating the violence into regional conflict and with minimal harm to the Palestinian population.

In a speech to the Knesset on April 8, 2002, Sharon announced:

> *IDF soldiers and officers have been given clear orders: to enter cities and villages which have become havens for terrorists; to catch and arrest terrorists and, primarily, their dispatchers and those who finance and support them; to confiscate weapons intended to be used against Israeli citizens; to expose and destroy terrorist facilities and explosives, laboratories, weapons production factories and secret installations. The orders are clear: target and paralyze anyone who takes up weapons and tries to oppose our troops, resists them or endangers them—and to avoid harming the civilian population.*

Israeli tanks, bulldozers, soldiers, helicopters, and other forces and units moved into and laid siege to cities and towns. On March 29, Israeli forces entered Ramallah where they surrounded and partially destroyed Arafat's compound. Israel also demanded that terrorist suspects hiding there be handed over. On April 1, Israel entered

Bethlehem, and Palestinian gunmen took refuge in the Church of the Nativity on April 3. This was followed by sporadic fighting, and the standoff continued for some time until arrangements were made for the exile of the gunmen to other locations. The forces also entered Tulkarm, Qalqilya, Nablus, and Jenin. Much of the terrorist infrastructure was destroyed, and the PA's facilities were largely devastated. Ramallah, Tulkarm, Qalqilya, Bethlehem, and Nablus were overrun quickly with few casualties. Only in the Jenin refugee camp did the IDF encounter stiff resistance, and there it suffered relatively heavy casualties.

Outcome of the Military Operation

Defensive Shield accomplished most of its aims. Much of the terrorist infrastructure was destroyed. Hundreds of Palestinian gunmen were killed, and many others wounded. Thousands of suspects were arrested, including hundreds known to have been involved in terrorist acts. On April 15, the IDF arrested Marwan Barghouti, head of Fatah and Tanzim in the West Bank. Barghouti, who served as the most senior official of the al-Aqsa Martyrs' Brigades, had planned numerous suicide bombings and had even participated in shooting attacks. Thousands of weapons were seized, mostly rifles and handguns, but including weaponry banned by the Oslo Accords, such as antitank rocket launchers, mortars, and rockets. Dozens of explosives laboratories and weapons factories were uncovered and destroyed. Headquarters were located, and documents and computers were confiscated. Prisoner interrogations and captured documents provided valuable information about terrorist organizations and their connection with the PA. Military pressure on the terrorist infrastructure also led to a steep decline in terrorist attacks while the operation went on, as Palestinians focused on protecting themselves.

The operation's political objective was to put pressure on Arafat by isolating him in his offices in Ramallah. The IDF took over the PA compound there and refrained only from entering the rooms in which Arafat and his aides were present. The discovery of documents linking Arafat and other Palestinian officials to known terrorists and the uncovering of caches of illegal weapons yielded unprecedented evidence of the depth of the PA's connection to terrorist activity. Within Arafat's Mukataah compound in Ramallah, IDF soldiers found scores of munitions, pistols, automatic rifles, and empty suicide bomber belts. Also within Arafat's compound, the IDF found official correspondence between the office of Fuad Shoubaki, PA chief finance and procurement officer, and the al-Aqsa Martyrs' Brigades. The correspondence included procurement requests for bombs and ammunition, revealing that the al-Aqsa Martyrs' Brigades was a bona fide group, with its own terrorist infrastructure and supply chain. In addition to the arrests of top Fatah officials and the discovery of documents linking Arafat to terror operations, the IDF found evidence of the close cooperation of Fatah with Hamas and Palestine Islamic Jihad, especially in Jenin.

Operation Defensive Shield was a significant Israeli effort to convince the Palestinians, and especially Arafat, that an end to terrorism and violence was essential and that a failure to achieve this would incur a substantial Israeli response. Whatever the Palestinians had achieved in the occupied territories in the economic and social sectors and in terms of public services was now in a shambles as a result of the failure of Palestinian authorities to prevent, stop, respond to, or otherwise discourage anti-Israel violence since September 2000.

U.S. Involvement in the Region

By April 2002, it was clear that the Middle East was in the throes of a period of violence perpetrated by Palestinian terrorists to which Israel had responded with military force. The military operation came under increasing international criticism for delivering only short-term benefits at what seemed to be a disproportionately high human cost on both the Israeli and Palestinian sides. It was widely believed in the region and beyond that only involvement by the United States could reduce the level of confrontation and perhaps guide the situation toward peace. In early April, U.S. president Bush gave a speech to that end and then sent Secretary of State Colin Powell, to the region. Bush argued that the Palestinians needed to abandon their suicide bombings and other violence, or their hopes for a state could not be realized. The Israelis would have to withdraw their military from the West Bank and recognize that the end of the occupation was essential to peace. This presaged increased U.S. involvement in the problem. But speaking about peace did not lessen the terrorist attacks against Israel, nor did it convince Israel to cease its military response to terror.

On the contrary, in response to President Bush's speech of April 4, calling on Israel to end its invasion of the West Bank, Israel increased its military force in the area. Although Bush had stated, "I meant what I said about withdrawal without delay, and I mean what I say when I call upon the Arab world to strongly condemn . . . terrorist activities," a subsequent delay in Powell's visit to the region was widely interpreted in the Arab world as giving Sharon additional time to complete his military operations. By late April, Israel began to withdraw from the West Bank cities.

Arafat Unconfined

Arafat's Ramallah confinement ended on May 2, when Israel lifted its 34-day siege of his headquarters. Arafat agreed to compromises with Israel to end stalemates at the Church of the Nativity and at his headquarters in Ramallah. In the former case, he agreed to the exile to Europe of 13 Palestinians regarded as terrorists by Israel; in the latter, he turned over six Palestinian prisoners wanted by Israel to the custody of British and U.S. jailers in the West Bank town of Jericho. On May 13, 2002, for the first time since December 2001, Arafat ventured out of Ramallah and toured some other West Bank cities by helicopter, but the Palestinian crowds that greeted Arafat were small and not especially enthusiastic.

Operation Determined Path

Despite the successes of Israel's security services in preventing a number of terrorist attacks on Israelis, they could not prevent all violence and terrorism. The surge in attacks after the end of Operation Defensive Shield came as little surprise.

After a grouping of terror attacks in Jerusalem and elsewhere in June, Sharon pledged, based on the recommendations of the security services, to retaliate even more harshly than he did with Defensive Shield. With Operation Determined Path, which began on June 19, 2002, Sharon promised to reoccupy parts of the West Bank ceded to Palestinian control under the Oslo Accords, but not for a matter of days, as in the past, but "as long as terror continues." On June 19, Israeli troops (including thousands of reservists called up for military service under emergency orders) moved into Palestinian cities. Their goal was to round up terrorists and to disrupt and destroy their infrastructure for future attacks.

On June 23, the office of Defense Minister Benjamin Ben-Eliezer clarified that Israel had no intention to establish IDF civil-administrative control over the residents of the cities that Israel had taken control of in order to fight terrorism. However, Defensive Shield had ended sooner than many in the security services and the IDF had wanted owing to significant U.S., European, and international pressure. Although many individuals responsible for terrorism against Israelis at various levels had been arrested or killed, portions of the main terrorist organizations had eluded Israeli forces because of the short and hasty nature of the operation. Determined Path would make up for these lapses by intensifying the counterterrorism operations and placing additional pressure on the PA to stop terrorism.

The Bush Vision

The violence of early June and Israel's response to it had come at a time and in a manner that threatened to disrupt the Bush administration's policy.

On June 24, 2002, Bush rearticulated his vision of two states living side by side in peace and security, and reaffirmed his support for a Palestinian state but only if its leadership was not compromised by terrorism: "Peace requires a new and different Palestinian leadership, so that a Palestinian state can be born. . . . I call on the Palestinian people to elect new leaders, leaders not compromised by terror." Arafat was essentially disqualified as a peace partner and was seen as directly linked to the violence and terrorism that had followed Camp David II. This seemed to match Israel's perspective. But Bush also called on Israeli forces to withdraw fully to the positions they held prior to September 28, 2000, and demanded that settlement activity in the occupied territories stop, consistent with the Mitchell Committee recommendations.

A Separation Fence

The idea of building a separation fence between Israel and the West Bank had been raised as early as 1995–96 in response to terror attacks and bombings, but it gained greater impetus with the al-Aqsa Intifada. The idea initially faced formidable political hurdles. Fearful that any physical barrier would predetermine future borders, Israeli governments refrained from erecting the integrated system of physical barriers, technological means, armed personnel, and command, control, and monitoring systems that might prevent at least some of the terrorists from entering Israel. The proposed fence would resemble those constructed on Israel's border with Jordan, including barriers of coiled barbed wire and trenches, with electronic sensors to detect intruders, as well as a road for military patrols. There would be no mines along the fence. *Fence* is a somewhat general term for a physical barrier of various forms in different areas or locations. The exact composition of the separation fence would vary at different points along its length.

The security fence separating Israel from the Palestinians in the West Bank; the photos illustrate the two main forms of construction—fence (top) and concrete barrier (below)—used depending on the terrain and population locations. (Israel National Photo Collection; top: Photographer: Amos Ben Gerson; below: Photographer: Avi Ohayon)

Where there were Israeli and Palestinian population centers close to each other, it might take the form of a concrete wall that would prevent the infiltration of terrorists as well as afford protection from light arms' fire. Elsewhere, it could take the form of an electronic fence. Under the

231

concept, passage into Israel would only be possible through supervised entry points, and the aim would be to detect and foil any unauthorized attempt to cross into Israel.

As late as December 2001, both Prime Minister Ariel Sharon and Defense Minister Benjamin Ben-Eliezer declared that it would be militarily impossible to put up a defensive wall along the entire length of the Green Line separating Israel from the West Bank and the Gaza Strip as established by the 1949 armistice agreements. But by midwinter, public-opinion polls showed that nearly 80 percent of the public was in favor of unilateral separation from the Palestinians. Left-wing advocates saw separation as a temporary measure, diffusing tension until final-status negotiations could resume but also as a means of ending the occupation. For right-wing supporters, separation would be the final status, determining the country's security borders and ensuring a united Jerusalem under Israeli rule. A somewhat informal "fence now" movement began to appear in early 2002 with bumper stickers in Israel: "A Protective Fence, the Only Way."

In April 2002, the government decided to construct a fence along part of the Green Line between Israel and the West Bank. On June 23, the government authorized the first stage of the project, involving 115 kilometers (71 miles) of fence. The cost was estimated at about $1 million per kilometer. Sharon and Ben-Eliezer repeatedly emphasized that this was "a security fence," with no political implications or intentions. The fence was constructed to roughly parallel the border inside the West Bank, with changes to incorporate some Israeli settlements. Its primary aim was to prevent terrorists from infiltrating into Israel from areas controlled by the PA.

Opposition to building the fence centered on a number of themes ranging from financial to political reasons. Some opponents argued that the fence would be very expensive; others argued that it would not necessarily stop terrorists from infiltrating into Israel. Some believed that it would be perceived as a unilateral Israeli demarcation of a political border between Israel and a Palestinian state, which would generate protests by Arabs and by Israelis who believe that the West Bank is part of the biblical prophecy and oppose any compromise of that territory. Many on the Right, including members of Sharon's own party, resisted the idea of a separation fence arguing that it would convey the political message that Israel was willing to accept a line close to the pre-1967 Green Line as its future border with a Palestinian state and manifest a willingness to abandon the settlers in settlements located on the Palestinian side of the fence. Despite these concerns, however, Sharon

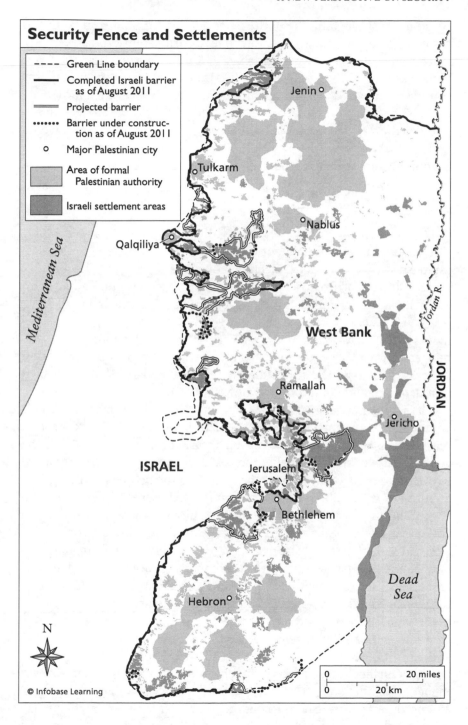

Security Fence and Settlements

- - - - - Green Line boundary

———— Completed Israeli barrier
as of August 2011

═════ Projected barrier

•••••• Barrier under construction as of August 2011

○ Major Palestinian city

Area of formal
Palestinian authority

Israeli settlement areas

Mediterranean Sea

Jenin ○

Tulkarm ○

Qalqiliya ○

Nablus ○

West Bank

Jordan R.

JORDAN

Ramallah ○

Jericho ○

ISRAEL

Jerusalem ○

Bethlehem ○

Hebron ○

Dead
Sea

N

0   20 miles
0   20 km

© Infobase Learning

could not stop the building of the fence because of public pressure and his inability to present another effective security solution.

The fence had many weaknesses. The line demarcating the West Bank was long (307 kilometers, or 190 miles), and the topography was complex and varied considerably from one sector to another. Moreover, densely populated areas of Israel often were close to Palestinian-populated areas, such as was the case in Jerusalem. Jerusalem, which had been the venue of the largest number of suicide bombings, was even more complex, given its mosaic of neighborhoods where effective separation would be practically impossible.

The NUG Collapses

The national unity government (NUG) of Prime Minister Ariel Sharon established after the 2001 election collapsed when, on October 30, 2002, Minister of Defense Benjamin Ben-Eliezer resigned along with other Labor Party ministers in the coalition. The precipitating issue was Ben-Eliezer's demand to cut $145 million in funds for Jewish settlements in the West Bank and Gaza Strip in the $57 billion 2003 state budget and reallocate the funds to finance social programs for weaker sectors of society including students and pensioners. Sharon rejected that demand, and compromise proposals failed.

The withdrawal ended the 20-month NUG formed by Sharon as a common front against the Palestinian intifada and the violence that marked it. Sharon characterized the Labor Party's decision to leave the government "over a political whim" as irresponsible behavior that led to the collapse of a government that reflected the people's will for unity. Sharon faced two alternatives: He could replace the NUG with a narrow coalition of right, extreme right, and ultra-Orthodox parties, or he could advance the date of the Knesset elections. Initially, Sharon sought alternative parliamentary support for the government from religious and nationalist parties but was faced with "unacceptable" demands and conditions to which he could not concede and which he characterized as "political blackmail." In particular, Sharon blamed Avigdor Lieberman and his National Union Party for the failure to retain his government coalition in power and avoid elections.

Sharon chose not to give in to the demands of the Right on such issues as further support for settlements and the altering of the government's guidelines so as to rule out any possibility of a Palestinian state, among other points. Sharon believed that such actions might undermine Israel's strategic understandings with the United States, break the budgetary framework, and cater to narrow political interests. Sharon instead reluctantly made the decision to call for early elections.

In a speech on November 5, Sharon announced that President Moshe Katsav had agreed to dissolve parliament and call for early elections in three months. Sharon retained the leadership of the caretaker government and added new members to it. Benjamin Netanyahu agreed to serve as foreign minister and Shaul Mofaz became defense minister. Mofaz was a former army chief of staff and was widely seen as shifting the government more to the right on issues relating to terrorism and security. Mofaz, for example, had advocated sending Arafat into exile.

The Kenya Attack

On November 28, 2002, two coordinated assaults on Israelis took place in Mombasa, Kenya. Terrorists fired two shoulder-launched SA-7 Strella missiles at an Israeli passenger jet but missed their target, and three suicide bombers drove to the doors of the Israeli-owned Paradise Hotel and crashed a vehicle packed with explosives into the building. The hotel burned down, at least 16 were killed, and scores injured. The Israeli government saw this as a dangerous escalation of terror. It was the first time that a terrorist organization had launched shoulder-fired missiles in an attempt to down a civilian aircraft. The attack showed that terror organizations and the regimes behind them were able to arm themselves with weapons that could cause mass casualties and be deployed anywhere. In a statement on December 2 on an Islamic Web site, a group calling itself the Political Office of al-Qaeda Jihad Organization took credit for the attack and reiterated its responsibility six days later.

On December 13, the UN Security Council, in Resolution 1450, formally condemned the attacks in Mombasa. This was the first time that the Security Council explicitly repudiated terrorism against Israeli victims in the action clauses of a resolution. The vote was 14 in favor; Syria voted against the resolution.

The 2003 Election Campaign

The January 2003 election posed a number of problems, including a very short campaign season and the fact that the Labor and the Likud Parties had both scheduled internal elections for party leadership. In Likud, the choice was between Sharon and Netanyahu, and in Labor, between Benjamin Ben-Eliezer, former minister, Knesset member, and chairman of the Histadrut Haim Ramon, and the mayor of Haifa, Amram Mitzna. Sharon remained leader of Likud while Mitzna ousted Ben-Eliezer from the Labor leadership.

The Labor Party under Amran Mitzna

Mitzna had been mayor of Haifa for nearly a decade, following a career in the IDF in which he rose to the rank of major general. In August 2002, Mitzna began his quest for the leadership of the Labor Party by making a very strong attack on Sharon's policies. In declaring his candidacy for the Labor Party leadership and thus also for prime minister, Mitzna stated that life in Israel was getting worse every day under Sharon's leadership and that Sharon was doing nothing to deal with Israel's security and economic problems. Consequently, Israelis had lost hope, and Labor's decision to remain in the government prevented it from offering an alternative to the government's policies. Mitzna argued that the conflict with the Palestinians could not be solved merely by talking about territorial concessions while continuing to use force and to build settlements. He called for a unilateral withdrawal from settlements, if an agreement could not be reached, and while a unilateral move was obviously less than ideal, it would achieve security separation and a secure border. He believed that only he could present a real alternative to the failing government and policies of Sharon.

Traditionally during times of crisis, Israelis have sought a cohesive government to deal with an emergency. During the 2003 election campaign, Israel was faced with two major security crises: the second intifada, and an escalating threat of war in the Persian Gulf. The al-Aqsa Intifada that had erupted 18 months previously had already led to thousands of casualties on both sides and led many Israelis to consider security and peace to be the nation's top priority. At the same time, rhetoric against Iraq was reaching a fevered pitch, and Israelis were concerned about the prospects of a war in the Persian Gulf and the effects it would have on Israel's security. With widespread public support, therefore, for a coalition government, it would have seemed prudent for Mitzna and Labor to agree to a NUG rather than run the risk of alienating voters.

Israel's last Labor government, under Barak, had fallen apart in 2002 for a number of reasons, but perhaps the most central was the issue of funding for the settlements in the Gaza Strip and the West Bank. Furthermore, Labor supporters were becoming disenchanted because they felt that their party was compromising on key issues, going so far as to acquiesce when Sharon decided to reoccupy most of the occupied territories. Thus, Mitzna found it necessary to move farther to the left in order to distance Labor from this stance. One of Mitzna's main policy initiatives was to take budgeted money away from the settlements and allocate it for social purposes. Mitzna believed that it was necessary for Labor to present a viable alternative to the hard-line stance endorsed

Knesset election campaigning, 2003 (Courtesy Daniel Aires)

by the right-wing parties. He advocated a position that would fit the mold of traditional Labor policies that encouraged negotiation over confrontation.

Shinui under Tomy Lapid

The secular Shinui Party headed by the charismatic Yosef (Tomy) Lapid became the arch-nemesis of the religious establishment during the 2003 campaign by promising to eradicate the influence of religious groups and parties on the government. Lapid was born in Yugoslavia in 1931, immigrated to Israel in 1948, and became a journalist. He began to reinvigorate the Shinui Party as its leader during the 1999 election campaign, when he first became a member of the Knesset.

In 2003, Shinui campaign ads criticized the ultra-Orthodox Jews for refusing military service. Shinui also opposed strict kosher laws and other religious laws that affected those who were not as religious. Shinui supporters favored a NUG, overwhelmingly supported the evacuation of settlements in the occupied territories, and were split over whether to conduct negotiations with Arafat. These positions allowed Shinui to appeal to centrist and leftist voters, while its virulent anti-Orthodox message was appealing to all secular voters.

Election Results

The election campaign focused primarily on the issues of security and peace. The religious-secular divide was also a significant element, and various other issues were championed by smaller political parties. The reinvigorated Shinui Party was targeted by many, especially the religious parties, which were concerned with Shinui's avowedly secular platform; however, Mitzna also attacked it by suggesting that Shinui was a problematic party because it carried "the flag of hostility" toward Israel's religious population. Mitzna's attack on Shinui foreshadowed his suggestion that Labor would renew its historic partnership with the religious parties in governing Israel. He also ruled out the idea of Labor's participation in a NUG headed by Likud and Sharon. This suggested to many observers his lack of national political experience, since the idea of a national unity government was high on the agenda of many Israeli voters.

The election of January 28, 2003, was in many respects a revolution in Israeli politics and suggested significant changes in both domestic and foreign policies. Voters were not confident about the situation facing them and the country as a whole. There was a feeling of inadequate security, and the economy had deteriorated significantly. Generally, depression characterized the political scene. The election results presented a snapshot of Israel in 2003.

Likud emerged as the largest political party in Israel, with twice the number of seats of the runner-up, its longtime rival, Labor. Clearly Likud was now the dominant power in Israeli political life, and Sharon emerged with a stronger mandate to deal with the Palestinians and the security issue. Sharon's substantial victory, coupled with the significant downturn in the electoral results for Labor, Meretz, and Shas, contributed to an usual combination of more right-wing, more secular perspectives in the government.

Prime Minister Ariel Sharon casts his ballot at a polling station in Jerusalem during elections for the 16th Knesset in 2003. (Israel National Photo Collection; Photographer: Avi Ohayon)

The Labor Party suffered the worst election defeat in its history. Labor obtained only 19 seats in the Knesset compared to the 38 seats held by its rival Likud. Most saw Labor's significant losses as a direct result of the failure of the party to project a strong image and of its leader to appreciate the need to match party policy with popular views. The party clearly suffered from the leadership of Mitzna, and his announced refusal to join a Likud-led NUG was probably a dominant factor in the defeat. By refusing to join a NUG, Labor was left with its principles intact but its credibility as a ruling party shaken.

Mitzna had called for negotiations with whichever leaders the Palestinians put forward, even if that was the PLO and Arafat. Mitzna underestimated the resentment voters had toward Arafat and the PLO after so many deaths and so much damage caused by the intifada. Mitzna continued to defend his positions even when his party members argued ardently against them.

Another factor was Labor's undistinguished party platform, which did not adequately address issues that differentiated them from the other parties, especially Shinui. Labor's foreign policy platform called for unilateral withdrawal from the occupied territories with two states for two nations and political separation alongside economic cooperation. This also distanced Labor from the typical Israeli voter.

On May 4, Mitzna resigned his position as leader of the Labor Party and lashed out at his rivals in the party. Peres became acting chairman.

Meanwhile, other parties declined in strength and popular support. Yisrael B'Aliya received enough votes to secure only two seats, and party leader Sharansky believed that the party had somehow lost its image and message. He resigned from the Knesset and effectively merged his party into Likud. He joined Sharon's government but noted that he would concentrate his efforts on rebuilding the Yisrael B'Aliya Party into a viable force. The other Russian group, Israel Beiteinu, which had been led by Lieberman, had merged into the National Union party prior to the 2003 elections. National Union won seven seats in the Knesset, and Lieberman became minister of transport in Sharon's government.

Among the religious parties, NRP gained a single seat to emerge with six positions in the Knesset; United Torah Judaism remained stable at five seats. Shas, whose spiritual leader, Rabbi Ovadia Yosef, had suggested that the party would grow from 17 seats to 26 seats, suffered a significant reversal and declined from its position as the third-largest party to 11 seats in the new parliament.

Besides Likud and Sharon, the big winner in the election was the Shinui Party under the leadership of Lapid. Lapid utilized his secular message to secure 15 seats in the Knesset, and Shinui became the third largest party by playing to public sentiment. His party joined the coalition government, and Lapid became minister of justice and deputy prime minister.

Meretz suffered a significant electoral loss of 40 percent of its seats, and Yossi Sarid resigned his leadership position. The Arab parties lost several seats in the parliament and shrank to a total of eight seats. One Nation secured three mandates but did not join the government.

Israel's 30th Government

As with all previous instances the new government would be formed by a coalition. Sharon's preference was a national unity government which he believed would better represent the strength and coherence of Israel in light of the existing situation—the continuing intifada, terrorist attacks against the civilian population, economic distress (partly resulting from the violence), and the prospects of conflict in Iraq that might involve Israel, directly or indirectly. He believed that the problems facing the state required cooperation and unity among all factions, foremost Labor because of Labor's still significant size and influence in Israel. However, Mitzna, the leader of Labor, rejected that idea.

Sharon presented his government to the Knesset on February 27, 2003, his 75th birthday. Sharon's coalition was composed of the centrist but stridently secular Shinui Party, the Orthodox, right-leaning NRP, and Likud and Yisrael B'Aliya, which had merged and together held 40 seats in parliament. This gave Sharon a narrow but valid parliamentary majority. Subsequently, an agreement with the far-right National Union Party, with seven seats, gave him a comfortable majority. The great surprise was the nonincorporation of two longtime Likud political allies, Shas and United Torah Judaism. Sharon had to choose between them and Shinui, which, under Lapid, had made it clear that the party would never serve with the ultra-religious in government.

The four principal cabinet posts were occupied by senior Likud figures: Sharon as prime minister, Mofaz as minister of defense, Netanyahu as minister of finance, and Silvan Shalom as deputy prime minister and minister of foreign affairs. Former mayor of Jerusalem Ehud Olmert became minister of industry and commerce and acting prime minister during Sharon's travels out of the country. The other coalition parties received posts they had sought as important to their agenda. Lapid was appointed deputy prime minister and minister of justice. Avraham Poraz, a longtime member of Shinui, became minister of the interior, suggesting that a major effort would be made to achieve the Shinui agenda through this important position. Sharansky became minister without portfolio with responsibility for Jerusalem Affairs, Society, and the Diaspora.

The 2003 election suggested several new directions toward dealing with the major issues facing the Israeli polity at the time, notably peace and security, prosperity, and what constitutes Jewishness. In presenting his government, Sharon noted that its primary mission would be to lead Israel back to the path of economic growth and prosperity. And, of course, he noted the importance of resolving the conflict between Israel and the Palestinians. However, Sharon also noted "we will work to complete a constitution which can be agreed upon by enacting the missing basic laws: the basic law to anchor the identity of Israel as a Jewish state and its national symbols and basic laws to complete the rights of the individual such as freedom of expression and the freedom to assemble, legal and social rights, etc."

The question of Who is a Jew? has appeared in Israel's political and religious-secular dialogue since before independence. In presenting his government, Sharon noted that one of his responsibilities was "to find fair and reasonable solutions to the problem of numerous citizens who cannot marry and divorce according to the Halacha." Sharon's government was to focus on mass Jewish immigration to Israel and noted that "aliya [immigration to Israel] is the lifeblood of Zionism," but there remained controversy about whether those immigrants would meet the extant criteria for being Jewish and be accepted as such.

Sharon's approach to the central issue of peace and security built on his previous views and was modified during and after the election campaign. He emphasized again that before one could return to the political track to negotiate, "the Palestinian Authority must stop terror and incitement, implement far-reaching reforms, and replace its current leadership." He suggested that after the violence stopped, and these related conditions were met, a political process could be initiated that would lead to genuine peace. The political process would be based on lessons learned from past failed attempts. For peace, which Israelis wanted, Sharon expressed his conviction that there was a willingness to make painful concessions. But, he also acknowledged, "creating a

WHO IS A JEW?

Israel is self-defined as a Jewish state, but exactly who is a Jew has been a matter of controversy since independence. In 1950, the Knesset passed the Law of Return, granting any Jew immigrating to Israel the right of immediate citizenship. The law did not define a Jew and left it to the minister of the interior to interpret the clause as he saw fit.

Since then, the religious segment of the population and their political parties and members of the Knesset have sought to sustain a narrow definition relying on halacha (Jewish law). Secularists have sought to broaden interpretation of these two elements to allow for a more lenient interpretation of identifying lineage and to permit conversion by other than recognized Orthodox Jewish authorities. No final legal determination has yet been made, and "Who is a Jew?" continues to be a central religious, social, and political issue.

Palestinian State under limited conditions in the framework of a political process is controversial among members of the coalition."

Sharon articulated a vision of a political settlement that "must ensure the historic, security and strategic interests of Israel" and should include such matters as "Palestinian renunciation of the groundless demand for 'The Right of Return' the sole purpose of which is to allow the entrance of masses of Palestinians into Israel." He also noted that any settlement would also have to preserve the unity of the capital of Israel, Jerusalem, which he described as "the united and undivided capital of Israel."

The New Government in Action

The government took office in early March 2003. Sharon began his term with a very sure view of the ability of his government to achieve its primary objectives: ensure the security of the people of Israel, achieve economic stability and growth, initiate an accelerated political process, and increase the number of immigrants to Israel.

Shinui's primary agenda was the secular-religious divide within the state. Newly appointed justice minister Lapid noted that he planned to propose legislation to shut down pirate radio stations serving the ultra-Orthodox and right-wing public. The ultra-Orthodox do not have television, theater, or similar entertainment and cannot bring secular newspapers into their homes because of the unacceptable pictures therein, which they believe, violate religious prohibitions. They thus stressed the importance of pirate radio stations to give access to their audience to readings from the Torah, Sephardic music, and related items. The ultra-Orthodox argued that the secular Israelis had a monopoly of personnel in official radio stations and catered to other audiences. In previous governments little had been done about eliminating these pirate stations, to a great extent because Shas supported the need for these stations and had substantial political clout. The new government excluded Shas and included Shinui; the Shinui faction thus seemed poised to move ahead on this issue.

The appointment of Shinui's Poraz as interior minister foretold change when he spoke of a more humane and liberal approach to immigration than under his predecessor. The ministry's powers are broad as it decides on citizenship for immigrants and visas for foreigners. For years, the ministry was run by members from religious parties, who openly declared that their primary interest was to control the composition of the immigration population in order to preserve the Orthodox dominance of daily activities in Israel. Poraz promised to reexamine this.

The War in Iraq

The effects on Israel of Operation Iraqi Freedom, the 2003 war in Iraq, launched by a coalition of forces led by the United States to terminate the regime of Saddam Hussein, have been extensive and long lasting. In the run-up to the war there was concern that Saddam Hussein might act as he had in the Persian Gulf War of 1990–91 and seek to split the anti-Iraq coalition and use the conflict as a pretext to attack Israel. Although the assessment of the chance of an Iraqi missile attack was low, there were extensive preparations in Israel, and elsewhere, for a potential attack that might employ Scud or other missiles with chemical or biological warheads. Shelters and safe rooms were prepared, and protective kits were updated and distributed, while the government tried to reduce public concern and avoid panic.

It was widely reported that, should Israel be a target of Iraq's missiles during a U.S. assault on Saddam Hussein, Israel would retaliate rather than be restrained, as it had been in 1991, and that Sharon had advised Bush of this policy. During the war, Israel deployed its Arrow missiles and the United States deployed its Patriot air defense system in Israel to protect Israel from Iraqi missile attacks. There were no attacks on Israel during the initial major hostilities. Once sites in western Iraq that could pose a threat to Israel were controlled by coalition forces and Israeli intelligence believed that the threat to Israel had been removed, Defense Minister Mofaz lowered the alert level in Israel; the population was no longer required to carry gas masks or maintain sealed rooms, and reserve soldiers who had been specially called up were released from military service.

In the aftermath of the initial hostilities that ousted Saddam Hussein and his regime, Israelis began to debate its effects on Israel's long-term security and the peace process. The termination of the Iraqi regime eliminated a significant and chronic threat to Israel. Iraq had been a participant in the 1948, 1967, and 1973 wars. The threat from Iraq's arsenal of weapons that might be employed in the future (as the Scud missiles had been in 1991) and its financial and logistical support for anti-Israel terrorist organizations and individuals had been minimized.

It was unclear, however, if the swift fall of Baghdad and the Saddam Hussein regime would convince other anti-Israel forces and factors in the region (Syria or Hizballah, for example) to modify their positions.

Some Israelis saw a window of opportunity in the changes wrought in Iraq that could presage a situation unknown since 1948. Others were more cautious. For Israel, Syria's weapons of mass destruction and its connections to various terrorist organizations hostile to Israel—such as Hamas, Palestine Islamic Jihad, PFLP, and Hizballah—were the main elements of importance. Growing American-articulated concern and long-standing Israeli perspectives about Syria coincided with elements of the U.S. global war on terrorism and against the countries that support terrorists and provide haven for them.

The Quartet and the Roadmap

During the war in Iraq, an international Quartet—the United States, the European Union, Russia, and the United Nations—came together and met informally to discuss the Israeli-Palestinian issue. In a speech made on June 24, 2002, President Bush called for an independent Palestinian state that would coexist peacefully with Israel. The plan would require the Palestinian Authority to make democratic reforms and renounce terrorism in exchange for statehood. Israel, in turn, would accept a Palestinian state and cease constructing settlements in the Gaza Strip and the West Bank.

A Roadmap first emerged in September 2002 as a mechanism for implementing Bush's articulated vision of two states, Israel and Palestine, living side by side in peace and security. It provided a timetable for concrete steps with dates for their accomplishment.

As initial hostilities in the war with Iraq drew to a close, the Roadmap emerged as an important element in Israel's quest for peace and security, but it also portended potential clashes and/or tensions with the Bush administration. Among Israel's concerns was the timing of the settlements issue: Sharon sought to deal with them at the end of the process; the Quartet proposed doing so at an initial stage. Israel was unwilling to accept the Roadmap until the Palestinians prevented terror and ceased violence. Compromises on security were unlikely, and Israel's definition of security was to be self-determined. Israel also expressed concerns about the return of Palestinian refugees to Israel. Among hard-liners in the government and outside it, the Roadmap, as originally drafted, was referred to as a potential national disaster.

In mid-April 2003, Sharon dispatched several close aides and advisers to Washington, D.C., to consult with the U.S. administration on his reservations and concerns about the Roadmap. Israel wanted references to the 2002 Saudi proposal presented by then Crown Prince Abdullah deleted since it was never formally presented to Israel and included unacceptable elements. Israel also wanted the Palestinians to recognize Israel's right to exist as a Jewish state. In addition, some elements were regarded as politically unacceptable because of the "symmetry" in their treatment of Israel and the Palestinians, despite the differences in their status and policies, and others because they reflected, in the eyes of the Israelis, the bias of the other members of the Quartet.

On April 30, 2003, the final version of the long-awaited Roadmap was presented by U.S. ambassador to Israel Dan Kurtzer to Israeli prime minister Ariel Sharon and by UN envoy Terje Larsen to the newly chosen Palestinian prime minister Mahmoud Abbas. In a formal White House statement, Bush urged Israelis and Palestinians to work "to immediately end the violence and return to a path of peace based on the principles and objectives outlined in my statement of June 24, 2002."

The aim of the Roadmap was to create by 2005 a viable, independent Palestinian state living in peace alongside Israel. It was replete with time lines, target dates, benchmarks, and steps to be taken by the parties to achieve goals and objectives of a security, political, economic, and humanitarian nature. The document was unbalanced in its identification of precise goals and strategies for the two sides. The ultimate Palestinian objective—the end of the Israeli occupation and the establishment of a sovereign, viable, democratic Palestinian state—was clear. The nature of the Palestinian state's sovereignty as well as its borders were not made specific. The Israeli equivalent was less precise. Israel's ultimate goal remained its acceptance as a Jewish state living securely in the region, where it is recognized and accepted as such by its Arab neighbors. This would mean an end to violence and recognition of Israel's Jewish character and would also mean that the Palestinian "right of return" would not remain as a viable Palestinian objective.

The Roadmap was constructed without direct input from the parties. It did not contain a design for or the specifics of a comprehensive Arab-Israeli peace settlement. Its basic concern seemed to be to put the parties on the road from violence to negotiation. To get to its destination, the Roadmap detoured around several central, if not critical, complex, and seemingly irreconcilable issues that were potential deal breakers: Jerusalem, refugees, and settlements. The Oslo process had not seriously addressed these core issues, saving them for final status negotiations, and ultimately failed because of that approach. The Roadmap made brief note of all of these, and other, issues but did not deal with them in any meaningful way. Sidelining Arafat and getting power to a relatively more moderate Abbas, however, provided a way to denounce and stop violence and suicide bombings and to stop Palestinian terrorists.

In its preamble, the document made clear that the Palestinian people would need a leadership "acting decisively against terror and willing and able to build a practicing democracy based on tolerance and liberty." The Roadmap also noted that there needed to be "Israel's readiness to do what is necessary for a democratic Palestinian state to be established." Both parties had to accept, clearly and unambiguously, a negotiated settlement. The Quartet would assist and facilitate implementation of the Roadmap. The settlement would be based on earlier foundations including the Madrid Conference; the principle of land for peace; UN Security Council Resolutions 242, 338, and 1397; agreements previously reached by the parties; and the Abdullah initiative endorsed by the Beirut Arab League Summit.

Abbas as Palestinian Prime Minister

The presentation of the Roadmap to Mahmoud Abbas (Abu Mazen) came just hours after he was sworn in as the first Palestinian prime minister and after the latest suicide bomber attack (at a Tel Aviv night spot). On April 29, Abbas and his government were endorsed by the Palestinian parliament by a vote of 51 to 18, with three abstentions. Abbas was sworn in the next day, the first time that a government was formed by a Palestinian prime minister rather than by Arafat, who was officially the president of the PA. The appointment suggested a potential for change. If Abbas had real power and could make tangible modifications in the situation, his appointment would open up possibilities for movement with the Israelis.

Abbas's selection came about because of a number of factors, not the least of which was the refusal of Israel and the United States to deal with Arafat and their desire to make him irrelevant in both description and reality. Although Arafat remained the icon of the Palestinian movement and revolution, Palestinian reformers, Israelis, the United States, and the international community all saw the need and value of having Abbas as prime minister for progress to be made on ending corruption, instituting reform, and moving along the peace process. The critical test of Abbas would be his willingness and ability to crack down on terror and terrorists.

In his speech to the Palestinian legislative body, from which he formally derived his position and his power, Abbas denounced terror and noted that weapons must be held only by the Palestinian government, not by independent militia forces. The situation was complicated for Abbas. If Abbas were to take actions against the military groups, he would be seen as a lackey of Israel and the United States, and this would hurt his credibility among the Palestinians and in the broader Arab world. His most immediate task was to deliver tangible improvements for the Palestinians: Their life had to get better; checkpoints needed to be relaxed, other controls lifted; prisoners had to be released, schools reopened; employment possibilities had to grow, and economic conditions had to improve.

Abbas outlined a program of domestic reform and commitment to diplomacy. He demonstrated both loyalty to Arafat and a desire for political change. His commitment to negotiations rather than violence as the path to Palestinian aspirations was punctuated by his assertion of the need to deal with the issue of unauthorized possession of arms and the primacy of the rule of law. In effect, he suggested that armed struggle should give way to diplomacy as the route to a solution to the Palestinian problem. But, he focused on the requirement for an immediate halt to Israeli settlement activity, especially in and around Jerusalem, and the building of the "separation wall" by Israel. The continuation of the settlements and fence, he argued, could destroy the Roadmap.

The Israeli reaction was mixed but hopeful. Israelis were relieved that Arafat had been "elbowed aside" and that Abbas focused on diplomacy not violence. However, Abbas did not change or give up traditional Palestinian demands, and Arafat continued to wield considerable authority; numerous loyalists were part of Abbas's government. Arafat also seemed to retain control over the security services. Indeed, it was Arafat who introduced Abbas to the Palestinian representatives when they convened in Ramallah and called on them to vote confidence in the new Abu Mazen government.

Powell, Sharon, and Abbas

Soon after the release of the Roadmap, Secretary of State Powell went to the Middle East and called on both sides to take quick steps for conciliatory action rather than getting bogged down in arguing about the details of the Roadmap. He seemed to focus on Sharon's efforts to revise the plan to accommodate some Israeli objections on such issues as the right of return. The PLO Executive Committee had announced on May 3 that it accepted the Roadmap and Powell noted that the new Palestinian leadership must dismantle the terrorist infrastructure and that Abbas understood the requirement that terror had to be ended.

During his visit, Powell met with Israeli foreign minister Shalom and with Sharon. On the Palestinian side, he met only with Abbas and his team, which took place in Jericho rather than in Ramallah, where Arafat was located and under Israeli siege.

On May 17, Sharon and Abbas met to discuss possible next steps to move the process forward, but the atmosphere was not conducive to that end. The day before they met, the senior Palestinian peace negotiator, Saeb Erekat, submitted his resignation suggesting significant divisions within the Palestinian camp between Arafat's loyalists and those more attuned to the views of Abbas. A spate of violence designed to destroy the Roadmap and the efforts to achieve peace followed. A Palestinian suicide bomber boarded a bus in Jerusalem and killed himself and a number of passengers while wounding many more. Another bomber killed only himself. A third bomber killed an Israeli couple in Hebron.

Sharon did not initially endorse the Roadmap and awaited the meeting scheduled for May 20 with Bush in Washington to do so. But then the violence by extremists brought the process to a brief halt, and Sharon postponed his visit. Sharon insisted that he would not sign on to the Roadmap until Abbas cracked down on Palestinian militant groups such as Hamas and Islamic Jihad. Abbas insisted that Sharon first accept the Roadmap and then he could begin to crack down on the Islamic terrorist movements.

After the renewed violence, Israel imposed a "general closure" on the West Bank, thus preventing Palestinians from crossing the line between Israel and the West Bank. Despite these actions, Sharon continued to meet with Abbas. At the same time, the Israelis suggested that Arafat was implicated in the recent terrorist efforts and announced that it would shun foreign representatives who met with Arafat.

A fifth suicide bombing in less than 48 hours took place on May 19 at the entrance to a shopping mall in Afula. The first four attacks were claimed by Hamas. The Afula bombing was claimed by Islamic Jihad and the al-Aqsa Martyrs' Brigades.

Bush, meanwhile, defended the Roadmap and sought to revive the Israeli-Palestinian discussions in the wake of the five bombings. He suggested that all parties were on the road to peace, but it was "going to be a bumpy road."

Accepting the Roadmap
On Friday, May 23, the government of Israel formally announced its acceptance of the steps outlined in the Roadmap. This followed intensive

negotiations between Israel and the U.S. government in which Israel's conditions were addressed, and its concerns were assuaged. Israel considered its 14 comments or reservations as part of the Roadmap, and this is the way they were conveyed to the U.S. administration. On May 23, Prime Minister Sharon's bureau released a statement:

> In view of the recent statement of the U.S. regarding the Israeli comments on the Roadmap, which shares the view of the Government of Israel that these are real concerns and in view of the U.S. promise to address those concerns fully and seriously in the implementation of the Roadmap to fulfill the President's vision of June 24, 2002, we are prepared to accept the steps set out in the Roadmap. I intend to submit this acceptance to the Government of Israel's approval.

On May 25, the government of Israel considered the prime minister's statement on the Roadmap and, like Sharon, accepted the various steps of the plan, rather than the overall plan, and indicated that it would continue to try to change it along the lines of the 14 objections it had earlier raised with the United States. An overriding concern of Sharon and some in the government was to be able to send a positive signal to the United States.

The Israeli "acceptance" was not clear and unequivocal. But, it was historic, because for the first time the Israeli government had formally committed itself to the formation of a Palestinian state on the western side of the Jordan River. Public reaction in Israel appeared to be positive, although there were many doubters and skeptics. As some of the Right pointed out, the Roadmap was in fact supported in a vote by only 12 out of the 23 ministers in the government. Netanyahu was among those abstaining. This majority was achieved after the prime minister said that the 14 reservations Israel had submitted to the United States, as well as the prohibition of the entrance of Palestinian refugees into the State of Israel, were red lines on which Israel would not compromise. Israel did not see the refugee issue as one of a "right of return" but a "demand to return," and in Israel's view the refugees did not have any right to return to Israel proper because the Arab refugee problem was the result of an act of aggression by the Arabs and was therefore up to them to solve it, not Israel. Also, Israel believed it was timely and appropriate to raise the claims of Jews from Arab countries as part of the negotiations of the refugee issue such as compensation for properties they left behind when forced to leave their homes in Arab states after 1948.

Although the resolution's reservations were important, the significance of the resolution could not be overstated. It constituted the first official Israeli government endorsement of a Palestinian state. But Sharon went further in his statement to the Likud parliamentary faction in which he noted that "occupation" of 3.5 million Palestinians was "bad for Israel and the Palestinians" and could not continue indefinitely. This was the first time that Sharon used the word *occupation,* which he had previously rejected as a description of the situation. Sharon suggested that it was the control of a foreign people that constituted occupation, focusing on the people, not the land in question. Israel did not want to control 3.5 million Palestinians with all the political, economic, and security implications of this action.

Middle East Summits

At the end of May 2003, the United States announced two summit meetings to secure support for the Roadmap in the wake of the conclusion of the initial large-scale hostilities in Iraq. On May 28, U.S. national security advisor Condoleezza Rice announced that President Bush would travel to Sharm el-Sheikh, Egypt, and meet there with President Mubarak of Egypt, Crown Prince Abdullah of Saudi Arabia, King Abdullah of Jordan, King Hamad of Bahrain, and Palestinian prime minister Abbas. He would then travel to Aqaba, Jordan, and meet individually with King Abdullah, then Sharon, and then Abbas, ending with a trilateral meeting with Sharon and Abbas. The overall purpose of the visit and the summits in the region was to achieve movement on the Roadmap to implement Bush's vision of June 24, 2002. This trip marked a substantial increase in presidential involvement in these issues, unlike the initial period of the Bush administration.

Moving the Roadmap Along

Sharon and Abbas both sought to reiterate their positions and gain support for their preferences. In an interview in *Haaretz* on May 27, Abbas stated that this was a historic opportunity to "return to a track of normalcy," the Roadmap should be implemented as written, and the violence should stop. He also noted that "Arafat is the elected president of the Palestinian Authority and should not be isolated." After a meeting on May 29, between Sharon and Abbas, Sharon announced that Israel would take a series of steps aimed at easing the living conditions of the Palestinians and seek to improve the Palestinian economy.

In early June, Israel lifted the general closure of the West Bank and Gaza and allowed an increase in the daily number of workers entering Israel from Gaza. Sharon also ordered the dismantling of some illegal outposts in the territories, but to Palestinian leaders and critics of the settlements, the action demonstrated how little Sharon was willing to do.

A Step Backward

The optimism that followed the issuance of the Roadmap and the June summits was soon tempered by continued violence. In the week following the summit, seven Israelis were killed. Israel's right wing criticized Sharon, described those Israelis as the first victims of the Roadmap policy, and predicted that more would follow. On June 8, the three main Palestinian terrorist groups—Hamas, Palestine Islamic Jihad, and al-Aqsa Martyrs' Brigades—staged a joint attack on an Israeli army outpost at Erez in Gaza, killing four Israeli soldiers. Thus, they recorded their violent opposition to the Roadmap and their resistance to the occupation.

From left to right: Prime Minister Ariel Sharon, President George W. Bush, and Palestinian prime minister Mahmoud Abbas at the Middle East Peace Summit in Aqaba, Jordan, June 2004 (Courtesy of the White House)

Israel responded to the attacks with targeted strikes against prominent Hamas figures and others who were involved in the assaults. The Bush administration's view of Hamas soon conformed to Israel's: that Hamas and like-minded groups were the primary obstacle to the Bush vision of a peaceful Middle East. On June 25, Bush said, "The true test for Hamas and terrorist organizations is the complete dismantlement of their terrorist networks, their capacity to blow up the peace process . . . We must see organizations such as Hamas dismantled."

On June 29, Hamas, Palestinian Islamic Jihad, and al-Aqsa Martyrs' Brigade agreed to a temporary truce (*hudna*) in which they would suspend attacks against Israelis.

From June to December 2003

Hopes for progress gave way to concern with the Abbas government's end; in fact, the resignation of Abbas suggested to many observers that the Roadmap was in danger of imminent collapse. The Roadmap sought a way for the parties to deal with each other without the involvement or interference of Arafat, but this proved futile.

In late August 2003, a suicide bomber, a 29-year-old Muslim cleric disguised as an ultra-Orthodox Jew, blew himself up on a bus full of Jewish families returning from prayers at a Jerusalem shrine and killed more than 18 people. This was seen by the Israelis as a *hudna*-breaker. Abbas launched a bid to salvage the shattered truce by cracking down on terrorists among the Palestinians. Other terrorist acts followed, and Israel's military soon retaliated. Ultimately, Abbas resigned out of frustration over Arafat's refusal to cede control over security and other issues, and Arafat made a phoenix-like comeback in fall 2003.

On September 9, Prime Minister Sharon instructed the security forces to act "relentlessly, continuously and determinedly" to eliminate the terrorist organizations and take all appropriate measures against their leaders, commanders, and operatives until their criminal activity was halted. This led Israel to decide, in principle, on September 11, 2003, to "remove" Arafat. A cabinet communiqué issued that day noted: "Events of recent days have reiterated and proven again that Yasser Arafat is a complete obstacle to any process of reconciliation between Israel and the Palestinians. Israel will work to remove this obstacle in a manner, and at a time, of its choosing." Secretary Powell rejected either the elimination or exile of Arafat as a flawed idea.

The remnants of a bus in Haifa after a terror attack by a Palestinian suicide bomber, 2001
(Israel National Photo Collection; Photographer: Moshe Milner)

By the third anniversary of the start of the al-Aqsa Intifada, the situation had deteriorated for both Israelis and Palestinians. Economic conditions had weakened and the general security situation was worse. On October 4, a suicide bomber ran into a crowded seaside restaurant in Haifa and detonated explosives that killed more than 19 people, including children. The United States condemned the act as a vicious act of terrorism and underlined the responsibility of the Palestinian authorities to fight terror and dismantle the infrastructure of terror.

The following day, October 5, Israeli warplanes bombed what they called an Islamic Jihad training base in Syria in retaliation for the suicide bombing. Israel noted that any country that harbors terrorism, trains terrorists, and supports and encourages them will have to answer for their actions. On October 6, President Bush said that Israel should not feel constrained in defending itself against terrorism. The United States would not condemn Sharon's decision to stage an air strike into Syria in response to the Haifa suicide bombing.

Replacing Abbas

The replacement of Abbas suggested a new period of potential. On November 12, the Palestinian parliament approved Ahmed Qureia (Abu

Ala) as prime minister and his cabinet by a narrow margin. Qureia was a member of the PLO who served as director of finance for Arafat and led the delegation that negotiated the Oslo Accords with Israel. In his first speech, Qureia called for a mutual and comprehensive cease-fire with Israel and urged Palestinians to reject the "chaos on the ground. . . . We are not terrorists and we shall never be. Our struggle has never been directed against children, women and civilians. . . . We reject it, we condemn it and we refuse it."

Sharon's Initiative: "Disengagement"

Toward the end of November, Prime Minister Sharon noted his pledge to carry out the Roadmap but warned that if negotiations with the Palestinians failed, Israel would have to take unilateral steps. Although he was not precise as to what those steps might be, he hinted that it would include "territorial concessions" and even suggested that Israel might evacuate isolated settlements and unauthorized outposts unilaterally. Nevertheless, he also made clear that he would continue construction of the security fence.

In a speech on December 18, Sharon reiterated his warning. In the short term, the prime minister suggested that he would ease travel restrictions on Palestinians and dismantle small and unauthorized outposts erected by settlers. He continued, "If, in a few months, the Palestinians continue to disregard their part in implementing the road map then Israel will initiate the unilateral security step of disengagement from the Palestinians." "Disengagement" would translate into Israel's unilaterally declaring new borders should the PA not take immediate action to halt terrorism. Sharon's disengagement plan would evacuate some settlements and draw a security line in the West Bank. Many assumed that it would be drawn along the lines of the security fence then under construction. He noted that Israel would strengthen its control over areas it intended to be part of Israel in the future. Sharon's remarks reflected an important turning point in the Israeli position.

On Israel's political Left, there were critics of several aspects of Sharon's speech and the initiative it described. Sharon sought to reduce friction between Israel and the Palestinians by relocating some settlements. The Left, however, continued to seek a full Israeli withdrawal from the Gaza Strip and also isolated settlements in the West Bank.

The Palestinian reaction was predictably negative, refusing to accept or agree to any unilateral Israeli action. The Palestinians argued that the only way to resolve the conflict was through a mutual agreement that would lead to a Palestinian state composed of the West Bank and Gaza Strip and with a capital in Jerusalem.

More Violence

As 2003 approached its end without a major terrorist event or a suicide bombing for almost three months, Israelis were beginning to believe, or hope, that its war against terrorism was having some success. Then on the seventh night of Hanukkah, December 25, 2003, a Palestinian suicide bomber, acting for the PFLP, struck at a bus stop in Petah Tikva and killed four people. This was the first attack to claim Israeli civilian lives since the October 4 attack in Haifa in which 21 people were killed. The United States strongly condemned the bombing and reiterated its long-standing view of the absolute and urgent need for the PA to confront terror and violence. The bombing served to remind participants and observers that the Israeli-Palestinian negotiations were stalemated and the long-awaited meeting between Sharon and Qureia still had not taken place. The Israeli government saw this as evidence that the Palestinians had not yet given up terrorism and that there was no Palestinian negotiating partner. Events therefore suggested the need for Israel to continue to assure its own security by taking actions against terrorist leadership and cells through targeted assassinations and attacks against those preparing or participating in attacks. At the same time, they reaffirmed the need for Israel to consider unilateral steps in order to ensure its security, such as accelerating construction of the security fence and disengaging from the Palestinians.

The Security Fence

Toward the end of 2003, Israel's security fence became the focal point of significant international attention. In early December, the UN General Assembly, at an emergency session, voted 90 in favor and 8 opposed, with 74 abstentions, to petition the International Court of Justice to rule on the legality of the fence. In October 2003, the assembly, by a vote of 144 to 4, had demanded that Israel tear down the barrier. On November 28, Secretary-General Kofi Annan issued a report calling the construction of the wall "a deeply counterproductive act" that was causing serious socioeconomic harm to the Palestinians.

Moving toward Security and Peace

The beginning of 2004 saw a continuation of Palestinian terrorist attacks against Israelis by Hamas, al-Aqsa Martyrs' Brigades, and

Palestine Islamic Jihad. As the attacks increased, Israel continued its policies of targeted assassinations of Hamas and other terrorist group leaders. An Israeli missile strike in March 2004 killed Hamas founder Sheikh Ahmed Yassin, and another strike killed the new Hamas leader, Abdel Aziz Rantisi, the following month.

Sharon also moved ahead on his plan for a unilateral Israeli withdrawal from Gaza. In a speech prior to his visit to Washington, D.C., in April 2004, Sharon noted that he was disposed to keep some Jewish settlements in the West Bank and suggested that these would include Ariel, Givat Zeev, Maaleh Adumim, the Etzion bloc, and Kiryat Arba and the Hebron enclave.

On April 14, President Bush, in a joint news conference with Sharon, recognized Israel's right to retain some West Bank settlements and called Sharon's plan "historic" and "courageous." Bush referred to "new realities on the ground" and suggested that it was unrealistic that the outcome of final status negotiations would be a full and complete return to the 1949 armistice lines and that the so-called right of return was effectively ruled out. On April 16, Prime Minister Tony Blair of Great

U.S. president George W. Bush (right) and Israeli prime minister Ariel Sharon at the White House, April 14, 2004 (Israel National Photo Collection; Photographer: Avi Ohayon)

Britain and President Bush, in a joint press conference in Washington, noted that Sharon's plan was not seen as a unilateral attempt to impose a settlement but as an opportunity to move forward to resolve the issue.

The Likud Party membership (with a relatively small voter turnout) rejected the plan on May 2, by a vote of 60 percent against to 40 percent in favor. It was clear that the opposition came primarily from the settler portion of Likud's membership and was contrary to the overwhelming popular support for the plan expressed in nationwide Israeli public-opinion polls.

Nevertheless, on May 4, the Quartet met in New York City to assess the status of the Roadmap and, after its deliberations, agreed with the Bush administration assessment that Sharon's plan to withdraw from the Gaza Strip and settlements in parts of the West Bank was a "rare moment of opportunity."

On June 4, Sharon removed National Union ministers Avigdor Lieberman and Benny Elon from his government coalition because of their opposition to his disengagement plan. The withdrawal of the support of the National Union's seven votes, in addition to threatened defections on the part of the NRP and right-wing elements of Sharon's Likud Party, left the prime minister without a secure majority in the Knesset. Sharon pledged to construct a new coalition to push through his proposals, and on June 7, his cabinet agreed to proceed with the Gaza disengagement plan, while deferring a vote on the dismantling of settlements.

In a landmark ruling on June 30, Israel's Supreme Court, while acknowledging the right of the state to build the West Bank fence on security grounds, nevertheless ordered it to change the route in order to reduce the suffering the fence was causing the Palestinians. The Sharon government immediately moved to implement this order.

On July 9, the International Court of Justice, in an Advisory Opinion said Israel's West Bank security fence violated international law and should be immediately dismantled. Israel and the United States rejected the opinion as one-sided and politicized. Israel said that it would be guided only by the rulings of its own Supreme Court and would continue to build the fence as long as it was required to protect Israel's citizens from terror.

Arafat's death in November 2004 and the opportunity presented by Sharon's disengagement proposal led the Labor Party, under Shimon Peres, to rejoin the coalition government. Labor was convinced that Sharon's Gaza disengagement plan was a crucial step for a settlement with the Palestinians and could fail without the party's support. In January 2005 the Knesset voted approval of a new coalition led by

Sharon by a vote of 58 to 56, with six abstentions. Overshadowing this issue was the change in the Palestinian camp and in the international negotiating process occasioned by the death of Arafat on November 11, 2004. On January 9, 2005, the Palestinians went to the polls to elect a new head of the Palestinian Authority. Abbas, who had already succeeded Arafat as chairman of the PLO, won the election handily. Abbas seemed to bring a new approach to the conflict with Israel—stating that violence was counterproductive—that suggested the prospect of improved relations with Israel.

The establishment of a new coalition government supporting the Sharon disengagement plan, the replacement of Arafat by Abbas, and the inauguration of a new Bush administration in Washington, with Condoleezza Rice as secretary of state, brightened the prospects for a potential end to the second intifada and the resumption of Israeli-Palestinian negotiations to move toward resolution of the conflict between them. On January 27, 2005, Prime Minister Ariel Sharon said that there was an opportunity for a historic breakthrough with the Palestinians if they took comprehensive and effective action to stop "terrorism, violence, and incitement." An early indicator of the new environment was a summit meeting between Sharon and Palestinian Authority president Mahmoud Abbas in Sharm el-Sheikh, Egypt, on February 8, at which they agreed to suspend the Palestinian attacks and Israeli counterterrorism actions that had marked the al-Aqsa Intifada since the fall of 2000. On February 20, the Israeli cabinet approved (by a vote of 17 to 5) Sharon's plan to withdraw Israeli settlers and soldiers from the Gaza Strip. The cabinet also voted (20 to 1) for a modified route for the security fence in the West Bank. The new route would generally move the fence closer to the 1967 Green Line (the 1949 Armistice Line). Maale Adumim and Gush Etzion would be on the Israeli side of the fence.

But, Sharon's coalition government and his plans for disengagement faced serious challenges in the form of a call for a national referendum on the plan and by the legal requirement that the state budget be approved by the end of March or the government would be deemed to have fallen and thus require new Knesset elections in early summer. On March 28, the Knesset rejected the call for a national referendum on the Gaza withdrawal plan, and on March 29, the Knesset approved the budget. These votes effectively allowed the Sharon-led government to continue in office, to proceed with the Gaza disengagements, and to move forward in negotiations with its Palestinian interlocutor to achieve a resolution of the conflict between them.

Disengagement

Amid much public anguish, the evacuation of the 8,500 residents from all 21 Israeli settlements in the Gaza Strip began on August 15, 2005, and was completed on August 21, 2005. The withdrawal of the civilian residents of the four isolated settlements in the northern West Bank affected by the disengagement was completed on August 23, 2005. The last IDF soldier left Gaza on September 12, 2005, and the northern West Bank settlements on September 20, 2005. The settlers were evacuated, the settlements were demolished, the troops were withdrawn, the military positions were abandoned and destroyed. Palestinian control replaced Israeli (since 1967) and Egyptian (1949 to 1967) control of the Gaza Strip.

In a speech to the Herzliya Conference on December 16, 2004, Sharon explained that the disengagement plan was motivated by Israel's recognition of the tremendous demographic imbalance in the Gaza Strip favoring the Palestinians; the need to distinguish between "goals which need to be fought for," such as the defense of Jerusalem, the security zones, the major settlement blocs, and "maintaining Israel's

IDF soldiers prevent protesters from marching to the Gaza Strip to prevent the disengagement in July 2005. (Israel National Photo Collection; Photographer: Avi Ohayon)

character as a Jewish state," and "goals where it is clear to all of us that they will not be realized"; denying the Gaza-based Palestinian terrorists the "excuse" for continued terrorism by ending Israel's occupation of Gaza; and protecting and enhancing Israel's international standing, especially with the United States.

In a historic speech in Hebrew to the United Nations General Assembly on September 15, 2005, Sharon articulated a critical principle to guide future Israeli policy concerning the territories and the nature of Israel-Palestinian relations: "The right of the Jewish people to the Land of Israel does not mean disregarding the rights of others in the land. The Palestinians will always be our neighbors. We respect them, and have no aspirations to rule over them. They are also entitled to freedom and to a national, sovereign existence in a state of their own."

The Israeli body politic overwhelmingly supported Sharon's proposals for the disengagement. Nevertheless, there was opposition to it in the Gaza Strip and the northern West Bank and orange was the color chosen by those who opposed the evacuation. Blue, the traditional color of the Israeli flag (blue and white), was used by those who supported the decision to disengage. The "orange rebellion" was unprecedented in nature and larger in size than any that had been seen previously in Israel. However, the blue camp was obviously larger, and support for disengagement was a clear majority perspective among Israelis.

Continuing Threat from Gaza

The Israeli withdrawal from Gaza and the reversion of the area to full Palestinian control was seen as having the potential for stabilizing that sector, but the area did not quiet down. Palestinian arms smuggling, much of which came through the Rafah crossing between the Gaza Strip and Egypt's Sinai Peninsula continued, including large quantities of rifles and ammunition and large amounts of explosives. This was a constant concern, as was the continued firing of Qassem rockets from Gaza that targeted populated areas of Israel's western Negev. The town of Sderot was hit particularly often. Many of the rockets exploded harmlessly, but some Israelis were killed or wounded and property was damaged or destroyed. From the onset, the Israelis were active in trying to stop the attacks. Israeli efforts involved the use of air strikes at the individuals firing the missiles, at the staging areas, and at the factories producing them. Periodic operations by ground forces were also employed.

Kadima Emerges

Ariel Sharon, one of the principal founders of the Likud, increasingly frustrated by the rebellion and intense opposition within the party to his altered approach to the Palestinians and the peace process, decided to leave the Likud Party and create a new party that he would lead in the Knesset elections and toward a resolution of the conflict with the Palestinians.

Sharon resigned from the Likud on November 12, 2005, to form the Kadima (Forward) Party. The move significantly altered Israel's political landscape, placing Kadima and the Labor Party at the center of the political spectrum, with parties both to the left and the right. Sharon took with him a number of Likud ministers and members of the Knesset (MKs), and was joined by some leading Labor Party members (including Shimon Peres) and other prominent Israelis. This political earthquake set in motion changes within the political system with a new "center" under Sharon's leadership. Sharon said he left Likud because he did not want to waste time with political wrangling or miss the opportunities resulting from Israel's withdrawal from Gaza. Riding a wave of popularity, Sharon seemed certain to be reelected by a huge margin, with a mandate to continue his policy of withdrawal from the occupied territories.

Amir Peretz, a Moroccan immigrant to Israel and head of the Histadrut (General Federation of Labor), defeated Shimon Peres for the leadership of the Labor Party in November 2005 by a margin of 2.4 percent. Peretz appealed to Israel's working class and Sephardic Jews of Middle Eastern origin, and he became the first Moroccan-born politician to lead a major Israeli political party. Peretz led Labor's departure from the government and, combined with the formation of Kadima and the turmoil within Likud, prepared the way for the next Knesset election.

Sharon suffered a minor stroke on December 18, 2005, but his condition improved rapidly. He remained lucid and in control of the government and was released quickly from the hospital. However, on the night of January 4, 2006, Sharon suffered a major stroke and fell into a coma (in which he remains). Unexpectedly, Sharon's career was over and Israel, as well as the peace process, was in search of new political leadership. When Sharon's deputy, Ehud Olmert, took over as acting prime minister, a relative unknown replaced a certainty.

11

A CONTINUING QUEST FOR PEACE (2006–PRESENT)

Israel's quest for peace with its neighbors, acceptance in the Middle East, and security has been a continuous theme in Israeli policy and politics since its independence. Momentous events and changing partners have led to reconsideration of approaches and methods, but the goal has remained consistent throughout.

No Partner for Peace

The death of Yasser Arafat had given hope to Israelis and others that the time might now be ripe for movement toward a peaceful resolution of the Israeli-Palestinian and Israeli-Arab conflicts. The choice of Mahmoud Abbas as Arafat's successor as head of the Palestinian Authority (PA) was initially welcomed as a positive indicator, despite some of Abbas's past comments and actions. Progress was slow and further compromised by the outcome of the Palestinian election of January 2006 that brought an end to Fatah control of the Palestinian leadership and put Hamas, a terrorist organization committed to replacing Israel with a Palestinian Islamic state, in control of the PA government. Abbas remained as president, albeit with diminished capacity to act on behalf of the Palestinians.

The success of Hamas at the polls generated two significant outcomes. One was a division within the PA concerning its relationship with Israel, and the other was the decision of the United States, the European powers, and various other international players not to provide funds to the Palestinians as long as the Hamas-led government remained in power. In addition, the Israeli government decided not to transfer tax revenues collected for the PA. This led to dire economic conditions within the Gaza Strip and, to a lesser degree, the West Bank.

After the election and the subsequent formation of the Hamas-led Palestinian government, substantial efforts were made by the major world powers (and others) to convince Hamas to accept three basic conditions in order to be deemed a relevant negotiating partner with Israel and the international community: to renounce violence, to accept the previous agreements between Israel and the Palestinians, and to recognize Israel's right to exist. Over the ensuing months, PA president Mahmoud Abbas and other Arab leaders made efforts to establish some form of a Palestinian unity government composed of Hamas and Fatah that would be acceptable as a negotiating partner with Israel and within the broader international community. At various times, they seemed close to agreement, and tentative power-sharing accords were announced, but these were followed by the ending of the dialogue and violence between the factions. Hamas, for its part, after its success in the Palestinian election and its formation of the new Palestinian government, pursued a consistent theme, insisting "We will not recognize Israel."

The Palestinian election results were as much a repudiation of Fatah (for corruption and ineffectiveness) as a vote for Hamas and its stated political objectives. Hamas won support in the election because of its platform of efficient, noncorrupt services and government for the Palestinians *not* because of its hard line on Israel. Nevertheless, the government led by Ismail Haniyeh brought deteriorating conditions to the Gaza Strip and to Israel's southern areas. Terror attacks, firing of rockets, kidnappings, digging of tunnels, and smuggling of arms continued and contributed to instability and economic deterioration, not to improved security and the prospects for negotiation and peace.

Knesset Election 2006

The Knesset was disbanded officially on December 8, 2005, preparing the way for the next election, to be held on March 29, 2006. In early April, with no change expected in Sharon's condition, the cabinet deemed him officially and permanently incapacitated and unable to discharge his duties of office and then chose Ehud Olmert to serve as interim prime minister.

The 2006 election marked the beginning of a new and significant period in Israel's political life. The voter turnout was only 63.2 percent, with 3,186,739 (of the 5,014,622 eligible) votes cast. Thirty-one

Campaign poster for the Kadima Party, 17th Knesset elections, 2006 (Israel National Photo Collection; Photographer: Moshe Milner)

political parties presented lists of candidates for election to the Knesset, and all parties that received more than 2 percent of the valid votes participated in the allocation of the mandates (seats) in the parliament. Twelve parties won sufficient votes to win seats and be represented in the 17th Knesset. Kadima won 29 seats with Labor-Meimad winning 19. Other successful parties were: Likud, 12; Shas, 12; Israel (Yisrael) Beiteinu, 11; HaIchud HaLeumi (National Union)-Mafdal (NRP), 9; Gil (Pensioners), 7; Torah and Shabbat Judaism (United Torah Judaism), 6; Meretz, 5; United Arab List-Arab Renewal, 4; Hadash, 3; and National Democratic Assembly (Balad), 3. Kadima won the March 2006 Knesset election on a promise to complete the process of separating Israel and the Palestinians by enacting a large-scale unilateral Israeli withdrawal from much of the West Bank.

The election results dramatically altered Israel's political landscape. The new Kadima Party, without its founder and initial leader, Ariel Sharon, became the largest party in the Knesset. Despite the pedigree of many of its prominent members, the party lacked formal institutions,

EHUD OLMERT
(SEPTEMBER 30, 1945–)

Ehud Olmert was born in Binyamina, Israel, in 1945. He graduated from Hebrew University with a degree in psychology and philosophy and, later, in law.

Olmert was first elected to the Knesset in 1973 at the age of 28 and served in various ministerial capacities (including minister of minority affairs from 1988 to 1990 and minister of health from 1990 to 1992). He served two terms as mayor of Jerusalem (1993–2003) before rejoining the Knesset in 2003 on the Likud list. In 2006, Olmert resigned from Likud and joined Ariel Sharon in the newly created Kadima Party.

With Sharon hospitalized and incapacitated in January 2006, Olmert was charged with the duties of prime minister, then formally became acting prime minister, and in April was named interim prime minister. He led the Kadima Party list in the 2006 Knesset election and became prime minister of Israel in May after Kadima's success in the election. Olmert led Israel through the Second Lebanon War and into a renewed peace process with Palestinian leader Mahmoud Abbas. He was widely criticized for his handling of the hostilities in the Second Lebanon War.

ideology, and leadership. It brought people from the Left and Right and adopted a position in the center under Ehud Olmert, a former mayor of Jerusalem and MK who had never before been prime minister.

Labor was the second largest party. The Left-Right balance and the religious-nonreligious balance seemed to focus on a centrist approach. Likud—led by Benjamin Netanyahu—which had dominated Israeli politics (and was the party in power) for nearly three decades (with brief interludes) shrank in size and influence. Shinui disappeared, and some of its leadership moved to other parties.

HaIchud HaLeumi focused on the theme that it was the new right-wing alternative and that Likud and Kadima had abandoned the historical legacy of Menachem Begin and Ze'ev Jabotinsky. Their leaders, HaIchud HaLeumi maintained, were no longer faithful public servants who could capture the admiration of Zionists everywhere, and their economic plans no longer considered the weaker segments of the population; they also no longer treasured such values as Jewish identity and tradition. HaIchud HaLeumi contended that Likud had adopted

---

In January 2007 a criminal investigation was initiated focusing on activities during his tenure as finance minister and decisions concerning the sale of Bank Leumi. In May 2007 the preliminary report of the Winograd Commission accused Olmert of failure in the management of the Second Lebanon War. At times, his popularity rating sank to single digits, but he persevered.

In November 2007 Olmert participated in the international conference sponsored by the United States at Annapolis, Maryland, to begin a process of direct negotiations to resolve the Israeli-Palestinian conflict. The negotiations ultimately failed. In December 2008 Olmert launched Operation Cast Lead against Hamas in the Gaza Strip.

On July 30, 2008, Olmert announced that he would not seek reelection as party leader, and on September 21, 2008, he formally resigned. He remained in office until the formation of the new government in March 2009. Investigations into accusations of corruption and related charges led to a formal indictment on August 30, 2009, on charges including fraud, breach of trust, and tax evasion. The trial opened in September 2009 and continued into 2012. On January 5, 2012, he was also indicted for taking bribes while mayor of Jerusalem.

the platform of the far Left and acted in opposition to the will of the majority of voters when it supported the evacuation of all Israelis from the Gaza Strip. By doing so, HaIchud HaLeumi reasoned, Likud and Kadima had handed Hamas a victory.

The newly established Gil (Pensioners Party), under the leadership of Rafi Eitan, won a surprising seven seats in the Knesset and joined the government in which Rafi Eitan, who was born in November 1926 in Ein Harod (then Palestine), served as minister of pensioner affairs. Gil emerged as an important player.

On May 4, 2006, Israel's 31st government, headed by Ehud Olmert, was presented to the Knesset, which voted its approval of the coalition of Kadima, Labor, Shas, and Gil with a majority of 65 for, 49 against, and 4 absent. The cabinet was large and a curious mix of individuals. Olmert served for the first time as prime minister. Labor Party leader Amir Peretz became minister of defense, despite a lack of significant military experience. Shimon Peres, Israel's elder statesman and former Labor Party leader and prime minister, who had left Labor after his defeat for the party leadership and joined Kadima, was given the post of regional development minister with a focus on the Galilee and the Negev. Avi Dichter, former head of the Shin Bet, became internal security minister.

Olmert said that he sought negotiations with the Palestinians for a solution to the conflict, but only with a Palestinian Authority that recognized Israel, upheld all previous agreements with Israel, and fought terror. If the Palestinian Authority continued to be led by terrorist factions, it would not be a partner in negotiations, nor would there be practical day-to-day relations. Failing a change and without an agreement, Olmert declared, Israel would act to establish defensible borders and ensure a solid Jewish majority in the Jewish state. In the government policy guidelines, Olmert noted that major settlement blocs in the West Bank were a prelude to his "convergence" proposal, which would move tens of thousands of Israelis from settlements scattered throughout the West Bank to several settlement blocs near the Green Line. He noted: "I, too, like many others, dreamed and wished that we could safeguard all of the territories of the Land of Israel for ourselves, and that the day would not come when we would need to give up parts of our land." But, he noted, this was needed for a "solid and stable" Jewish majority in the state.

Palestinian Violence and the Second Lebanon War

Hamas's election victory led to growing violence. The Palestinians took advantage of the end of the Israeli presence in Gaza to launch daily

Residents of Majdal Krum village in northern Israel after a Katyusha rocket attack by Hizballah during the Second Lebanon War (Israel National Photo Collection; Photographer: Moshe Milner)

rocket barrages on Israeli towns near the border. On June 25, 2006, Palestinians tunneled under the international border between Israel and Gaza, attacked an Israeli patrol, killed two soldiers, and kidnapped a third one, Gilad Shalit. Israel responded by attacking a series of terrorist and infrastructure targets in the Gaza Strip, but the kidnapped Israeli soldier remained in captivity somewhere in Palestinian territory.

Shortly after Hamas's capture of Shalit, Hizballah opened a second front on Israel's northern border. Hizballah, a terrorist organization trained, financed, and armed by Iran and Syria and with seats in the Lebanese government, had built up an enormous rocket capability after Israel's unilateral withdrawal from southern Lebanon to the recognized international border (the Blue Line) in May 2000.

On July 12, 2006, fighters crossed the Blue Line into Israel, attacked Israeli soldiers, killed eight of them, and kidnapped two others—Ehud Goldwasser and Eldad Regev—who were taken into Lebanon. Prime Minister Ehud Olmert called this an "act of war," and the Israel Defense Forces (IDF) launched a massive air campaign in response, bomb-

GILAD SHALIT
(AUGUST 28, 1986–   )

Gilad Shalit, born on August 28, 1986, was abducted from Israel, by Hamas and other Islamic militants operating from the Gaza Strip, on June 25, 2006, in a cross-border raid. Since his abduction, Shalit has been held incommunicado in an undisclosed location. Hamas consistently has refused all requests (including from the International Committee of the Red Cross) to visit Shalit or to prove that he is still alive. In exchange for his release, Hamas has made various demands. In July 2011 Hamas released some details of the abduction operation that it called "Shattered Illusions" and noted that "he was taken to a place that had been prepared in advance and secured as a prison for the captive."

In September 2009 Israel released 20 Palestinian women from custody in exchange for a videotape in which Shalit was alive and holding a newspaper dated September 14.

By the fourth anniversary of his captivity, the Shalit matter had become the subject of an extensive public campaign in Israel. There have been numerous calls for Shalit's release and demonstrations and marches to publicize his captivity. It has become a matter of public discourse and debate.

Netanyahu said that despite his fervent wish to bring Shalit home, he had to consider the security of all of the country's citizens. "The State of Israel is willing to pay a heavy price for the release of Gilad Shalit, but it cannot say, 'at any price.'" In October 2011 Shalit was exchanged, following delicate and extensive negotiations between Israel and Hamas, for 1,027 Palestinians prisoners, many "with blood on their hands," held by Israel. The arrangement was widely supported at all levels of Israeli society, but its price was the subject of extensive debate.

---

ing Hizballah strongholds in southern Lebanon. Operation Change of Direction sought to prevent the supply of arms from Syria and Iran to Hizballah; Israel also launched air attacks against Beirut's airport and major land routes, while a naval blockade prevented shipping from entering or leaving Lebanese ports. Israel attacked Hizballah targets, including weapons storehouses and missile launching points, across the country.

Meanwhile, Hizballah attacked Israel with Katyusha rockets fired on northern Israeli cities, towns, and villages, including Haifa, Israel's third-largest city and a major port. Israel called up reservists, and a ground incursion by the IDF led to the taking of villages and towns in Lebanon south of the Litani River. Israeli forces met fierce resistance from Hizballah fighters entrenched in underground bunkers, tunnels, and caves who were armed with sophisticated antitank and other weapons that appeared to have been supplied by Iran and Syria.

The Israeli war effort was aimed at restoring Israel's deterrent power, removing the Hizballah rocket threat, and creating conditions for the return of the abducted soldiers. The initial air strikes were successful: On the night of July 12, the Israeli air force destroyed most of Hizballah's Iranian-made Zilzal long-range rockets, which were believed to be capable of hitting Tel Aviv. Over the next few days, the air force reduced Hizballah's Beirut headquarters to rubble, destroyed weapons stores, and killed dozens of elite Hizballah fighters. However, it soon became apparent that incessant Hizballah rocket fire from mobile launchers, such as Katyushas, could only be stopped by a large-scale ground operation. This did not materialize until the last days of the war, and Hizballah was able to continue firing more than 100 rockets a day at Israeli civilians in northern Israel and to claim victory on the grounds that Israel had been unable to stop the Katyushas from being launched.

The fighting lasted for 34 days until UN Security Council Resolution 1701 achieved a cease-fire on August 14, 2006, and an agreement for a "robust" version of UNIFIL (the United Nations Interim Force in Lebanon), with a larger number of troops and new and different multinational components drawn from a variety of countries (primarily European), to be installed in southern Lebanon, essentially between the Litani River and the Blue Line, to prevent Hizballah from reestablishing itself there and using the area to attack Israel. The resolution also called for an embargo on arms to be imposed on Hizballah, for its forces to be removed from southern Lebanon, and for the area to be patrolled by the Lebanese army. Israel's army completed its withdrawal from Lebanon on October 1, 2006.

Estimates of the number of Lebanese killed varied from about 850 to 1,200. The number of Israelis killed was put at 43 civilians and 117 soldiers between July 12 and August 14, with 4,262 civilians wounded. Others were killed after the cease-fire. UN officials estimated that 1 million Lebanese and 300,000 Israelis had been displaced by the fighting. More than 1 million Israelis were forced to live in shelters as some 4,000 rockets landed on Israel, of which more than 900 hit communities in more than 160 Israeli cities, towns, villages, kibbutzim, and moshavim.

The Second Lebanon War had both positive and negative aspects. The deployment to southern Lebanon of a stronger UNIFIL, with new and different multinational components drawn from a variety of countries, was a positive feature of the outcome of hostilities. At the same time, the Lebanese Armed Forces deployed in southern Lebanon for the first time in decades. Militarily, Israel dealt Hizballah a severe blow. Hizballah lost its control of, and position on, the Lebanon-Israel border; its weapons systems were destroyed and degraded; it lost much of its arsenal of long-range missiles; and it suffered serious casualties, both killed and wounded. But, at the same time, Hizballah survived (as did Hassan Nasrallah, Hizballah's secretary-general) and could sustain what it termed "its resistance" against Israel. Perhaps most significant was that the war ended inconclusively after more than a month of fighting, and at the end Hizballah was still able to fire more than 100 rockets a day against Israeli civilian targets. Subsequently, it restored much of its arsenal of weapons.

The war also identified the links between Hizballah, Syria, and Iran. It reminded the international (and especially the Arab and broader Middle Eastern) community of the destabilizing nature of Iran as reflected in its current leadership. Clearly Iran provided missiles and other munitions to Hizballah, and many saw it as the guiding hand in providing other armaments, as well as training and other support for Hizballah's mission.

Within several months of the end of hostilities, the Israel-Lebanon frontier was quiet, with a reasonable prospect that it might remain that way for some time, despite bellicose statements from Hizballah. But the issues that triggered the conflict were not resolved. The kidnapping of Israeli soldiers by Hamas and Hizballah and Iran's growing effort to become a major regional player continued to loom large. Militants in the Gaza Strip seemed eager to emulate what Hizballah did on Israel's northern border. They smuggled weapons, built tunnels, and continued firing rockets at Israel.

The Altered Political Environment

Instead of an anticipated brief postelection "honeymoon," Israel's new prime minister was faced with a war, followed by a changed perception of the region and of appropriate policies to pursue. Rather than concentrating his efforts on fulfilling his campaign pledge to move ahead with further unilateral withdrawals in the absence of a Palestinian peace partner, Olmert was now forced into the defensive posture of explaining the "failures" of the summer, consolidating his hold on power, and searching for an alternative to a now-discredited unilateral withdrawal scheme that could be applied to the West Bank. In fall 2006, he removed the idea of further unilateral withdrawals from the public agenda. His rationale was that the 2000 Israeli withdrawal to the international border from Lebanon and the 2005 withdrawal to the international border from Gaza did not prevent Hamas and Hizballah from attacking Israel in 2006.

As with previous wars that ended without clear success for Israel, the war altered the political environment. The Olmert government came under harsh criticism for its handling of the conflict and the related diplomacy. The kidnapped Israeli soldiers remained in their captors' hands, and the image of Israel as an overwhelmingly successful military power seemed diminished. This led to protests and demonstrations, calls for commissions to evaluate the handling of the conflict, and for an evaluation of the IDF and of Israel's political leadership. Some called for changes in the government, others for changes at the senior levels of the IDF. Critics cited the lack of military experience of both Prime Minister Olmert and Defense Minister Amir Peretz, the leader of the Labor Party. Pressure mounted on Olmert to set up a formal, independent state commission of inquiry with the power to subpoena witnesses, impound evidence, and recommend the dismissal of political and military leaders. In mid-September, the Winograd Commission, appointed by Olmert and established by a cabinet vote, convened to set the parameters for its investigation into the war in Lebanon. The inquiry itself came under challenge because it was not an official and independent state inquiry. Discontent and concern lingered into the winter.

Malaise and Concern: Losing Faith in the Leadership

Frustration over the outcome of the war with Hizballah led many Israelis to question their new generation of leaders. With the incapacitation of Sharon and the marginalization of Peres, the generation of the founders of the state was now being replaced with a new generation of younger and less historic figures. The older leadership, mostly East European immigrants and their offspring or protégés, that had comprised the elite of the Yishuv in the period of the Palestine Mandate and the State of Israel in its first decades was being replaced by a generation generally born, or at least raised, primarily in Israel itself. This new leadership was increasingly ethnically different (for example, President Moshe Katsav was born in Iran, and Labor Party leader Amir Peretz in Morocco) and ideologically more diverse. The generations of the socialist (labor-oriented) founders was being replaced by a more capitalist, free market–oriented group with a different style of political leadership. Much of the older leadership had risen through the ranks of the labor movement, the political parties, the kibbutz movement, or the military. In contrast, the new generation of leaders is as likely to come from the private sector as from the traditional parties. While Peretz is from the labor movement, Olmert was previously a lawyer in private practice, although he served as both a member of the Knesset and mayor of Jerusalem before becoming prime minister.

Public opinion polls suggested that most Israelis regarded the older generation of leaders as more competent than the current one when queried after the war with Hizballah. There seemed to be both displeasure and disappointment with the newly chosen leadership of the state.

Polls also suggested that there was a significant decline in the support for, and positive view of, the IDF and its senior leadership, an unusual occurrence in Israel. The IDF had always been viewed as the country's premier and most-esteemed institution, but now it came under close scrutiny for its "failures" in combat and deficiencies of leadership and its need to launch a significant investigation of itself. Among reserve officers there was anger and criticism of military commanders and civilian leadership for insufficient equipment and supplies during the hostilities and a tentativeness and insufficiency on the battle plan and the approach to the fighting.

Many Israelis saw this as a war that Israel did not "win," with all the implications that had for Israel's ability to deter its enemies. A loss of confidence in the senior military or political leadership was not unprecedented, but both at the same time was unusual, and the lack of confidence persisted long after the hostilities had ended.

Further aggravating this loss of faith in the country's leadership were a number of scandals involving the president and other senior figures on charges of corruption and immorality. In mid-October 2006, a joint statement by the Justice Ministry and the police said there was evidence that President Moshe Katsav committed "rape, aggravated sexual assault, indecent acts without permission and offenses under the law to prevent sexual harassment" against several women in his office. According to the police, the inquiry also found evidence that the president had committed fraud and was engaged in illegal wiretapping. In January 2007, Attorney General Menachem Mazuz decided to indict the president, and Katsav recused himself from official duties. In a statement, Katsav's office said: "The President reiterates and emphasizes that he is a victim to a low plot spun against him and . . . it will be proven that the allegations against him are false stories and a lie, and the truth will be brought to light."

Fallout after the War: Domestic Politics

In light of the public's criticism and the increasing threat posed by Iran, Olmert sought to expand and reinforce the coalition. Although Labor was an important partner, it had lost respect during the war, due to the insistence of its leader, Amir Peretz, that he keep the portfolio of defense minister, a post for which he was not well qualified. Eventually, Olmert turned to the Right.

On October 30, 2006, Olmert won the approval of Israel's cabinet for Yisrael Beiteinu (Israel, Our Home), founded in 1999 and led by Avigdor Lieberman, to join the government. Lieberman would become a deputy prime minister with special responsibility for strategic issues, primarily focusing on the potential threat from Iran.

Avigdor Lieberman immigrated to Israel from Moldova in the Soviet Union in 1978 and lived with his family in the West Bank settlement of Nokdim. He held strong views about the future of the West Bank and was widely known for his provocative proposals and statements (for example, supporting the death penalty for Arab parliamentarians who met with Hizballah or Hamas, both classified as terrorist groups by Israel). He retained wide popularity among Soviet immigrants to Israel. Lieberman suggested that there be a swap between Israel and the Palestinians in which Israel would keep portions of the West Bank with its Jewish settler population and trade portions of Israel that had a large Arab Israeli population, reducing the number of Arabs in Israel.

Olmert's ability to have Yisrael Beiteinu join the government while retaining the participation of Labor was an important achievement—given the long-standing and often acrimonious differences between the two parties. By co-opting Yisrael Beiteinu, the government gained the support of its 11 seats in the Knesset. This increased to 78 (out of 120) the number of seats supporting the coalition in parliament, a substantial majority.

In January 2007, Dan Halutz, chief of staff of the IDF, tendered his resignation, becoming the first IDF chief of staff to voluntarily resign. He cited the internal probes of the Second Lebanon War as his main reason for resigning and said that he was taking full responsibility for the war.

In late May, Israel's Labor Party ousted its populist leader, Amir Peretz, who had also been sharply criticized for his role as defense minister during the 2006 Lebanon war. In the first round of elections, former

Swearing-in ceremony of Shimon Peres as Israel's ninth president (Israel National Photo Collection; Photographer: Amos Ben Gershom)

prime minister Ehud Barak and a former head of Shin Bet (General Security Service), Ami Ayalon, emerged as the two top candidates. In mid-June, Barak defeated Ayalon, returning to his former position as leader of the Labor Party.

President Moshe Katsav's resignation took effect on July 1. In December 2010, he was found guilty of rape, sexual assault, sexual abuse, sexual harassment, and obstruction of justice.

In June 2007, Shimon Peres, a member of the founding generation and a distinguished statesman, was elected the ninth president of Israel. This was widely seen in Israel and beyond as bringing honor to public life and as a corrective to much of the malaise of the previous year. As *Haaretz* noted in an editorial on June 16, 2007: "No one is better suited to restore the dignity of the presidency in the world's eyes and to represent Israel."

In August 2007, Benjamin Netanyahu was reelected as leader of Likud, easily defeating Moshe Feiglin, thus increasing the probability that Netanyahu would again seek to become prime minister in the next Israeli national election.

Iran as an Existential Threat

With its strong natural and human resource base, Iran had increasingly emerged as a powerful state in the Middle East. In Israel's view, the international community had to prevent Iran from achieving the capability to produce nuclear weapons. Israel saw Iran's nuclear program as an existential threat to Israel and a threat to world peace. Iranian president Mahmoud Ahmadinejad had sustained a rhetorical campaign against Israel, labeling Israel "illegitimate" and calling for its destruction. He had said Israel had been "imposed" on the region and could not survive. He had described the Holocaust as a "myth" and stated that Israel should be "wiped off the map." Ahmadinejad labeled Israel the cause of 60 years of war, 60 years of displacement, 60 years of conflict, and not one day of peace. He argued that the Palestinian people should decide their fate and the "people with no roots" who are ruling the land should be replaced: "Israel currently occupies Palestine. Where did they come from? They should return."

When Hizballah forces launched an attack on Israel and then, in response to an Israeli counterattack, showed that they had been well prepared by Iran (and Syria) for their military role, the threat to Israel posed by Iran became more tangible. At the same time, the war also led to something of a de facto alliance of perspective between Israel and some Arab states, which had become more concerned about the potential threats posed by a powerful Iran than they were about the threats posed by Israel. Israeli concerns also dovetailed with those of the United States and some European states that saw Iran as developing a nuclear capability leading to a nuclear weapon, even though Iran claimed its nuclear program was purely peaceful, with energy as its primary objective.

The Palestinian Unity Government

In the aftermath of the Second Lebanon War, Israel continued to search for a partner with which it could make peace. The Palestinian Authority had a Hamas-led government that would not meet the minimal preconditions outlined by Israel and the international community that would enable it to be a possible partner for peace negotiations. It failed to recognize the State of Israel, to accept and implement the agreements signed between Israel and the Palestinian Authority, and to act to terminate violence and eradicate terrorism, which included rocket attacks on Israel's southern communities. On numerous occasions, and in various venues, Ismail Haniya and other senior Hamas leaders and officials repeated that the Hamas movement would not recognize Israel under any circumstances and would not deal with it. At the same time, Israel sought the release of Gilad Shalit, the soldier kidnapped in the summer of 2006.

On December 23, 2006, Olmert and Abbas met, in their respective leadership positions, for the first time in an attempt to revive the peace process and to bolster Abbas against Hamas in the internal Palestinian arena. This was the first formal session between Israel and the Palestinians in nearly two years. Olmert promised to transfer frozen tax revenues to Abbas in an effort to ease the Palestinian economic situation.

Palestinian efforts to establish a unity government intensified in early 2007. On February 6, 2007, the leaders of Hamas and Fatah, the two main Palestinian groups, began a Saudi-brokered effort to agree on a unity government that could end the violence between them in the Gaza Strip and the West Bank. The effort was intended to yield a Palestinian government that would include members of both Hamas and Fatah and be acceptable to Western governments so that they could resume relations with, and provide aid to, the Palestinians and restart the peace negotiations with the Israelis that had been stalled since Hamas's election victory in 2006. The agreement that was signed on February 8 by Mahmoud Abbas, PA president, and Khaled Mashal, leader of the political wing of Hamas, included measures to end the internecine violence and an arrangement for the appointment of a new government and steps to incorporate Hamas and Islamic Jihad into the PLO.

On March 17, the Palestinian parliament approved the new unity government. Abbas called for peace and equality with Israel and urged international donors to end the economic aid boycott that had been in place since Hamas took over the government. However, Prime Minister Ismail Haniyeh stated that the new government "affirms that resistance in all its forms . . . is a legitimate right of the Palestinian people." On March 18, 2007, the Israeli cabinet voted to limit future talks—even with moderate Palestinian officials—to shared security and humanitarian concerns. It thereby ruled out a formal peace process until the new Palestinian government recognized Israel and renounced terrorism and violence.

The uneasy alliance between Hamas and Fatah ended when Hamas seized full control of the Gaza Strip in June 2007, thereby terminating the power-sharing arrangement with Fatah. Abbas dismissed the unity government and appointed a caretaker Fatah-affiliated government in the West Bank, headed by Salam Fayyad. Hamas refused to recognize its authority and continued to govern in the Gaza Strip, leading to two distinct Palestinian authorities in two territories. Each claimed to be the legitimate Palestinian government, and each sought to gain Arab and international legitimacy and support.

The takeover of the Gaza Strip by Hamas led to a continually deteriorating situation on the border between Israel and Gaza. Hamas operatives, and those of other Palestinian terrorist organizations and groups, continued to strike at Israel, occasionally with suicide bombers entering the country and usually with rocket attacks across the

Sderot exhibit of remnants of rockets that hit the city. (Israel National Photo Collection; Photographer: Moshe Milner)

border at Israeli towns and villages, kibbutzim, and other residential and commercial facilities. While the rockets generally were not targeted with precision, they were effective in inflicting terror upon Israel's population and destroyed property and killed and maimed individuals. Between 2000 and 2008, more than 7,000 rockets and mortars were fired at Israel from the Gaza Strip. Most of the rockets fell on Israel's southern city of Sderot.

The continuation of the attacks and the unwillingness of the Hamas-led government to engage in peacemaking led Israel's government to declare the Gaza Strip "hostile territory." On September 19, 2007, Israel's security cabinet determined: "Hamas is a terrorist organization that has taken control of the Gaza Strip and turned it into hostile territory. This organization engages in hostile activity against the State of Israel and its citizens and bears responsibility for this activity." As an "enemy entity" Gaza would be subjected to economic sanctions, including import restrictions and reductions in supplies of electricity and fuel from Israel.

The United States, Israel, and Europe sought to bolster Abbas and his Fatah-led government in the West Bank, strengthening his security forces and facilitating peace talks with Israel. To further strengthen

Abbas's position and to demonstrate to the Palestinians the benefits of moderation, Israel released tax revenues that had been collected on behalf of the Palestinian Authority and then withheld after Hamas came to power. Israel also released 250 Palestinians from Israeli jails and gave immunity to some members of the al-Aqsa Martyrs' Brigades linked to Fatah. West Bank Palestinian terrorists were taken off Israel's wanted list in exchange for handing in weapons and signing pledges to cease violence against Israel. Israel also gave permission for several exiled PLO officials to attend a meeting of the group's central council in Ramallah, West Bank.

Movement toward Peace

Until May 2007, the Bush administration was hesitant in its approach to the Arab-Israeli peace process: Bush made it clear that he would not follow the Clinton policy of extensive personal involvement. In mid-July 2007, the United States launched a diplomatic effort to revive the moribund peace process. President Bush, on July 16, announced $80 million in aid to the Palestinian government in the West Bank and called for an international conference in the fall to prepare for the creation of a Palestinian state side by side with Israel. The goal was to rebuild faith in the peace process among Palestinians and Israelis. Bush called upon the Palestinians to reject Hamas and, with it, war, terror, and death and to choose peace and hope instead, by making the Palestinian state a reality.

In a historic visit in late July, the foreign ministers of Egypt and Jordan traveled to Israel to promote an Arab peace plan. This was the first visit by official representatives of the Arab League to Israel. However, the meeting produced no immediate breakthroughs. On August 6, Olmert met with Abbas in Jericho, West Bank. A statement released by the prime minister's office noted: "It is our intention to bring about two states for two peoples living side by side in security, as soon as possible." This was the first meeting between senior Israeli and Palestinian leaders in the West Bank since the start of the intifada in 2000.

On August 16, the United States and Israel signed an arrangement in which Israel would receive $30 billion in military aid over the next decade to counter the perceived threat by Iran. U.S. secretary of state Condoleezza Rice told reporters: "There isn't any doubt, I think, that Iran constitutes the single most important concrete challenge to U.S. interests in the Middle East and to the kind of Middle East we want to see." At the same time, Secretary of State Condoleezza Rice and Defense Secretary Robert Gates announced plans to provide some $20 billion in military aid to the Arab states of the Persian Gulf, primarily Saudi Arabia, to further contain the Iranian threat.

The Middle East Peace Conference at Annapolis

On November 27, 2007, an international conference was convened at the U.S. Naval Academy in Annapolis, Maryland, at the invitation of the United States. It was chaired by Secretary of State Condoleezza Rice and brought together Israel, the Palestinian Authority, and 49 states and international organizations. The purpose was to begin a process of direct negotiations leading to peace between Israel and the Palestinians, based on the two-state solution envisioned by President George Bush and partly detailed in the Quartet Roadmap. In his opening address to the conference President Bush noted:

> We meet to lay the foundation for the establishment of a new nation—a democratic Palestinian state that will live side by side with Israel in peace and security. We meet to help bring an end to the violence that has been the true enemy of the aspirations of both the Israelis and Palestinians.

Israel was represented by its three most senior government figures—Prime Minister Ehud Olmert, Defense Minister Ehud Barak, and Foreign Minister Tzipi Livni. The trio reflected the seriousness of Israel's participation in the peace effort but also reflected their rivalry on the issues involved in the peace process as well as their personal ambitions for leadership of Israel. Israel and the Palestinian Authority under Abbas agreed to begin immediate negotiations with the goal of reaching a peace treaty by the end of 2008. The joint understanding between Olmert and Abbas read in part:

> We express our determination to bring an end to bloodshed, suffering and decades of conflict between our peoples; to usher in a new era of peace, based on freedom, security, justice, dignity, respect and mutual recognition; to propagate a culture of peace and nonviolence; to confront terrorism and incitement, whether committed by Palestinians or Israelis. In furtherance of the goal of two states, Israel and Palestine living side by side in peace and security, we agree to immediately launch good-faith bilateral negotiations in order to conclude a peace treaty, resolving all outstanding issues, including all core issues, without exception, as specified

> *in previous agreements. We agree to engage in vigorous, ongoing and continuous negotiations, and shall make every effort to conclude an agreement before the end of 2008.*

In the immediate aftermath of the Annapolis conference, the negotiations process moved ahead, albeit very slowly. No appreciable progress, no working groups to deal with the core issues of borders, security, Jerusalem, refugees, water issues, and related matters, developed in the initial weeks.

In January 2008, President George W. Bush traveled to the Middle East primarily to maintain the momentum and facilitate the process relaunched at Annapolis. This was his first visit to Israel since becoming president of the United States. Bush met with Prime Minister Ehud Olmert in Jerusalem and with Palestinian Authority president Mahmoud Abbas in the West Bank city of Ramallah and expressed confidence that an Israeli-Palestinian agreement could be reached by the end of 2008. President Bush, at a press conference in Jerusalem, said:

> *I share with these two leaders the vision of two democratic states, Israel and Palestine, living side by side in peace and security. Both of these leaders believe that the outcome is in the interest of their peoples and are determined to arrive at a negotiated solution to achieve it.*
>
> *The point of departure for permanent status negotiations to realize this vision seems clear: There should be an end to the occupation that began in 1967. The agreement must establish Palestine as a homeland for the Palestinian people, just as Israel is a homeland for the Jewish people. These negotiations must ensure that Israel has secure, recognized, and defensible borders. And they must ensure that the state of Palestine is viable, contiguous, sovereign, and independent.*

Reaction in Israel

The reactions in Israel showed a wide division about the wisdom of the process, the content of the negotiations, and the positions taken on the various issues. Shas and others from the religious factions were most concerned about discussions concerning the status of Jerusalem. On the Right, verbal concerns led to specific actions. On January 16, 2008, Minister of Strategic Affairs in the Prime Minister's Office and Deputy Prime Minister Avigdor Lieberman resigned from the cabinet, and the Yisrael Beiteinu Party withdrew from the Kadima-led coalition government, focusing specifically on the negotiating strategy with the Palestinians adopted by the Olmert government. Lieberman had threatened to leave the coalition once Israel's talks with the Palestinians touched on the core issues of the conflict, especially the status of Jerusalem, but also including borders and refugees. Lieberman said that he did not expect the Israeli-Palestinian negotiations to lead anywhere. At a press conference, he noted that his purpose in government was "to stop the Annapolis process." This departure narrowed the government coalition by 11 members, reducing its control to 67 out of 120 seats in the Knesset.

Rockets from Gaza

As the post-Annapolis peace talks continued in an effort to reach a solution to the issues in dispute, violence and terror emanating from the Hamas-controlled Gaza Strip continued to escalate. New groups espousing Islamic causes, some associated with al-Qaeda, emerged with militant anti-Israel agendas seeking to harm Israelis and to prevent movement toward peace between Israel and the Palestinians. Their common feature was to liberate all of the territory of Palestine (i.e., all of Israel) and secure the holy places in Jerusalem through armed struggle.

In the months following the Annapolis summit, there were periodic escalations of rocket fire and some mortar shells from the Gaza Strip toward the town of Sderot, although some also reached Ashkelon. In Israel there were growing calls for government action in response to the rocket fire, to include more air strikes and/or a ground offensive.

The Siege of Gaza

In mid-January 2008, Defense Minister Ehud Barak halted all imports into the Gaza Strip, including food and fuel, and stepped up Israeli military operations and actions as a way to convince Hamas to discontinue its attacks. This had limited success. Under intense international pressure, Israel eased the blockade on January 22, 2008, despite the continuing attacks. The growing boycott and restrictions on travel in and out of Gaza for both people and goods produced a seriously deteriorating situation in the area but did not generate any movement toward negotiation for peace by Hamas with Israel.

After the Israeli disengagement from Gaza, a series of security measures had been put in place that sought to assure that the border crossings to and from Gaza would be appropriate and peaceful. After the Hamas takeover of Gaza, it became clear that these crossings were increasingly used for contraband—routes for terrorists on their way to attacks in Israel and for guns, funds, explosives, and rocket-making material for strikes on Israel. With the growing threats, Israel increased the security measures at the crossings between Gaza and Israel. This was partly successful in reducing the threats, but it also created a growing siege of the Gaza Strip leading to a deteriorated economic situation.

In early February 2008, Israel decided to again tighten the siege on the Gaza Strip in an effort to convince the Palestinians to end their attacks, without Israel using force. Israel reduced the amount of electricity it sold to Gaza but noted that it would continue to provide the minimum to prevent harm to the health or safety of the residents, as well as the requisite amount of gasoline and diesel fuel.

On February 4, 2008, an Israeli civilian was killed and 11 others wounded when a suicide bombing took place in the city of Dimona. One bomber detonated his weapon; the second bomber was killed before he could detonate his bomb. Several Palestinian groups claimed responsibility for this attack, which was the first of this type in Israel for more than a year, but the claim by the Qassem Brigades, a wing of Hamas, seemed to be the most credible. The attack was glorified, and further such efforts were threatened by Hamas spokesmen in Tehran, Iran, and in Gaza. Gazans expressed their joy at the attack: Children handed out candy and flowers in the streets to celebrate the event. The attack marked an end to a self-imposed moratorium by Hamas on such attacks over the previous months.

Winograd Report

On January 30, 2008, the Winograd Commission issued its long-awaited final report on the Second Lebanon War (2006), calling it a "serious missed opportunity" for Israel that ended "without its clear military victory" and that had "far-reaching implications for us, as well as for our enemies, our neighbors, and our friends in the region and around the world." It placed responsibility mainly with the IDF command. Although it found failings with their management of the war, the report essentially exonerated Prime Minister Ehud Olmert and then defense minister Amir Peretz on the decision to approve the plan for a controversial ground operation against Hizballah in Lebanon. It laid responsibility with the IDF leadership at the time of the fighting and those who had preceded them, whom they blamed for a deterioration in overall preparedness, decision making, and strategic thinking.

The report reviewed the preparations and the execution of the military and diplomatic objectives of the Israeli leadership and concluded

THE WINOGRAD REPORT: EXCERPT FROM THE OFFICIAL SUMMARY

1. . . . The Final Report of the Commission to investigate the Lebanon Campaign in 2006 [was submitted] to the Prime Minister, Mr. Ehud Olmert, and to the Minister of Defense, Mr. Ehud Barak [on 30 January 2008]. . . .

11. Overall, we regard the 2nd Lebanon War as a serious missed opportunity. Israel initiated a long war, which ended without its clear military victory. A semi-military organization of a few thousand men resisted, for a few weeks, the strongest army in the Middle East, which enjoyed full air superiority and size and technology advantages. The barrage of rockets aimed at Israel's civilian population lasted throughout the war, and the IDF did not provide an effective response to it. The fabric of life under fire was seriously disrupted, and many civilians either left their home temporarily or spent their time in shelters. After a long period of using only stand-off fire power and limited ground activities, Israel initiated a large scale ground offensive, very close to the Security Council resolution imposing a cease fire. This offensive did not result in military gains and was not completed. These facts had far-reaching implications for us, as well as for our enemies, our neighbors, and our friends in the region and around the world. . . .

12. . . . We found serious failings and shortcomings in the decision-making processes and staffwork in the political and the military echelons and their interface.

We found serious failings and flaws in the quality of preparedness, decision-making and performance in the IDF high command, especially in the Army.

We found serious failings and flaws in the lack of strategic think-ing and planning, in both the political and the military echelons.

We found severe failings and flaws in the defense of the civilian population and in coping with its being attacked by rockets.

(continues)

THE WINOGRAD REPORT *(continued)*

These weaknesses resulted in part from inadequacies of preparedness and strategic and operative planning which go back long before the 2nd Lebanon War. . . .

18. The overall image of the war was a result of a mixture of flawed conduct of the political and the military echelons and the interface between them, of flawed performance by the IDF, and especially the ground forces, and of deficient Israeli preparedness. Israel did not use its military force well and effectively, despite the fact that it was a limited war initiated by Israel itself. At the end of the day, Israel did not gain a political achievement because of military successes; rather, it relied on a political agreement, which included positive elements for Israel, which permitted it to stop a war which it had failed to win. . . .

20. All in all, the IDF failed, especially because of the conduct of the high command and the ground forces, to provide an effective military response to the challenge posed to it by the war in Lebanon, and thus failed to provide the political echelon with a military achievement that could have served as the basis for political and diplomatic action. Responsibility for this outcome lies mainly with IDF, but the misfit between the mode of action and the goals determined by the political echelon share responsibility. . . .

37. The 2nd Lebanon War has brought again to the foreground for thought and discussion issues that some parts of Israeli society had preferred to suppress: Israel cannot survive in this region, and cannot live in it in peace or at least non-war, unless people in Israel itself and in its surroundings believe that Israel has the political and military leadership, military capabilities, and social robustness that will allow her to deter those of its neighbors who wish to harm her, and to prevent them—if necessary through the use of military force—from achieving their goal. . . .

---

that the war failed to meet those objectives. No clear recommendations were made concerning the prime minister.

Olmert remained in power despite low popular ratings, ongoing investigations of "criminal" activity, and divisions in the government coalition over the peace talks with the Palestinians.

Continued Clashes

On February 12, 2008, Imad Fayez Mughniyeh (also known as Hajj Rudwan), long regarded as a senior member of Hizballah's military wing and in charge of Hizballah's special operations and a terrorist responsible for numerous major terrorist attacks against the United States and other Western targets, as well as against Israeli and Jewish facilities (such as the Buenos Aires bombings in the 1990s), was killed by a car bomb in Damascus, Syria.

Hizballah leader Hassan Nasrallah noted in a speech broadcast on February 14 that Israel was responsible for the killing and threatened that Hizballah was ready for "open war" with Israel as a consequence. "Zionists, if you want this type of open war, then let it be. . . ." Israel, for its part, rejected Nasrallah's claims of Israeli culpability but placed its missions worldwide on high alert and reinforced its positions and forces on the border with Lebanon.

Winter and spring 2008 were punctuated by Qassem and other missiles fired into Israel from Gaza. When in July 2008 U.S. presidential candidate Barack Obama visited the southern town of Sderot, which had become a symbol of the threat from Gaza since Israel's withdrawal in 2005, he noted: "If somebody was sending rockets into my house . . . I'm going to do everything in my power to stop that. . . . And I would expect Israelis to do the same thing."

On June 19, 2008 an Egyptian-brokered "lull" or "pause" in hostilities between Hamas in Gaza and Israel went into effect. The arrangement required that Hamas end rocket and mortar attacks on Israel and Egypt would cease to allow the smuggling of military equipment across its border into Gaza. Hamas was to end its military buildup in Gaza and there would be movement toward the release of Gilad Shalit. Israel would ease the blockade of Gaza and cease its defensive military raids into the territory. The arrangement was not formalized, but persisted, with violations, until it collapsed in December when Hamas launched scores of mortar shells and rockets into Israel.

Sixty Years of Independence

As Israel celebrated 60 years of independence in May 2008 it continued to face a host of challenges. Domestically, the scene was dominated by scandals concerning the sitting prime minister, Ehud Olmert, and the former president Moshe Katsav, but it involved other political figures as well. The lessons of the second Lebanon War were being debated. The conflict with the Palestinians and other Arabs remained to be resolved.

Hizballah (in Lebanon) and Hamas (in Gaza) continued to call for Israel's demise and its replacement by an Islamic entity, for preparations for the next encounter, and to stir tensions in Israel and on its frontiers. The peace process initiated at Annapolis in November 2007 continued but with little real progress. Iran grew as a threat as it developed nuclear power (and perhaps a nuclear weapon) and sophisticated missiles to deliver new weapons.

Olmert Opts-Out

In July 2008, Ehud Olmert announced: ". . . I have always believed that when a prime minister is elected in Israel, even those who voted against him at the polls are obligated to desire his success. Instead . . . I found myself subject to a wave of investigations, examinations and criticism immediately after being elected." He asserted that, despite his struggle for personal justice, the good of the state was more important, and, thus, he decided not to run in the Kadima elections to retain his party leadership. Tzipi Livni replaced Olmert as head of the party by a slim-margin in the internal party election, defeating Shaul Mofaz with 43.1 percent of the vote to Mofaz's 42 percent. Analysts noted that she won "despite being a woman."

On September 21, 2008, Ehud Olmert met with President Shimon Peres and formally submitted his resignation. Peres tasked Livni to establish a new coalition government. However, by late October, she had failed, due, she maintained, to demands by the ultra-Orthodox Shas party for hundreds of millions of dollars in government assistance for its constituents as the price for joining the coalition. Shas's leadership said it was mostly concerned about the potential division of Jerusalem.

Stymied by the religious parties, Livni recommended that new Knesset elections be held, and agreement was reached to hold them on February 10, 2009. Under Israeli law, Olmert and the government remained in office, with full authority, pending the formation of a viable successor coalition government. It was in this caretaker capacity that the Olmert-led government launched Operation Cast Lead in Gaza.

The War in Gaza

Violations of the six-month "lull" were recorded in the early days of the arrangement, and both Israel and Hamas accused each other of violations throughout its six-month term. Hamas and other Palestinian groups in Gaza had continued to launch rockets, mortars, and missiles into Israel and to wound and kill Israelis and destroy civilian property, despite the arrangement. Israel responded with military strikes on occasion.

After the "lull" ended formally in December, Israel launched Operation Cast Lead. It had a specific set of objectives: to stop the bombardment of Israeli civilians by destroying and damaging the mortar and rocket launching apparatus and its supporting infrastructure and to improve the safety and security of southern Israel and its residents by reducing the ability of Hamas and other terrorist organizations in Gaza to carry out future attacks. It began with air strikes into Gaza, followed by a ground assault.

Late morning on December 27, 2008, Israel began air strikes by F-16 fighter jets and AH-64 Apache helicopters against planned targets. The objectives were military targets, police stations, and government buildings. In addition to weapons caches and military facilities, Israel targeted elements of Gaza's infrastructure that it believed supported Hamas's military and terrorist objectives, including a network of smugglers' tunnels along the border with Egypt. Air strikes also killed several senior Hamas leaders.

On January 3, 2009, Israel began a ground offensive—sending thousands of troops over Gaza's northern border, along with tanks, armored personnel carriers, and artillery. The ground troops targeted areas responsible for launching rockets into Israel, as well as tunnels, bunkers, and training facilities affiliated with Hamas. The ground operation began in the north largely to disable rocket launch sites that took advantage of the area's relative proximity to targets in southern Israel, such as Ashkelon. Having captured military targets in the northern sector of Gaza, the Israeli forces positioned themselves around Gaza City, after taking control of Gaza's main north-south highway. There was also limited close-quarters fighting between Israeli forces and Hamas gunmen in various Gaza City neighborhoods and in towns in the immediate vicinity. Hamas's mortar and rocket attacks escalated against the southern portions of Israel, eventually reaching the areas of Beersheba and Ashdod.

On January 4, Olmert set out conditions for a cease-fire: a halt to rocket attacks and terror, international supervision of the cease-fire, and an end to Hamas's military buildup. Israel would not open its borders with Gaza unless Hamas released Gilad Shalit.

On January 17, 2009, Israel unilaterally declared a cease-fire. Hamas rejected the call for a cease-fire but announced its own shortly thereafter. Israel completed the withdrawal of its forces from Gaza on January 21, 2009. Operation Cast Lead lasted for three weeks. There was almost unanimous public support in Israel for the operation as necessary to end the unrelenting Hamas rocket fire on Israeli population centers in the southern Negev region and the smuggling of weapons into Gaza for future attacks against Israel.

Political Aftermath

Operation Cast Lead generated substantial international debate, much of it castigating Israel for the number of Palestinian casualties, especially civilians, and the destruction of property, which were considered disproportionate to the small number of Israeli losses. Although reports of casualties varied, some 1,400 Palestinian deaths were reported, while Israeli deaths were small in number. Critics charged that Israel did not take adequate care to prevent civilian casualties. Other observers blamed the high number of civilian losses on Hamas, which placed personnel and military equipment in civilian areas, thus leading to a higher casualty level.

Regardless, Israel saw itself as morally justified; it could not allow its people and its territory to be attacked (rocketed and shelled) with impunity. Indeed, it had an obligation to protect its people and its territory, to provide for their security. Israel carefully studied the conflict and the actions of its forces, and ultimately, there were trials of some who had violated Israeli norms in dealing with the civilian populations in the war zone.

On April 3, 2009, the United Nations Human Rights Council (UNHRC) created a four member Fact-Finding Mission headed by Justice Richard Goldstone, a former member of the Supreme Court of South Africa. Israel refused to cooperate with the mission because, it argued, the mission's mandate and the resolution establishing it prejudged the outcome of any investigation and gave legitimacy to the Hamas terrorist organization. The Goldstone Report (formally "Gaza Fact-Finding Mission Report") was released on September 15, 2009. It found both Israel and unspecified Palestinian armed forces guilty of war crimes and possibly crimes against humanity. It focused primarily on Israel, concluding that it had deliberately targeted civilians and sought to destroy the viable infrastructure of Gazan life. Recommendations for legal action were made. The report was hailed by those critical of Israel but regarded as fundamentally flawed by others. The UNHRC endorsed the report. Israel regarded the report as biased and one-sided, and it formally criticized it. Israel disputed the report's findings and argued that it essentially ignored Israel's right of self-defense and made inaccurate claims about the intent of the operation. It also ignored Hamas's actions that put the civilian population of Gaza in harm's way. Israel considered the Goldstone Report to be one of the most harmful events of recent years and believed that it contributed to Israel's delegitimization because of accusations that Israel intentionally killed Palestinian civilians. In April 2011, in an opinion article in the *Washington Post,* Goldstone wrote: "If I had known then what I know now, the Goldstone Report would have been a different document." He retracted a central assertion of his report by noting that investigations by Israel "indicate that civilians were not intentionally targeted as a matter of [Israeli] policy."

Election 2009

Israel's Knesset election campaign began after Cast Lead. It focused on security (especially the threat posed by Iran), the peace process, and the failures of the Olmert government. Kadima leader Tzipi Livni endorsed the basic principles adopted at the Annapolis conference in November 2007, including expedited bilateral negotiations leading to a viable two-state solution coupled with a zero tolerance approach to Hamas rocket attacks from the Gaza Strip. Benjamin Netanyahu and Likud were skeptical of the Annapolis efforts, calling instead for a return to the performance-based Roadmap initially formulated by U.S. president George Bush in 2002. Netanyahu presented himself to the electorate with a focus on security but also as someone who would successfully manage the economy and be able to form a broad government coalition. Avigdor Lieberman's Yisrael Beiteinu party appealed to Israel's Russian-immigrant vote and focused on the threat from Iran. Lieberman raised questions about Israel's Arab citizens, suggesting they undermine the state and calling on them to take a loyalty oath, and proposed trading areas of Israel heavily populated by Israeli Arabs in a peace arrangement with the Palestinians.

Kadima won 28 seats in the election, one more than Likud. Avigdor Lieberman's Yisrael Beiteinu party rose to third place, with 15 seats. Ehud Barak's Labor Party won only 13 mandates. Shas won 11 seats. Altogether, 12 parties won seats in the new Knesset. The right wing of Israeli politics (Likud, Yisrael Beiteinu, Habayit Hayehudi, National Union) gained 18 seats, while the left-of-center parties (Meretz, Labor, Kadima) lost eight seats. The religious parties focused primarily on religious issues (thus not political Right or Left, despite their tilt toward positions of the right wing on foreign and security policy–related issues). Israeli voters were more supportive of parties skeptical of, or opposed to, peace talks with the Palestinians than those more compromising in approach.

Netanyahu clearly achieved a comeback with Likud gaining 15 seats. Kadima lost ground, 29 to 28, although Livni emerged as the leader of the moderate Left. The Arab political parties also registered gains. Yisrael Beiteinu greatly expanded its influence; winning 15 seats in the Knesset, it became the third-largest party. Avigdor Lieberman essentially became a kingmaker during the coalition-building process, and by joining the Likud-led coalition before any other major party he was able to demand one of the three central cabinet positions. Lieberman was appointed foreign minister, despite being widely regarded as racist by the Arab world and in spite of his view of Israeli Arabs as mainly a fifth column.

Despite the fact that Kadima won the largest number of seats in the Knesset, it seemed clear that Israel had moved to the right politically. After considering the election outcome and the configuration of the new Knesset, and after consulting the parties, President Shimon Peres invited Netanyahu on February 20 to form Israel's 32nd government.

Netanyahu entered into relatively lengthy negotiations with numerous potential partners over the ensuing weeks. He sought to get Kadima to join with Likud and form a national unity government, but Livni rebuffed Netanyahu's overtures, based primarily on significant foreign-

---

TZIPI LIVNI
(JULY 8, 1958–)

Tzipi Livni was born in Tel Aviv, Israel, in 1958. She graduated from Bar Ilan University with an LL.B. and worked for the Mossad from 1980 to 1984. She was first elected to the Knesset on the Likud Party list in 1999 and became minister of regional cooperation in July 2001. She later served as minister of justice. Livni followed Ariel Sharon from Likud into the Kadima party in November 2005 and became minister of foreign affairs in January 2006. She was elected head of Kadima in September 2008 but failed to form a coalition government to replace the Olmert-led coalition after his resignation. Livni led Kadima in the 18th Knesset election in February 2009 and became chairperson of the opposition in Israel's 18th Knesset.

policy disagreements, especially Netanyahu's refusal to endorse a two-state solution with the Palestinians and to return the Golan Heights to Syria. The government Netanyahu established was less narrow and hawkish than many had anticipated, primarily because of the addition of Labor, Likud's historical opponent, now led by Ehud Barak. A broader coalition government was seen as in the national interest. Likud was the clear leader of the coalition, with Netanyahu serving as prime minister and minister for economic strategies. Labor had won only 13 seats and joined the coalition with five cabinet posts; Barak retained his position as defense minister, but Labor was clearly the junior partner. Yisrael Beiteinu, led by Avigdor Lieberman, became the number-two player.

The Decline of the Israel Labor Policy

One of the election's outcomes was the growing marginalization of the Labor Party. For decades, the Labor Party, in its various incarnations, had been the dominant party in Yishuv and Israeli politics. It controlled the government, parliament, Histadrut (Labor Federation), and virtually all senior public organizations in the state. It had been closely linked with the founding and building of the State of Israel and the military service (the kibbutz system and the IDF officer corps) that protected its inhabitants. That identification had slowly eroded over time. Consequently, the party became increasingly identified with economic and business elites; it no longer seemed to represent the interests of labor, and it lost its image as the protector of the underprivileged. By 2009, the Labor Party was only the fourth-largest party in the Knesset.

In the peace effort, Labor seemed to move more to the dovish Left at the same time that Israeli society seemed to move in the opposite direction. Oslo and the peace process, associated with Labor, had been increasingly discredited. Barak's positions at Camp David 2000 and afterward, including on the ultimate status of Jerusalem, contributed to the public's concerns about Labor and Barak. Labor also failed to gain supporters from the growing Sephardic population (much of which maintained a traditional religious perspective and supported Shas) and the very large and secular Russian immigrant population that clearly was oriented to the right-wing, secular, nationalist perspectives of Likud and Yisrael Beiteinu.

Barak's decision to join the Netanyahu-led government was emblematic of a divided Labor Party, some of whose members saw Labor playing a more effective role in the government than in the opposition.

Those who questioned the move feared that the decision to join a right-of-center-led government would mark the end of Labor's dominant role in creating and shaping the Jewish state. The central committee vote (680 to 507) reflected the split.

The 32nd Government of Israel

On March 31, 2009, the Knesset approved the establishment of the 32nd government of Israel by a vote of 69 to 45. The government coalition included Likud, with 27 mandates; Yisrael Beiteinu, with 15 mandates; Labor, with 13 mandates. Shas, with 11 mandates; Habayit Hayehudi, with three mandates. Benjamin Netanyahu served as prime minister but also held several other portfolios. Silvan Shalom and Moshe Ya'alom were vice prime ministers, Avigdor Lieberman was minister of foreign affairs, and Ehud Barak was appointed minister of defense. United Torah Judaism (UTJ), with five mandates, joined the government and secured two deputy minister positions and chairmanship of two Knesset committees, and as part of the arrangement the status quo on matters pertaining to religion was retained. It was the largest government in Israel's history.

As with all governments in Israel, the Knesset voted its confidence in the coalition government presented by the prospective prime minister Benjamin Netanyahu but also approved the broad policy guidelines of the new government: "The 32nd Government of Israel will strive to achieve security and social justice, improve the economy, advance peace with all of Israel's neighbors, and maintain the Jewish character of the country while ensuring the rights of all religions."

Obama Administration

At the end of the Bush administration the peace process resumed at Annapolis was moribund. The Obama administration moved quickly to demonstrate its commitment to a negotiated two-state solution of the Arab-Israeli conflict. On his first full day in office, January 21, President Obama telephoned Palestinian Authority president Mahmoud Abbas, Israeli prime minister Ehud Olmert, Egyptian president Hosni Mubarak, and Jordanian king Abdullah II, "to communicate his commitment to active engagement in pursuit of Arab-Israeli peace from the beginning of his term." The next day, the president and Secretary of State Hillary Clinton jointly announced the appointment of former senator George J. Mitchell as the special envoy for Middle East peace to deal with the Arab-Israeli conflict. Mitchell visited the region often to meet with Israeli and Palestinian leaders, as well as other Arab leaders, in an effort to restart Israeli-Palestinian negotiations toward an overall peace settlement.

The Obama administration's policy conception was articulated by the president on June 4, 2009, in a speech at Cairo University in Egypt. "I've come here to Cairo to seek a new beginning between the United States and Muslims around the world, one based on mutual interest and mutual respect. . . ." President Barack Obama restated the goal of U.S. policy as establishing a Palestinian state in the West Bank and Gaza Strip, alongside Israel, pursuing land for peace based on the principles of UN Security Council Resolutions 242 and 338. He said that "just as Israel's right to exist cannot be denied, neither can Palestine's." Obama focused on the settlement issue.

> The United States does not accept the legitimacy of continued Israeli settlements. The construction violates previous agreements and undermines efforts to achieve peace. It is time for these settlements to stop. . . . The only resolution is for the aspirations of both sides to be met through two states, where Israelis and Palestinians each live in peace and security. That is in Israel's interest, Palestine's interest, America's interest, and the world's interest. And that is why I intend to personally pursue this outcome with all the patience and dedication the task requires.

Netanyahu at Bar Ilan University

In a speech at Bar Ilan University on June 14, 2009, Netanyahu described what he saw as Israel's national consensus on achieving a peace agreement. For the first time, Netanyahu publicly contemplated establishment of a Palestinian state—albeit a state without an army, without control of its air space, and with effective measures to prevent weapons from being smuggled into its territory and for international guarantees of this principle—alongside a Jewish state. Israel would retain a military presence in the West Bank. He welcomed the resumption of negotiations with the Palestinians without preconditions but also insisted that in any peace agreement the PLO would need to recognize unequivocally that Israel is "the nation state of the Jewish people" because, he maintained, the root cause of the conflict is the refusal to recognize that right. Thus, Netanyahu accepted the principle of two states for two peoples. He also declared that Jerusalem must remain undivided as the capital of Israel and that the Palestinian refugee problem must be solved outside of Israel, thereby rejecting a "right of return." Netanyahu stated that Israel would not build new settlements or confiscate land for that purpose but rejected a settlement freeze, insisting that settlers must be allowed to have "normal lives," implying a right to "natural growth" as the settlement population grows.

Abbas rejected the conditions Netanyahu placed on a two-state solution and insisted that the PLO would resume negotiations only if there was a complete settlement construction freeze.

Moving toward Negotiations

In September 2009, Barack Obama hosted the first meeting between Israeli and Palestinian leaders since taking office. In those nine months George Mitchell had made numerous visits to the parties in an effort to relaunch meaningful final status negotiations that offered the prospect of success. The United States had focused on stopping settlement construction, as the Palestinians demanded, as a prelude to talks.

On November 25, 2009, Netanyahu proposed the suspension of new permits for new construction in Judea and Samaria (West Bank) for a period of 10 months as part of an effort to revive the peace talks. The "moratorium" was not to apply to housing units under construction, to schools and synagogues and public buildings, and to infrastructure needed for national security, or to Jerusalem. He later said that Israel would revert to the policies of previous governments in relation to construction at the end of the 10 months.

The Obama administration renewed its effort to restart negotiations in early 2010. It focused on Israel's willingness to have a 10-month moratorium on settlements and argued that this was more than any previous government of Israel had conceded during the 40 years of the settlement process.

In March 2010, Vice President Joe Biden visited Israel to get indirect talks ("proximity talks") to move forward. He reiterated the U.S. commitment to unyielding support for Israeli security. As he arrived, Israel's interior minister announced 1,600 new housing units for Jews in Ramat Shlomo in East Jerusalem. This surprised both Netanyahu and Biden. Netanyahu was embarrassed and noted his displeasure at the ill-timed move in a meeting with Interior Minister Eli Yishai of Shas, who apologized for the timing of the announcement. Biden denounced the decision: "I condemn the decision by the government of Israel to advance planning for new housing units in East Jerusalem."

He complained that the substance and timing of the announcement undermined the trust needed to move the proximity talks and the peace process forward. The imbroglio was soon overshadowed by the Gaza flotilla episode.

The Gaza Flotilla Episode

Israel had established a land and sea blockade of the Gaza Strip in accordance with international law and the laws of armed conflict when Hamas, a self-declared enemy of Israel, seized full control of the area in 2007 and used the territory for the launching of rockets and attacks against Israel. The blockade was established to prevent the entry of war matériel and items that might facilitate terror as well as stifle economic growth and weaken the Gaza economy in order to put pressure on the population to generate opposition to Hamas. Restrictions were authorized on the transfer of goods as well as the movement of people to and from Gaza. Israel's blockade did not prevent nonmilitary goods from reaching the civilian population.

Various groups sought to breach the blockade of Gaza. A flotilla of six ships described as a humanitarian mission to the besieged Gaza Strip was organized in 2010 to break the blockade. On board were also activists who sought to provoke an Israeli response that would lead to international condemnation of Israel and its blockade. On May 30, the flotilla left northern Cyprus with more than 700 people from some 35 countries and cargo bound for Gaza. Israel warned that they would not be allowed to reach Gaza but could dock to offload the cargo at Ashdod, from where, after inspection for prohibited items, the humanitarian goods could be delivered overland to Gaza. The flotilla leadership rejected these offers.

On May 31, IDF naval commandos intercepted the ships in international waters to enforce the blockade. Five of the six ships allowed the Israelis to board without violent incident, and those then sailed to Ashdod. However, on board the *Mavi Marmara*, a ship that sailed under Turkey's flag and was organized and financed by a Turkish group, *Insani Yardim Vakfi* (IHH; Turkish Humanitarian Relief Foundation; The Foundation for Human Rights and Freedoms and Humanitarian Relief), were some activists prepared for violence.

The Israeli commandos, from the navy's Shayetet 13, who boarded the vessel, were dropped from helicopters to the deck of the ship, where they were met with a violent reception and were attacked by some on board who were armed with knives, clubs, metal bars, and other weapons. Nine Turkish activists aboard were killed. According to an Israeli military report, the commandos acted in self-defense and were lauded as "professional and courageous." The violence they met was not spontaneous but organized and premeditated, and the activists were well prepared.

The international reaction was sharp and negative, condemning Israel and its actions. The United Nations Human Rights Council was particularly vociferous in its negative views. The UN Security Council called for an "impartial, credible and transparent investigation." On June 14, 2010, Israel's government decided to establish a special Independent Public Commission to Examine the Maritime Incident of 31 May 2010. The commission was tasked to conclude whether the actions taken and their objectives (preventing vessels from reaching the coast of the Gaza Strip) and related matters were in conformity with the rules of international law. The commission was chaired by Emeritus Supreme Court Judge Yaacov (Jacob) Turkel, with Professor Shabtai Rosenne and Major General (res.) Amos Horev as members. Two international observers were included—Nobel Peace laureate Lord (David) Trimble from Northern Ireland and retired Brigadier General Kenneth Watkins (former judge advocate general) from Canada. On July 25, the cabinet appointed Reuven Merhav and Professor Miguel Deutch to the commission. With the death of Professor Rosenne in September 2010, the cabinet modified the procedure and decided that Judge Turkel would have a double vote in the event of a tie. The Turkel Commission released the first part of its detailed report in January 2011. Among its key findings is that Israel's blockade of Gaza, imposed for military-security reasons, was "legal pursuant to the rules of international law." The IDF forces were justified in capturing the vessels in the flotilla because they were attempting to breach a naval blockade that was legally imposed. The capture in international waters was legal. The IDF soldiers boarding the *Mavi Marmara* acted professionally and in a "measured manner" in the face of unanticipated and extensive violence.

Israel also established a military investigation into its naval operations, led by retired IDF major general Giora Eiland. It determined that the killing of nine Turks (one a dual U.S.-Turkish citizen) on the ship was justified. It noted that at least 65 Turkish Islamic militants were armed with knives and metal rods and had pledged to fight the Israeli navy's efforts to board the ship. But the investigation identified Israeli errors of planning, intelligence, and coordination. It concluded that not all possible intelligence had been gathered before the ship was boarded and that coordination between IDF intelligence and navy intelligence was insufficient. Also, the level of anticipated violence was underestimated. "The team determined that the Navy Commando soldiers operated properly, with professionalism, bravery and resourcefulness and that the commanders exhibited correct decision making. The report further determines that the use of live fire was justified and that the entire operation is estimable."

Several subsequent efforts were made to break the blockade, emanating from various ports and organized by various groups and countries (including Libya, Lebanon, and Iran). These efforts were either stillborn or defused with no significant confrontation. Ships seeking to land at Gaza were diverted to alternative ports, usually Ashdod in Israel, where their cargoes were inspected for security purposes, and transferred to Gaza by land. Some went to El-Arish, where the cargoes were transferred via the Rafah border crossing from Egypt into Gaza. In the spring and early summer of 2011, a group of organizers made an attempt at a second flotilla, consisting of activists, media and a limited amount of supplies for Gaza, designed to challenge Israel's naval blockade of Gaza, to embarrass Israel, and to cast it in a negative political light. It was to set sail from various Mediterranean ports, meet at sea, and then sail to Gaza in defiance of Israel's blockade. The flotilla encountered technical and logistical problems, bureaucratic and political difficulties (the Greek government ordered some ships to remain in port), and ultimately the Turks withdrew the *Mavi Marmara* and no large passenger ships participated. The flotilla stalled and a confrontation at sea was averted.

Easing the Restrictions on Gaza

Three years after imposing the blockade of Gaza, Israel assessed that the effort designed to weaken Hamas and to oust it from power had been unsuccessful. The Security Cabinet met to examine various proposals and restated its goal of protecting Israelis against terror, rocket, and other attacks from Gaza. The security regime for Gaza would be maintained, and Israel would keep weapons and war matériel out of Gaza while liberalizing the system by which civilian goods enter Gaza and increase the inflow of materials for civilian projects. In late June 2010, Israel formally announced that it was easing its blockade of Gaza. The action would, and soon did, lead to a significant increase in the flow of goods into the territory. It also streamlined the movement of people to and from Gaza. Subsequently, Israel allowed the export of goods from Gaza to the West Bank and abroad, further easing the blockade.

Israeli-Turkish Relationship

Over the decades, Turkey had acquired a reputation as a secular, Western-oriented, Muslim friend of Israel. Turkey voted against the partition of Palestine in 1947 but extended recognition to Israel on March 28, 1949, and established diplomatic relations. Various agreements followed, and early on, Turkey viewed Israel as a potential ally in its ongoing territorial disputes with Syria and in combating terrorism. In addition to commercial exchanges, significant growth occurred in security cooperation, joint military training, and counterterrorism. The Israeli-Turkish relationship was strained after the electoral victory in October 2002 of the AKP (Islamic Justice and Development Party), a conservative Turkish party with Islamic roots. Turkey's interests and ambitions in the Middle East and farther to the east, amid its rebuff by the EU, contributed to the downturn. The bombings of two synagogues in Istanbul on November 15, 2003, by groups associated with al-Qaeda also adversely affected relations between Ankara and Jerusalem. However, the bilateral relationship proved resilient, driven in large measure by the similar regional concerns shared by Israelis and Turks, including Syrian and Iranian military adventurism, the instability in post-Saddam Iraq, the proliferation of weapons of mass destruction, the challenge of Islamic radicalism, and the geopolitical destiny of central Asia. Israel and Turkey built strong military and economic ties, and Turkey was Israel's closest ally in the Muslim world.

Relations between the two countries deteriorated with Turkey's increasingly vociferous criticism of Israel's treatment of Palestinians and especially of Operation Cast Lead and the Gaza blockade. They reached a low point in May 2010, when Israeli naval commandos killed nine Turkish activists aboard the *Mavi Marmara* during the Gaza flotilla episode. Turkey denounced Israel on numerous occasions, but over the ensuing months, efforts were made to improve the strained relationship. Turkey noted that Israel would have to apologize and offer compensation for the deadly raid. Israel insisted that Turkey recognize that Israel acted in self-defense and not with malicious intent. Israel would not formally apologize for the actions of its commandos during the incident, although in December 2010, Netanyahu said that Israel was willing to express regret over the loss of life. Israel saw it in its best interests to resolve the matter and to reduce tensions with Turkey. Turkey and Israel continued efforts to mend relations but these were complicated by the Arab Spring that brought about changes in Arab leadership and policies and generated increased Turkish attention to, and involvement in, various Arab states.

Hopes and Opportunities

On May 9, 2010, the United States announced that indirect, U.S.-brokered Israel-Palestinian talks had resumed. Under the revived process, Mitchell would shuttle between Israel and the Palestinians (and other Arabs) to mediate the indirect (proximity) talks. The next round of discussions took place in mid-July 2010, culminating in meetings in Cairo between Netanyahu and Egyptian president Hosni Mubarak "about ways to accelerate the entry into direct negotiations between us and the Palestinians."

Efforts to end the Arab-Israeli conflict have been the central concern of Israel throughout its history. Various external powers, notably the United States, have also hoped to start or restart peace negotiations in order to try to reach a settlement of all outstanding issues. At the end of August 2010, the United States announced that, after proximity talks and consultations, there would be a resumption of direct negotiations between Israel and the Palestinians. U.S. Secretary of State Clinton invited Netanyahu and Abbas to meet in Washington on September 2 to resume direct negotiations to resolve all final status issues.

In early September, President Obama and Secretary of State Clinton joined in a two-day summit meeting that sought to translate hopes and opportunities into steps that would lead to an Israel-Palestinian peace agreement based on a two-state solution ensuring security and dignity for Israelis and Palestinians. It was believed that such an agreement would help to reduce other regional tensions and facilitate U.S. efforts in Iraq and Afghanistan and assist in dealing with threats from terrorists in the region and beyond. Secretary Clinton acknowledged that "we've been here before, and we know how difficult the road ahead will be" but expressed confidence that the core disputes separating the two sides could be resolved and a peace accord could be achieved within a year. Obama met with Israeli prime minister Benjamin Netanyahu, Palestinian Authority president Mahmoud Abbas, Egyptian president Hosni Mubarak, and Jordanian king Abdullah II before a dinner at the White House. The next day, September 2, 2010, direct negotiations between Israel and the Palestinians were formally relaunched in a ceremony at the State Department. The goal was to achieve a comprehensive peace in the Middle East that would include a two-state solution ensuring security and dignity for Israelis and Palestinians.

Netanyahu articulated the Israeli perspective on August 29:

> *Our goal is to seriously and responsibly advance a peace agreement that will be based on the following principles: First of all,*

the recognition of Israel as the national state of the Jewish People, the end of the conflict and of claims on Israel, that will stem from recognizing it as the national state of the Jewish People, and the establishment of tangible security measures on the ground so as to ensure that there will not be a repeat in Judea and Samaria of what happened in Lebanon and the Gaza Strip after Israel withdrew from these areas. Of course, there are many other issues but I note these three principles as the basic components of Israel's approach.

Netanyahu and Abbas met again on September 15, in Jerusalem; however, despite the initial optimism, by early October the talks had stopped. The Palestinians said there would be no negotiations without a halt to Israeli settlement construction in the West Bank. Netanyahu called for continuing the negotiations, but Israel would not renew the settlement construction moratorium, despite pressure from Washington. Israel argued that halting construction should not be a precondition nor would it affect the final borders to be negotiated. Netanyahu noted: "For 17 years the Palestinians conducted direct talks with Israeli governments while building went on in Judea and Samaria." After weeks of discussions the United States and Israel gave up on the proposed "construction freeze for assurances" package as a means of getting the parties to resume meaningful direct negotiations that could be sustained over time.

Instead, on December 10, 2010, Secretary Clinton outlined the new U.S. approach in a speech at the Brookings Institution in Washington. "We will push the parties to lay out their positions on the core issues without delay and with real specificity." The United States went back to indirect talks. Special envoy George Mitchell began holding meetings on ways to restart the process by bridging the gaps between the parties.

The Unexpected "Arab Spring"

What became known as the Arab Spring evolved from an initially overlooked event in a small village in Tunisia in December 2010, that led in 2011 to an uprising that stretched from Morocco in the west to Bahrain in the east, generating domestic turbulence and dramatic changes in Israel's neighbors that would affect Israel's near and long-term future. The self-immolation of Mohamed Bouazizi, a Tunisian street vendor, in protest of his treatment by the police resulted not from Israel's existence nor from the Arab-Israeli conflict but from depravation and exclusion and from opposition to despotic and autocratic regimes. Nevertheless, by the anniversary of Israel's independence and the Arab commemoration of Nakba Day, Israel increasingly became a focus of the ire of demonstrators. For Israel, the mushrooming size, scope, and volatility of the Arab Spring generated anxiety and became a matter of concern and security considerations.

The protests and demonstrations and the instability in the Arab world in early 2011 raised numerous questions for the future of those states and the region. For Israel, the more immediate issue was how it would reconcile itself with the new or revamped governments in these states. Israel seemed concerned but hopeful that the new regimes and their policies would bring change of a positive nature. Would reform progress? Would democracy bring positive movements and "partners for peace"?

Mubarak's sudden departure from power in February 2011 jeopardized the Egypt-Israel Peace Treaty of 1979, the framework of Israeli security and foreign-policy calculations for the ensuing three decades. The military leadership administering the post-Mubarak transition and the new participants in the government produced uncertainties in the political equation. Popular sentiment in Egypt favored the termination of the arrangement with Israel, while the military council pledged to maintain the peace treaty. Potential changes affected communications routes (such as the Suez Canal, for both Israel and its adversaries), the opening of the Egypt-Gaza border as a supply route for armaments and terrorists, and energy, especially natural gas, supplies to Israel.

Demonstrations in Jordan, also formally at peace with Israel, were of a different nature and more limited in size and scope. Protesters generally sought reforms rather than the end of the monarchy and the ouster of the king (who sustained the peaceful relationship with Israel established by his father). Although Jordan's population included substantial numbers of Palestinians and many Jordanians were opposed to the peace treaty with Israel, the relationship with Israel was much warmer and seemed not to be in jeopardy.

In Syria, protests and demonstrations against the regime's repression grew in intensity, and the response was bloody. The regime sought to divert anger to the front with Israel with suggestions of Israeli complicity in the internal disorder and by facilitating the breaching of the border fence on the Golan Heights. These ploys failed, and demonstrations and military responses escalated, generating uncertainty for Israeli decision-makers.

Israel's Independence Day celebrations in May 2011 marked some great achievements but were accompanied by reminders of the ongoing Arab-Israeli conflict on Nakba Day, when the Palestinian Arabs and their brethren marked the "catastrophe" of Israel's independence on May 15, 1948. On Nakba Day, some sought to merge the anti-Israel actions with the Arab Spring. The demonstrations were larger than in the past. Palestinians and their supporters marched to the fences and barricades marking Israel's frontiers with the Golan Heights and Syria, Lebanon, Gaza, and the West Bank; clashed with Israeli forces; and burst across where possible. The actions clearly were coordinated by Hizballah in Lebanon and by the Assad government in Syria, which facilitated the arrival of the Palestinians at the Lebanon and Golan Heights frontiers.

On May 3, Hamas and Fatah signed a reconciliation declaration, in which they agreed to hold elections in 2012 and merge their efforts to achieve recognition for an independent Palestinian state at the United Nations in September. This unilateral political-diplomatic initiative would occur outside the scope of Israeli-Palestinian negotiations.

Israel was concerned about stability and security in the region and the impact on the prospects for resolving the Arab-Israeli conflict and reaching peace and security. The failure of recent Arab-Israeli peace efforts seemed to be symbolized by the resignation of George Mitchell in May after more than two years of attempts to bring Israel and the Palestinians to the table to resolve the outstanding peace issues.

A Sense of Siege and Isolation

Events in summer and fall 2011 added to Israeli anxieties and concerns. The Arab Spring continued and expanded, leading to a civil war and the death of Muammar al-Qaddafi in Libya, ongoing massive demonstrations in Syria, and challenges to the regimes in Bahrain, Yemen, Saudi Arabia, Jordan, and Morocco, events that raised questions about regional stability and security and how that might affect Israel's situation.

Relations between Egypt and Israel deteriorated rapidly in August after an incident in which Egyptian soldiers were killed when Israeli troops pursued terrorists who had crossed from the Sinai Peninsula into Israel, where they killed eight Israelis and wounded dozens.

The Palestinian decision to seek UN membership by a General Assembly vote without negotiations with Israel caused diplomatic and political concerns. The matter was ultimately sent to the attention of the Security Council. However, in late October UNESCO voted for full membership for the Palestinians, further challenging both Israeli and U.S. diplomatic efforts and adding increased complexity to the Arab-Israeli peace efforts.

Conclusion

ISRAEL AT SIXTY-THREE

In May 2011, Israel celebrated the 63rd anniversary of its independence as a state with significant accomplishments yet faced with substantial uncertainties. Its economic achievements were remarkable and obvious. Its technical and scientific progress and skills (such as satellite capability) were celebrated.

Economic Well-being

Israel's economy has made substantial progress, and the economic well-being of its people has improved significantly since independence, when Israel was a poor country with weak agricultural and industrial sectors and a dependence on imported consumer goods, raw materials, and food. Although virtually bereft of natural resources and faced with substantial burdens of immigrant absorption and defense, Israel had become an economic power by regional standards by the beginning of the 21st century.

Massive immigration created problems in Israel's early years, but it also endowed Israel with a motivated and skilled labor force. Israel has developed its own highly regarded educational and scientific establishment. Illiteracy is virtually nonexistent, and Israel's population is one of the most highly educated in the world. It is in the forefront of scientific accomplishment in fields such as irrigation and water usage, energy technology, computer science, aerospace technology, and medical-scientific research. Its people are relatively prosperous, and its economy is well managed.

The unanimous decision of the 31 member states of the Organisation for Economic Co-operation and Development (OECD) in May 2010 to invite Israel to become a member recognized Israel's achievements as well as its ability to contribute to the OECD and to the overall world economy. In effect, the invitation and subsequent membership (formally signed in November 2010) signifies Israel's admittance into the "club of developed states" but also requires Israel to continue to work to achieve OECD standards in various areas, such as fighting corruption, protecting intellectual property, legislating international bribery, improving in the performance of the educational system, and addressing the gap between the wealthiest and poorest Israelis.

At the end of 2010, Israel's Central Bureau of Statistics (CBS) reported that Israel's economy was the fastest-growing in the West. Israel's gross national product (GNP) grew by 4.5 percent in 2010 (compared to a 2.7 percent average in the 33 other OECD members), and GNP per capita grew by 2.7 percent.

Despite Israel's significant achievements there were those who felt they had been bypassed by the system. A tent city movement, initially focusing on housing costs, began to appear in Tel Aviv in July 2011 and had expanded by mid-August and subsequently into demonstrations involving hundreds of thousands of protesters in several cities focusing on the widening gap between rich and poor and related economic and social issues. They sought a revision of the social contract. Negotiations with various government bodies soon followed. In response to the protests, Netanyahu's government established a panel of experts, led by Professor Manuel Trachtenberg, to suggest socioeconomic reforms (new housing, education, and tax measures) that would address the protestors' demands. The process continued into fall and winter 2011.

Israel's accomplishments are especially notable in the fields of science and technology. One indicator of Israel's scientific prowess is its

Ofeq 9 *satellite being launched, June 22, 2010 (Israel Aerospace Industries)*

satellite technology capability. On June 23, 2010, Israel launched the *Ofeq* (*Ofek*) 9 satellite, widely referred to as a "spy satellite," from an air base in Israel. It was placed by an Israel Aerospace Industries–manufactured Shavit booster rocket in a low orbit, where it joined a number of predecessors, mostly designed for intelligence gathering. Israel remained one of a few countries that could launch a satellite based on domestic technology and the achievements of its own industries.

The Special Relationship

Israel's unique and special relationship with the United States continues to be an overriding factor in all that Israel does. The U.S. relationship has evolved from being that of a power providing limited direct support to that of an indispensable ally. The complex and multifaceted special relationship with the United States originated prior to the independence of Israel, when it was grounded primarily in humanitarian concerns, religious and historical links, and a moral-emotional-political arena rather than a strategic military one. Today, the United States provides Israel, through one form or another, with economic (governmental and private), technical, military, political, diplomatic, and moral support. It had been seen as the ultimate resource against the Soviet Union and is a central participant in the campaign against Islamic terrorism; it is the source of Israel's sophisticated military hardware; and it is central to the Arab-Israeli peace process.

Israel's special relationship with the United States, which is based on substantial positive perception and sentiment evident in public opinion and official statements and manifest in political support and military and economic assistance, has not been enshrined in a formal, legally binding document joining the two states in an alliance. Israel has no mutual security treaty with the United States, nor is it a member of any alliance system requiring the United States to take up arms automatically on its behalf. The U.S. commitment to Israel has taken the form of presidential statements that have reaffirmed the U.S. interest in supporting the political independence and territorial integrity of Israel. On February 1, 2006, President George W. Bush said: "Israel is a solid ally of the United States, we will rise to Israel's defense if need be." When asked if he meant that the United States would rise to Israel's defense militarily, Bush said: "You bet, we'll defend Israel."

The Obama administration has reaffirmed the centrality of the special relationship. In a joint press conference with Prime Minister Netanyahu on May 18, 2009, President Obama said: "It is in U.S. national security interest to assure that Israel's security as an independent, Jewish state is maintained." In November 2010, Vice President Joe Biden reaffirmed the special relationship: "This administration represents an unbroken chain of American leaders who have understood this critical strategic relationship, one in which we will not yield one single inch. . . . The ties between our countries are literally, literally unbreakable. Our common values are interwoven in our cultures, in our mutual interests, and none more urgent than the shared struggle against the scourge of violent extremism and terrorists."

And, while the United States–Israel special relationship was again capped by presidential statements concerning the "ironclad" and unbreakable nature of the U.S.-Israeli bond and the U.S. commitment to Israel's long-term security, there was, again, a brief episode of tension in May 2011. President Obama and Prime Minister Netanyahu each articulated their views of the next steps in the peace process between Israel and the Palestinians in speeches and public and private meetings, including Netanyahu's speech to a joint meeting of Congress.

As President Obama said in a speech on May 19, 2011: "As for Israel, our friendship is rooted deeply in a shared history and shared values. Our commitment to Israel's security is unshakeable." On May 22, 2011, he elaborated: ". . . even while we may at times disagree, as friends sometimes will, the bonds between the United States and Israel are unbreakable and the commitment of the United States to the security of Israel is ironclad."

Israel as the Jewish State

Despite the various scientific and economic achievements and the general and overall prosperity and well-being of its people, Israel did not begin its 64th year with the attainment of the ultimate goal of peace with the Palestinians or acceptance by the Arab and Muslim world. Israel's capital, Jerusalem, remained a city divided in reality, if not formally, and its future was a subject of dispute and negotiation with other powers. The special relationship with the United States continued to elicit words and deeds of support concerning Israel's existence and security, but periodically it also was marked by tension and concern.

Sixty-four years after the United Nations voted to partition the Mandate of Palestine into a Jewish state and an Arab state, with an international regime for Jerusalem, and after Israel declared its independence, peace remained elusive, and Israel continued to seek Palestinian and Arab recognition as the Jewish state.

Appendix 1

Basic Facts About Israel

Official Name
Medinat Yisrael (State of Israel)

Government
Israel is a parliamentary democracy but has no formal written constitution. A series of Basic Laws has been enacted since independence that guide Israel's actions and are intended to form portions of a consolidated constitutional document. These include: The Knesset; The Lands of Israel; The President; The Government; The State Economy; The Army; Jerusalem, the Capital of Israel; The Judiciary; The State Comptroller; Human Dignity and Liberty; and Freedom of Occupation.

Executive Branch
Chief of state: president (*nasi*); elected by the Knesset for a seven-year term.
Head of government: prime minister.
Government (cabinet): chosen by prime minister and approved by the Knesset.

Legislative Branch
Knesset (unicameral parliament): 120 members; elected by popular vote for a four-year term.

Judicial Branch
Supreme Court: justices; appointed for life by the president.

Political Parties
Many of Israel's political parties trace their origins to the 1920s and 1930s when three categories of parties developed: the labor or socialist

left, the center and nationalist right, and the religious parties. These parties had grown out of movements, clubs, and other groups that began to develop around the Zionist movement in Europe at the turn of the century.

New parties, mostly small, have developed out of Israel's recent political experiences, for example, Sephardic parties, parties taking a dovish stand on the Arab-Israeli conflict, and parties representing new immigrant communities, such as those from the former Soviet Union. These special-interest parties are often active for relatively short periods before disbanding or merging into larger parties. There are also parties representing Israel's Arab citizens.

Legal System

Israel's legal system is a mixture of English common law and British mandate regulations. For personal status matters, Jewish, Muslim, or Christian law is applied accordingly. Laws are enacted by the Knesset.

Political Divisions

Capital

Jerusalem, as proclaimed by Israel in 1950. Most countries maintain their embassies in Tel Aviv.

Districts

There are six districts: Central, Northern, Southern, Jerusalem, Tel Aviv, and Haifa.

Geography

Area

20,770 square kilometers (about 8,100 square miles; approximately the size of New Jersey).

Coastline

273 kilometers

Boundaries

Mediterranean Sea, Egypt, Jordan, Lebanon, Syria, West Bank, Gaza Strip.

Climate

Temperate; hot and dry in southern and eastern desert areas.

Terrain
Negev Desert in the south; low coastal plain; central mountains; Jordan Rift Valley

Elevation
Lowest point: Dead Sea (408 meters [1,339 feet] below sea level)
Highest point: Har Meron (1,208 meters [3,963 feet])

Natural Resources
Timber, potash, copper ore, natural gas, phosphate rock, magnesium bromide, clays, sand

Demographics

Population (May 2011)
7.746 million

Population Growth Rate (2011)
1.6 percent

Infant Mortality Rate (2011 estimate)
4.12 deaths/1,000 live births

Life Expectancy at Birth (2011 estimate)
80.96 years

Ethnic groups (May 2011)
Jewish, 76.4 percent
Non-Jewish, 23.6 percent

Religions (2008 census)
Jewish, 75.6 percent
Muslim (predominantly Sunni), 16.9 percent
Christian, 2.0 percent
Druze, 1.7 percent
Other, 3.8 percent

Literacy (2004 estimate)
97.1 percent (age 15 and over who can read and write)

Major Cities
Jerusalem, Tel Aviv-Yafo, Haifa, Rishon Lezion, Ashdod

Languages
Hebrew (official), Arabic (official), Russian, English

Economy
Israel has a technologically advanced market economy with substantial but decreasing government participation. It depends on imports of crude oil, grains, raw materials, and military equipment. Despite limited natural resources, Israel has intensively developed its agricultural and industrial sectors. Cut diamonds, high-technology equipment, and agricultural products (fruits and vegetables) are the leading exports.

GDP (2010 estimate)
$219.4 billion
Composition by sector: agriculture 2.4 percent; industry 32.6 percent; service 65 percent (2010 estimate)

Real Growth Rate (2010 estimate)
4.6 percent

GDP–per Capita (2010 estimate)
$29,800

Currency
New Israeli shekel (NIS)

Agricultural Products
Citrus, vegetables, cotton, beef, poultry, dairy products

Industries
High-technology products (aviation, communications, computer design and manufacture, medical electronic), wood and paper products, potash, phosphates, processed foods, chemicals, diamond cutting and polishing, metal products

Exports—Commodities
Machinery and equipment, software, cut and polished diamonds, agricultural products, chemicals, textiles, apparel, electronics, and computer products

Imports—Commodities
Raw materials, military equipment, investment goods, rough diamonds, fuels, grain, consumer goods

Appendix 2

Knesset Election Results

Knesset Seats Won, by Party, 1949–1969							
	Election Year						
Party	1949	1951	1955	1959	1961	1965	1969
Mapai (Israel Workers)	46	45	40	47	42	IA	IA
Mapam (United Workers)	19	15	9	9	9	8	IA
Ahdut Ha'avodah (Unity of Labor)	–	–	10	7	8	IA	IA
Herut (Freedom)	14	8	15	17	17	–	–
General Zionists	7	20	13	8	–	–	–
Progressives	5	4	5	6	–	–	–
Liberal	–	–	–	–	17	–	–
United Religious Front	16	–	–	–	–	–	–
Mizrahi	–	2	–	–	–	–	–
Hapoel Hamizrahi	–	8	–	–	–	–	–
National Religious (NRP)	–	–	11	12	12	11	12
Agudat Israel	–	–	–	–	4	4	4
Poalei Agudat Israel	–	–	–	–	2	2	2
Torah Religious Front	–	5	6	6	–	–	–
Arab Democratic List	2	3	2	–	–	–	–

Note: IA = In Alignment

Knesset Seats Won, by Party, 1949–1969 *(continued)*							
	Election Year						
Party	1949	1951	1955	1959	1961	1965	1969
Arab Progress and Work	–	1	2	2	2	2	–
Arab Farmers and Development	–	1	1	1	–	–	–
Arab Cooperation and Brotherhood	–	–	–	2	2	2	–
Communist	4	5	6	3	5	–	–
Sephardim	4	2	–	–	–	–	–
Fighters List	1	–	–	–	–	–	–
Women's International Zionist Organization (WIZO)	1	–	–	–	–	–	–
Yemenites	1	1	–	–	–	–	–
Alignment (Mapai and Ahdut Ha'avodah)	–	–	–	–	–	45	–
Rafi (Israel Labor List)	–	–	–	–	–	10	IA
Israel Labor	–	–	–	–	–	–	IA
Maarach (Israel Labor and Mapam)	–	–	–	–	–	–	56
State List	–	–	–	–	–	–	4
Gahal (Gush Herut Liberalim)	–	–	–	–	–	26	26
Independent Liberals	–	–	–	–	–	5	4
Free Center	–	–	–	–	–	–	2
Alignment-affiliated Arab and Druze lists	–	–	–	–	–	–	4
Haolam Hazeh	–	–	–	–	–	1	2
New Communists	–	–	–	–	–	3	3
Israel Communists	–	–	–	–	–	1	1

Note: IA = In Alignment

Knesset Seats Won, by Party, 1973–1996							
	Election Year						
Party	1973	1977	1981	1984	1988	1992	1996
Mapai (Israel Workers)	IA	IA	IA	IA	–	–	–
Mapam (United Workers)	IA	IA	IA	IA	3	–	–
Ahdut Ha'avodah (Unity of Labor)	IA	IA	IA	IA	–	–	–
Rafi (Israel Labor List)	IA	IA	IA	IA	–	–	–
Israel Labor	IA	IA	IA	IA	39	44	34
Maarach (Israel Labor and Mapam)	51	32	47	44	–	–	–
State List	–	–	–	–	–	–	–
Independent Liberals	4	1	–	–	–	–	–
Shlomzion	–	2	–	–	–	–	–
Likud	39	43	48	41	40	32	32
National Religious Party (NRP)	10	12	6	4	5	6	9
Agudat Israel	–	4	4	2	5	–	–
Poalei Agudat Israel	–	1	–	–	–	–	–
Torah Religious Front	5	–	–	–	–	–	–
Tami (Traditional Movement of Israel)	–	–	3	1	–	–	–
Morasha (Heritage)	–	–	–	2	–	–	–
Shas (Sephardi Torah Guardians)	–	–	–	4	6	6	10
Alignment-affiliated Arab and Druze lists	3	–	–	–	–	–	–
United Arab List	–	1	–	–	–	–	–
Rakah (New Communist List)	4	–	–	–	–	–	–

Note: IA = In Alignment

(continues)

Knesset Seats Won, by Party, 1973–1996 _(continued)_							
	Election Year						
Party	1973	1977	1981	1984	1988	1992	1996
Democratic Front for Peace and Equality (Hadash)	–	5	4	4	4	3	5
Moked	1	–	–	–	–	–	–
Flatto-Sharon	–	1	–	–	–	–	–
Citizens Rights Movement (CRM)	3	1	1	3	5	–	–
Democratic Movement for Change (DMC)	–	15	–	–	–	–	–
Shinui (Change)	–	–	2	3	2	–	–
Shelli (Shalom Lemaan Israel)	–	2	–	–	–	–	–
Progressive List for Peace	–	–	–	2	1	–	–
Telem	–	–	2	–	–	–	–
Ometz (Courage to Cure the Economy)	–	–	–	1	–	–	–
Yahad	–	–	–	3	–	–	–
Kach	–	–	–	1	–	–	–
Tehiya	–	–	3	5	3	–	–
Tzomet	–	–	–	–	2	8	–
Moledet	–	–	–	–	2	3	2
Arab Democratic Party	–	–	–	–	1	2	–
Meretz	–	–	–	–	–	12	9
Degel HaTorah	–	–	–	–	2	–	–
United Torah Judaism	–	–	–	–	–	4	4
United Arab List	–	–	–	–	–	–	4
Yisrael Beiteinu	–	–	–	–	–	–	7
Third Way	–	–	–	–	–	–	4

Note: IA = In Alignment

Knesset Seats Won, by Party, 1999–2009

Party	Election Year			
	1999	2003	2006	2009
One Israel (Labor, Gesher, Meimad)	26	–	–	–
Labor—Meimad	–	19	19	13
Shinui (Change)	6	15	–	–
Meretz—New Movement	10	6	5	3
Likud	19	38	12	27
National Religious Party (NRP)	5	6	–	–
United Torah Judaism	5	5	6	5
Shas	17	11	12	11
Democratic Front for Peace and Equality (Hadash)	3	3	3	4
Israel B'Aliya	6	2	–	–
United Arab List	5	–	4	–
Center Party	6	–	–	–
National Union (Ichud Leumi)	4	7	–	–
Yisrael Beiteinu (Israel Our Home)	4	–	11	15
National Democratic Alliance (Balad)	2	3	3	3
One Nation (Am Ehad)	2	3	–	–
Ra'am	–	2	–	4
Gil	–	–	7	–
Ichud Leumi–Mafdal (National Union—NRP)	–	–	9	4
Kadima	–	–	29	28
Habayit Hayehudi	–	–	–	3

Appendix 3

GLOSSARY OF POLITICAL PARTIES

Agudat Israel (also Aguda)   Part of the TORAH RELIGIOUS FRONT until the 1961 election and again in the 1973 election. Ultra-Orthodox Ashkenazi religious political party with a non-Zionist ideology.

Ahavat Israel   Sephardic-based Haredi party that contested unsuccessfully in the 2003 election.

Ahdut Ha'avodah (Unity of Labor)   Formed in 1919 by a merger of POALEI ZION and smaller socialist Zionist groups. Dominant in the politics of the Yishuv. Included in MAPAM in 1949 and 1951. Joined MAPAI and RAFI in 1968 to form the ISRAEL LABOR PARTY.

Alignment (Maarach)   Name of election list in 1965 composed of MAPAI and AHDUT HA'AVODAH. Name of election list between 1969 and 1984 composed of LABOR PARTY and MAPAM.

Arab Democratic Party   Founded in 1988 by Abd el-Wahab Darawshe.

Atzmaut (Independence)   A Zionist, centrist, democratic party established by Ehud Barak and others who split from the LABOR PARTY in January 2011.

Balad (National Democratic Alliance)   Arab party that emphasized the granting of full political and civil rights to Israeli Arabs.

Black Panthers   Jewish protest movement to better social and economic status of Sephardim. Affiliated in electoral list with RAKAH.

Center Party   First competed in 1999 Knesset election. Led by prominent individuals seeking to create a middle ground party between LIKUD and the LABOR PARTY.

Citizens' Rights Movement (CRM) (Ratz)   Left-wing Zionist party. Now part of MERETZ.

Communist Party The communist movement began during the Palestine Mandate and has existed continuously since, despite internal divisions. The ISRAEL COMMUNIST Party (Miflaga Kommunistit Yisraelit-Maki) was founded in 1948 and split in 1965. The splinter group, the New Communist List (Reshima Kommunistit Hadasha, RAKAH) was primarily Arab in membership.

Degel HaTorah (Flag of the Torah) Ultra-Orthodox Ashkenazi non-Zionist party, formed in 1988 by a split from AGUDAT ISRAEL. Part of UNITED TORAH JUDAISM coalition.

Democracy and Aliyah (Da, Yes) The Russian initials for *demokratia v'aliyah*. Formed in 1992 to represent the interests of Jewish immigrants from the former Soviet Union.

Democratic Choice Dovish immigrant-based party. Joined the MERETZ coalition prior to the 2003 elections.

Democratic Front for Peace and Equality (Hadash) (DFPE) Formed in 1977 by a merger of RAKAH and some BLACK PANTHERS. Arab communist and nationalist list, dominated by Rakah. Joined with TA'AL in 2003 election campaign.

Democratic Movement for Change (DMC) Formed in 1976 by SHINUI, Democratic Movement, FREE CENTER, Zionist Panthers, and various individuals. Led by Yigael Yadin. Split in September 1978.

Free Center Formed in 1968 by a splinter group from HERUT. Part of LIKUD between 1973 and 1977 and a component of the DEMOCRATIC MOVEMENT FOR CHANGE in 1977.

Gahal Formed in 1965 as a joint merger of HERUT and the majority of the LIBERAL PARTY. Originally an acronym for the Herut-Liberal bloc. Expanded in 1973 and called the LIKUD.

General Zionists Right-of-center party that joined with the PROGRESSIVES between 1961 and 1965 and became known as the LIBERAL PARTY.

Gesher List headed by David Levy after leaving LIKUD before the 1996 election. Eventually formed a joint list with Likud and TZOMET. Disqualified in the 2003 election.

Gil (Pensioners Party) A political party led by Rafi Eitan established to contest the 2006 Knesset election. It focused on the rights of pensioners in Israel.

Habayit Hayehudi (Jewish Home)   Right-wing party formed in 2008 by the merger of the NATIONAL RELIGIOUS PARTY, MOLEDET and TEKUMA. Defection of Moledet and Tekuma prior to 2009 election, left it as the New National Religious Party (The New Mafdal).

Haolam Hazeh   Founded in 1965. Called for negotiations for a peace settlement between Israel and a Palestinian Arab state.

Hapoel Hamizrahi   Religious workers' movement and a major component of the NATIONAL RELIGIOUS PARTY.

Hapoel Hatzair (Young Worker)   A political party in the Yishuv period representing labor.

Hashomer Hatzair (Young Watchman)   First developed in Galicia in 1915 with followers from Poland and Lithuania, it had a collectivist vision of the Jewish state, combining Zionism and Marxism.

Herut (Freedom)   Founded by Menachem Begin in 1948. Nationalist ideology and a major component if the LIKUD.

Herut–National Movement   A party on the extreme Right that broke away from NATIONAL UNION–ISRAEL BEITEINU for the 16th Knesset election.

Ichud Leumi-Mafdal   A merger of the NATIONAL UNION and the NATIONAL RELIGIOUS PARTY for the 2006 Knesset election.

Independent Liberal Party   Minority of LIBERAL PARTY not joining in merger with HERUT. Formerly the PROGRESSIVES. Part of the Liberal Party between 1961 and 1965. In 1984, part of the LABOR-MAPAM ALIGNMENT.

Israel B'Aliya   A Russian immigrant-based party led by Natan Sharansky. Merged with LIKUD after 2003 Knesset election.

Israel Communist (Maki) (Miflaga Kommunistit Israelit)   Split of COMMUNIST PARTY in 1965 resulted in the formation of RAKAH and MAKI.

Israel Labor Party   Formed in 1968 by a merger of MAPAI, RAFI, AHDUT HA'AVODAH. Leftist Zionist party.

Kach   Jewish Defense League list. Founded and originally led by Rabbi Meir Kahane. Not permitted to run in Knesset elections since 1988 because of its racist ideology.

Kadima (Forward)   A centrist party established in November 2005 and initially led by Ariel Sharon. Under Ehud Olmert, it won 29 seats in the 2006 Knesset election and formed the 31st government of Israel. Led by Tzipi Livni in the 2009 election.

La'am   A political party that developed from the RAFI faction of MAPAI; in 1968, it refused to support the LABOR PARTY, then joined the LIKUD.

Labor Alignment   *See* LABOR-MAPAM ALIGNMENT.

Labor-Mapam Alignment   List that included the LABOR PARTY and MAPAM, 1969–84.

Labor Party   Formed in 1988 through a merger of ISRAEL LABOR and YAHAD. One of Israel's major political parties as a continuation of the Socialist Party dominant in the prestate era and during the first three decades of independence.

Liberal Party   Formed in 1961 by a merger of GENERAL ZIONISTS and PROGRESSIVES. Middle-class party; a member of GAHAL and LIKUD. Formerly the General Zionists.

Likud (Union)   One of Israel's major parties, this right-of-center secular nationalist party has historically been opposed to the return of territories taken in 1967 war. Likud was established in 1973 as an alliance of the GAHAL alliance (HERUT and the LIBERAL PARTY), the LA'AM alliance (the STATE LIST and the FREE CENTER), and SHLOMZION (Ariel Sharon's former party). Led by Menachem Begin, Likud came to power in 1977 with Begin as prime minister.

Maarach   Hebrew for ALIGNMENT.

Mapai (Israel Workers Party)   Created in 1930. Dominant party in Israel until its merger in 1968 with AHDUT HA'AVODAH and RAFI to form the ISRAEL LABOR PARTY.

Mapam   Formed in 1948 by merger of HASHOMER HATZAIR, AHDUT HA'AVODAH, and POALEI ZION.

Meretz   Formed in 1992 as a coalition of small left-wing Zionist parties, including MAPAM, the CITIZENS RIGHTS MOVEMENT, and SHINUI. Changed its name to YACHAD AND THE DEMOCRATIC CHOICE in 2004 and, in 2009 to Meretz–The New Movement (Hatnua Hahadasha).

Meimad (Dimension-Movement of the Religious Center)   Moderate Orthodox movement that broke away from the NATIONAL RELIGIOUS PARTY in the 1980s. Joined with LABOR to form ONE ISRAEL prior to the 1999 election.

Mizrahi   A major component of the NATIONAL RELIGIOUS PARTY.

Moked   Israel Communist Party and Tchelet Adom (Blue-Red) Movement.

Moledet (Homeland)   A right-wing secular nationalist party formed in 1988. Led by Rehavam (Gandhi) Ze'evi. Party called for the voluntary transfer of Arabs from Israel. It joined others to form the NATIONAL UNION (Ichud Leumi) in 1999.

Morasha (Heritage) Splinter party from the NATIONAL RELIGIOUS PARTY and POALEI AGUDAT ISRAEL.

Moriah A religious party formed by Rabbi Yitzhak Peretz, who had broken away from SHAS. Merged into UNITED TORAH JUDAISM in 1992.

National Democratic Alliance *See* BALAD.

National Religious Party (NRP) (Mafdal) Formed by a merger of MIZRAHI and HAPOEL HAMIZRAHI. Zionist Orthodox party active in settlements in the West Bank and in Gaza (until 2005). It merged with NATIONAL UNION in 2008. Former members dominate HABAYIT HAYEHUDI.

National Union (Ichud Leumi) Coalition of right-wing political parties headed by Ze'ev Benjamin Begin that ran for the first time in the May 1999 election.

National Union–Israel Beiteinu Coalition of both parties, along with MOLEDET and TEKUMA.

New Herut (Herut Hahadasha) A right-wing party formed by Ze'ev Binyamin Begin in late 1998. It joined with other small right-wing parties to form NATIONAL UNION (Ichud Leumi) in 1999.

New Liberal Party Formed in 1987 as a merger of SHINUI, the Liberal Center Party, and the INDEPENDENT LIBERAL PARTY.

New Way Dalia Rabin-Pelessof's single-member party established after the collapse of the CENTER PARTY, of which she was a member.

Ometz (Courage to Cure the Economy) Founded in 1982 by Yigael Hurvitz advocating drastic measures to deal with Israel's substantial economic problems.

One Israel Formed in 1999 as an electoral coalition of LABOR, GESHER, and MEIMAD. Reconfigured version of ISRAEL LABOR PARTY.

One Nation (Am Ehad) A centrist party in 1999 and 2003 elections that promoted increased social and economic assistance to the weakest sectors of Israeli society. It merged with the LABOR PARTY in 2004.

Poalei Agudat Israel Part of the TORAH RELIGIOUS FRONT until the 1961 elections and again in the 1973 elections. Ultra-Orthodox religious party with a worker orientation. In 1984, it was a component of MORASHA.

Poalei Zion A major socialist political party in the Yishuv period.

Progressive List for Peace (PLP) Established in 1984 as a joint Arab-Jewish list supporting the creation of a Palestinian state alongside Israel.

Progressives Party originally supported and dominated by German immigrants. In 1961, merged with GENERAL ZIONISTS to form the LIBERAL PARTY. The latter split in 1965, and the Progressives took the name INDEPENDENT LIBERAL PARTY. In 1984, it was part of the ALIGNMENT.

Ra'am An Arab political party known also as the United Arab List.

Rafi (Israel Labor List) Formed 1965 as a Ben-Gurion splinter group from MAPAI. Won 10 seats. In 1968, most of the activists (excluding Ben-Gurion) returned and formed, along with Mapai and AHDUT HA'AVODAH, the ISRAEL LABOR PARTY.

Rakah (New Communist List) Broke off from the ISRAEL COMMUNIST Party in 1965. Based primarily on Arab support. In 1977, it formed the DEMOCRATIC FRONT FOR PEACE AND EQUALITY as a joint list with the BLACK PANTHERS.

Shas (Sephardi Torah Guardians) Ultra-Orthodox religious party established in 1984 by a split from AGUDAT ISRAEL. Special appeal to Sephardim.

Shelli (Shalom Lemaan Israel) (Peace for Israel) Formed in 1977 by a merger of MOKED, HAOLAM HAZEH, Independent Socialists, and some BLACK PANTHERS.

Shinui (Change) Centrist party established as a protest movement after the 1973 Yom Kippur War. Part of the DEMOCRATIC MOVEMENT FOR CHANGE in 1977 and of MERETZ in 1992 and 1996. Ran as a separate party in 1999 and 2003. Under Yosef (Tomy) Lapid it ran an anti-ultra-Orthodox campaign in the 2003 election winning 15 mandates.

Shlomzion Right-wing party headed by Ariel Sharon. Joined LIKUD after 1977 election,

State List Ben-Gurion splinter group from ISRAEL LABOR PARTY. Made up originally of RAFI members who refused to reunite with MAPAI in 1968. Later part of LIKUD (in 1977 as part of LA'AM).

Ta'al (Arab Movement for Change) Arab political party led by Ahmed Tibi.

Tami (Tenuah Lemassoret Yisrael—Movement for Jewish Tradition) Founded in 1981 by then Religious Affairs Minister

Aharon Abuhatzeira drawing mainly on Sephardim to seek elimination of anti-Moroccan sentiment.

Tehiya Formed in 1981. Extreme nationalist party, which claimed Israel's right to the land of Israel and opposed the peace treaty with Egypt. Last elected in 1988.

Tekuma A breakaway from the NATIONAL RELIGIOUS PARTY, it joined with others to form NATIONAL UNION (Ichud Leumi) in 1999.

Telem Formed in 1981 and led by Moshe Dayan to contest that year's election. Dissolved after Dayan's death.

Third Way Political party that promoted a third way, that is, one other than LABOR PARTY or LIKUD. Concerned by the political concessions by Rabin and Peres in negotiations with Syria over the Golan Heights.

Torah Religious Front Joint list of AGUDAT ISRAEL and POALEI AGUDAT ISRAEL.

Tzomet Formed in 1988 as a splinter from TEHIYA-Tzomet. Right-wing party established by "Raful" Eitan, former IFD chief of staff. Formed a joint list with LIKUD and GESHER in 1996.

United Arab List *See* RA'AM.

United Religious Front A coalition of HAPOEL HAMIZRAHI, MIZRAHI, AGUDAT ISRAEL and POALEI AGUDAT ISRAEL that won 16 mandates in the first Knesset election in 1949.

United Torah Jewry (Yahadut HaTorah) Joint list of ultra-Orthodox non-Zionist parties, AGUDAT ISRAEL, and DEGEL HATORAH.

United Torah Judaism (UTJ) (Yahadut HaTorah Hameukhedet) Formed in 1992 by a merger of AGUDAT ISRAEL, DEGEL HATORAH, and MORIAH.

Yahad A centrist party formed and led by Ezer Weizman to contest the 1984 Knesset election,

Yachad and the Democratic Choice New name for MERETZ adopted in 2004. Led by Yossi Beilin. Changed to MERETZ–THE NEW MOVEMENT (Hatnua Hahadasha) in 2009.

Yisrael Beiteinu (Israel Our Home) A secular-nationalist party founded in 1999. Rooted in the Russian immigrant community. Moved further to the right under the leadership of Avigor Lieberman.

APPENDIX 4

CHRONOLOGY

ca. 17th century B.C.E.	Jewish patriarchs period: Abraham, Isaac, and Jacob
ca. 1250–1210	Exodus of the Jews from Egypt, wandering in the Sinai Desert, and the conquest of Canaan under Joshua
ca. 1020–1004	Establishment of the Israelite kingdom under King Saul
ca. 1004–965	Consolidation and expansion of the kingdom under King David
1004	King David establishes Jerusalem as his capital
ca. 961–928	The Temple is built in Jerusalem under King Solomon
ca. 928	Division of the state into the Kingdoms of Judah (South) and Israel (North)
ca. 722	Assyrian conquest of Samaria and Kingdom of Israel; large number of Jews exiled (Ten Lost Tribes)
ca. 586	Jerusalem is conquered and the Temple is destroyed; mass deportation of Jews to Babylon
ca. 520–515	Jews permitted to return; the Temple is rebuilt
ca. 167–160	Hasmonean rebellion under Judah Maccabee
164	Jerusalem is liberated and the Temple is rededicated
37–4	Reign of King Herod
ca. 19 B.C.E.	The Temple is rebuilt
C.E. ca. 35–40	Death of Jesus and the birth of Christianity
66	Jewish revolt against Rome
70	Siege of Jerusalem; destruction of the Second Temple by Romans; direct Roman rule is

	imposed (lasting until 395); beginning of the Jewish Diaspora
73	Fall of Masada
132–135	Revolt of Shimon Bar Kochba
135	Jews are expelled from "Palestine," the name given to Judea by Rome
313–636	Byzantine rule of region
ca. 636–1071	Arab rule of region
638	Muslim Arab armies conquer Jerusalem
1071–98	Seljuk rule
1099	Jerusalem is captured by the Crusaders
1099–1291	Crusader rule, with interruptions
1187	Jerusalem is captured by Saladin
1291–1516	Mamluk rule
ca. 1517–1917	Ottoman rule

The Creation of the State of Israel

1882	Hibbat Zion movement begins; Rishon le Zion is founded
1882–1903	First Aliyah: about 25,000 immigrants, primarily from Russia
1894	Dreyfus trial in France
1896	Publication of *Der Judenstaat* by Theodor Herzl
1897	First Zionist Congress is held in Basle, Switzerland; World Zionist Organization is established
1901	Jewish National Fund is established
1904	Herzl dies
1904–14	Second Aliyah: about 40,000 immigrants, mostly from Russia
1909	Kibbutz Degania is founded; Tel Aviv is established
1917	British army captures Jerusalem
November 2, 1917	Balfour Declaration is issued
1919–23	Third Aliyah: about 35,000 immigrants, mostly from Russia; the Arabs react in 1921 in a wave of murderous attacks against Jews
1920	British mandate over Palestine is granted at San Remo; Herbert Samuel is appointed high commissioner for Palestine; the Histadrut and Haganah are founded

1921	Moshav Nahalal is founded
1922	Churchill Memorandum (White Paper) is issued
July 1922	Palestine mandate ratified by League of Nations; Britain separates area east of Jordan River from Palestine mandate and establishes Transjordan
1924–28	Fourth Aliyah: about 80,000 immigrants, mostly from Poland
1925	Hebrew University is inaugurated on Mt. Scopus, Jerusalem
1929	Arab riots take place in Jerusalem; massacres of Jews occur in Hebron and Safed: 68 Jews are slaughtered in Hebron, and 500 others leave the city
1929–39	Fifth Aliyah: about 245,000 immigrants, most from German-speaking countries but also Poland
1935	Revisionist Zionist movement, headed by Vladimir Ze'ev Jabotinsky, establishes the New Zionist Organization
1936–39	Arab revolt
1937	Peel Commission report is issued: first proposal to partition Palestine
1939	British White Paper further limits Jewish immigration to Palestine and land purchases
May 1942	Biltmore Program is promulgated by the Zionists
November 1945	Anglo-American Committee of Inquiry is established
July 22, 1946	British headquarters in King David Hotel, Jerusalem, are bombed by Irgun
February 15, 1947	Great Britain turns the Palestine issue over to the United Nations; United Nations Special Committee on Palestine examines the problem and recommends solution
November 29, 1947	UN General Assembly adopts Resolution 181(II), providing for an independent Jewish state and an independent Arab state in the area of the Palestine mandate linked by an economic union; an international regime (corpus separatum) is to be established in Jerusalem; plan is accepted by Jewish leadership in Yishuv, but rejected by the Arabs; United States and Soviet Union support the partition plan

December 1947	Jewish-Arab communal strife in Palestine intensifies after adoption of UN partition plan
May 14, 1948	Proclamation of the independence of the State of Israel; David Ben-Gurion becomes first prime minister of Israel
May 15, 1948	British mandate for Palestine is terminated; Arab armies of Egypt, Iraq, Jordan, Lebanon, and Syria invade and the first Arab-Israeli war (Israel's War of Independence) officially begins; United States and Soviet Union recognize Israel

Political, Economic, and Military Consolidation

January 25, 1949	Election for the first Knesset
February 16, 1949	Chaim Weizmann is elected first president of Israel
February 24, 1949	Armistice agreement with Egypt
March 10, 1949	First regular government is established, with Ben-Gurion as prime minister
March 23, 1949	Armistice agreement with Lebanon
April 3, 1949	Armistice agreement with Jordan
May 4, 1949	Israel declares Jerusalem its capital city
May 11, 1949	Israel becomes a member of the Untied Nations
July 20, 1949	Armistice agreement with Syria
September 12, 1949	Compulsory Education Law is passed
November 2, 1949	Weizmann Institute of Science is inaugurated
December 1949	King Abdullah of Transjordan annexes that part of Palestine occupied by the Arab Legion (West Bank) and East Jerusalem
December 13, 1949	A resolution to transfer the Knesset and the government to Jerusalem is adopted
January 4, 1950	The Knesset ratifies a government statement opposing the internationalization of Jerusalem
May 25, 1950	Tripartite Declaration (by Britain, France, and United States) regulates arms flow to the Middle East
July 1950	Beginning of large-scale immigration to Israel from Iraq
July 5, 1950	Law of Return, confirming the right of every Jew to settle in Israel, is passed by the Knesset
September 24, 1950	Airlift of Jews from Yemen to Israel in Operation Magic Carpet is concluded

September 1, 1951	UN Security Council condemns Egyptian anti-Israel blockade in Suez Canal
1952	Knesset ratifies the reparations agreement with West Germany
November 9, 1952	President Weizmann dies
December 8, 1952	Itzhak-Ben Zvi becomes Israel's second president
1953	Ben-Gurion resigns as prime minister; Moshe Sharett becomes prime minister
October 14, 1953	Israel Defense Forces (IDF) troops carry out a reprisal raid against Jordanian village of Kibya
1954	Moshe Dayan becomes chief of staff of IDF; Gamal Abdul Nasser becomes prime minister and president of Egypt; Lavon Affair occurs
June 2, 1954	Hebrew University dedicates its new campus in Jerusalem
September 28, 1954	Egypt seizes the *Bat Galim,* an Israel-flag merchant vessel, when it attempts to transit the Suez Canal
February 28, 1955	Israel raids Gaza Strip in retaliation for guerrilla activity against Israel
November 3, 1955	Ben-Gurion becomes prime minister of Israel
October 29, 1956	Israel invades Sinai Peninsula to eliminate fedayeen and supporting bases; Sinai Campaign (second Arab-Israel war) begins
November 5, 1956	France and the United Kingdom invade the Suez Canal Zone
November 6, 1956	Israel announces acceptance of a cease-fire in the Sinai Peninsula
December 22, 1956	Anglo-French troops complete their withdrawal from the Suez Canal Zone
January 22, 1957	Israel evacuates all of Sinai except Gaza and Sharm el-Sheikh
March 1, 1957	Israel agrees to evacuate Gaza and Sharm el-Sheikh
March 8, 1957	United Nations Emergency Force (UNEF) take over from Israel the garrisoning of Sharm el-Sheikh and the administration of the Gaza Strip
April 26, 1960	Israel approves a plan for laying a giant conduit to carry water from the Sea of Galilee to southern Israel

May 23, 1960	Adolf Eichmann is kidnapped from Argentina for trial in Israel
April 11, 1961	Eichmann trial opens in Jerusalem
July 30, 1961	Cornerstone of the deep-sea port of Ashdod is laid; the millionth immigrant since the establishment of the state arrives
August 15, 1961	Election for the fifth Knesset
May 31, 1962	Eichmann is executed
September 27, 1962	Israel announces that the United States has agreed to supply Israel with Hawk ground-to-air missiles for defense: first direct sale of significant American weapons to Israel
November 21, 1962	New town of Arad is officially inaugurated
April 23, 1963	President Ben-Zvi dies
May 21, 1963	Shneur Zalman Shazar is elected Israel's third president
June 16, 1963	Ben-Gurion resigns as prime minister and minister of defense
June 26, 1963	A new government, with Levi Eshkol as prime minister, takes office
October 21, 1963	Prime Minister Eshkol announces relaxation of military government restrictions on Israel's Arab citizens
January 1964	Palestine Liberation Organization (PLO) is created; Ahmed Shukairi becomes its first chairman; Palestine National Covenant calls for the destruction of Israel
January 5, 1964	Pope Paul VI begins a pilgrimage to Christian holy sites in the Holy Land
June 9, 1964	National Water Carrier begins operation
September 5, 1964	Arab Summit decides to divert the sources of the Jordan River in Syria and Lebanon
January 1, 1965	Fatah is established and launches its first attack against Israel
November 2, 1965	Election for the sixth Knesset
January 1966	Golda Meir resigns as foreign minister and is succeeded by Abba Eban
November 12, 1966	An Israeli patrol car detonates a land mine near the Jordan frontier, incurring casualties
November 13, 1966	Israeli forces launch an attack on the Jordanian village of es-Samu in response to killing of Israelis

December 10, 1966	S. Y. (Shmuel Yosef) Agnon is awarded Nobel Prize in literature
April 7, 1967	During an air clash, six Syrian MIG-21s are shot down by Israeli planes
May 15, 1967	United Arab Republic (UAR) puts its forces on a state of alert and begins extensive redeployment of military units
May 18, 1967	UAR asks the United Nations to remove UNEF from the Egypt-Israel armistice line; United Nations complies; Israel announces it is taking "appropriate measures" in response to the UAR military buildup in Sinai
May22/May 23, 1967	President Nasser announces an Egyptian blockade of the Gulf of Aqaba
May 24, 1967	Jordan announces it has given permission for Iraqi and Saudi Arabian forces to enter Jordan and that general mobilization in Jordan has been completed
June 1, 1967	Prime Minister Eshkol forms a broadly based national unity government (NUG) with Moshe Dayan as minster of defense

From the Six-Day War to the Yom Kippur War and Its Aftermath

June 5, 1967	Hostilities commence between Israel and the Arab states in the Six-Day War (third Arab-Israeli war)
June 7, 1967	Jordan and Israel accept the UN call for a cease-fire; Israel has established itself at the Jordan River and has control of the West Bank
June 8, 1967	Cease-fire goes into effect between the UAR and Israel; Israeli forces have occupied the Gaza Strip and the Sinai Peninsula
June 10, 1967	Soviet Union breaks diplomatic relations with Israel; Other Soviet-bloc European countries, except Romania, follow suit
June 11, 1967	Cease-fire goes into effect between Israel and Syria; Israel establishes itself on the Golan Heights
June 12, 1967	Eshkol declares to parliament that Israel will not return to the prewar situation and demands

	that the Arabs make peace with Israel; Israel has reunited Jerusalem and gained control of the West Bank (Judea and Samaria), Sinai Peninsula, Gaza Strip, and Golan Heights
June 28, 1967	Israel announces new municipal boundaries for Jerusalem that include former Jordanian-held East Jerusalem
August/September 1967	Arab Summit meeting, in Khartoum, Sudan, declares "no recognition, no negotiation, and no peace with Israel"
October 21, 1967	Israeli destroyer *Eilat* is sunk by the UAR off the Sinai coast; in reprisal, on October 24, Israel shells Suez and its oil refineries
November 22, 1967	UN Security Council adopts Resolution 242
December 1967	Mission of Gunnar Jarring to implement UN Resolution 242 begins
January 27, 1968	Israeli submarine *Dakar* disappears in the Mediterranean Sea
December 26, 1968	Arab fedayeen from Beirut attack an El-Al plane at Athens airport
December 28, 1968	Israeli helicopter-borne commandos launch retaliatory attack against aircraft at Beirut airport
1969	Egypt launches sustained artillery barrages against Israelis along the Suez Canal, marking a new phase in the War of Attrition (fourth Arab-Israeli war)
February 1969	Yasser Arafat becomes chairman of the PLO
February 26, 1969	Eshkol dies
March 7, 1969	Meir becomes prime minster
October 28, 1969	Election for the seventh Knesset
1970	Bar-Lev line is completed
August 7, 1970	War of Attrition is ended by a cease-fire
September 1970	Jordan civil war between armed forces and the PLO takes place; PLO is ousted from Jordan
September 28, 1970	Nasser dies; Anwar Sadat becomes president of Egypt
May 30, 1972	Japanese gunmen, acting for the Popular Front for the Liberation of Palestine (PFLP), shoot up Lod Airport
September 5, 1972	Munich Olympics massacre of Israeli athletes by Black September terrorists

April 10, 1973	Ephraim Katzir is elected fourth president of Israel
October 6, 1973	Yom Kippur War (fifth Arab-Israeli war) begins, as Egypt and Syria launch surprise attack on Israel
October 22, 1973	Resolution 338 is adopted by the United Nations Security Council
December 21, 1973	Geneva Peace Conference is convened
December 31, 1973	Election for the eighth Knesset
January 17, 1974	Egypt-Israel Disengagement Agreement is signed at Kilometer 101
April 10, 1974	Meir resigns as prime minister
April 22, 1974	Yitzhak Rabin becomes prime minister
May 15, 1974	Palestinian infiltrators hold schoolchildren hostage in Maalot; 21 are killed
May 31, 1974	Israel and Syria sign a disengagement of forces agreement in Geneva
October 28, 1974	Arab League summit meeting at Rabat, Morocco, declares the PLO the "sole legitimate representative of the Palestinian people"
September 4, 1975	Egypt and Israel sign the Sinai II agreement brokered by U.S. secretary of state Henry Kissinger
November 10, 1975	The UN General Assembly adopts a resolution declaring Zionism to be a form of racism

Peace with Egypt

July 4, 1976	Israeli commandos free hostages held at Entebbe Airport in Uganda
April 1977	Rabin resigns as prime minister; Shimon Peres is chosen as Labor Party leader
May 17, 1977	Election for the ninth Knesset; Likud, under the leadership of Menachem Begin, emerges as the largest party
June 21, 1977	Begin forms the government coalition with himself as prime minister, the first non-Labor government in Israel
November 1977	Egyptian president Sadat announces his willingness to visit Israel to discuss peace; the Israeli Knesset overwhelmingly approves an invitation

	to Sadat; Sadat addresses the Israeli Knesset on November 19; negotiations begin
December 25–26, 1977	Begin meets Sadat in Ismailia, Egypt
March 14, 1978	Following an attack on an Israeli bus, Israel launches Operation Litani against Palestinian bases in Lebanon
April 19, 1978	Yitzhak Navon is elected fifth president
June 13, 1978	Israel completes the withdrawal of its armed forces from Lebanon; United Nations Interim Force in Lebanon takes up positions there
September 5–17, 1978	Sadat, Begin, and U.S. president Jimmy Carter meet at Camp David, Maryland; the Camp David Accords are signed at the White House in Washington, D.C., on September 17
October 12, 1978	Egypt and Israel begin peace negotiations at Blair House in Washington, D.C., to implement the Camp David Accords
December 10, 1978	Nobel Peace Prize is awarded to Sadat and Begin
March 26, 1979	Egypt-Israel Peace Treaty is signed in Washington, D.C.
May 25, 1979	Israel begins withdrawal from the Sinai Peninsula; Egypt and Israel begin discussion of autonomy issues
October 1979	Dayan resigns as foreign minister
February 1980	Egypt and Israel exchange ambassadors
March 1980	Yitzhak Shamir is appointed foreign minister

Renewed Hostilities and the First Intifada

July 30, 1980	Knesset adopts the Basic Law reaffirming united Jerusalem as Israel's capital
June 7, 1981	Israel destroys Iraq's Osirak nuclear reactor near Baghdad
June 30, 1981	Election for the 10th Knesset; Likud secures the largest number of seats
August 1981	Begin-led coalition government secures a vote of confidence from the Knesset
October 6, 1981	Sadat is assassinated
November 30, 1981	United States and Israel sign a Memorandum of Understanding on Strategic Cooperation

December 14, 1981	Israel extends its "law and jurisdiction" to the Golan Heights
April 25, 1982	Israel completes its withdrawal from the Sinai Peninsula and returns it to Egypt
June 6, 1982	War in Lebanon (Operation Peace for Galilee) begins; Israel invades Lebanon in an attempt to destroy PLO bases
July/August 1982	Israeli siege of Beirut; PLO and Syrian forces are expelled
September 1982	Bashir Gemayel, president-elect of Lebanon, is assassinated; Christian Phalangist forces massacre Palestinians at Sabra and Shatila refugee camps; Israel establishes Kahan Commission to inquire into the massacres
September 1, 1982	U.S. president Ronald Reagan outlines his "fresh start" initiative for peace in the Middle East
February 1983	Kahan Commission of Inquiry reports its findings; Ariel Sharon resigns as defense minister and is replaced by Moshe Arens
March 22, 1983	Chaim Herzog is elected sixth president
May 17, 1983	Israel and Lebanon sign an agreement concluded with the assistance of U.S. secretary of state George Shultz
September 16, 1983	Begin resigns as prime minister
October 1983	Shamir forms a new government and takes office as prime minister
March 5, 1984	Lebanon abrogates the May 17, 1983, agreement with Israel
July 23, 1984	Election for the 11th Knesset
September 1984	NUG is formed by Labor and Likud with Peres as prime minister and Shamir as alternate prime minister and foreign minister; mass immigration of Ethiopian Jews to Israel in Operation Moses takes place
January 1985	Israel announces its intent to withdraw unilaterally from Lebanon
July 1985	IDF completes its withdrawal from Lebanon; a "security zone" is established in southern Lebanon astride the Israeli-Lebanese frontier in which a contingent remains

September 11–12, 1985   Prime Minister Peres and Egyptian president Hosni Mubarak hold a summit meeting in Egypt

July 1986   Peres visits King Hassan II in Morocco

October 20, 1986   NUG rotation shifts Shamir to the position of prime minister and Peres to the post of foreign minister

December 8, 1987   An Israeli truck hits a Palestinian car in Gaza killing four people; anti-Israeli violence erupts in Gaza

December 9, 1987   The Arab uprising, Intifada, begins in the West Bank and the Gaza Strip, challenging Israel's authority in the territories

December 14, 1987   Hamas is created in Gaza

September 19, 1988   Israel launches its first space satellite, *Ofeq-1*.

November 1, 1988   Election for the 12th Knesset

November 15, 1988   Palestine National Council meeting in Algiers declares an independent Palestinian state

December 14, 1988   Arafat, at press conference, recognizes Israel's right to exist, accepts UN Security Council Resolutions 242 and 338, and renounces terrorism; United States announces that it will begin a dialogue with the PLO in Tunis

December 22, 1988   Shamir's coalition government is approved by the Knesset

March 15, 1989   Egypt takes control of Taba

May 14, 1989   Israel's cabinet formally approves the "Shamir Plan" peace initiative

January 1990   Soviet Jews begin to arrive in Israel in large numbers

March 13, 1990   Shamir dismisses deputy prime minister Peres from the government, and the other Labor Party cabinet ministers resign

March 15, 1990   Knesset passes a motion of no confidence in the government led by Shamir by a vote of 60-55

April 26, 1990   After failing in his efforts, Labor Party leader Peres returns the mandate to form a government to President Chaim Herzog

June 11, 1990   Knesset approves Shamir's government composed of Likud and right-wing and religious parties

June 20, 1990   U.S. president George H. W. Bush suspends dialogue with the PLO

August 2, 1990	Iraq invades Kuwait
September 30, 1990	Consular relations are reestablished between Israel and the Soviet Union
November 5, 1990	Rabbi Meir Kahane, leader of the Kach Party, is assassinated in New York

The Persian Gulf War and the Peace Process

January 16, 1991	U.S.-led coalition forces launch a massive air campaign against Iraq (Operation Desert Storm)
January 17, 1991	Iraq launches the first of 39 Scud missiles against Israel
February 3, 1991	Rehavam Ze'evi of Moledet joins the cabinet as minister without portfolio
October 18, 1991	Israel and the Soviet Union restore diplomatic relations
October 30, 1991	Peace conference organized by the United States and the Soviet Union meets in Madrid, Spain
December 10, 1991	Beginning of Washington rounds of bilateral Arab-Israeli negotiations
December 16, 1991	UN General Assembly repeals the "Zionism Is Racism" resolution
January 24, 1992	Israel and China establish diplomatic relations
January 29, 1992	India announces it will establish formal diplomatic relations with Israel
March 17, 1992	Thirty are killed and more than 200 wounded in bombing of Israeli embassy in Buenos Aires, Argentina
March 18, 1992	Knesset approves electoral reform that includes direct election of the prime minister
June 23, 1992	Election for the 13th Knesset; Israel Labor Party wins under leadership of Rabin
July 13, 1992	Rabin's coalition with Meretz and Shas assumes power, with Rabin serving as prime minister and defense minister and Peres as foreign minister and deputy prime minister
August 24, 1992	Sixth round of bilateral Israel-Arab peace talks convenes in Washington, the first since Rabin's election

December 17, 1992	Israel orders temporary expulsion to Lebanon of some 415 Muslim extremists in response to terrorist attacks on Israeli soldiers
January 19, 1993	Knesset repeals legislation prohibiting PLO contacts
January–February 1993	Deputy Foreign Minister Yossi Beilin discloses existence of Oslo talks to Peres, who in turn informs Rabin; talks continue
March 11, 1993	U.S. president Bill Clinton pledges to Rabin to "minimize risks" of peace for Israel
March 23, 1993	Benjamin Netanyahu is elected leader of the Likud Party, replacing Shamir
March 24, 1993	Ezer Weizman is elected seventh president of Israel
May 1993	Rabin agrees to upgrade Oslo talks to official level
July 25, 1993	Israel mounts Operation Accountability against Hizballah bases in southern Lebanon
September 9, 1993	Rabin and Arafat exchange letters of mutual recognition on behalf of Israel and the PLO
September 13, 1993	Israel-PLO Declaration of Principles (DOP) is signed by Peres and Mahmoud Abbas on the White House lawn in Washington; Prime Minister Rabin and PLO leader Arafat shake hands
September 14, 1993	Israel and Jordan sign Common Agenda for future negotiations; Rabin meets with King Hassan II in Morocco
September 23, 1993	Knesset approves DOP by vote of 61-50, with eight abstentions
October 1993	Rabin visits Indonesia, the world's most populous Muslim country
October 6, 1993	Rabin and Arafat meet with Egypt's Mubarak in Cairo to coordinate implementation of Gaza-Jericho First agreement
November 2, 1993	Longtime Jerusalem mayor Teddy Kollek is defeated by Likud's Ehud Olmert in a municipal election
December 1993	Third round of Israel-Palestinian talks on implementing Oslo Accords takes place in Cairo, Oslo, and Paris

December 14, 1993	By a vote of 155-3 (Iran, Syria, and Lebanon against), with one abstention (Libya) and 25 absences, the UN General Assembly adopts resolution 48/59 expressing "full support" for Israel-Palestinian peace process
December 30, 1993	Israel and the Vatican sign the Basic Agreement to establish diplomatic ties
January 1994	President Weizman becomes first Israeli head of state to visit Turkey
February 9, 1994	Clinton reaffirms U.S. "ironclad" commitment to Israel's security
February 25, 1994	Jewish settler Baruch Goldstein kills 29 Palestinian worshipers and wounds more than 100 others in Hebron's Tomb of the Patriarchs; Supreme Court president Meir Shamgar heads commission of inquiry
March 13, 1994	Israel outlaws Kach and Kahane Chai as terrorist groups
March 31, 1994	Israel and the PLO agree on Temporary International Presence in Hebron (TIPH)
April 29, 1994	Israel-PLO economic cooperation agreement signed in Paris
May 4, 1994	Israel and the PLO sign Cairo agreement for establishing self-rule in Gaza Strip and Jericho
May 13, 1994	IDF withdraws from Jericho, transferring authority to the PLO
May 18, 1994	IDF completes withdrawal from the Gaza Strip, except for security positions near several small settlements in the north
June 15, 1994	Israel and the Vatican establish full diplomatic relations
July 1, 1994	Arafat visits the Gaza Strip for the first time in 27 years
July 18, 1994	One hundred and two people are killed and hundreds wounded in bombing of Jewish community offices in Buenos Aires, Argentina
July 25, 1994	Washington Declaration on Israel-Jordan peace is issued
August 3, 1994	Knesset approves resolution reaffirming Jerusalem's status as the "eternal capital of Israel, and Israel alone"

August 8, 1994	Rabin visits King Hussein of Jordan in the first official visit to Jordan by an Israeli leader
August 29, 1994	"Early empowerment" agreement on transfer of civilian authority in parts of the West Bank and Gaza Strip is signed
September 1, 1994	Israel and Morocco sign agreement to open liaison offices in Tel Aviv and Rabat
October 26, 1994	Israel and Jordan sign a peace treaty; King Hussein subsequently makes first official visit to Israel during which he and Rabin formally exchange copies of the treaty
November 3, 1994	Tansu Ciller makes first visit by Turkish prime minister to Israel
November 27, 1994	Israel and Jordan establish diplomatic relations
December 1994	IDF chief of staff Ehud Barak and his Syrian counterpart, Hikmat Shihabi, meet in Washington, D.C., to discuss security arrangements for the Golan Heights and related matters
December 10, 1994	Rabin, Peres, and Arafat receive the Nobel Peace Prize in Oslo, Norway
December 12–15, 1994	Rabin visits Japan and South Korea
December 21, 1994	Israel and India sign a wide-ranging trade agreement
December 26, 1994	Rabin becomes first Israeli prime minister to visit the Persian Gulf Sultanate of Oman
December 26, 1994	Knesset, by vote of 56-6, with 32 abstentions, passes Gaza-Jericho Agreement Implementation Law (Limiting of Activities), barring any PLO or Palestinian Authority (PA) political activity in East Jerusalem and the rest of Israel and areas of the West Bank and Gaza still under Israeli control
February 7–8, 1995	Officials from the United States, Israel, Egypt, Jordan, and the PLO meeting in Taba, Egypt, sign a joint declaration calling for end to the boycott of Israel
March 14, 1995	Israel and Syria agree to resume direct peace talks involving their ambassadors in Washington, D.C.
August 11, 1995	Israeli and Palestinian delegations meeting in Taba, Egypt, reach partial agreement on IDF redeployment in West Bank

September 28, 1995	Israeli-Palestinian Interim Agreement on the West Bank and Gaza Strip (Oslo II) is signed in Washington, D.C.
October 24, 1995	U.S. Congress passes the Jerusalem Embassy Relocation Act, requiring transfer of U.S. embassy to Jerusalem by May 1999
November 4, 1995	Rabin is assassinated by Yigal Amir in Tel Aviv; Peres becomes interim prime minister; inquiry headed by retired Supreme Court president Meir Shamgar finds serious lapse in security around Rabin but no evidence of conspiracy
November 22, 1995	Knesset votes its confidence in government of Peres
December 11–27, 1995	IDF completes withdrawal from six major West Bank cities
December 27, 1995	Israel and Syria meet at Wye Plantation in Maryland
February 12, 1996	Arafat is sworn in as president of the PA
March 13, 1996	Summit of the Peacemakers is held at Sharm el-Sheikh, Egypt
April 14–16, 1996	Thirteen are wounded by Katyusha rockets fired into northern Galilee from Hizballah bases in Lebanon; in retaliation, Israel launches air and missile barrage (Operation Grapes of Wrath) to push Hizballah out of firing range of the Galilee and the south Lebanon security zone
April 18, 1996	IDF bombardment of suspected Hizballah missile emplacements results in the death of 11 Lebanese civilians in the village of Nabatiya al-Fawqa and 102 at the UN refugee base at Kfar Qana; Israel is widely condemned for these deaths
April 22, 1996	Palestine National Council meeting in Gaza resolves that the PLO Charter is "hereby amended by canceling the articles that are contrary to the letters exchanged between the P.L.O. and the Government of Israel 9–10 September 1993," and instructs its legal committee to present a redrafted charter within six months
May 5–6, 1996	First session of Israel-PLO permanent status talks convenes at Taba, Egypt

The Netanyahu and Barak Governments

May 29, 1996	In the first direct election of the prime minister, Netanyahu defeats Peres by less than 1 percent of votes cast; concurrent election to 14th Knesset is held
June 17, 1996	New governing coalition (holding 66 of 120 seats) is presented to the Knesset
September 4, 1996	Netanyahu and Arafat meet for the first time
October 1–2, 1996	Netanyahu and Arafat join King Hussein of Jordan and U.S. president Clinton at summit in Washington, D.C.; Israeli and Palestinian leaders reaffirm commitment to abide by obligations undertaken in the Oslo Accords
October 6, 1996	Nonstop talks toward implementing outstanding aspects of interim agreements begin between delegations headed by former IDF chief of staff Dan Shomron and chief Palestinian negotiator Saeb Erekat
January 15, 1997	Israel and the PA conclude Protocol Concerning the Redeployment in Hebron
January 16, 1997	Knesset endorses the Hebron agreement by a vote of 87-17
February 4, 1997	Seventy-three Israeli soldiers die when two IDF helicopters collide near the Lebanon border
March 9, 1997	Jordan's King Hussein sends letter to Netanyahu expressing "distress" over stalemate in negotiations with the Palestinians and questioning whether it is Netanyahu's "intent to destroy" the peace process
March 28, 1997	Jewish worshipers are temporarily evacuated from the plaza in front of the Western Wall when Palestinian demonstrators throw stones from the Temple Mount above
March 31, 1997	Arab foreign ministers recommend that Arab countries cease normalizing relations with Israel, restore the economic boycott, and suspend participation in multilateral peace talks to protest the absence of progress in bilateral talks
May 29, 1997	Israel and Jordan sign agreement to share international airports at Eilat and Aqaba; the "Shalom Airport" goes into service in November 1997

September 25, 1997	Khaled Mashal, head of the Hamas political office in Jordan, is wounded in an assassination attempt in Amman; two Mossad agents are arrested by Jordanian police
October 1, 1997	Israel frees Hamas spiritual leader Sheikh Ahmed Yassin
January 4, 1998	Defense Minister Yitzhak Mordechai declares Israel's readiness to negotiate IDF withdrawal from southern Lebanon on the basis of UN Security Council Resolution 425 (1978); David Levy resigns as foreign minister and withdraws his Gesher faction from the governing coalition to protest stalemate in peace process and proposed budget cuts
March 18, 1998	Eighty-one U.S. senators sign letter to President Clinton expressing concern about reported White House pressure on Israel to make unsafe concessions in negotiations with the PA
October 9, 1998	Sharon is named foreign minister and Israel's chief negotiator of final-status agreements with the PA
October 23, 1998	Netanyahu and Arafat conclude the Wye River Memorandum, and it is signed
October 30, 1998	United States and Israel sign Memorandum of Agreement on strategic security cooperation
November 17, 1998	Knesset ratifies the Wye River Memorandum
November 18, 1998	Foreign Minister Sharon and PA minister Abbas formally launch final-status negotiations
December 9, 1998	For the first time, the UN General Assembly includes anti-Semitism in its definition of racism
December 14, 1998	At a special meeting in Gaza, in the presence of U.S. president Bill Clinton, the Palestine National Council ratifies changes to its covenant; Israel calls the changes "satisfactory"
December 21, 1998	Faced with likely defections of key coalition partners in Knesset no-confidence vote over his government's handling of the peace process, Netanyahu supports legislation to prepare for general elections
December 28, 1998	Ze'ev Benjamin Begin quits Likud, announcing intention to enter race for prime minister as

	head of New Herut (Herut Hahadasha) Party; this party is subsequently incorporated into new right-wing National Union coalition, with Begin as its candidate for prime minister
March 25, 1999	Azmi (Ahmed) Bishara becomes first Israeli Arab to declare his candidacy for prime minister
May 15–16, 1999	On the eve of general elections, Bishara, Mordechai, and Begin withdraw from prime ministerial race, creating two-way contest between Netanyahu and Ehud Barak
May 17, 1999	Israel Labor Party/One Israel leader Barak defeats Netanyahu in the direct election for prime minister, receiving 56.08 percent of the popular vote, compared to 43.92 percent for Netanyahu; in elections for the 15th Knesset, One Israel wins 26 seats, Likud 19, and Shas 17
May 18, 1999	Netanyahu resigns as head of Likud
July 6, 1999	Knesset approves Barak's government and its policy guidelines
August 5, 1999	Knesset member Nawaf Massalha is appointed to the post of deputy foreign minister, the first Israeli Arab to hold that post
August 30, 1999	Morocco renews political contacts with Israel
September 2, 1999	Sharon is elected leader of the Likud Party
September 4, 1999	Barak and Arafat sign agreement at Sharm el-Sheikh to implement outstanding elements of the October 1998 Wye River Memorandum; target date for completing final-status peace negotiations is set for September 2000
September 13, 1999	Foreign Minister Levy and Palestinian negotiator Abbas formally launch the final status peace talks between Israel and the Palestinians
October 28, 1999	Mauritania establishes diplomatic ties with Israel, becoming the third Arab country (after Egypt and Jordan) to do so
November 10, 1999	Barak cabinet approves additional 5 percent redeployment in the West Bank, but Arafat refuses to sign the maps, claiming that the areas affected by the proposed redeployment are "not significant enough" for the Palestinians

December15–16,1999	Barak and Syrian foreign minister Farouk al-Sharaa meet with Clinton in Washington, D.C.
January 3–10, 2000	Barak and al-Sharaa and their respective delegations meet with U.S mediators in Shepherdstown, West Virginia
January 6, 2000	Israel concludes a scheduled redeployment from 5 percent of the West Bank
March 21, 2000	Pope John Paul II begins visit to Israel
May 2000	IDF completes withdrawal from south Lebanon security zone
July 10, 2000	President Weizman resigns
July 11, 2000	Camp David II summit of Clinton, Barak, and Arafat convenes
July 25, 2000	Camp David summit ends without an agreement
July 31, 2000	Moshe Katsav is elected president of Israel

The Second Intifada

September 28, 2000	Sharon visits the Temple Mount; clashes occur between Palestinians and Israeli security and spread in the territories; second Palestinian intifada (al-Aqsa Intifada) begins
October 16, 2000	Crisis summit convenes at Sharm el-Sheikh; Arafat, Barak, Clinton, and Jordan's king Abdullah meet to end the violence
December 9, 2000	Barak announces he will resign as prime minister
January 27, 2001	Taba talks between Israelis and Palestinians end without an agreement; both sides say they have never been closer to peace
February 6, 2001	Sharon is elected prime minister over Barak by a landslide of 62.6 percent to 37.2 percent
March 7, 2001	Sharon government is sworn in
October 17, 2001	Tourism Minister Rehavam Ze'evi is assassinated in Jerusalem by PFLP
December 13, 2001	Israel declares Arafat "irrelevant" in the struggle against terrorism
January 3, 2002	Palestinian ship Karine A is intercepted carrying arms to Gaza
March 12, 2002	By a vote of 14 for, 0 against, with 1 abstention (Syria), the UN Security Council adopts Resolution 1397, articulating, for the first time, the

council's "vision of a region where two States, Israel and Palestine, live side by side within secure and recognized borders"; the resolution also demands an "immediate cessation of all acts of violence, including all forms of terror, provocation, incitement and destruction" and affirms the council's support for an immediate and unconditional cease-fire as called for in the Mitchell report and Tenet work plan

March 27–28, 2002   Saudi Arabia formally presents peace proposal at Arab League summit meeting in Beirut

A New Perspective on Security

March 29, 2002   Israel's security cabinet declares Arafat an "enemy" who "set up a coalition of terror against Israel" and was to be "isolated"; the cabinet approves "a wide-ranging operational action plan against Palestinian terror"; the first target of Operation Defensive Shield is Arafat's command compound in Ramallah, where the IDF imposes a siege

March 31, 2002   Prime Minister Sharon and the cabinet declare "war against terrorism" and label Arafat "the enemy of the entire free world"

April–June, 2002   Operations Defensive Shield and Determined Path are undertaken; reoccupation of Palestinian areas by the IDF occurs

April 4, 2002   U.S. president George W. Bush demands action to implement sustainable cease-fire based on Tenet and Mitchell proposals, criticizes Arafat for his failure to end violence and terror and for his failure to lead Palestinian people toward statehood, calls on Israel to end its military operations in Palestinian cities, including Ramallah, and announces that Secretary of State Colin Powell will be traveling to the region to facilitate talks toward a cease-fire

June 24, 2002   Bush articulates his vision of Israel-Palestine peace and a two-state solution

October 30, 2002   Labor leaves the NUG

November 5, 2002	Sharon calls for elections
November 28, 2002	Terror attacks against Israelis in Mombasa, Kenya
January 16, 2003	The U.S. National Aeronautics and Space Agency launches the space shuttle *Columbia* on mission STS-107, with the first Israeli astronaut, Ilan Ramon, on board
January 28, 2003	Elections for the 16th Knesset
February 1, 2003	Space shuttle disintegrates on reentry to earth; all on board are killed
March 2003	U.S.-led coalition begins war against Iraq
April 29, 2003	Abbas and his cabinet are approved by the Palestinian legislature
April 30, 2003	The Roadmap is presented to Sharon and Abbas
June 4, 2003	Middle East Peace Summit at Aqaba, Jordan, is held; President Bush meets with King Abdullah of Jordan and Prime Ministers Sharon and Abbas
September 6, 2003	Abbas resigns as Palestinian prime minister, citing lack of support from Arafat
March 22, 2004	Israel kills Hamas leader Sheikh Ahmed Yassin in Gaza City
April 14, 2004	In an historic statement, Bush endorses Sharon's unilateral withdrawal plan
May 2, 2004	The Likud Party membership votes 60 percent to 40 percent to reject Sharon's Gaza withdrawal plan
June 7, 2004	Israel's cabinet agrees to proceed with Gaza disengagement plan
June 30, 2004	Israel's Supreme Court orders changes in the route of Israel's security fence; Sharon moves to implement the order
July 9, 2004	The International Court of Justice rules that Israel's security fence violates international law and should be dismantled
November 11, 2004	Yasser Arafat dies
December 2004	Labor rejoins coalition government led by Sharon
January 2005	Mahmoud Abbas is elected to replace Arafat as head of the PA
January 10, 2005	Knesset approves Sharon's new coalition government

February 8, 2005	Sharon and Abbas meet at Sharm el-Sheikh, Egypt
February 20, 2005	Israeli cabinet approves Sharon's disengagement plan for Gaza and the new route for the security fence in the West Bank
March 13, 2005	The Israeli government formally approves the appointment of Air Force Major General Dan Halutz as the chief of staff of the IDF
April 11, 2005	Sharon meets with President Bush at his ranch at Crawford, Texas
August 15, 2005	Israel begins withdrawing settlers and troops from the Gaza Strip
October 11, 2005	Robert J. Aumann is announced as joint recipient of the Nobel Prize in Economics
November 10, 2005	Amir Peretz is elected head of the Labor Party
November 21, 2005	Ariel Sharon announces his departure from the Likud Party and the formation of a new centrist political party (called Kadima)
December 18, 2005	Ariel Sharon is hospitalized after a mild stroke
January 4, 2006	Ariel Sharon suffers a massive cerebral hermorrhage
January 18, 2006	Tzipi Livni is appointed foreign minister

A Continuing Quest for Peace

January 25, 2006	Palestinian parliamentary elections. Hamas wins
March 28, 2006	Israeli election for 17th Knesset
March 29, 2006	Kadima Party emerges from Knesset election with 28 seats. Labor Party wins 19
June 25, 2006	Hamas attacks across the border from Gaza, kills two Israeli soldiers, and kidnaps Corporal Gilad Shalit
June 28, 2006	IDF forces enter the southern Gaza Strip
July 12, 2006	Hizballah forces cross into Israel and kidnap two Israeli soldiers. Israel launches a military counterattack. Second Lebanon War begins
August 14, 2006	Israel-Hizballah cease-fire takes effect
September 18, 2006	Winograd Commission begins its investigation into the war in Lebanon
October 1, 2006	Israel completes military withdrawal from Lebanon

December 23, 2006	Prime Minister Ehud Olmert meets at his Jerusalem residence with Palestinian Authority president Mahmoud Abbas
January 16, 2007	IDF chief of staff Lt. Gen. Dan Halutz resigns
January 22, 2007	General Gabi Ashkenazi is appointed as the new chief of staff of the IDF
January 23, 2007	Israel's attorney general, Menachem Mazuz, decides to charge President Moshe Katsav with rape, sexual harassment, obstruction of justice, fraud, and breach of trust
June 2007	Hamas seizes control of the Gaza Strip by force
June 13, 2007	Shimon Peres is elected president of Israel
August 6, 2007	Olmert and Abbas meet in Jericho, on the West Bank, to continue talks
September 19, 2007	Israel's security cabinet unanimously determines: "Hamas is a terrorist organization that has taken control of the Gaza Strip and turned it into hostile territory"
November 27, 2007	An international conference is convened at the U.S. Naval Academy in Annapolis, Maryland, to begin direct Israeli-Palestinian negotiations to achieve peace between the parties
January 9–11, 2008	George W. Bush makes his first visit to Israel since becoming president of the United States. He meets with Ehud Olmert and Mahmoud Abbas and expresses confidence that an agreement can be reached before the end of his term of office
January 16, 2008	Avigdor Lieberman resigns from the cabinet and Yisrael Beiteinu party withdraws from the government over Israel's negotiations with the Palestinians
January 21, 2008	Israel launches a sophisticated reconnaissance satellite from a site in India
January 30, 2008	The Winograd Commission issues its final report concerning the Second Lebanon War
February 4, 2008	A Palestinian suicide bombing at a shopping mall in Dimona kills one and injures numerous others
February 28, 2008	Operation Hot Winter is launched by the IDF to halt Qassam rocket fire into Israel from Gaza

March 3, 2008	Operation Hot Winter is concluded
March 6, 2008	A terrorist kills eight at the Mercaz Harav Yeshiva in Jerusalem
June 19, 2008	Israel and Hamas agree to a six-month "lull" in hostilities
September 17, 2008	Tzipi Livni wins Kadima primary to replace Ehud Olmert
September 21, 2008	Olmert formally submits his resignation to President Peres
October 26, 2008	Tzipi Livni announces that she is unable to form a government
December 19, 2008	Hamas announces that its "lull" with Israel has expired and will not be renewed. Rocket attacks from Gaza resume
December 27, 2008	IDF launches Operation Cast Lead in Gaza
January 18, 2009	Israel declares a unilateral cease-fire and an end to major operations in Gaza
February 19, 2009	18th Knesset election; Right-wing parties win a commanding majority of seats: Kadima wins 29, Likud 28
March 31, 2009	Knesset approves the Netanyahu-led 32nd government by a vote of 69 to 45
June 4, 2009	U.S. president Barak Obama speaks at Cairo University
June 14, 2009	Prime Minister Netanyahu speaks at Bar-Ilan University
September 12, 2009	United Nations Human Rights Council issues the Goldstone report
September 14, 2009	Hamas releases first video of Gilad Shalit
September 25, 2009	Ehud Olmert's corruption trial begins
October 15, 2009	United Nations Human Rights Council endorses the Goldstone Report
March 9, 2010	Interior Ministry announces the construction of 1,600 new housing units for Jews in East Jerusalem
May 9, 2010	United States announces that American-brokered indirect (proximity) talks between Israel and the Palestinians resume
May 31, 2010	IDF naval forces intercept six ships attempting to break the naval blockade of the Gaza Strip. Naval commandos storm the *Mavi Marmara*

	after it refuses to heed requests to allow inspection at Ashdod port
June 1, 2010	Turkey condemns Israel for the raid on *Mavi Marmara*
June 13, 2010	Israel forms Commission of Inquiry into the Gaza flotilla incident, headed by retired justice Jacob Turkel
June 20, 2010	Israel eases Gaza Blockade
June 23, 2010	Israel launches *Ofeq* (*Ofek*) 9 satellite
August 2, 2010	UN secretary-general Ban Ki-moon establishes a panel of inquiry led by Sir Geoffrey Palmer to examine the *Mavi Marmara* flotilla incident
September 2, 2010	Resumption in Washington, D.C., of direct negotiations between Prime Minister Netanyahu and President Abbas to resolve all final status issues
December 17, 2010	In Tunisia, Mohamed Bouazizi sets himself on fire, sparking protests and demonstrations that lead to the ouster of President Ben Ali and inauguration of the "Arab Spring"
December 21, 2010	Prime Minister Netanyahu "decided to accede to Jonathan Pollard's personal request" and "officially and publicly appeal" to U.S. president Barack Obama for the release of Pollard
December 30, 2010	Former president Moshe Katsav is found guilty of rape, sexual assault, sexual abuse, sexual harassment, and obstruction of justice in a Tel Aviv district court
January 17, 2011	Ehud Barak announces his departure from the Labor Party and the formation of a new political party to be named Atzmaut (Independence)
January 23, 2011	The Turkel Commission releases the first part of its report
January 25, 2011	Large protests and demonstrations against the Mubarak regime in Egypt begin
February 11, 2011	Mubarak is ousted as president of Egypt
March 22, 2011	Former president Katsav is sentenced to seven years in prison for rape and other offenses
April 27, 2011	Fatah and Hamas initial a reconciliation agreement in Cairo
May 3–4, 2011	The Palestinian reconciliation agreement is signed and celebrated in Cairo

May 12, 2011	Ehud Barak officially launches his breakaway Atzmaut political party
May 13, 2011	Former senator George J. Mitchell submits his resignation as U.S. Special Envoy for Middle East Peace, effective May 20
May 15, 2011	Palestinians marching from Lebanon, Syria, Gaza, and the West Bank during Nakba Day clash with Israeli border forces
May 20, 2011	President Obama and Prime Minister Netanyahu meet at the White House to discuss the future of the peace efforts
June 5, 2011	Palestinians and Israeli forces clash on the Golan Heights on Naksa Day
July 28, 2011	Israel and the Republic of South Sudan decide to establish diplomatic relations at the ambassadorial level
July–August 2011	Social protests, beginning as a tent city movement, focusing on the high cost of living, housing prices, the widening gap between rich and poor, and other economic and social issues, grow to involve hundreds of thousands of Israelis
July–October 2011	Protests and demonstrations, beginning as a tent city movement, grow to involve hundreds of thousands of Israelis; calling for social justice, they focus on the high cost of living, lack of affordable housing, the widening gap between rich and poor, and other economic and social issues
August 7, 2011	Netanyahu announces a panel of ministers and experts, headed by Professor Manuel Trachtenberg, to devise a plan with "real solutions" for socioeconomic issues facing Israel
August 18, 2011	Eight Israelis are killed in cross-border attacks by Gazan terrorists north of Eilat, near Israel's border with Egypt
September 2, 2011	UN secretary-general Ban Ki-moon receives the report of the Palmer panel of inquiry examining the flotilla incident. It concludes that Israel's Gaza naval blockade was a "legitimate security measure," the flotilla acted "recklessly" in its attempt to break the blockade, and Israel's use

	of force was "excessive and unreasonable." Turkey downgrades its relations with Israel and expels Israel's ambassador
September 9, 2011	Israel's embassy in Cairo is attacked by Egyptian protesters, trapping some staff members, who are rescued and evacuated
September 21, 2011	Shelly Yachimovich is elected leader of the Labor Party in a run-off election against Amir Peretz
September 23, 2011	Mahmoud Abbas announces his request for admission of a Palestinian state to full membership in the United Nations
October 18, 2011	Staff Sergeant Gilad Shalit is released from captivity and returns to Israeli custody
October 31, 2011	UNESCO votes to admit Palestine as a member
November 10, 2011	Israel's Supreme Court upholds the conviction of rape and other sexual offenses, as well as the prison sentence of seven years, of former President Moshe Katsav

APPENDIX 5

BIBLIOGRAPHY

Israeli government statements, press conferences, speeches, and other materials may be found in a number of locations, including on the World Wide Web, such as at http://www.mfa.gov.il and http:// www. pmo.gov.il and in the 18 volumes of *Israel's Foreign Relations, Selected Documents, 1947–2001* (Jerusalem: Ministry of Foreign Affairs, 1976–2002), which are also available online at http://www. mfa.gov.il. Items can be found by date and often by subject matter as well.

U.S. government statements, press conferences, speeches, and other materials may be found at two Web sites: http://www.whitehouse.gov, which focuses primarily on materials of the president and other White House offices, and http://www.state.gov, which focuses primarily on materials issued by the Department of State. In both cases, items can be found by subject matter and/or date of the item.

Aharoni, Yohanan, and Michael Avi-Yonah, eds. *The Macmillan Bible Atlas.* New York: Macmillan, 1968.

Arian, Asher (Alan). *The Choosing People: Voting Behavior in Israel.* Cleveland and London: Case Western Reserve University Press, 1973.

———. *Ideological Change in Israel.* Cleveland: Case Western Reserve University Press, 1968.

———. *Politics in Israel: The Second Generation.* Chatham, N.J.: Chatham House Publishers, 1989.

———. *The Second Republic: Politics in Israel.* Chatham, N.J.: Chatham House Publishers, 1998.

Arian, Asher (Alan), ed. *The Elections in Israel: 1969.* Jerusalem: Jerusalem Academic Press, 1972.

———. *The Elections in Israel: 1973.* New Brunswick, N.J.: Transaction Books, 1975.

———. *The Elections in Israel: 1977.* New Brunswick, N.J.: Transaction Books, 1980.

————. *The Elections in Israel: 1981.* New Brunswick, N.J.: Transaction Books, 1984.

Arian, Alan, and Michal Shamir, eds. *The Elections in Israel: 1984.* New Brunswick, N.J.: Transaction Books, 1986.

————. *The Elections in Israel, 1988.* Boulder, Colo.: Westview Press, 1990.

————. *The Elections in Israel, 1992.* Albany State University of New York Press, 1995.

————. *The Elections in Israel, 1996.* Albany: State University of New York Press, 1999.

————. *The Elections in Israel, 1999.* Albany: State University of New York Press, 2002.

_____. *The Elections in Israel, 2006.* New Brunswick, N.J. and London: Transaction Publishers, 2008.

_____. *The Elections in Israel 2009.* New Brunswick, N.J.: Transaction Publishers, 2001.

Atlas of Israel. New York: Macmillan, 1985.

Avineri, Shlomo. *The Making of Modern Zionism: The Intellectual Origins of the Jewish State.* New York: Basic Books, 1981.

Avner, Yehuda. *The Prime Ministers: An Intimate Narrative of Israeli Leadership.* New Milford, Conn., London, Jerusalem: The Toby Press, 2010.

Badi, Joseph. *The Government of the State of Israel: A Critical Account of Its Parliament, Executive and Judiciary.* New York: Twayne, 1963.

Badi, Joseph, ed. *Fundamental Laws of the State of Israel.* New York: Twayne, 1961.

Baker, Henry E. *The Legal System of Israel.* Jerusalem: Israel Universities Press, 1968.

Baskin, Juith R., and Kenneth Seeskin, eds. *The Cambridge Guide to Jewish History, Religion and Culture.* New York: Cambridge University Press, 2010.

Bein, Alex. *Theodore Herzl: A Biography.* Philadelphia: Jewish Publication Society of America, 1940.

Ben-Gurion, David. *Israel: A Personal History.* New York and Tel Aviv: Sabra Books, 1971.

————. *Israel: Years of Challenge.* New York: Holt, Rinehart, and Winston, 1963.

————. *The Jews in Their Land.* Garden City, N.Y.: Doubleday, 1966.

Bentwich, Norman. *Israel Resurgent.* New York: Praeger, 1960.

Bentwich, Norman, and Helen Bentwich. *Mandate Memories, 1918–1948.* London: Hogarth, 1965.

Bermant, Chaim. *Israel*. New York: Walker, 1967.

Bernstein, Marver H. *The Politics of Israel: The First Decade of Statehood*. Princeton, N.J.: Princeton University Press, 1957.

Bregman, Ahron. *Israel's Wars: A History since 1947*. 3rd ed. London and New York: Routledge, 2010.

Brenner, Michael. *Zionism: A Brief History*. Translated by Shelley L. Frisch, Princeton, N.J.: Markus Wiener Publishers, 2003.

Central Bureau of Statistics. *Statistical Abstract of Israel*. Jerusalem: Central Bureau of Statistics, 1949– .

Eban, Abba. *My Country: The Story of Modern Israel*. New York: Random House, 1972.

––––––. *My People: The Story of the Jews*. New York: Random House, 1969.

Efrat, Elisha, ed. *Geography and Politics in Israel since 1967*. London: Frank Cass, 1988.

Elon, Amos. *Herzl*. New York: Holt, Rinehart and Winston, 1975.

Encyclopedia Judaica. 16 vols. Jerusalem: Keter, 1972.

Finklestein, Louis, ed. *The Jews: Their History, Culture and Religion*. New York: Schocken, 1949.

Friedlander, Dov, and Calvin Goldscheider. *The Population of Israel*. New York: Columbia University Press, 1979.

Garcia-Granados, Jorge. *The Birth of Israel: The Drama as I Saw It*. New York: Alfred A. Knopf, 1948.

Gilbert, Martin. *The Atlas of Jewish History*. 5th ed. London: J. M. Dent, 1993.

––––––. *Atlas of the Arab-Israeli Conflict*. 6th ed. New York: Oxford University Press, 1993.

––––––. *Israel: A History*. London: Doubleday, 1998.

––––––. *Israel: A History*. Rev, ed. Santa Barbara, Calif.: McNally and Loftin, 2008.

––––––. *The Routledge Atlas of the Arab-Israeli Conflict*, 9th ed. London and New York: Routledge, 2008.

Golan, Galia. *Israel and Palestine: Peace Plans and Proposals from Oslo to Disengagement*. Updated ed. Princeton, N.J.: Markus Wiener Publishers, 2008.

Halevy, Efraim. *Man in the Shadows: Inside the Middle East Crisis with the Man Who Led the Mossad*. New York: St. Martin's Press, Griffin, 2008.

Halpern, Ben. *The Idea of the Jewish State*. 2d ed. Cambridge, Mass.: Harvard University Press, 1970.

Herzl, Theodor. *Complete Diaries*. 5 vols. Edited by Raphael Patai. New York: Herzl Press, 1960.

Historical Atlas of Israel. Jerusalem: Carta, 1983.

Horowitz, David. *The Economics of Israel.* Oxford: Pergamon Press, 1967.

Hurewitz, Jacob C. *The Struggle for Palestine.* New York: W. W. Norton, 1950

The Israel Yearbook. Tel Aviv: Israel Yearbook Publishers, 1950– .

Israel Government Yearbook. Jerusalem: Government Printer, 1950– .

Israel's Foreign Relations, Selected Documents, 1947–2001. 18 vols. Jerusalem: Ministry of Foreign Affairs, 1976–2002.

Janowsky, Oscar I. *Foundations of Israel: Emergence of a Welfare State.* Princeton, N.J.: D. Van Nostrand, 1959.

Karsh, Efraim. *Palestine Betrayed.* New Haven, Conn., and London: Yale University Press, 2010.

Kieval, Gershon R. *Party Politics in Israel and the Occupied Territories.* Westport, Conn.: Greenwood, 1983.

Kraines, Oscar. *Israel: The Emergence of a New Nation.* Washington, D.C.: Public Affairs Press, 1954.

Lucas, Noah. *The Modern History of Israel.* New York and Washington, D.C.: Praeger, 1975.

Mahler, Gregory S. *Israel: Government and Politics in a Maturing State.* San Diego, Calif.: Harcourt Brace Jovanovich, 1990.

———. *The Knesset: Parliament in the Israeli Political System.* Rutherford, N.J.: Fairleigh Dickenson University Press, 1981.

Maoz Zeev. *Defending the Holy Land: A Critical Analysis of Israel's Security and Foreign Policy.* Ann Arbor: University of Michigan Press, 2006.

Metz, Helen Chapin, ed. *Israel: A Country Study.* Washington, D.C.: Federal Research Division, Library of Congress, 1990.

Meyer, Herrmann M. Z., comp. *Israel: Pocket Atlas and Handbook.* Jerusalem: Universitas Booksellers, 1961.

Ministry of Justice. *Laws of the State of Israel: Authorized Translation.* Jerusalem: Government Printer, 1948– .

Parkes, James. *A History of Palestine from 135 A.D. to Modern Times.* Oxford: Clarendon, 1949.

Pedahzur, Ami. *The Israeli Secret Services and the Struggle Against Terrorism.* New York: Columbia University Press, 2009.

Penniman, Howard R., ed. *Israel at the Polls: The Knesset Elections of 1977.* Washington, D.C.: American Enterprise Institute for Public Policy Research, 1979.

Penniman, Howard R., and Daniel Elazar, eds. *Israel at the Polls, 1981.* Washington, D.C.: American Enterprise Institute for Public Policy Research, 1986.

Peri, Yoram. Generals in the Cabinet Room: How the Military Shapes Israeli Policy. Washington, D.C.: United States Institute of Peace Press, 2006.

Reich, Bernard. *Historical Dictionary of Israel*. Lanham, Md.: Scarecrow Press, 1992.

———. *Israel and the Occupied Territories*. Washington, D.C.: U.S. Department of State, 1973.

———. *Quest for Peace: United States–Israel Relations and the Arab-Israeli Conflict*. New Brunswick, N.J.: Transaction Books, 1977.

———. *Securing the Covenant: United States–Israel Relations After the Cold War*. Westport, Conn.: Greenwood Press, 1995.

———. *The United States and Israel: Influence in the Special Relationship*. New York: Praeger, 1984.

Reich, Bernard, ed. *Arab-Israeli Conflict and Conciliation: A Documentary History*. Westport, Conn., and London: Praeger, 1995.

———. *An Historical Encyclopedia of the Arab-Israeli Conflict*. Westport, Conn.: Greenwood Press, 1996.

Reich, Bernard, and David Goldberg. *Historical Dictionary of Israel*. Metuchen, N.J.: Scarecrow Press, 1992.

Reich, Bernard, and David H. Goldberg. *Political Dictionary of Israel*. Lanham, Md., and London: Scarecrow Press, 2000.

Reich, Bernard, and Gershon R. Kieval. *Israel: Land of Tradition and Conflict*. 2d ed. Boulder, Colo.: Westview Press, 1993.

Reich, Bernard, and Gershon R. Kieval, eds. *Israel Faces the Future*. New York: Praeger, 1986.

———. *Israeli National Security Policy: Political Actors and Perspectives*. Westport, Conn.: Greenwood Press, 1988.

———. *Israeli Politics in the 1990s: Key Domestic and Foreign Policy Factors*. Westport, Conn.: Greenwood Press, 1988.

Ross, Dennis, and David Makovsky. *Myths, Illusions, and Peace: Finding a New Direction for America in the Middle East*. New York: Penguin Books, 2010.

Sachar, Howard M. *A History of Israel: From the Rise of Zionism to Our Time*. New York: Alfred A. Knopf, 1976.

———. *A History of Israel*. Vol. 2: *From the Aftermath of the Yom Kippur War*. New York: Oxford University Press, 1987.

Senor, Dan, and Saul Singer. *Start-Up Nation: The Story of Israel's Economic Miracle*. New York: Twelve, 2009.

Shapira, Anita. *Yigal Allon, Native Son: A Biography*. Translated by Evelyn Abel. Philadelphia: University of Pennsylvania Press, 2008.

Sher, Gilead. *The Israeli-Palestinian Peace Negotiation, 1999–2001: Within Reach.* London and New York: Routledge, 2006.

Stein, Leslie. *The Hope Fulfilled: The Rise of Modern Israel.* Westport, Conn., London: Praeger, 2003.

Strober, Deborah Hart, and Gerald S. Strober. *Israel at Sixty: A Pictorial and Oral History of a Nation Reborn.* Hoboken, N.J.: John Wiley & Sons, 2008.

Sykes, Christopher. *Crossroads to Israel.* Cleveland and New York: World Publishing, 1965.

Vilnay, Zev. *The New Israel Atlas: Bible to Present Day.* New York: McGraw-Hill, 1969.

Waxman, Charles I., and Rafael Medoff. *Historical Dictionary of Zionism.* Lanham, Md.: Scarecrow Press, 2000.

Weymouth, Lally. "Terror, Iraq and 'Full Security.'" *Newsweek,* August 11, 2003, 32.

APPENDIX 6

SUGGESTED READING

Israel is a country on which a great deal has been written, in numerous languages, covering all aspects of society and politics. The following listing of English-language works constitutes but a small portion of the available materials and should be considered with the items listed in the bibliography as the corpus of materials available to the reader and researcher interested in Israel. They cover primarily the history, politics, economics, foreign policy, and international relations of Israel. These books and numerous others are available to the reader seeking to learn more about Israel. There is a much larger number of periodical articles and a plethora of Internet sources that consider virtually every perspective and all aspects of the State of Israel. The English online edition of the daily newspaper *Ha'aretz* may be found at www.haartez. com. The English-language *Jerusalem Post* publishes its online edition at www.jpost.com.

Directories, Yearbooks, and Encyclopedias
Bank of Israel. *Annual Report*. Jerusalem: Bank of Israel, 1955–   .

Encyclopedia Judaica. 2d ed., 22 vols. Fred Skolnik, editor in chief. Michael Berenbaum, executive editor. Detroit: Macmillan Reference USA in association with Keter Pub. House, 2007.

Hill, Helen, ed. *Zionist Year Book*. London: Zionist Federation of Great Britain and Ireland, 1951–   .

Patai, Raphael, ed. *Encyclopedia of Zionism and Israel*. 2 vols. New York: Herzl, McGraw-Hill, 1971.

General
Aharoni, Yair. *The Israeli Economy: Dreams and Realities*. London and New York: Routledge, 1991.

Aronoff, Myron J. *Israeli Visions and Divisions: Cultural Change and Political Conflict*. New Brunswick, N.J.: Transaction Books, 1989.

Aronson, Shlomo. *David Ben-Gurion and the Jewish Renaissance.* Translated by Naftali Greenwood. New York: Cambridge University Press, 2011.

Bar-Zohar, Michael. *Ben-Gurion: A Biography.* Translated by Peretz Kidron. New York: Delacorte Press, 1979.

———. *Ben-Gurion: The Armed Prophet.* Englewood Cliffs, N.J.: Prentice Hall, 1966.

Begin, Menachem. *The Revolt.* New York: Nash, 1981.

Ben-Gurion, David. *Rebirth and Destiny of Israel.* New York: Philosophical Library, 1954.

Ben-Meir, Alon. *Israel: The Challenge of the Fourth Decade.* New York and London: Cyrco Press, 1978.

Ben-Porat, Amir. *Divided We Stand: Class Structure in Israel from 1948 to the 1980s.* Westport, Conn.: Greenwood Press, 1989.

Ben-Rafael, Eliezer. *Status, Power and Conflict in the Kibbutz.* Brookfield, Vt.: Gower Publishing, 1988.

Benziman, Uzi. *Sharon: An Israeli Caesar.* New York: Adama Books, 1975.

Berlin, Isaiah. *Chaim Weizmann.* New York: Farrar, Straus and Cudahy, 1958.

Cameron, James. *The Making of Israel.* London: Secker and Warburg, 1976.

Chafets, Ze'ev. *Heroes and Hustlers, Hard Hats and Holy Men: Inside the New Israel.* New York: Morrow, 1986.

Cooke, Hedley V. *Israel: A Blessing and a Curse.* London: Stevens and Sons, 1960.

Cristol, Jay. *The Liberty Incident: The 1967 Israeli Attack on the U.S. Navy Spy Ship*, Washington, D.C.: Brassey's, 2002.

Crossman, Richard H. S. *A Nation Reborn: The Israel of Weizmann, Bevin, and Ben-Gurion.* London: Hamish Hamilton, 1960.

Davis, Moshe, ed. *Israel: Its Role in Civilization.* New York: Harper and Row, 1956.

Dayan, Moshe. *Breakthrough: A Personal Account of the Egypt-Israel Peace Negotiations.* New York: Knopf, 1981.

———. *Story of My Life: An Autobiography.* New York: William Morrow, 1976.

DeGaury, Gerald. *The New State of Israel.* New York: Praeger, 1952.

Dershowitz, Alan M. *The Case for Israel.* Hoboken, N.J.: John Wiley, 2003.

Dunner, Joseph. *Democratic Bulwark in the Middle East: A Review and Analysis of Israel's Social, Economic, and Political Problems during the*

Period from 1948 to 1953. Grinnell, Iowa: Grinnell College Press, 1953.

Eisenstadt, Samuel N. *Israeli Society*. New York: Praeger, 1967.

————. *The Transformation of Israeli Society*. London: Weidenfeld and Nicolson, 1985.

Elon, Amos. *The Israelis: Founders and Sons*. New York: Bantam Books, 1972.

Elston, D. R. *Israel: The Making of a Nation*. Oxford: Oxford University Press, 1963.

————. *No Alternative: Israel Observed*. London: Hutchinson, 1960.

Farrell, James T. *It Has Come to Pass*. New York: Herzl, 1958.

Feis, Herbert. *The Birth of Israel: The Tousled Diplomatic Bed*. New York: W. W. Norton, 1969.

Frank, Waldo. *Bridgehead: The Drama of Israel*. New York: George Braziller, 1957.

Frankel, William. *Israel Observed: An Anatomy of the State*. London: Thames and Hudson, 1980.

Frishwasser-Ra'anan, H. F. *The Frontiers of a Nation*. London: Batchworth, 1955.

Fuchs, Esther, ed. *Israeli Women's Studies: A Reader*. New Brunswick, N.J.: Rutgers University Press, 2005.

Gavron, Daniel. *Israel after Begin*. Boston: Houghton Mifflin, 1984.

Gervasi, Frank. *The Life and Times of Menachem Begin: Rebel to Statesman*. New York: Putnam, 1979.

Golan, Matti. *Shimon Peres: A Biography*. New York: St. Martin's Press, 1982.

Grose, Peter. *A Changing Israel*. New York: Vintage Books, 1985.

Haber, Eitan. *Menachem Begin: The Legend and the Man*. Translated by Louis Williams. New York: Delacorte Press, 1978.

Halperin-Kaddari, Ruth. *Women in Israel: A State of Their Own*. Philadelphia: University of Pennsylvania Press, 2004.

Hertzog, Esther, ed. *Perspectives on Israeli Anthropology*. Detroit: Wayne State University Press, 2010.

Heschel, Abraham H. *Israel: An Echo of Eternity*. New York: Farrar, Straus, and Giroux, 1969.

Horowitz, Dan, and Moshe Lissak. *Trouble in Utopia: The Overburdened Polity of Israel*. Albany: State University of New York Press, 1989.

Israeli, Raphael. *Jerusalem Divided: The Armistice Regime, 1947–1967*. London: Frank Cass, 2002.

Kaplan, Eran. *The Jewish Radical Right: Revisionist Zionism and Its Ideological Legacy*. Madison: University of Wisconsin Press, 2004.

Kimche, Jon, and David Kimche. *A Clash of Destinies: The Arab-Jewish War and the Founding of the State of Israel*. New York: Praeger, 1960.

Kimmerling, Baruch, ed. *The Israeli State and Society: Boundaries and Frontiers*. Albany: State University of New York Press, 1989.

Kurzman, Dan. *Ben-Gurion: Prophet of Fire*. New York: Simon and Schuster, 1983.

Kyle, Keith, and Joel Peters, ed. *Whither Israel? The Domestic Challenges*. New York: I.B. Tauris, 1993.

Landau, Jacob M. *The Arabs in Israel: A Political Study*. London: Oxford University Press, 1969.

Lau-Lavie, Naftali. *Moshe Dayan: A Biography*. London: Vallentine, Mitchell, 1969.

Lehrman, Hal. *Israel, the Beginning and Tomorrow*. New York: William Sloane, 1951.

Lissak, Moshe, ed. *Israeli Society and Defense Establishment: The Social and Political Impact of a Protracted Violent Conflict*. London: Frank Cass, 1984.

Litvinoff, Barnet. *Ben-Gurion of Israel*. New York: Praeger, 1954.

———. *Weizmann: Last of the Patriarchs*. New York: Putman, 1976.

Mautner, Menachem. *Law and the Culture of Israel*. Oxford and New York: Oxford University Press, 2011.

Meinertzhagen, Richard. *Middle East Diary: 1917–1956*. New York: Yoseloff, 1960.

Meir, Golda. *A Land of Our Own: An Oral Autobiography*. Ed. Marie Syrkin. New York: G.P. Putnam's Sons, 1973.

———. *My Life*. New York: Putnam, 1975.

Meyer, Lawrence. *Israel Now: Portrait of a Troubled Land*. New York: Delacorte, 1982.

Morris, Benny. *Righteous Victims: A History of the Zionist-Arab Conflict, 1881–1999*. New York: Alfred A. Knopf, 1999.

Mort, Jo-Ann, and Gary Brenner. *Our Hearts Invented a Place: Can Kibbutzim Survive in Today's Israel*. Ithaca, N.Y.: Cornell University Press, 2003.

Naamani, Israel T. *Israel: A Profile*. New York: Praeger, 1972.

———. *Israel: Its Politics and Philosophy; an Annotated Reader*. New York: Behrman, 1974.

O'Brian, Connor Cruise. *The Seige: The Saga of Israel and Zionism*. New York: Simon and Schuster, 1986.

Oren, Michael B. *Six Days of War: June 1967 and the Making of the Modern Middle East*. Oxford and New York: Oxford University Press, 2002.

Orni, Ephraim, and Elisha Efrat. *Geography of Israel*. 3rd rev. ed. Jerusalem: Keter, 1971.

Oz, Amos. *In the Land of Israel*. New York: Harcourt, Brace and Jovanovich, 1983.

Perlmutter, Amos. *The Life and Times of Menachem Begin*. Garden City, N.Y.: Doubleday, 1987.

Postal, Bernard, and Henry W. Levy. *And the Hills Shouted for Joy: The Day Israel Was Born*. New York: David McKay, 1973.

Prittie, Terence. *Eshkol: The Man and the Nation*. New York: Putnam, 1969.

―――. *Israel: Miracle in the Desert*. New York: Praeger, 1967.

Rabin, Yitzhak. *The Rabin Memoirs*. Boston: Little, Brown, 1979.

Rabinovich, Itamar, and Jehuda Reinharz, eds. *Israel in the Middle East: Documents and Readings on Society, Politics, and Foreign Relations, 1948–Present*. New York: Oxford University Press, 1984.

Reich, Bernard, and David H. Goldberg. *The A to Z of Israel*. Lanham, Md., Toronto, Plymouth, U.K.: The Scarecrow Press, 2010.

Reinharz, Jehuda. *Chaim Weizmann: The Making of a Zionist Leader*. New York: Oxford University Press, 1985.

Rivlin, Paul. *The Israeli Economy from the Foundation of the State through the 21st Century*. Cambridge and New York: Cambridge University Press, 2011.

Roman, Michael, and Alex Weingrod. *Living Together, Living Separately: Arabs and Jews in Contemporary Jerusalem*. Princeton, N.J.: Princeton University Press, 1991.

Safran, Nadav. *Israel: The Embattled Ally*. Cambridge, Mass.: Belknap Press of Harvard University Press, 1981.

St. John, Robert. *Tongue of the Prophets: The Life Story of Eliezer Ben-Yehuda*. New York: Doubleday, 1952.

Sanbar, Moshe, ed. *Economic and Social Policy in Israel: The First Generation*. Lanham, Md.: University Press of America, 1990.

Schechtman, Joseph B. *Fighter and Prophet: The Last Years*. Vol. 2: *The Vladimir Jabotinsky Story*. New York: Thomas Yoseloff, 1961.

―――. *Rebel and Statesman: The Vladimir Jabotinsky Story*. Vol. 1: *The Early Years*. New York: Thomas Yoseloff, 1956.

Schoenbrun, David, with Robert Szekely and Lucy Szekely. *The New Israelis*. New York: Atheneum, 1973.

Segev, Tom. *1949: The First Israelis*. New York: Free Press, 1986.

Shalev, Michael. *Labour and the Political Economy in Israel*. London: Oxford University Press, 1989.

Shihor, Samuel. *Hollow Glory: The Last Days of Chaim Weizmann, First President of Israel.* New York: Thomas Yoseloff, 1960.

Shuval, Judith T. *Immigrants on the Threshold.* New York: Atherton Press, 1963.

Silver, Eric. *Begin: The Haunted Prophet.* New York: Random House, 1984.

Simon, Merrill. *Moshe Arens: Statesman and Scientist Speaks Out.* Middle Island, N.Y.: Dean Books, 1988.

Slater, Robert. *Rabin of Israel.* New York: St. Martin's Press, 1993.

Sofer, Sasson. *Begin: An Anatomy of Leadership.* Oxford: Basil Blackwell, 1988.

Stein, Leslie. *The Hope Fulfilled: The Rise of Modern Israel.* London and Westport, Conn.: Praeger, 2003.

Stock, Ernest. *Israel on the Road to Sinai, 1949–1956.* Ithaca, N.Y.: Cornell University Press, 1967.

Syrkin, Marie. *Golda Meir: Woman with a Cause.* New York: Putnam, 1963.

Temko, Ned. *To Win or to Die: A Personal Portrait of Menachem Begin.* New York: William Morrow, 1987.

Teveth, Shabtai. *Ben-Gurion: The Burning Ground, 1886–1948.* Boston: Houghton Mifflin, 1987.

———. *Ben-Gurion and the Palestinian Arabs: From Peace to War.* New York: Oxford University Press, 1985.

———. *Moshe Dayan: The Soldier, the Man, the Legend.* Boston: Houghton Mifflin, 1973.

Weingrod, Alex. *Israel: Group Relations in a New Society.* New York: Frederick A. Praeger Publishers for the Institute of Race Relations, 1965.

Weisgal, Meyer S., and Joel Carmichael, eds. *Chaim Weizmann: A Biography by Several Hands.* New York: Atheneum, 1963.

Weizmann, Chaim. *Trial and Error: The Autobiography of Chaim Weizmann, First President of Israel.* New York: Harper and Row, 1949.

Weizman, Ezer. *The Battle for Peace.* Toronto, New York, and London: Bantam Books, 1981.

Williams, L. F. Rushbrook. *The State of Israel.* New York: Macmillan, 1957.

Defense and Security

Allon, Yigal. *The Making of Israel's Army.* New York: Bantam Books, 1971.

Banks, Lynne Reid. *Torn Country: An Oral History of the Israeli War of Independence.* New York: Watts, 1982.

Bar-Siman-Tov, Yaacov. *The Israeli-Egyptian War of Attrition, 1969–1970: A Case Study of Limited Local War.* New York: Columbia University Press, 1980.

Ben-Meir, Yehuda. *National Security Decision-Making: The Israeli Case.* Boulder, Colo.: Westview Press, 1986.

Byman, Daniel. *A High Price: The Triumphs and Failures of Israeli Counterterrorism.* New York: Oxford University Press, 2011.

Claire, Rodger W. *Raid on the Sun: Israels Secret Campaign That Denied Saddam the Bomb.* New York: Broadway Books, 2004.

Cohen, Avner. *Israel and the Bomb.* Cambridge, Mass.: Harvard University Press, 1998.

Churchill, Randolph S., and Winston S. Churchill. *The Six-Day War.* Boston: Houghton Mifflin, 1967.

Dayan, Moshe. *Diary of the Sinai Campaign.* New York: Harper and Row, 1966.

Feldman, Shai. *Israeli Nuclear Deterrence: A Strategy for the 1980s.* New York: Columbia University Press, 1982.

Henriques, Robert. *A Hundred Hours to Suez: An Account of Israel's Campaign in the Sinai Peninsula.* New York: Viking Press, 1957.

Herzog, Chaim. *The War of Atonement: October, 1973.* Boston: Little, Brown, 1975.

———. *The Arab-Israeli Wars: War and Peace in the Middle East.* New York: Random House, 1982.

Ilan, Amitzur. *The Origins of the Arab-Israeli Arms Race: Arms, Embargo, Military Power and Peace in the 1948 Palestine War.* New York: New York University Press, 1996.

Kimche, David, and Dan Bawly. *The Six-Day War: Prologue and Aftermath.* New York: Stein and Day, 1971.

Kimche, Jon, and David Kimche. *A Clash of Destinies: The Arab-Jewish War and the Founding of the State of Israel.* New York: Praeger, 1960.

Klieman, Aaron, and Ariel Levite, eds. *Deterrence in the Middle East: Where Theory and Practice Converge.* Jaffee Center for Strategic Studies Study no. 22. Boulder, Colo.: Westview Press, 1993.

Kober, Avi. *Coalition Defection: The Dissolution of Arab Anti-Israel Coalitions in War and Peace.* Westport, Conn.: Praeger, 2002.

Levite, Ariel. *Offense and Defense in Israeli Military Doctrine.* Boulder, Colo.: Westview Press, 1989.

Lorch, Netanel. *The Edge of the Sword: Israel's War of Independence, 1947–1949.* New York: Putnam, 1961.

Luttwak, Edward, and Dan Horowitz. *The Israeli Army.* New York: Harper and Row, 1975.

Middle East Military Balance. Tel Aviv: Jaffee Center for Strategic Studies, Tel Aviv University, 1979–.

Morris, Benny. *Israel's Border Wars, 1949–1956: Arab Infiltration, Israeli Retaliation, and the Countdown to the Suez War.* New York: Oxford University Press, 1993.

O'Ballance, Edgar. *The Third Arab-Israeli War.* London: Faber, 1972.

———. *No Victor, No Vanquished: The Yom Kippur War.* San Rafael, Calif.: Presidio Press, 1978.

Peres, Shimon. *David's Sling: The Arming of Israel.* London: Weidenfeld and Nicolson, 1970.

Perlmutter, Amos. *Military and Politics in Israel: Nation-Building and Role Expansion.* London: Frank Cass, 1969.

Rabinovich, Abraham. *The Yom Kippur War: The War That Transformed the Middle East.* New York: Schocken Books, 2004.

Rabinovich, Itamar. *The War for Lebanon, 1970–1983.* Ithaca, N.Y.: Cornell University Press, 1984.

Reiser, Stewart. *The Israeli Arms Industry: Foreign Policy, Arms Transfers, and Military Doctrine of a Small State.* New York: Holmes and Meier, 1989.

Schiff, Ze'ev. *A History of the Israeli Army: 1874 to the Present.* New York: Macmillan Publishing, 1985.

Schiff, Ze'ev, and Eitan Haber, eds, and Arie Hashavia, assoc. ed. *A Lexicon of Israel's Defense.* Israel: Zmora, Bitan, Modan, 1976.

Schiff, Ze'ev, and Ehud Ya'ari. *Israel's Lebanon War.* New York: Simon and Schuster, 1984.

Shalev, Aryeh. *The Israel-Syria Armistice Regime, 1949–1955.* Boulder, Colo.: Westview, 1993.

Shalev, Aryeh. *Israel's Intelligence Assessment before the Yom Kippur War: Disentangling Deception and Distraction.* Portland, Ore.: Sussex Academic Press, 2010.

Sheffer, Gabriel, and Oren Barak, eds. *Militarism and Israeli Society.* Bloomington: Indiana University Press, 2010.

Shimshoni, Jonathan. *Israel and Conventional Deterrence: Border Warfare from 1953 to 1970.* Ithaca, N.Y.: Cornell University Press, 1988.

Tamir, Avraham. *A Soldier in Search of Peace: An Inside Look at Israel's Strategy.* New York: Harper and Row, 1988.

Thomas, Gordon. *Gideon's Spies: The Secret History of the Mossad.* New York: Thomas Dunne Books, 2009.

Tzalel, Moshe. *From Ice-Breaker to Missile Boat: The Evolution of Israel's Naval Strategy.* Westport, Conn.: Greenwood Press, 2000.

Van Creveld, Martin. *The Sword and the Olive: A Critical History of the Israeli Defense Force*. New York: Public Affairs, Perseus Books Group, 1998.

Wallach, Jehuda L. *Israeli Military History: A Guide to the Sources*. New York: Garland Publishers, 1984.

Government and Politics

Akzin, Benjamin and Yehezkel Dror. *Israel: High-Pressure Planning*. Syracuse, N.Y.: Syracuse University Press, 1966.

Aronoff, Myron J. *Frontiertown: The Politics of Community Building in Israel*. Manchester, U.K.: Manchester University Press, 1974.

———. *Power and Ritual in the Israel Labor Party*. Rev. ed. Armonk, N.Y.: M.E. Sharpe, 1993.

Bayne, E. A. *Four Ways of Politics: State and Nation in Italy, Somalia, Israel, Iran*. New York: American Universities Field Staff, 1965.

Ben-Meir, Yehuda. *Civil-Military Relations in Israel*. New York: Columbia University Press, 1995.

Bradley, ca. Paul. *Electoral Politics in Israel*. Grantham, N.H.: Tompson and Rutter, 1981.

Caiden, Gerald E. *Israel's Administrative Culture*. Berkeley: Institute of Governmental Studies, University of California Press, 1970.

Caspi, Dan, Abraham Diskin, and Emanuel Gutmann, eds. *The Roots of Begin's Success: The 1981 Israeli Elections*. New York: St. Martin's Press, 1984.

Deshen, Shlomo. *Immigrant Voters in Israel*. Manchester, U.K.: Manchester University Press, 1970.

Diskin, Abraham. *Elections and Voters in Israel*. New York: Praeger, 1991.

———. *The Last Days in Israel*. London: Frank Cass, 2003.

Drezon-Tepler, Marcia. *Interest Groups and Political Change in Israel*. Albany: State University of New York Press, 1990.

Dror, Yehezkel, and Emanuel Gutmann, eds. *The Government of Israel*. Jerusalem: Eliezer Kaplan School of Economics and Social Sciences, Hebrew University, 1961.

Eisenstadt, S. N. *Israeli Society*. London: Weidenfeld and Nicolson, 1967.

Elazar, Daniel J. *The Other Jews: The Sephardim Today*. New York: Basic Books, 1989.

Elazar, Daniel J., and Howard R. Penniman, eds. *Israel at the Polls 1981*. Bloomington: Indiana University Press, 1986.

Elazar, Daniel J., and Shmuel Sandler, eds. *Israel at the Polls, 1992*. Lanham, Md.: Rowman and Littlefield, 1995.

————. *Israel's Odd Couple: The Nineteen Eighty-Four Knesset Elections and the National Unity Government.* Detroit, Mich.: Wayne State University Press, 1990.

————. *Who's the Boss in Israel: Israel at the Polls, 1988–89.* Detroit, Mich.: Wayne State University Press, 1992.

Elizur, Yuval, and Eliahu Salpeter. *Who Rules Israel?* New York: Harper and Row, 1973.

Etzioni-Halevy, Eva, with Rina Shapira. *Political Culture in Israel: Cleavage and Integration among Israeli Jews.* New York and London: Praeger, 1977.

Fein, Leonard J. *Israel: Politics and People.* Boston: Little, Brown, 1968.

Freudenheim, Yehoshua. *Government in Israel.* Dobbs Ferry, N.Y.: Oceana, 1967.

Gerson, Allan. *Israel, the West Bank and International Law.* Totowa, N.J.: Cass, 1978.

Hall-Cathala, David. *The Peace Movement in Israel, 1967–1987.* New York: St. Martin's Press, 1990.

Harkabi, Yehoshafat. *The Bar-Kokhba Syndrome: Risks and Realism in International Politics.* Chappaqua, N.Y.: Rossel, 1983.

Horowitz, Dan, and Moshe Lissak. *The Origins of the Israeli Polity.* Chicago: University of Chicago Press, 1978.

————. *Trouble in Utopia: The Overburdened Polity of Israel.* Albany: State University of New York Press, 1989.

Horowitz, David. *State in the Making.* New York: Alfred A. Knopf, 1953.

Isaac, Rael Jean. *Israel Divided: Ideological Politics in the Jewish State.* Baltimore, Md.: Johns Hopkins University Press, 1976.

————. *Party and Politics in Israel: Three Visions of a Jewish State.* New York: Longman, 1981.

Kimmerling, Baruch. *Zionism and Territory: The Socio-Territorial Dimension of Zionist Politics.* Berkeley, Calif.: Institute of International Studies, 1983.

Kraines, Oscar. *Government and Politics in Israel.* Boston: Houghton Mifflin, 1961.

Landau, Jacob M. *The Arab Minority in Israel, 1967–1991: Political Aspects.* Oxford, U.K.: Clarendon Press, 1993.

————. *The Arabs in Israel: A Political Study.* London: Oxford University Press, 1969.

Lehman-Wilzig, Sam N. *Stiff-Necked People, Bottle-Necked System: The Evolution and Roots of Israeli Public Protest, 1949–1986.* Bloomington: Indiana University Press, 1991.

Liebman, Charles S., and Eliezer Don-Yehiya. *Religion and Politics in Israel*. Bloomington: Indiana University Press, 1984.

Likhovski, Eliahu S. *Israel's Parliament: The Law of the Knesset*. London: Oxford University Press, 1971.

Mahler, Gregory S. *Politics and Government in Israel: The Maturation of a Modern State*, 2d ed. Lanham, Boulder, New York, Toronto, Plymouth, U.K.: Rowman & Littlefield, 2011.

Medding, Peter Y. *The Founding of Israeli Democracy, 1948–1988*. London: Oxford University Press, 1989.

———. *Mapai in Israel: Political Organization and Government in a New Society*. Cambridge, U.K.: Cambridge University Press, 1972.

Mendilow, Jonathan. *Ideology, Party Change, and Electoral Campaigns in Israel, 1965–2001*. Albany: State University of New York Press, 2003.

Merhav, Peretz. *The Israeli Left: History, Problems, Documents*. Cranbury, N.J.: A. S. Barnes, 1980.

Norell, Magnus. *Dissenting Democracy: The Israeli Movement "Peace Now."* London: Frank Cass, 2002.

Peri, Yoram. *Between Battles and Ballots: Israeli Military in Politics*. Cambridge, U.K.: Cambridge University Press, 1983.

———. *Generals in the Cabinet Room: How the Military Shapes Israeli Policy*. Washington, D.C.: United States Institute of Peace Press, 2006.

Perlmutter, Amos. *Anatomy of Political Institutionalization: The Case of Israel and Some Comparative Analyses*. Cambridge, Mass.: Center for International Affairs, Harvard University, 1970.

———. *Israel: The Partitioned State*. New York: Scribner, 1985.

———. *Military and Politics in Israel*. London: Frank Cass, 1969.

Rackman, Emmanuel. *Israel's Emerging Constitution, 1948–51*. New York: Columbia University Press, 1955.

Rubinstein, Amnon. *The Zionist Dream Revisited: From Herzl to Gush Emunim and Back*. New York: Schocken, 1984.

Sager, Samuel. *The Parliamentary System of Israel*. Syracuse, N.Y.: Syracuse University Press, 1985.

Samuel, Edwin. *Problems of Government in the State of Israel*. Jerusalem: Rubin Mass, 1956.

Schnall, David J. *Radical Dissent in Contemporary Israeli Politics: Cracks in the Wall*. New York: Praeger, 1979.

Seligman, Lester G. *Leadership in a New Nation: Political Development in Israel*. New York: Atherton, 1964.

Shapiro, Yonathan. *The Road to Power: Herut Party in Israel*. Albany: State University of New York Press, 1991.

Sharkansky, Ira. *The Political Economy of Israel*. New Brunswick, N.J.: Transaction Books, 1987.

———. *What Makes Israel Tick? How Domestic Policy-Makers Cope with Constraints*. Chicago: Nelson-Hall, 1985.

———. *Wither the State? Politics and Public Enterprise in Three Countries*. Chatham, N.J.: Chatham House Publishers, 1979.

Shimshoni, Daniel. *Israel Democracy: The Middle of the Journey*. New York: Free Press, 1982.

Sprinzak, Ehud. *The Ascendance of Israel's Radical Right*. New York: Oxford University Press, 1991.

Sprinzak, Ehud, and Larry Diamond, eds. *Israeli Democracy under Stress*. Boulder, Colo.: Lynne Rienner Publishers, 1993.

Vlavianos, Basil J., and Feliks Gross, eds. *Struggle for Tomorrow: Modern Political Ideologies of the Jewish People*. New York: Arts, 1954.

Wolfsfeld, Gadi. *The Politics of Provocation : Participation and Protest in Israel*. Albany: State University of New York Press, 1988.

Yaacobi, Gad. *The Government of Israel*. New York: Praeger, 1982.

Yanai, Nathan. *Party Leadership in Israel*. Philadelphia: Turtledove, 1981.

Yaniv, Avner, ed. *National Security and Democracy in Israel*. Boulder, Colo.: Lynne Rienner Publishers, 1993.

Yishai, Yael. *Between the Flag and the Banner: Women in Israeli Politics*. Albany: State University of New York Press, 1997.

———. *Land of Paradoxes: Interest Politics in Israel*. Albany: State University of New York Press, 1991.

Zidon, Asher. *Knesset: The Parliament of Israel*. New York: Herzl Press, 1967.

Zohar, David M. *Political Parties in Israel: The Evolution of Israeli Democracy*. New York: Praeger, 1974.

History

Barbour, Neville. *Palestine, Star or Crescent?* New York: Odyssey, 1947.

Bauer, Yehuda. *From Diplomacy to Resistance: A History of Jewish Palestine, 1939–1945*. Philadelphia: Jewish Publication Society, 1970.

Bentsur, Eytan. *Making Peace: A First-Hand Account of the Arab-Israeli Peace Process*. Westport, Conn., and London: Praeger, 2001.

Blum, Howard. *The Eve of Destruction: The Untold Story of the Yom Kippur War*. New York: HarperCollins, 2003.

Buber, Martin. *Israel and Palestine*. New York: Farrar, Straus, and Young, 1952.

Cohen, Amnon. *Palestine in the 18th Century: Patterns of Government and Administration.* Jerusalem: Magnes, 1973.

Crossman, Richard H. S. *A Nation Reborn.* New York: Atheneum, 1960.

Dunner, Joseph. *Republic of Israel: Its History and Its Promise.* New York: McGraw-Hill, 1950.

Garcia-Granados, Jorge. *The Birth of Israel, the Drama as I Saw It.* New York: Alfred A. Knopf, 1948.

Gazit, Mordechai. *Israeli Diplomacy and the Quest for Peace.* London: Frank Cass, 2002.

Graetz, Heinrich. *History of the Jews.* 6 Vols. Philadelphia: Jewish Publication Society of America, 1891–98.

Horowitz, Dan, and Moshe Lissak. *Origins of the Israeli Polity: Palestine under the Mandate.* Chicago: Chicago University Press, 1978.

Israeli, Raphael. *Jerusalem Divided: The Armistice Regime, 1947–1967.* London: Frank Cass, 2002.

Jones, Philip, comp. *Britain and Palestine 1914–1948: Archival Sources for the History of the British Mandate.* London: Oxford University Press, 1979.

Katznelson, Rachel Shazar. *The Plough Woman: Memoirs of the Pioneer Women of Palestine.* 2d ed. New York: Herzl, 1975.

Koestler, Arthur. *Promise and Fulfillment: Palestine 1917–1949.* New York: Macmillan, 1949.

Lowdermilk, W. C. *Palestine: Land of Promise.* New York: Harper and Row, 1944.

Maoz, Moshe, ed. *Studies on Palestine during the Ottoman Period.* Jerusalem: Magnes, 1975.

Marlowe, John. *The Seat of Pilate: An Account of the Palestine Mandate.* London: Cresset Press, 1959.

Morris, Benny. *The Road to Jerusalem: Glubb Pasha, Palestine, and the Jews.* New York: Palgrave Macmillan, 2002.

Nathan, Robert, Oscar Gass, and Daniel Kraemer. *Palestine: Problem and Promise.* Washington, D.C.: Public Affairs Press, 1946.

Rabinovich, Abraham. *The Yom Kippur War: The Epic Encounter That Transformed the Middle East.* New York: Schocken Books, 2004.

Rabinovich, Itamar. *Waging Peace: Israel and the Arabs, 1948–2003.* Princeton, N.J.: Princeton University Press, 2004.

Ross, Dennis. *The Missing Peace: The Inside Story of the Fight for Middle East Peace.* New York: Farrar, Straus and Giroux, 2004.

Sacher, Harry. *Israel: The Establishment of a State.* London: Weidenfeld and Nicolson, 1952.

Samuel, Maurice. *Harvest in the Desert*. Philadelphia: Jewish Publication Society, 1944.

————. *Level Sunlight*. New York: Alfred A. Knopf, 1953.

Sanders, Ronald. *The High Walls of Jerusalem: A History of the Balfour Declaration, the Birth of the British Mandate for Palestine*. New York: Holt, Rinehart, and Winston, 1984.

Schneer, Jonathan. *The Balfour Declaration: The Origins of the Arab-Israeli Conflict*. New York: Random House, 2010.

Segev, Tom. *One Palestine Complete: Jews and Arabs under the British Mandate*. New York: Owl Books, 2001.

Shapira, Anita, and Derek J. Penslar. *Israeli Historical Revisionism: From Left to Right*. London: Frank Cass, 2003.

Sharef, Zeev. *Three Days: An Account of the Last Days of the British Mandate and the Birth of Israel*. New York: Doubleday, 1962.

Sykes, Christopher. *Crossroads to Israel*. Cleveland and New York: World Publishing, 1965.

Tuchman, Barbara W. *Bible and Sword: England and Palestine from the Bronze Age to Balfour*. New York: Minerva Press, 1968.

International Relations

Abadi, Jacob. *Israel's Quest for Recognition and Acceptance in Asia: Garrison State Diplomacy*. London: Frank Cass, 2004.

Amir, Shimeon. *Israel's Development Cooperation with Africa, Asia and Latin America*. New York: Praeger, 1974.

Arbel, Andrea S. *Riding the Wave: The Jewish Agency's Role in the Mass Aliyah of Soviet and Ethiopian Jewry to Israel, 1987–1995*. Jerusalem: Gefen Publishing House, 2001.

Argov, Shlomo. *An Ambassador Speaks Out*. London: Weidenfeld and Nicolson, with the Van Leer Institute, 1983.

Beker, Avi. *The United Nations and Israel: From Recognition to Reprehension*. Lexington, Mass.: Lexington Books, 1988.

Ben-Ami, Shlomo. *Scars of War, Wounds of Peace: The Israeli-Arab Tragedy*. New York: Oxford University Press, 2006.

Ben-Ezer, Gadi. *The Ethiopian Jewish Exodus: Narratives of the Migration Journey to Israel 1977–1985*. London: Routledge, 2002.

Bengio, Ofra. *The Turkish-Israeli Relationship: Changing Ties of Middle Eastern Outsiders*. New York: Palgrave Macmillan, 2004.

Bentsur, Eytan. *Making Peace: A First-Hand Account of the Arab-Israeli Peace Process*. Westport, Conn., and London: Praeger, 2001.

Ben-Zvi, Abraham. *The United States and Israel: The Limits of the Special Relationship.* New York: Columbia University Press, 1993.

Bialer, Uri. *Between East and West: Israel's Foreign Policy Orientation, 1948–1956.* Cambridge: Cambridge University Press, 1990.

———. *Mapai and Israel's Foreign Policy, 1947–1952.* Jerusalem: Hebrew University, 1981.

———. *Cross on the Star of David: The Christian World in Israel's Foreign Policy, 1948–1967.* Bloomington: Indiana University Press, 2005.

Brecher, Michael. *Decisions in Israel's Foreign Policy.* New Haven, Conn.: Yale University Press, 1975.

———. *The Foreign Policy System of Israel: Setting, Images, Process.* New Haven, Conn.: Yale University Press, 1972.

———. *Israel, The Korean War, and China.* New Brunswick, N.J.: Transaction Books, 1974.

Brecher, Michael, with Benjamin Geist. *Decisions in Crisis: Israel, 1967 and 1973.* Berkeley: University of California Press, 1980.

Curtis, Michael R., and Susan Aurelia Gitelson, eds. *Israel in the Third World.* New Brunswick, N.J.: Transaction Books, 1976.

Decalo, Samuel. *Israel and Africa: Forty Years, 1956–1996.* Gainesville: Florida Academic Press, 1998.

Draper, Theodore. *Israel and World Politics: Roots of the Third Arab-Israeli War.* New York: Viking Press, 1968.

Eban, Abba. *Voice of Israel.* New York: Horizon, 1957.

Elath, Eliahu. *Israel and Her Neighbors.* London: James Barrie, 1956.

Eytan, Walter. *The First Ten Years: A Diplomatic History of Israel.* New York: Simon and Schuster, 1958.

Gazit, Mordechai. *Israeli Diplomacy and the Quest for Peace.* London: Frank Cass, 2002.

Glick, Edward B. *Latin America and the Palestine Problem.* New York: Theodor Herzl Foundation, 1958.

Golan, Galia. *Yom Kippur and After.* Cambridge: Cambridge University Press, 1977.

Harkabi, Yehoshafat. *Arab Strategies and Israel's Response.* New York: Free Press, 1977.

———. *Israel's Fateful Decisions.* Translated by Lenn Schramm. London: I.B. Tauris, 1988.

Heller, Mark A. *A Palestinian State: The Implications for Israel.* Cambridge, Mass.: Harvard University Press, 1983.

Herzog, Chaim. *Who Stands Accused? Israel Answers Its Critics.* New York: Random House, 1978.

Hillel, Shlomo. *Operation Babylon.* New York: Doubleday, 1987.

Joseph, Benjamin M. *Besieged Bedfellows: Israel and the Land of Apartheid.* Westport, Conn.: Greenwood, 1988.

Kaufman, Edy, Yoram Shapira, and Joel Barromi. *Israel–Latin American Relations.* New Brunswick, N.J.: Transaction Books, 1979.

Kay, Zachariah. *The Diplomacy of Prudence: Canada and Israel, 1948–1958.* Montreal and Kingston: Queen's University Press, 1996.

Klieman, Aaron. *Israel and the World after 40 Years.* Elmsford, N.Y.: Pergamon, 1989.

————. *Israel's Global Reach: Arms Sales as Diplomacy.* Elmsford, N.Y.: Pergamon-Brassey's International Defense Publishers, 1985.

————. *Statecraft in the Dark: Israel's Practice of Quiet Diplomacy.* Boulder, Colo.: Westview Press, 1988.

Krammer, Arnold P. *The Forgotten Friendship: Israel and the Soviet Bloc, 1947–1953.* Urbana: University of Illinois Press, 1974.

Kreinin, Mordechai. *Israel and Africa: A Study in Technical Cooperation.* New York: Praeger, 1964.

Laufer, Leopold. *Israel and the Developing Countries: New Approaches to Cooperation.* New York: Twentieth Century Fund, 1967.

Liebman, Charles. *Pressure without Sanctions: The Influence of World Jewry on Israeli Policy.* Rutherford, N.J.: Fairleigh Dickinson University Press, 1977.

Pardo, Sharon, and Joel Peters. *Uneasy Neighbors: Israel and the European Union.* Lanham, Md: Lexington Books, 2010.

Peleg, Ilan. *Begin's Foreign Policy, 1977–1983: Israel's Move to the Right.* Westport, Conn.: Greenwood, 1987.

Raphael, Gideon. *Destination Peace: Three Decades of Israeli Foreign Policy.* New York: Stein and Day, 1981.

Roberts, Samuel J. *Survival or Hegemony? The Foundations of Israeli Foreign Policy.* Baltimore, Md., and London: Johns Hopkins University Press, 1973.

Romberg, Otto R., and George Schwinghammer, eds. *Twenty Years of Diplomatic Relations between the Federal Republic of Germany and Israel.* Frankfurt, West Germany: Tribune Books, 1985.

Sheffer, Gabriel, ed. *Dynamics of a Conflict: A Re-examination of the Arab-Israeli Conflict.* Atlantic Highlands, N.J.: Humanities Press, 1975.

Slater, Robert. *Israel's Aid to Developing Nations.* New York: Friendly House Publishers, 1973.

Spector, Stephen. *Operation Solomon: The Daring Rescue of the Ethiopian Jews.* New York: Oxford University Press, 2005.

Tekoah, Yosef. *In the Face of Nations: Israel's Struggle for Peace.* New York: Simon and Schuster, 1976.

Wilson, Harold. *The Chariot of Israel: Britain, America and the State of Israel.* London: Weidenfeld and Nicolson, 1981.

Yaniv, Avner. *Dilemmas of Security: Politics, Strategy, and the Israeli Experience in Lebanon.* New York: Oxford University Press, 1987.

Religion

Abramov, S. Zalman. *Perpetual Dilemma: Jewish Religion in the Jewish State.* Rutherford, N.J.: Fairleigh Dickinson University Press, 1979.

Badi, Joseph. *Religion in Israel Today: The Relationship between State and Religion.* New York: Bookman Associates, 1959.

Birnbaum, Ervin. *The Politics of Compromise: State and Religion in Israel.* Rutherford, N.J.: Fairleigh Dickinson University Press, 1970.

Kraines, Oscar. *The Impossible Dilemma: Who Is a Jew in the State of Israel.* New York: Bloch, 1976.

Leslie, Samuel C. *The Rift in Israel: Religious Authority and Secular Democracy.* New York: Schocken, 1971.

Liebman, Charles S., and Eliezer Don-Yehiya. *Civil Religion in Israel: Traditional Judaism and Political Culture in the Jewish State.* Berkeley, Los Angeles, and London: University of California Press, 1983.

―――. *Religion and Politics in Israel.* Bloomington: Indiana University Press, 1984.

Liebman, Charles S., and Elihu Katz, eds. *The Jewishness of Israel.* Albany: State University of New York Press, 1997.

Marmorstein, Emile. *Heaven at Bay: The Jewish Kulturkampf in the Holy Land.* London: Oxford University Press, 1969.

Rabinowicz, Harry M. *Hasidism and the State of Israel.* Rutherford, N.J.: Fairleigh Dickinson University Press, 1982.

Sacks, Jonathan. *Future Tense: Jews, Judaism, and Israel in the Twenty-first Century.* New York: Schocken Books, 2009.

Schiff, Gary S. *Tradition and Politics: The Religious Parties of Israel.* Detroit, Mich.: Wayne State University Press, 1977.

Sharansky, Ira. *Rituals of Conflict: Religion, Politics, and Public Policy in Israel.* Boulder, Colo.: Lynne Rienner Publishers, 1996.

Zucker, Norman L. *The Coming Crisis in Israel: Private Faith and Public Policy.* Cambridge, Mass.: MIT Press, 1973.

Zionism

Laqueur, Walter. *A History of Zionism.* New York: Holt, Rinehart and Winston, 1972.

Rubinstein, Amnon. *The Zionist Dream Revisited: From Herzl to Gush Emunim and Back*. New York: Schocken. 1984.

Vital, David. *The Origins of Zionism*. London: Oxford University Press, 1975.

———. *Zionism: The Crucial Phase*. New York: Oxford University Press, 1987.

———. *Zionism: The Formative Years*. New York: Oxford University Press, 1982.

INDEX

Note: **Boldface** page numbers indicate primary discussion of a topic. Page numbers in *italic* indicate illustrations. The letters *c* and *m* indicate chronology and maps, respectively.